THE FALL OF JERUSALEM
AND THE CHRISTIAN CHURCH

" And they shall fall by the edge of the sword, and shall be led captive into all the nations; and Jerusalem shall be trodden down of the Gentiles, until the times of the Gentiles be fulfilled."— Luke 21. 24. A bas-relief from the Arch of Titus in the Forum Romanum depicting the spoils of the Temple, the seven-branched candlestick, the altar of shew-bread and the silver trumpets, being borne in triumph through the streets of Rome by the victorious legionaries of Titus. (See page 202, n. 2.)

THE FALL OF JERUSALEM

AND

THE CHRISTIAN CHURCH

A Study of the Effects of the Jewish Overthrow of
A.D. 70 on Christianity

BY

S. G. F. BRANDON, M.A., D.D.

LONDON

S·P·C·K

1951

First published in 1951
by S.P.C.K.,
Northumberland Avenue, W.C.2.

Printed and bound in Great Britain by
William Clowes and Sons, Limited,
London and Beccles.

VXORI MEAE

CONTENTS

FRONTISPIECE. THE SPOILS OF THE TEMPLE : A BAS-RELIEF ON THE
ARCH OF TITUS IN ROME.

PREFACE

THE subject of the present study has been one of long-standing interest to the writer. Its importance was first suggested by certain remarks made by the late Dr. Streeter [1] in his great work on Gospel Origins; one example will suffice to show his appreciation of the momentous nature of the destruction of Jerusalem in A.D. 70 for the Christian Church: "It is impossible for us nowadays to realize the shock of A.D. 70 to a community in which Jewish and Gentile members alike had been reared in the profoundest veneration of the immemorial sanctity of the Holy City and the Temple." [2]

Unfortunately Dr. Streeter never seems to have undertaken any special study of the matter in order to demonstrate his judgement about its crucial nature. However, the mere formulation of the suggestion that the overthrow of the Jewish national state in A.D. 70 may have had important repercussions for nascent Christianity at once set in train a number of *a priori* considerations which seemed to confirm its reasonableness. It was surprising, therefore, that when a definitive search was undertaken of the relevant modern literature, it was found that writer after writer either completely neglected to consider the possible significance of the event or discounted it peremptorily, and the logical conclusion of this consistency of verdict seemed to be reached in the categorical assertion of that great authority on the ancient world, Eduard Meyer, that the crucial developments of Christianity had been effected before A.D. 70, so that the Jewish catastrophe had really nothing more than an academic interest for Christians. [3]

Mindful of this curious divergence of evaluation, the writer undertook an investigation of the relevant ancient documents in the hope of reaching a solution of it. The result has been, as the following pages show at length, that, in seeking a solution of the mystery of the significance of the events of A.D. 70 for Christianity, he has been led to study many aspects of Christian Origins, to question several established positions, and to propose an evaluation of the effect of the destruction of the Jewish state on the development of Christianity which, on the most moderate estimate, will undoubtedly be described as novel.

The temerity of proposing new and radical solutions of the problems of Christian Origins must be obvious to anyone who has a working knowledge of New Testament studies, and no wise man will lightly undertake

[1] See Appendix to Chapter One, p. 12.
[2] *The Four Gospels*, p. 516.
[3] See n. 1 above.

ix

the risks involved.   It is submitted that those risks are fully realized here and that the solution set forth in this study is offered as a tentative interpretation of data which contain real and urgent problems and accordingly demand consideration.

The late Professor Guignebert has written that [1]   "*Tous ces débuts de l'Église chrétienne sont si incertains et si obscurs que presque chaque fois que l'exégète se risque à une affirmation, il aperçoit tout aussitôt une raison de la contredire.*" The truth of this statement has been constantly realized by the present writer, and it is certain that those who read the succeeding pages will often find themselves preferring some other interpretation of a specific passage to that which is set forth here.   Such divergence of opinion is inevitable where the data are so ambiguous, and there is no useful alternative to the obvious and usual way of submitting one's interpretation, supported by all the evidence which seems to be relevant, to other scholars and abiding their fair consideration.   As Professor Goguel has well said, in the study of Christian Origins every possible interpretation must be sought and examined.   Accordingly, the following interpretation is advanced in the hope that it will stimulate others to consider the well-known data with a fresh orientation of reference.

Attention has already been drawn to the curious neglect scholars have shown towards the subject of the significance of the destruction of Jerusalem for the infant Christian Church.   What has been the cause of this neglect is not certain, but it appears likely that it may reside in an unconscious reaction to a certain earlier development of New Testament exegesis.   The general criticism is consequently anticipated that here many of the old ghosts of Tübingen have been recalled and allowed to stalk freely through the discussion.   If such an objection be made, the answer must surely be that those ghosts were never really laid and that they are found on closer scrutiny to be very substantial beings. While a doctrinaire application of Hegelian metaphysic to the elucidation of the history of primitive Christianity may justly be condemned, the hard facts, which may have been utilized for this, must not be disregarded as having thereby lost their force or relevancy for subsequent research.

It remains for the author to put on record his sincere gratitude to Professor T. W. Manson of the Rylands Chair of Biblical Exegesis in the University of Manchester for his constant encouragement over many years.   Without this encouragement the work of preparation for the press must long ago have been abandoned; however, Professor Manson's kind advice was given on the evidence of the original draft of the work and he is in no way responsible for the novel suggestions put forth in the present completed version.

The author also desires to express his great indebtedness to Dr. Robert Eisler for his encouragement and advice so freely and so richly given.

[1] *Le Christ* (Paris, 1943), p. 90.

Despite the many divergences of opinion, Dr. Eisler will best know to what extent his own great learning has been drawn upon in this work, and it is hoped that some indication of the debt will be apparent to readers in the notes.

Catterick Camp,

July 5th, 1947.

Postscriptum

Since the completion of the manuscript several events have encouraged the author in his belief in the importance of the theme. On reading Professor M. Goguel's fine study entitled *La Naissance du Christianisme* (Paris, 1946), he was gratified to find that, while no specific consideration was given therein to the question of the significance of the Jewish over-throw in A.D. 70, on many important points his own interpretation received considerable support, directly or indirectly, from the great French scholar; such instances have been indicated in the notes. Similarly he has found valuable confirmation in the important work which Professor H. J. Schoeps has recently published under the title of *Theologie und Geschichte des Judenchristentums* (Tübingen, 1949); because this study, which will surely remain for many years one of the most authoritative interpretations of Jewish Christianity, provides both powerful support on some of the points set forth here and divergent views on others, a *critique* of it has accordingly been appended to Bibliography II. In 1948 the author was invited to lecture on his subject in the University of Vienna. In the invitation he saw further recognition of the significance of the Fall of Jerusalem for Christianity, and he accordingly desires to acknow-ledge here the kind interest of Professor G. Entz, Dean of the Faculty of Theology (*Evangelisch-theologischen Fakultät*) in the University of Vienna, from whom the invitation came.

The author gratefully acknowledges the permission kindly given by the following publishers to quote from the works indicated: The Cambridge University Press (M. P. Charlesworth, *Documents illustrating the Reigns of Claudius and Nero*); Messrs. Macmillan and Co., Ltd. (J. B. Lightfoot and J. R. Harmer, *The Apostolic Fathers*); Messrs. J. C. B. Mohr (Paul Siebeck) of Tübingen (H. J. Schoeps, *Theologie und Geschichte des Juden-christentums*); Messrs. Payot of Paris (M. Goguel, *La Naissance du Christianisme*).

Since the present work was set in type the death of Dr. Robert Eisler has been announced. The author accordingly hopes that his book may be regarded as a tribute to the memory of a great scholar from one who has been effectively stimulated by his published work and who was privileged privately to draw upon his vast erudition—a privilege which was always so willingly and so kindly given.

Finally, grateful acknowledgement must be made of the immense care which has been so generously given by the editorial staff of The Society for Promoting Christian Knowledge to the preparation of the manuscript for the press while its author has been serving overseas.

Klagenfurt, Austria.

  July 27th, 1950.

SYNOPSIS OF CHAPTERS

CHAPTER ONE. *Introductory: The Nature of the Problem of Christian Origins.* That the apparent emphasis upon historicity in the New Testament documents is found on analysis to raise a problem of basic significance, since this emphasis finds comparatively late literary expression (pp. 1–4). Related problems concerning rival interpretations of Jesus (p. 4); the leadership of the Jerusalem Church (p. 5); the origins of Christianity in Egypt (pp. 5–6); the conflicting evidence of the Pauline Epistles and the Acts on the Judaistic question (pp. 6–7); the fate of Paul and his work (pp. 7–8); the extant condition of the *Corpus Paulinum* (pp. 8–9); the complete disappearance of documents representative of the Jerusalem Church (pp. 9–10); the silence of the primitive Christian records about the Jewish overthrow of A.D. 70 (p. 10). That *a priori* consideration of these problems reveals a tunnel-period in Christian history between A.D. 60 and 80 and thus suggests that A.D. 70 constituted a unique crisis (pp. 10–11).

CHAPTER TWO. *The Primitive Church: Its Territorial Extent and Internal Constitution according to the Evidence* (a) *of the Writings of Paul and* (b) *of the Acts of the Apostles.* That Paul's writings attest the unique status of the Jerusalem Church and reveal that the Jerusalem Christians had organized successful missionary work among Gentiles outside Palestine (pp. 16–17). Paul's references to Apollos suggest that the teaching of the Alexandrian Church differed from his own (pp. 17–18). Pauline evidence of the leadership of James, the Lord's brother (p. 20). The significance of the collection of alms for "the saints" of Jerusalem (p. 21). Paul's unconscious witness to the predominance of Jewish culture in the Church (pp. 21–3). That the account in Acts of Apollos reveals on analysis an antipathy to Alexandrian Christianity (pp. 24–6). The witness of the Acts to the unique status of the Jerusalem Church and to the primacy of James (pp. 26–8). The comparative numerical strengths of the Jewish and the Gentile Christians (p. 28). The zeal of the Jerusalem Christians for Judaism as indicated in the Acts (p. 29). That the evidence of Paul and Acts indicates a situation, fraught with problems and possibilities for the future, which demands closer investigation (pp. 30–1).

CHAPTER THREE. *The Church in Palestine according to the Evidence of the Synoptic Gospels and other Palestinian Sources.* The problem of obtaining other evidence of Palestinian Christianity: from the Synoptic Gospels, Josephus, and Hegesippus (pp. 31–3). The story of the Syro-Phœnician woman as illustrating original Jewish Christian attitude towards Gentile converts (pp. 33–4). Matthean and Lukan evidence of Jewish Christian superciliousness towards the Gentiles and the grudging admission of their right to enter the Church (pp. 34–7). Synoptic evidence of the devotion of the Jewish Christians to Jerusalem and the Temple (p. 37). That the alleged charge of "the false witnesses", that Jesus threatened to destroy the Temple, is found on examination to attest the devotion of the Jerusalem Christians to the national sanctuary (pp. 37–40). The Lament over Jerusalem interpreted as evidence of the prolonged effort of the *Urgemeinde* to convert the inhabitants of the metropolis (pp. 40–1). That the Synoptic Gospels indicate the existence of Christian communities in Galilee and Samaria which accepted the supremacy of the Jerusalem Church (pp. 41–4). Examination of the problem raised by Paul's witness to the existence of a triumvirate of James (the Lord's brother), Peter, and John in the *Urgemeinde*, and the Synoptic tradition of a triumvirate of Peter, James (son of Zebedee), and John. The curious silence maintained about the antecedents of James, the Lord's brother. The dynastic factor in Jewish Christianity, and the personality of James (pp. 45–52). Evidence of Josephus and Hegesippus attesting the reputation of James (pp. 52–3).

CHAPTER FOUR. *The Pauline Interpretation of Christianity.* Paul's witness to the existence of two rival gospels (pp. 54–5). Paul's attempt to base his teaching on the authority of Spirit-mediated revelation against his opponents' doctrine of "the Jesus of History" (pp. 55–8). That the origin of Paul's gospel is to be found in the peculiar nature of his conversion: Paul believed that God had converted him in order to make a new revelation of his Son to the Gentiles (pp. 58–60). That Paul's belief that he was divinely commissioned to evangelize the Gentiles indicates his possession of a sympathetic insight into Græco-Roman culture and its needs (pp. 61–3). Résumé of Paul's doctrine (pp. 63–6). The question of the origin of Paul's concept of an incarnated Saviour-God (pp. 66–9). That Paul's experience of the Risen Jesus overcame his original detestation of the scandal of the Cross and led him, in contradistinction to the Jewish Christians, to find a soteriological meaning in the Crucifixion (pp. 69–71). That the logic of Paul's soteriology inevitably brought him into serious conflict with the Jewish Christians, who were the exponents of the traditional teaching (pp. 71–3).

CHAPTER FIVE. *Christianity according to the Church of Jerusalem.* That the Markan Passion narrative points to an original concentration of interest on the part of the Jewish Christians on the Crucifixion; this was due to the need of explaining the death of Jesus, if he were the Messiah (pp. 74–5). Development of an apologetic: that the Crucifixion was a tragic accident which had been foretold in the Isaianic Servant Sagas (p. 76). Soteriological possibilities of Suffering Servant concept not developed by Jewish Christians, since emphasis on the Crucifixion was calculated to constitute an obstacle to Pharisaic sympathy and support (p. 77). Consequently, interpretation of the Crucifixion was a basic cause of conflict between Jewish Christians and Paul (pp. 77–8). Jewish Christian interpretation of Jesus maintained distinction between human and divine (pp. 78–9). Jesus as the Messiah (pp. 79–80), as the Son of Man (p. 81). That Jewish Christian Christology remained static theologically and nationalist in outlook (pp. 81–2). The Christological passage of Philippians 2 interpreted as a formal Jewish Christian repudiation of the deification of Jesus (pp. 82–3). That the *Weltanschauung* of the Jewish Christians was essentially nationalistic (pp. 84–6). Hence the need to investigate the question of the degree to which the Jewish Christians were affected by the political aspirations of their ancestral faith (p. 87).

CHAPTER SIX. *The Jewish Christians and their Nation's Cause against Rome.* The problematical nature of the evidence of Acts concerning Palestinian Christianity: doubt about the true significance of Stephen's teaching and martyrdom and the death of James, the Apostle (pp. 88–90). General conclusion that Acts shows the Jerusalem Church as flourishing and unmolested by the authorities (pp. 90–1). That investigation of the data relating to Paul's persecuting activities suggests that the locality of his operations was Damascus, not Judæa (pp. 91–2). Reference in 1 Thess. to persecution of Christians in Judæa not authentic (pp. 92–3). Examination of references to persecution in the Synoptic Gospels reveals no serious attempt to suppress Christianity in Palestine (pp. 93–5). Examination of the accounts of Josephus, Hegesippus, and the *Clementine Recognitions* concerning the death of James, the Lord's brother: conclusion that it was due to the high-handed action of the High Priest and was condemned by the Pharisees (pp. 95–100). Since the Palestinian Christians were not an outcast body from Israel, the question arises of why Acts depicts them as living in idyllic insulation from contemporary affairs (pp. 100–1). Evidence pointing to the existence of a political element in the original Christian movement: Jesus crucified by the Romans; armed resistance to his arrest; his triumphal entry into Jerusalem; the attack on the Temple bank; Barabbas; the question about tribute; inclusion of a Zealot among the disciples; the slaughter of the Galilæans and the fall of the Siloam tower (pp. 101–7). Evidence from the Little Apocalypse that the Palestinian Christians shared in the common agitation occasioned by Caligula's attempt to desecrate the Temple (pp. 107–9). Conclusion: that the extant evidence indicates that the primitive Christian movement in Palestine was closely concerned with the cause of Jewish nationalism and that the author of Acts found the fact inconvenient to his theme (pp. 109–110). Examination of the *Testimonia Flaviana* shows that Josephus regarded Jesus as a claimant to Messiahship in a political sense (pp. 110–14). That the Slavonic version of Josephus' *Wars* indicates that Josephus regarded Christianity as primarily a revolutionary movement against Roman suzerainty in Palestine (pp. 114–19). Further evidence of the political aspect of primitive Christianity provided by an edict of the Emperor Claudius against the robbery of tombs in Palestine and by the account of Sulpicius Severus of the Roman decision to destroy the Temple (pp. 119–21). Johannine evidence concurs (p. 124).

CHAPTER SEVEN. *The Crisis of A.D. 55 to 66.* A priori considerations concerning the tendentious character of the record of Acts (p. 126). The inadequacy of the accounts of Stephen, the conversion of the Samaritans, and the Cornelius episode; however, Acts witnesses to a fundamental cleavage in Christian interpretation originating from the primitive Palestinian period (pp. 127–9). The episode of Stephen used in Acts to carry theme from Palestinian stage to cycle of stories concerning Paul (pp. 129–30). That the author of Acts regarded Paul as the Apostle to the Gentiles *par excellence*, although giving no adequate explanation of what predisposed Paul to this work (p. 130). The unsatisfactory nature of Acts' account of the Council of Jerusalem (pp. 130–2), and of its sequel at Antioch (p. 132). That the account in Acts of Paul's last journey to Jerusalem is found on analysis to indicate a most serious crisis in Paul's relations with the Jerusalem Church and the defeat of his cause (pp. 133–5). Examination of the Pauline evidence: that Paul's account of his second visit to Jerusalem reveals the weakness of his position *vis-à-vis* to the Jerusalem leaders (pp. 136–8); that the episode at Antioch proves the opposition of James and Peter (p. 138); that the polemic of the Galatian Epistle shows how serious was the dispute and the fundamental doctrinal factor involved (pp. 138–9). That the parties at Corinth reflect the conflict between Paul and his Jerusalem opponents (pp. 139–40). Analysis of 1 Corinthians showing Paul's defence of his authority against the Jerusalem leaders (pp. 140–1). That 2 Corinthians reveals Paul fighting bitterly to maintain his authority against the attacks of the Jerusalem leaders or their emissaries (pp. 141–5). That the Epistle to the Romans provides evidence that Paul in turn tried to win over the Gentile Christians of Rome in the period after the expulsion of the Jews from the capital (pp. 145–8). Conclusions: that the Jerusalem Christians regarded Paul's teaching as unsound and likely to endanger their own position with the Pharisees; hence, they conducted a campaign against him by seeking to undermine his authority with his converts, and he in self-defence was obliged to disparage the traditional teaching concerning "the Jesus of History" (pp. 148–9). Reconstruction of the situation which led to Paul's last journey to Jerusalem to seek some *modus vivendi* with his enemies there (pp. 149–50). He is trapped by James into compromising himself with his Gentile followers and his arrest removes him from further effective action in the Church (pp. 150–1). That Paul's appeal to Cæsar probably ended in his execution (pp. 151–2). That after Paul's removal his converts were subjected to the unopposed propaganda of the Jerusalem Church, so that the decade A.D. 55–65 was a period of profound crisis for the future of Christianity. In 66 this crisis was merged in an even greater one occasioned by the Jewish revolt against Rome (pp. 152–3).

CHAPTER EIGHT. *The Jewish War against Rome,* A.D. *66 to 70.* That the true cause of the Jewish war against Rome was religious: the Jews cherished the ideal of Israel as a theocracy. The Romans not only failed to conciliate Jewish religious susceptibilities, but inflamed them by many senseless acts (pp. 154–5). Economic and social factors (pp. 155–6). The value of Josephus' evidence for the Jewish War (pp. 156–7). The outbreak of rebellion in Palestine required the intervention of the governor of Syria, C. Gallus; he delayed his expedition for three months (p. 157). The Jewish situation during this period. Gentile and Jewish reprisals. The inspiration of the Zealots (pp. 157–9). The attack of C. Gallus and its amazing defeat confirm the Jews in their trust in Yahweh's succour (pp. 159–61). Josephus' account of his defence of Galilee (p. 161). Vespasian's campaign of A.D. 67 results in the subjugation of Galilee, Samaria, and the coastal area of Judæa (pp. 161–2). The Zealots, under John of Gischala, and the Idumæans gain control of Jerusalem (pp. 162–3). The cautious campaign of Vespasian during A.D. 68–9 succeeds in subduing all insurgent Palestine outside Jerusalem and three minor strongholds; it ends when Vespasian is elected emperor. The unspectacular progress of the Romans encourages Jewish faith in divine protection (pp. 163–4). The siege of Jerusalem by Titus in A.D. 70 ends with the destruction of the Temple and the overthrow of Israel as a national state. The Jewish losses and sufferings (pp. 164–6).

CHAPTER NINE. *The Fate of the Palestinian Church.* The Jewish reaction to the fall of Jerusalem (p. 167). The strange silence about the Jewish disaster in the primitive Christian records (pp. 167–8). The accounts by Eusebius and Epiphanius of the flight of the Jerusalem Christians to Pella; the strong objections to its historicity; that the tradition probably grew out of the memory of some (non-Jerusalem) Christian Jews who settled in Pella (pp. 168–73). Matthean evidence indicating that there was no concerted flight; the possibility of a certain amount of persecution when the nationalist spirit was aflame (pp. 173–6). Discussion of a suggested reference in the Apocalypse to the flight of the Jewish Christians (pp. 176–7). Summary: evidence of a concerted flight of Jerusalem Christians to Pella not sufficient; possibility of some small-scale unorganized flights (p. 177). Probability that many Jewish Christians sought refuge in Egypt (p. 178). That the Christian community in Cæsarea probably survived the Jewish catastrophe (pp. 178–9). That the silence about the fate of the Jerusalem Church in early Christian tradition is probably due to the fact that many Jewish Christians made common cause with their countrymen in the struggle against Rome. The probable fate of the more pacific of the Jewish Christians (pp. 179–80). The impoverishment of the Jewish Christians who survived in Palestine. Their mental outlook; tendency to revert to Judaism; the significance of the Apocalypse vision of the new Jerusalem (pp. 180–3). Summary: the effective elimination of the Church of Jerusalem and the resolution of the crisis of A.D. 55–66 (pp. 183–4).

CHAPTER TEN. *The Markan Reaction to A.D. 70.* That Mark, purporting to be an historical narrative of the career of Jesus, is an innovation in Christian thought and practice; need to explain this (pp. 185–6). That Mark must have been produced in response to some specific situation. *A priori* reasons in favour of that created by the fall of Jerusalem. Does internal evidence of the Gospel agree? (p. 186). That in Mark's treatment of the Jewish leaders there is developed an apologetic designed to demonstrate Jesus' independence of Jewish national life. The significance of the Son of David and the Tribute Money incidents and of the intention to shift the blame of the Crucifixion from the Romans to the Jews (pp. 186–94). The same apologetical theme apparent in Mark's treatment of the Jewish people (p. 194). Mark's defamatory

2

account of the Lord's family further illustrates his desire to separate Jesus from his Jewish origins and *milieu* (pp. 195–6). Mark's disparagement of the Twelve inspired by same motive. The Cæsarea Philippi Confession intended to commemorate limitations of Jewish Christian Christology (pp. 196–7). The same theme is found in Mark's treatment of Galilee and Jerusalem (pp. 197–8). Summary: that this consistent tendency to separate Jesus from his native *milieu* and to condemn all that was Jewish and associated with Jerusalem points to a situation after the destruction of Jerusalem (p. 198). The significance of Mark's failure to explain the title "the Cananæan" (pp. 198–9). That the form of Mark, i.e. historical narrative, is a consequence of the predominance of Jewish Christian teaching in the Gentile churches between 55 and 66 (pp. 199–200). Evidence in Mark of a rehabilitation of Paul and his teaching consequent on the fall of Jerusalem (pp. 200–1). That the Markan Apocalypse presupposes a situation just after A.D. 70 (pp. 201–4). Summary: that the very *raison d'être* of Mark is the situation which faced the Gentile Christians immediately after the fall of Jerusalem (pp. 204–5).

CHAPTER ELEVEN. *The Lukan Literature and the Rehabilitation of Paul.* That the Lukan writings show a relative detachment of concern about Judaism and the fate of the Jews which corresponds to the later date of their composition (pp. 206–7). That the Acts represents a further stage in the rehabilitation of Paul: its picture of primitive Christianity idealized (pp. 208–10). Evidence that when Luke wrote the Church of Alexandria had succeeded Jerusalem as the citadel of Jewish Christianity and of opposition to Pauline teaching. Consequently Acts contains a covert polemic against Alexandrian Christianity (pp. 210–12). The significance of the *Corpus Paulinum* in the course of the rehabilitation of Paul. Evidence that the *Corpus* was known and used in circles which had little or no knowledge of Acts; that Acts was not the likely cause of the formation of the *Corpus* (pp. 213–14). The testimony of the *Corpus* to an eclipse of Paul's reputation which continued sufficiently long to permit of the loss of several of his writings (214–15). The unknown compiler's keen appreciation of the issues involved in Paul's controversies and his honesty of purpose in preserving the Letters unchanged. That the Epistle to the Ephesians was probably intended to be the preface to the *Corpus* (pp. 215–16). Summary (p. 216).

CHAPTER TWELVE. *The Gospel of Matthew and the Origins of Alexandrian Christianity.* The problem of determining the situation which produced the Gospel of Matthew. Examination of the theory of the Antiochene origin of Matthew; its rejection in favour of an Alexandrian origin (pp. 217–21). The problem of the origins of Christianity in Alexandria. The evidence of the Letter of Claudius and of the Alexandrians' insult to Agrippa I pointing to the early arrival of the faith in Alexandria (pp. 221–4). That Alexandria was evangelized by Jerusalem Christians and became a stronghold of Jewish Christian teaching (pp. 224–5). The catastrophe of A.D. 70 smashed this Jewish Christian axis, leaving the Alexandrian Church as the only effective representative of the Jewish Christian position. The situation facing the Alexandrian

Christians after A.D. 70; out of this situation the Gospel of Matthew was born (pp. 225–6). The evidence of the story of the Flight into Egypt for the Egyptian origin of Matthew (pp. 226–7). Matthew's concern to explain the overthrow of the Jewish nation (pp. 227–30). Matthew's severe attitude towards the Gentiles: the significance of the Parables of the Wedding Garment and the Labourers in the Vineyard (pp. 230–1). Matthew and the rehabilitation of Paul. The counter-exaltation of Peter; veiled polemic against Paul (pp. 231–6). That Matthew's Christology, while revealing traces of older Jerusalem teaching, shows signs of emendation to meet the challenge of Pauline doctrine (pp. 236–7). The decline of Jewish predominance in the Alexandrian Church. The significance of the preservation of Philo's works (p. 237). That the Epistles of James and to the Hebrews, *Barnabas*, and *II Clement* represent successive phases of the evolution of Alexandrian Christianity from its Jewish origins to its second-century form (pp. 238–42). Summary and conclusion (pp. 242–2).

EPILOGUE. Christianity twice-born. The Jewish overthrow of A.D. 70 emancipated the infant faith from its Jewish cradle, thus making possible its career as a world-religion. The synthesis of the tradition of the historical Jesus and the concept of the universalist Saviour-God. The destruction of Jerusalem gave other cities decisive parts in the life of the Church, especially Rome. The Jewish catastrophe of A.D. 70 probably the next most crucial event for Christianity after the Resurrection experiences (pp. 249–51).

ABBREVIATIONS

B.C.   *Beginnings of Christianity*, edited by F. J. Foakes Jackson and Kirsopp Lake.

G.J.V.   Schürer, E., *Geschichte des jüdischen Volkes im Zeitalter Jesu Christi.*

Huck, *Synopse.*   Huck, A., *Synopse der drei ersten Evangelien.*

I.C.C.   *International Critical Commentary.*

Jos. *Ant.*   Josephus, *The Antiquities of the Jews.*

Jos. *Wars.*   Josephus, *The Wars of the Jews.*

Jos. *Life.*   Josephus, *Autobiography.*

J.T.S.   *Journal of Theological Studies.*

Knox, *Jerusalem.*   Knox, W. L., *St. Paul and the Church of Jerusalem.*

Knox, *Gentiles.*   *St. Paul and the Church of the Gentiles.*

Knox, *Some Hellenistic Elements.*   *Some Hellenistic Elements in Primitive Christianity.*

Lake, *Landmarks.*   Lake, K., *Landmarks in the History of Early Christianity.*

New. Com. N.T.   *A New Commentary of Holy Scripture* : section on the New Testament.

R.H.P.R.   *Revue d'Histoire et de Philosophie Religieuses.*

Z.N.T.W.   *Zeitschrift für die Neutestamentliche Wissenschaft.*

Introductory: The Nature of the Problem of Christian Origins

THE development of the comparative study of religion has progressively shown how much primitive Christianity had in common with other religions and cults of the ancient Near East and in what it uniquely differed from them. Generally this research has tended to demonstrate the extraordinary nature of the original Christian movement. This result may indeed be fairly regarded as one which was to be expected, since a contrary conclusion would necessarily raise a new and suspiciously paradoxical problem, namely that of explaining the sudden emergence of the faith in history and its successful struggle against mighty rivals, which, besides being already well established, would accordingly have differed but little from it in nature and function.

In the writings of Christian scholars on various aspects of the subject, it has become customary to distinguish among those factors which are held to have contributed to the uniqueness of Christianity one which may fairly be regarded as constituting the very quintessence of its genius. This factor is generally described as the historicity of the new faith. What exactly is meant by historicity as a contributory factor in the constitution of a religion is rarely defined, but what it is assumed to mean in the case of Christianity is to be gathered from the remarks which are generally made as *obiter dicta* with reference to other religions.[1]

It is usual in this connection for a comparison to be drawn along the following lines: that the various religions and cults of the ancient civilizations of the Near East conformed to certain common patterns of belief and practice, which corresponded in turn to the needs of certain specific stages of cultural development; that the ritual acts of these religions and cults were generally provided with a kind of libretto which served as their rationale; that the myths which were set forth in this libretto had only the vaguest chronological reference, amounting in most cases

---

[1] E.g. Dodd, *History and the Gospels*, pp. 29–30, 55, *Apostolic Preaching*, pp. 87 *seq.*; Bevan, *Christianity*, pp. 35–6; R. Niebuhr, *The Nature and Destiny of Man* (London, 1941, 1943), vol. i, pp. 10 *seq.*, vol. ii, pp. 2 *seq.*; N. Berdyaev, *The Meaning of History* (London, 1936), pp. 33 *seq.*; Angus, *The Mystery Religions and Christianity*, pp. 309 *seq.*; E. O. James, *Comparative Religion* (London, 1938), pp. 271, 349, in *The Study of Theology* (ed. K. E. Kirk, London, 1939), pp. 114–5; G. F. Moore, *History of Religions* (Edinburgh, 1920), vol. ii, pp. 128–9; C. Gore, *The Reconstruction of Belief* (ed. 1930), pp. 171 *seq.*; O. C. Quick, *Doctrines of the Creed* (London, 1943), pp. 66–7, 91, 94. Cf. W. Windelband, *Storia della Filosofia* (Italian trans., Palermo-Milan, 1937), vol. i, pp. 297–9; Martinetti, *Jésus Christ et le Christianisme*, p. 108; C. C. J. Webb, *The Historical Element in Religion* (London, 1935), pp. 35 *seq.*; A. N. Whitehead, *Religion in the Making* (Cambridge, 1927), pp. 40–1; O. Cullmann, *Christus und die Zeit*, pp. 15 *seq.*, 107 *seq.*

merely to that of an imaginary primæval age, and that history was without any apparent significance for their *Weltanschauungen*; that Christianity, on the other hand, was the true child of Hebrew Religion, which was distinguished from its contemporaries by its dynamic interpretation of the significance of history, its literature constituting a veritable *Heilsgeschichte*, in which Yahweh's providence for his people was demonstrated on the stage of human history. It is held that Christianity, heir to such a tradition, was from its very genesis conscious of the supreme significance of history and that, in striking contradistinction to other faiths, it based its claims to authority upon the fact that the crucial events of its ἱερός λόγος were enacted at a definitive time in history and not in some far-off mythical past.

The assumption is generally made that this emphasis upon history was original and that it can be traced back to the very beginnings of the faith. Evidence of this appears to be forthcoming from the earliest Christian writings, for more than one half of the contents of the New Testament comprises works of historical narration. In the Gospels the life of Jesus of Nazareth is related in apparent chronological sequence, and in one of these documents an elaborate synchronization is attempted between the events of, or relative to, the career of Jesus and secular history.[1] The Acts of the Apostles also purports to be an historical record describing the foundation and initial expansion of the Church. These five documents by their very nature dominate the New Testament corpus and clearly indicate that the first Christians were supremely interested in the events from which they believed that their faith had derived; and this interest, moreover, does not appear to be primarily concerned with the theological significance of these happenings, but was a true appreciation of their concrete historicity as they were set forth against their contemporary topographical background.

Approached in the light of these vivid historical narratives, the other documents of the New Testament corpus tend to be seen as theological interpretations of the original history, the validity of which essentially depends upon the soundness and constancy of their reference to the vital historical data. But herein lies a problem of fundamental seriousness for the study of Christian Origins. If the powerful appeal of the narrative portions of the New Testament can be resisted and the investigation of Christianity be approached through the documents taken in their proper chronological order, quite a different situation is found to obtain with regard to what is held to be the essential historicity of the original form of the faith. Moreover, so fundamental is the problem involved here that, when its true proportions are realized, it at once becomes evident that it is but a particularly serious aspect of a much wider problem, the ramifications of which are seen to extend in so many directions as

---

[1] Luke 2. 1, 2; 3. 1–3, 23; cf. 23. 7, 12. See the valuable comment of W. L. Knox, *Some Hellenistic Elements*, p. 22, on the Hellenic element in Luke's appreciation of history.

to constitute a veritable questioning of the accuracy of the generally accepted picture of Christian Origins.

Having thus summarily indicated that there exist grounds for raising so serious a problem, we must now turn our attention to establishing a fuller appreciation of these grounds and the various related questions which they entail.

By the general consensus of critical opinion the authentic writings of Saint Paul are held to antedate our earliest extant Gospel, namely the Gospel of Mark, by at least some twenty years. Hence the Pauline documents may fairly be regarded as giving the earliest and most certain insight into the life and thought of primitive Christianity, for although it is reasonable to assume that the Gospels are based upon earlier sources of information, in their extant forms they are compositions designed for Greek-speaking publics and are thus considerably removed both in space and time from the environment and the generation of which they purport to record such notable events. Moreover, so far as we have knowledge, the Markan Gospel was a novel creation and represents a new departure in Christian thought and practice.[1]

The primary nature of Paul's writings, therefore, gives their testimony a unique value in any reconstruction of the evolution of primitive Christianity. Hence the contrast which they afford in matters of interest and emphasis to the Gospels is significant. When proper allowance has been made for the peculiar circumstances of the production of each of these Letters of Paul, the overwhelming impression which their study gives is that of the dynamic existence of a highly mystical and esoterical faith and teaching concerning the nature of Jesus Christ and his work. This faith seems almost totally independent of any relation to the historical Jesus, so vividly depicted in the Gospels, and the teaching at times almost appears to be consciously impatient of the authority of any such historical tradition.[2] Many New Testament scholars have specially set themselves the task of showing that Paul was acquainted with all the chief moments of the Gospel tradition,[3] but the very undertaking is itself significant, for not only is the catena of references to the earthly life of Jesus which they succeed in culling singularly unimpressive when compared with the rich treasury of the Gospel narrative, but the fact that the need of such an undertaking is felt clearly reveals a general recognition

[1] This is true, even if the existence of some *Ur-Marcus* be assumed; cf. Moffatt, *Intro. to N.T.*, p. 192; Streeter, *Four Gospels*, pp. 495 *seq.*; V. Taylor, *Formation of Gospel Tradition*, pp. 176–80; Dibelius, *From Tradition to Gospel*, pp. 56–7.

[2] Cf. Guignebert, *Jesus*, p. 25, *Le Christ*, pp. 347 *seq.*; Nock, *St. Paul*, p. 243; Knox, *Jerusalem*, pp. 149, 184; Martinetti, op. cit., pp. 247–8; Schweitzer, *Paul and his Interpreters*, pp. 123, n. 3, 245–6; Klausner, *From Jesus to Paul*, pp. 313–15, 413–17, 477; Loisy, *Les Mystères Païens et le Mystère Chrétien*, pp. 242–3; Deissmann, *St. Paul*, p. 195; Angus, *Religious Quests of the Graeco-Roman World*, p. 389; Windisch, *Der zweite Korinthbrief*, p. 188.

[3] E.g. Hoskyns and Davey, *Riddle of the New Test.*, pp. 217–31; Scott, *Christianity according to St. Paul*, pp. 13–16; Dodd, *Apostolic Preaching*, pp. 16 *seq.*, *History and the Gospel*, pp. 53, 63–8; Goguel, *Jesus*, pp. 112–13, 119, n. 1; H. L. Goudge, *New Com. N.T.*, pp. 411–12; Cave, *Gospel of St. Paul*, pp. 55–6. Cf. Schweitzer, op. cit. pp. 42–3, 123, n. 3, 158–9, n. 1; A. M. Hunter, *Paul and his Predecessors*, pp. 9–11.

that Paul's writings constitute a real problem relative to what is believed to be the original emphasis of primitive Christianity on historical fact.

It would appear, therefore, that at least among the Pauline churches there was not current that interest in the life of Jesus of Nazareth, as it was lived out in Palestine, which is the primary *raison d'être* of the later Gospels. There is thus provided a legitimate cause for speculation about why such an interest did not manifest itself in these Christian circles, and, consequently, about the *milieu* in which such interest was current and the factors which led to its apparent literary quiescence for so many vital years until it finally received expression outside Palestine in a Greek form somewhere about A.D. 70.

The problem constituted by the seeming indifference manifested in the Pauline writings to the subject of what we should now term the Jesus of History is paralleled by another which may conceivably be related in some way to it. Paul's Letters are admittedly concerned with many matters which in the light of modern missionary experience can reasonably be understood as natural consequences following from the situation produced by the taking of a faith which has grown up under one cultural tradition to people who have hitherto been living under another. From such an impact many difficulties and anomalies in thought and practice must almost inevitably result, and much controversy is likely to flourish before satisfactory adjustments or solutions can be achieved. The writings of Paul, however, besides showing concern for such things, reveal an atmosphere of conflict and tension with regard to a matter of a very strange and unexpected nature, and one which appears to concern the very foundations of the faith. Thus in two of his Epistles, addressed to different churches, Paul seeks to combat the influence of opponents whom he describes as preaching "another Jesus" and setting forth "a different gospel".[1] The situation which these charges necessarily indicate is certainly a remarkable one, and its serious character is manifest in the deep agitation shown by the Apostle and in the fact that, while they are never actually named, these opponents clearly had such standing and authority that they were able to enter into Paul's own mission-field and to challenge his position to the degree apparent in the concern which he displays about the matter in his writings. Hence a situation in the primitive Church is implied which constitutes a problem of fundamental importance, for obviously within some twenty-odd years of the Crucifixion there were current in the Church two distinct, and apparently mutually hostile, "gospels", or, presumably, interpretations of the nature and work of Jesus. This general problem naturally resolves itself into a number of more detailed related problems, concerning the nature and source of these rival interpretations, the identity of Paul's opponents in this dispute, and the final issue.

Comparison between Paul's references to the organization of the Church

---

[1] Gal. 1. 6–9; 2 Cor. 11. 4.

and what might reasonably be inferred in this respect from the Gospels is naturally provoked in considering the conflict of interpretation indicated by his Letters, and it consequently raises another problem of considerable significance. The various Letters agree in representing the control of the Christian movement as strongly centralized at Jerusalem. There it would seem that three men, named as James, Cephas, and John, are regarded as στύλοι (pillars) and exercise a decisive authority in matters affecting the faith and practice of the Church.[1] Of these three, moreover, James, described significantly as "the brother of the Lord", is clearly the leader [2]—a position which incidentally is attested by several references made by the writer of the later Acts of the Apostles.[3] This situation with regard to the leadership of the Church certainly does not correspond with that which the Gospels seem to presuppose. In these writings Jesus is represented as having a special band of twelve disciples "to be with him", and among these Cephas or Peter is obviously the leader.[4] James, the Lord's brother, is definitely not reckoned among these twelve, and, moreover, he is represented by inference as unsympathetic and perhaps even hostile to the mission of Jesus.[5] Peter, on the other hand, is not only depicted as the spokesman and leader of the twelve, but also singled out as the recipient of special attention from Jesus, and in one Gospel he is actually described as receiving a unique spiritual authority from the Master.[6] Thus a strange lacuna appears in our picture of the constitution of the Church in the matter of government as we move from the later Gospels to the earlier Epistles. If the Gospel version be true, then clearly in some unexplained way Peter had been ousted from his original primacy by James, the erstwhile sceptical brother of the Lord. How such an unexpected change was effected during the two vital decades after the Crucifixion obviously presents a problem of considerable moment for a proper understanding of Christian Origins.

Another aspect of the problem of Christian Origins, which is related to those which we have just noticed, is indicated by the Epistles of Paul and the Acts of the Apostles in two matters about which they respectively agree and disagree. In the first instance they agree in the general picture which they give of the direction in which the infant faith expanded beyond the borders of Palestine. From Paul's Letters we learn that he had communities of believers at Corinth [7] and Cenchreæ,[8] in Galatia,[9] Ephesus,[10] Philippi,[11] Colossæ,[12] Laodicea,[13] Hierapolis,[14] Thessalonica,[15]

[1] Gal. 2. 9. [2] Gal. 1. 18, 19; 2. 12.
[3] Acts 12. 17; 15. 13, 19; 21. 18.
[4] Mark 3. 13–19; Matt. 10. 1–4; Luke 6. 12–16. Cf. Mark 8. 29; 9. 2–8; 10. 28; 11. 21; 13. 3; 14. 33; 16. 7; Matt. 16. 16–19; 17. 1–8, 24–27; Luke 9. 20, 28–36; 22. 31, 32; 24. 34.
[5] Mark 3. 21, 31–35; 6. 3; Matt. 12. 46–50; Luke 8. 19–21.
[6] Matt. 16. 17–19.
[7] Epistles to the Corinthians.
[8] Rom. 16. 1.
[9] Gal. 1. 8.
[10] I Cor. 16. 8, 9.
[11] Phil. 1. 1–7.
[12] Col. 1. 1–8.
[13] Col. 2. 1.
[14] Col. 4. 13.
[15] I Thess. 1. 1–6.

and Crete [1]; indeed we may take the Apostle's words to the Roman Christians as a fair comprehensive summary of the field of his missionary effort: "From Jerusalem and round about even unto Illyricum I have fully preached the gospel of Christ".[2] Besides these indications of the scope of his own churches, the fact of his Epistle to the Romans attests the existence, in the metropolis of the Empire, of a notable Christian community, which certainly had been founded by Christians other than Paul and his band of missionaries. Thus the Pauline picture of the expansion of the Church represents it as a northward movement from its original home in Palestine to Antioch in Syria, whence it turned in a north-westward direction through Asia Minor and Greece to Rome. The evidence of the later Acts agrees with this picture, adding only the names of further places within the area and tending to represent Paul's coming to Rome as the effective commencement of Christian teaching there.[3] This agreement in so depicting the geographical aspect of the primitive Christian movement is seen on reflection to involve a remarkable silence about any spread of the faith southwards from Palestine and, particularly, to the great city of Alexandria, with its enormous Jewish population. That there were Christians of some kind in the Egyptian metropolis at this early period is attested by a curious reference in the Acts,[4] but certainly Paul had not worked in the city or corresponded with any Church there, so far as we know from his extant writings, and the author of the Acts obviously was not concerned to describe the origins of the faith in that area. This silence about the beginnings of either Egyptian or Alexandrian Christianity in the New Testament documents certainly appears to be very odd when the proximity of Egypt to Palestine and its age-long attraction to the Jews are duly considered, and it fairly invites investigation into its cause, whatever that may be.

The matter upon which the Pauline Letters and the Acts disagree is that of the nature of the conflict occasioned by the taking of the new faith to the Gentiles. Briefly the Acts recognizes that there was at first a conflict between the more zealous members of the Jerusalem Church and those who initiated a liberalist policy on the subject of admitting Gentile converts to the full fellowship of the Church, but an edifying account is given of how the difference was amicably and effectively settled in common council.[5] This general picture of the pacific settlement of the issue is slightly obscured by the record of the deference shown to Jewish prejudice by the Jerusalem Church on the occasion of Paul's last visit to the city,[6] but beyond this the Acts gives no reason for doubting that the Gentile problem in this respect was speedily and finally settled

---

[1] Titus 1. 5. Whatever view be held of the authenticity of this document, it is likely that it preserves some tradition that Paul had caused a Church to be founded in Crete or that he had had dealings with Christians on the island.
[2] Rom. 15. 19.
[3] Acts 28. 22.
[4] Acts 18. 24; see below, pp. 24–6, for a discussion of the matter.
[5] Acts 15. 1–33.
[6] Acts 21. 20–24.

by the Church early on in the course of Paul's ministry. This idyllic picture is completely contradicted by the Pauline evidence. Throughout the majority of the Epistles there are references to what is considered as the adverse activity of certain Judaistic teachers, and one Epistle, namely that to the Galatians, is a veritable polemic against those who maintained the necessity of the Gentiles' submitting to the rite of circumcision. But what is especially surprising after reading the record of the Acts is Paul's complete failure to invoke the decision of the so-called Council of Jerusalem in support of his contention in this matter. Many scholars have sought, with very dubious success, to reconcile the evident conflict here between the Acts and the testimony of the Galatian Epistle on grounds of date,[1] but, whatever may be the conclusion reached upon this particular point, the fact remains that not only do the extant writings of Paul afford no indication whatever that an amicable settlement was reached between himself and his opponents with regard to the issue of the question of the Gentiles' ritual obligations, but the very logic of Paul's emphasis on the absolute saving power of faith in Christ confirmed the truth of the alleged charge against him which the author of the Acts puts into the mouth of the Jerusalem Christians when they proposed the act which was calculated to exonerate him therefrom—"They are informed concerning thee, that thou teachest all the Jews which are among the Gentiles to forsake Moses, telling them not to circumcise their children, neither to walk after the customs".[2]

The problem which is caused by the conflict between the Pauline evidence and that of the Acts on the Judaistic question is further aggravated by our lack of knowledge about the eventual fate of Paul and his work. Paul's own writings on their internal evidence provide no certain clue, and the record of the Acts fails us by reason of its curious contentment to end its narrative with Paul's arrival and sojourn at Rome, with his fate still undecided. Whether the Apostle's career ended as a result of his trial before Cæsar, or whether later Christian tradition is correct in telling of his martyrdom during the Neronian persecution, we have no certain means of knowing, but we have the significant fact that the author of the Acts did not record any further effective action on the part of the great exponent of Christianity as a religion of universal validity. The proper significance of this fact is, however, very difficult to determine. It may be interpreted as the logical result of the purpose of the writer of the Acts, namely that of tracing the growth of Christianity from a tiny band of men and women at Jerusalem to a religion preached at Rome, the capital of the world, with "none forbidding". A decision about the rightness of such an interpretation must obviously depend upon what is considered to be the historical cause of the production of the Acts, which means that we are but led back to the general problem of the evolution

---

[1] Cf. K. Lake, *B.C.*, vol. v, pp. 195–212; Moffatt, *Intro. to N.T.*, pp. 99–106.
[2] Acts 21. 21.

of Christianity in the first century. Another possible line of interpretation would be that the author of the Acts made Paul's coming to Rome and preaching there the conclusion of his narrative since this offered the most convenient point for stopping, because thereafter his hero ceased to play any further part in the development of Gentile Christianity which was worthy of commemoration in the interests of his theme. Whichever of these hypotheses may be preferred, they both ultimately raise the same question: what was the fate of Paul's interpretation of Christianity for which he had fought so strenuously against powerful opponents? Many scholars, among whom pre-eminently is the great historian of the Ancient World, Eduard Meyer,[1] believe that before his death Paul's cause had already triumphed and that the future of his achievement was assured. This view, however, appears to run counter to two groups of facts, the evidential force of which does not seem to have been sufficiently appreciated. There is first to be considered the general evidence of Paul's writings with regard to his great controversy about the two gospels and the Judaistic propaganda. The only conclusion that would appear to be justifiably drawn from this matter is that the dispute had not been settled and that it is not certain that Paul felt that he was winning. However, although one may hesitate to invoke an *argumentum a silentio*, it must also be fairly noted that no Pauline letter has survived which records a settlement in his favour—a lack which must certainly be regarded as significant, for, considering the constitution of Paul's Letters in this connection, we might legitimately wonder at the strange fact therein implied, namely that apparently the Apostle only wrote letters during the throes of controversy, or that for some curious and unknown reason the churches to which he wrote thought that his controversial writings only were worthy of preservation. This consideration brings us to the second factor for doubt about the triumph of Paul's cause during his own lifetime, and, consequently, to a matter for further speculation about the development of Christian affairs during the two or three decades after the Apostle's death.

The group of documents in the New Testament canon attributed to Paul is recognized by general critical opinion as involving a great many problems of authenticity, of varying degrees of complexity. Even when those writings are put aside which are by common consent not the original productions of the Apostle, the group of documents regarded as of genuinely Pauline authorship reveals in some of its members a truly amazing confusion of text. To take just two obvious examples of this, the Second Epistle to the Corinthians appears in its extant form as an almost unintelligible mosaic of fragments of Paul's Letters,[2] while it is widely thought that the present chapter 16 of the Epistle to the Romans was

---

[1] *Ursprung und Anfänge des Christentums*, III, p. 584. Cf. Harnack, *Die Mission und Ausbreitung des Christentums*, I, p. 72; Ropes, J. H., in *Studies of Early Christianity*, pp. 364–5; Klausner *From Jesus to Paul*, p. 598; Knox, *Gentiles*, p. 181.

[2] Cf. Moffatt, op. cit., pp. 126–8.

originally an independent document.[1]   Furthermore in this connection, we have evidence that one quite important Letter, namely that addressed to the Church at Laodicea, has completely disappeared,[2] while so simple a personal note as the Epistle to Philemon has survived.   This remarkable state of textual fragmentation and dislocation, together with the proof of the absolute loss of at least one Letter, is hardly consistent with the picture of a revered Apostle, triumphant in his championship of the Gentile cause, whose Letters were carefully treasured both during his lifetime and after his death as precious souvenirs of a holy and inspired leader.   It would appear rather that there intervened a period during which Paul's reputation suffered such an eclipse that his writings were neglected and their preservation left to the chance of circumstance, so that when that period of oblivion ended and Paul's work was once more valued, a search for his writings was only able to produce those which, in their varying degrees of completeness, have gone to form the *Corpus Paulinum*.   Having considered these matters, therefore, we find ourselves in turn faced with two further problems of great pertinence to a proper understanding of Christian Origins, namely those of the cause and the nature of Paul's apparent loss of reputation and his subsequent rehabilitation.

The literary remains of primitive Christianity involve yet another, and apparently related, problem.   The Epistles of Paul clearly attest the position of the Church at Jerusalem as the Mother Church of the Christian Faith.   There, as we have noted, were the members of the original community of disciples and the "pillars" of the Church; thither Paul, despite all his assertion of spiritual independence, felt himself obliged to go for approval of his work, for there was the original and accepted source of tradition and authority.[3]   The later Gospels and the Acts in their turn similarly agree in representing Jerusalem as the first effective centre of the new faith.   The position of the Jerusalem Church then being such, it is certainly remarkable that, except for a few minor documents of more than doubtful authorship,[4] there has survived no important authentic writing of the leaders of this Church.   That these leaders should have written letters as Paul did, dealing with various matters of faith and practice which must inevitably have required authoritative direction from time to time, would seem to be a reasonable assumption to make; and such indeed was the belief of the author of the Acts when he recorded the writing of a general letter to the Gentile churches embodying the decision of the Council of Jerusalem.[5]   Therefore, this lack of literary representation in the New Testament corpus is truly strange, and the fact is not adequately explained by the supposition that

[1] Cf. Moffat, op. cit., pp. 134–9.
[2] Col. 4. 16.   Cf. Moffatt, op. cit., pp. 159, 161.
[3] Gal. 2. 1, 2.   Cf. 1. 17, 18.
[4] I.e. the so-called Epistles of Peter, James, Jude, and John.
[5] Acts 15. 23, 30.

the destruction of Jerusalem in A.D. 70 was likely to have involved the archives of the Church there, for copies of its letters would have been circulated far beyond the confines of Palestine and thus, on *a priori* grounds, would have stood as good a chance of ultimate preservation as the writings of Paul. Accordingly we see another problem of Christian Origins to be involved here: what has caused the apparent loss of all literary documents representing the mind of the Church of Jerusalem, the fount of authority and the source of tradition for the Christian Faith, when the writings of Paul, who had been deeply involved in controversy with its leaders, have survived, howbeit in fragmentary form, in the sacred canon of scripture of the Universal Church?

The fact of the destruction of Jerusalem in A.D. 70 brings us to a question of general significance with regard to the literature of primitive Christianity. It is that of the almost complete silence maintained in the Christian documents, both within and without the New Testament canon, about this event. When we reflect on the magnitude of the disaster which the Jewish nation experienced through the war with Rome, which started in A.D. 66 and virtually ended with the destruction of the Jewish metropolis four years later, and of which Josephus has left us so graphic and circumstantial an account, the failure of the Christian writers to show any interest in these mighty and pregnant events is truly amazing. But far more amazing is the fact that, except for the few remarks of Hegesippus in the second century,[1] Christian literature contains no record of the fate of its Mother Church in this calamity. The original Jewish Church is suffered to pass away into complete oblivion until its pathetic remnants are noted with orthodox scorn some three centuries later by Epiphanius and Jerome.[2] Thus when we recall that the Gospels and the Acts were probably all written after A.D. 70 and that they are all essentially concerned with a period of Palestinian history just anterior to the war with Rome, this silence about the catastrophe of the Jewish nation and its consequences is seen also to constitute a problem of very considerable significance for our understanding of the nature of Christianity in the first century.

As we have proceeded in our survey the impression has steadily grown that in these various problems concerning the primitive Christian Church there appears to be involved a common time factor, which in each instance presents itself as either a lacuna in the thread of development, or a kind of tunnel-period from which we emerge to find a situation which is unexpected in terms of the situation which went before. For example,

---

[1] Preserved by Eusebius, *Ecclesiastical History*, III. v. 3. For Eusebius' dependence upon Hegesippus in this account, see Lawlor and Oulton, *Eusebius, Eccl. Hist.*, vol. ii, p. 82. The statements of Epiphanius about the flight of the Jerusalem Christians to Pella are perhaps derived from Hegesippus; see Lawlor, *Eusebiana*, pp. 5–9, 10 *seq.*, 28–34, and the discussion below, pp. 168–173.

[2] Cf. Lietzmann, *Geschichte der alten Kirche*, I, pp. 189 *seq.*; Meyer, *Ursprung und Anfänge des Christentums*, III, pp. 597 *seq.*; Harnack, *Die Mission und Ausbreitung des Christentums*, II, pp. 80–1; Schmidtke, *Neue Fragmente u. Untersuchungen z. den judenchristlichen Evangelien*, pp. 175–242.

the picture of the Christian faith presented in the Gospels, with its essential emphasis on historical data, is not that which might reasonably have been inferred from the earlier writings of Saint Paul; here a gap of some ten to twenty years from about A.D. 60 seems to separate these two different pictures of Christian belief. A similar hiatus, but of greater extent, shows itself, as we have also seen, between the Pauline presentation and that of the Acts of the Apostles.

Now since this intervening period coincides with the Jewish War against Rome and its epoch-making consequence of the destruction of Jerusalem, we seem to have an obvious *a priori* case for attributing to this catastrophe of Jewish national life a powerfully decisive effect upon the development of the infant Christian Church. Indeed so obviously does this appear that a newcomer to the study of Christian Origins, who had been pursuing his investigations along the lines which we have so far followed, might naturally conclude at this point that here was a matter which must already have been exhaustively studied by New Testament scholars, and he would turn to inquire, in reasonable expectation, for the relevant works. He would then learn, undoubtedly with considerable surprise, that there were no such works, and at the most he would only gather a few *obiter dicta* in the writings of various authorities to the effect that the event had no crucial importance for nascent Christianity, since the main lines of its subsequent development had already been laid down.[1]

This general disregard of the possible repercussions of the destruction of Jerusalem for primitive Christianity, or the summary judgement that the event had no significant consequence, is certainly remarkable, especially when we reflect upon the fact that every other factor which might conceivably have affected the infant Church has been minutely investigated. The matter is possibly to be explained as due to a natural reaction which was felt in New Testament scholarship against the extravagant theories which were current, about the end of the last and the beginning of the present century, concerning the part played by Paul in his conflict with the Judaistic Christians in the evolution of primitive Christianity. However that may be, we have seen that there are a number of important questions about Christian Origins which all appear in some way to be connected with the tunnel-period of Christian history which runs from about A.D. 60 to 80. Consequently a special attempt to investigate the general problem of the significance of the destruction of Jerusalem for the Christian Church would appear to be well merited and timely.

From the brief outline of the related questions given in this chapter it is clear that such an attempt, if it is to be at all adequate, will involve an investigation of a very large part of the wide and complex subject of Christian Origins and much ground still open to debate will have to be

[1] See the Appendix which follows this chapter.

traversed. This will inevitably mean that many conclusions which may be drawn will be of an essentially tentative character and subject to rejection or revision in the light of new judgements which may be established with regard to matters still under discussion. However, although such a process may be foreseen, the present essay will be justified if it succeeds in directing the attention of New Testament scholars to a subject which has been too long neglected.

APPENDIX

A selection of the opinions of some modern scholars on the effect of the destruction of Jerusalem on Christianity

An interesting catena of the views of previous writers down to 1908 is given by G. Hoennicke in his *Das Judenchristentum im ersten und zweiten Jahrhundert* (Berlin, 1908). In the chapter "*Die Beurteilung des Judenchristentums seit F. Ch. Baur*", the notes on the views of G. V. Lechler (p. 4), A. Ritschl (p. 6), and G. Holsten (p. 8) are particularly interesting. Hoennicke's own estimate (p. 104), which was limited to the effect of the overthrow of Jerusalem on the Jewish Christians, is brief: "*Die Missionskraft wurde gelähmt; die Hoffnung der Christen auf eine Gewinnung des jüdischen Volkes schwand mehr und mehr.*" Since that time the only work comparable to a monograph on the subject seems to be a fairly short article contributed to the *Theologisch Tijdschrift* in 1914 by Professor H. Windisch; and even this article divided its attention between the effects of the fall of Jerusalem on the Christians and on the Jews. The conclusion reached by this scholar was very meagre, namely that, "*den Christen bedeutete der Untergang der heiligen Stadt und ihres Tempels in erster Linie eine Bestätigung der Weissagung ihres Herrn und ein Strafgericht für die Kreuzigung ihres Herrn. Namentlich den Judenchristen wird es Schmerz bereitet haben, eine Gefährdung ihres Glaubens war es nicht.*" The significance of the opinion of Eduard Meyer on the subject has already been noted, but it will be useful to give his words *in extenso* (*Ursprung und Anfänge*, III, p. 584): "*Aber den Tatsachen entspricht diese Auffassung nicht; der Bruch und die Loslösung von Jerusalem ist vielmehr bereits von Paulus vollzogen. Die weiteren dortigen Vorgänge haben natürlich das Interesse der Christen erregt, die Zerstörung von Stadt und Tempel erschien ihnen als Erfüllung der Weissagungen und als das verdiente Strafgericht über das halsstarrige Volk, als Bestätigung dafür, dass die Juden in der Tat Offenbarung und Schrift vollkommen missverstanden hätten, dass allein die Christen das wahre Israel, das auserwählte Volk und die Träger der göttlichen Verheissung seien; aber eine weitere Bedeutung für ihre Auffassung des Christentums kam dem nicht mehr zu, die war vielmehr längst von Paulus festgelegt.*"

Dr. Streeter's appreciation of the importance of the event has also been already noted, and it will suffice here to give some further references to his views: *Four Gospels*, pp. 13 *seq.*, 231, 465, 512; *The Primitive Church*, pp. 40, 49, 62.

The opinion of Ernest Renan (*Antichrist*, Eng. trans., pp. 276–8), although his work comes in the earlier period surveyed by Hoennicke, is particularly noteworthy. He saw the chief significance of the destruction of Jerusalem in A.D. 70 in the consequent emancipation of Christianity from the tyranny of the Church of Jerusalem, and he drew a then topical comparison between the reactionary power exercised by the papal Curia and the Judaic conservatism of the original Christian community in Jerusalem. But it is interesting to note also that his English translator, W. G. Hutchinson, did not agree with this evaluation. He writes in his preface to his translation of Renan's book (p. xlii) that, "while one may concede, with Renan, an importance at least secondary to the fall of Jerusalem in the rise of Christianity, he attaches to it, I think, a significance too far reaching". This opinion, it may indeed be fairly said, is representative of the views of the majority of other modern scholars, in so far as they have noticed the matter, in its assigning of only a secondary importance to the destruction of Jerusalem in the evolution of Christianity, and it represents them too in its arbitrary character.

Various forms of this opinion, mainly of the nature of *obiter dicta*, are to be found in the works of the following writers: K. Kohler, *Jewish Encyclopedia*, vol. 4, p. 53; F. C. Burkitt, *Christian Beginnings*, pp. 71–2; H. J. Schonfield, *History of Jewish Christianity*, p. 54; H. M. Gwatkin, *Early Church History*, vol. ii, p. 9; O. Holtzmann, *Das Ende des jüdischen Staatswesens und die Entstehung des Christentums*, p. 657; F. J. Hort, *Judaistic Christianity*, pp. 175–6; L. Hartmann e G. Kromayer, *Storia Romana*, parte seconda, p. 62; J. Klausner, *From Jesus to Paul*, p. 599; A. von Harnack, *Die Mission und Ausbreitung des Christentums*, I, p. 55; O. Spengler, *The Decline of the West* (E.T., London, 1928), vol. 2, pp. 210–12; H. Lietzmann, *Geschichte der alten Kirche*, I, p. 189; A. J. Toynbee, *A Study of History*, vol. v, p. 75.

The thesis of R. Eisler (*ΙΗΣΟΥΣ ΒΑΣΙΛΕΥΣ ΟΥ ΒΑΣΙΛΕΥΣΑΣ* and *The Messiah Jesus and John the Baptist*), that Christianity was in origin a political movement against Rome, implies so thorough a reorientation of the usual view of Christian Origins that the significance of the fall of Jerusalem is dwarfed in that of the profound involvement of the Palestinian Christians in the nationalist movement. Indeed, in the light of Eisler's interpretation, the fall of Jerusalem but constitutes the inevitable final cause of the disappearance of Jewish Christianity and ensures the triumph of the "Hellenization" of the Jewish Messiah, initiated by Paul. The value of Eisler's work is discussed below in Chapter Six.

It is particularly unfortunate that Professor Ch. Guignebert did not live to complete his great trilogy on Christian Origins in the fine French series of studies on the development of human culture edited for the *Bibliothèque de Synthèse historique*, under the title of *L'Évolution de l'Humanité*, by M. Henri Berr. In the narrative of his last volume, *Le Christ* (Paris, 1943), Professor Guignebert did not reach A.D. 70, and so his opinion on the effect of the Jewish overthrow has remained unpublished.

The general comment of H. J. Schoeps in his recent monograph, entitled *Die Tempelzerstörung des Jahres 70 in der jüdischen Religionsgeschichte* (Uppsala, 1942), might well be noticed here. Although not primarily concerned with the Christian reaction to the Jewish overthrow, Schoeps remarks that, "*Schliesslich sei noch bemerkt, dass es* (i.e. his subject) *sich um Zusammenhänge handelt, die sich trotz ihrer grossen Bedeutung für frühchristliche Geschichte einer auffälligen Unbekanntheit erfreuen*" (p. 1).

The great study of Christian Origins recently published by Professor M. Goguel (*La Naissance du Christianisme*, Paris, 1946) deserves special attention. Although specific consideration is, curiously, nowhere given to the question of the possible effects of the Jewish overthrow of A.D. 70 on the Christian Church, Professor Goguel makes a number of brief references to the event which are tantalizing in their suggestion of an awareness of its importance which is never fully faced. The following are the most significant of these references. On p. 32 Goguel recognizes the crucial nature of A.D. 70: "*Dans la période qui va de la mort de Jésus à la fin du iie. siècle, une coupure assez nette se marque autour de l'an 70.*" However, although he proceeds to give several reasons why A.D. 70 was thus a turning-point, Goguel strangely omits all mention of the destruction of Jerusalem, and of the disappearance of the

3

Christian community of the city he merely remarks: "*C'est le moment où disparaît la première génération, où, par suite, l'Église n'est plus reliée que par l'intermédiaire d'une tradition aux témoins des faits générateurs de la foi et à ceux qui avaient donné les premières formules de la doctrine.*" In another passage (p. 171) he writes of the evolution of Christianity from its primitive Jewish form ("*christianisme dynastique*") to early Catholicism ("*l'ancien catholicisme*"). He notes that this process involved an effective degree of emancipation from the ideas and claims of Judaism; he continues: "*Leur élimination aurait sans doute été moins rapide et moins complète sans les événements de 66–70 et la catastrophe nationale qui a frappé alors le judaïsme.*" However, he thinks that the Christians primarily interpreted these events as the judgement of God upon the Jewish people for rejecting and slaying the Messiah. In support of this opinion he goes on to write: "*La conservation, dans la tradition, de paroles sévères de Jésus sur Jérusalem, l'annonce de sa destruction, la réduction du ministère jérusalémite à une brève série de conflits et surtout l'attribution aux Juifs de toute la responsabilité de la mort de Jésus sont autant de symptômes de cette condamnation du peuple juif qui a assuré la définitive autonomie du christianisme et fait du judéochristianisme une religion périmée.*" The effect of the catastrophe on Jewish Christianity he briefly describes as follows (loc. cit.): "*D'offensive qu'elle était avant 70, la position des judéochrétiens est devenue défensive après cette date. En renonçant à essayer d'imposer ses manières de voir aux Chrétiens helléniques, il s'est privé de l'une des forces qui l'avaient galvanisé.*" On pp. 282–3 Goguel briefly states, without explanation, that the events of A.D. 70 favoured and hastened a fusion of Palestinian and other types of Christianity. That the Jewish downfall of A.D. 70 ensured the victory of Pauline universalism is his opinion on pp. 347–9. After 70 there was no place in Judaism for heretics, so that the Jewish Christians had to choose between Judaism and what was to be Catholic Christianity. Goguel concludes with the significant comment: "*Si, sauf en ce qui concerne les petits groupes judéochrétiens restés réfractaires à l'action du Christianisme hellénique, l'Église a pu, sans que cela paraisse avoir provoqué de crise, s'adapter à la situation dans laquelle elle s'est trouvée après 70, n'est-ce pas parce que le paulinisme avait préparé pour elle une structure et un équilibre nouveaux?*" Then on pp. 596–7 is the pregnant observation: "*C'est seulement après 70 que la discussion avec le judaïsme a pris vraiment un caractère apologétique.*" Goguel sees two stages of this discussion in the Gospels of Mark and Matthew and in that of John. In his subsequent book *L'Église Primitive* (Paris, 1947), p. 185, n. 3, Professor Goguel writes: "*Ce n'est pourtant pas l'opposition paulinienne qui a diminué la position de l'Église de Jérusalem, ce sont les événements de 70.*"

Professor M. Simon in his important study, *Verus Israel: Étude sur les Relations entre Chrétiens et Juifs dans l'Empire Romain (133–425)* (Paris, 1948), recognizes the importance of A.D. 70 for Christianity (pp. 12–13, 87–88), but maintains that it had no definitive effect on the relations with which he is dealing as had the Jewish defeat of A.D. 135 (pp. 13 *seq.*). In making this judgement Professor Simon shows no appreciation of the complexity of the problem constituted by the relevant New Testament documents (e.g. see p. 88, n. 2), and he accepts the Eusebian story of the flight of the Jerusalem Christians to Pella at its face value and without comment (pp. 88, n. 3, 89, 304–5). Consequently, masterly though his handling of the complex theme is for the period which he selects, the study suffers seriously from his failure to investigate adequately the vital problems of the years before A.D. 135.

2

The Primitive Church: Its Territorial Extent and Internal Constitution according to the Evidence (a) of the Writings of Paul and (b) of the Acts of the Apostles

OUR brief survey of the various problems of Christian Origins which seem to point to the crucial nature of the two decades between A.D. 60 and 80 naturally demands that first a carefully constructed estimate of the situation of the Christian Church during this period, with regard to both its internal character and its external relations with its environment, be attempted. As we have already had reason to see, such an attempt, so far as the internal character of the Church is concerned, will inevitably be made on the basis of two distinct groups of evidence, namely the Epistles of Paul and the Acts of the Apostles, supplemented by any pertinent data which may be justifiably culled from other New Testament documents.

In trying to use Paul's writings for this purpose, however, we at once encounter a difficulty which we have already touched upon as an important part of the general problem of Christian Origins which we have set ourselves to study here. The *Corpus Paulinum*, as we have seen, provides some complicated critical questions about the authenticity of several of its component documents in their extant form. The evidence of loss and textual fragmentation and dislocation, which we noted, pointing, as it does, to the intervention of a period when Paul's writings were not valued generally by the Church, renders the very origin of the present *Corpus* a problem which is only likely to be elucidated after the prior problem of the apparent eclipse of Paul's reputation and its subsequent rehabilitation has been duly investigated. Fortunately, however, the dilemma is not absolute, and, while the problem of the origin of the *Corpus Paulinum* can be properly studied only after we have reached our conclusions on many other complicated matters, we can with confidence at this initial stage use certain at least of the Pauline documents as genuine writings of the Apostle. The documents which we may thus regard as authentic, either in whole or in substantial part, are those about which there is a significant consensus of critical opinion concerning their internal testimony in this respect; they comprise the Epistle to the Galatians, the two Epistles to the Thessalonians and the two to the Corinthians, and the Epistles to the Romans, to the Philippians, to the Colossians, and to Philemon.[1]

[1] Cf. Moffatt, *Intro. to N.T.*, pp. 62–4; K. and S. Lake, *Intro. to N.T.*, pp. 100–1; Guignebert, *Le Christ*, pp. 132–44.

15

It will obviously be best to begin our study of the situation obtaining in the Christian Church prior to A.D. 60 by dealing first with those factors of geographical extent and internal organization which may fairly be regarded as more free from the complications inevitably entailed where vital theological issues were at stake.

Of the geographical aspect of the Christian movement, as it is indicated in Paul's writings, we have already given a summary description. Here it will suffice to add that Paul's mission-field appears to have been roughly a crescent of which the eastern horn lay in the western provinces of Asia Minor and the western horn in Macedonia and Achaia. In this area were situate many famous cities of the Hellenistic world, and, although the Jewish Diaspora appears to have been strongly represented, the cultural tradition of its society was essentially Hellenistic.[1] Of Paul's reasons for preferring to work in this particular field we have no information in his Epistles. He does tell us that he left Palestine after his conversion and, after visiting Arabia, returned to what had apparently been a former centre for him at Damascus; then some two or three years later he travelled on to Syria and Cilicia.[2] His frequently repeated claim to be the Apostle of the Gentiles [3] must certainly indicate some natural sympathy for the non-Jewish peoples and would be consistent with the assertion of the Acts that he was a native of Tarsus, the celebrated university city of Cilicia.[4] It would thus also appear to be certain that the majority of the converts in his various churches were of Gentile extraction.

Paul's writings afford us no definite account of the extension of Christianity in regions beyond the limits of his own selected area of activity, but we can obtain some useful information on this subject from various chance allusions in his Letters. There was the Church at Jerusalem and there were churches in Judæa; [5] the mention of these latter is interesting, for, on the reasonable assumption that Judæa at this time would have meant the procuratorial district of that name,[6] it suggests that Paul differentiated in his mind between the Church in the metropolis and the churches in other parts of Palestine, thus attributing to the former a unique status in comparison with, presumably, the churches in Galilee, the reputed home of Jesus. According to the Galatian Epistle a Church already existed at Antioch in Syria,[7] and the Epistle

---

[1] Cf. P. Jouguet, *L'Impérialisme Macédonien et l'Hellénisation de l'Orient*, pp. 424 *seq.*; H. Gressmann, *Die orientalischen Religionen im hellenistisch-römischen Zeitalter*, pp. 13–14; V. Macchioro, *Zagreus*, pp. 473–82; Guignebert, *Le Monde Juif vers le Temps de Jésus*, pp. 307–26, *Le Christ*, pp. 155–88; G. Murray, *Five Stages of Greek Religion*, pp. 125–65.

[2] Gal. 1. 17–21.

[3] Gal. 1. 16; 2. 2, 7, 9; Rom. 1. 13; 11. 13; 15. 16.

[4] Acts 21. 39; 22. 3; cf. 9. 11, 30; 11. 25. Cf. Knox, *Jerusalem*, pp. 104–5; Klausner, *From Jesus to Paul*, p. 345; Guignebert, *Le Christ*, pp. 213–18, 221 *seq.*

[5] E.g. Gal. 1. 17, 18; 1 Cor. 16. 3; Gal. 1. 22.

[6] On the death of Agrippa I in 44 his kingdom, comprising mainly Judæa, Samaria, and Galilee, was put under Roman procuratorial administration, and it appears to have been popularly known as Provincia Judæa ; see Tacitus, *Ann.*, xii. 23, *Hist.*, v. 9; Suetonius, *Claudius*, 28. Cf. Schürer, *G.J.V.*, I, pp. 564, 456, n. 29.

[7] Gal. 2. 11 ff.

to the Romans witnesses to the existence of a Church of non-Pauline foundation in the capital city of the Empire. The fact that these churches at Rome and Antioch were established by Christians other than Paul and his companions indicates that there was successful missionary effort beyond the confines of the Pauline mission-field, and, it may well be noted, an effort which produced many Gentile conversions to the new faith. We are not, of course, expressly informed about the origin of this missionary activity, but, in default of evidence to the contrary and in consideration of the fact that Peter apparently operated even in Paul's special territory,[1] it might fairly be concluded that either the effort originated from the Church at Jerusalem or it was closely connected with it. This means in effect that, despite Paul's own careful definition of himself as the Apostle to the Gentiles *par excellence* and his claim in the Galatian Letter that this especial office had been recognized by the three leading members of the Church of Jerusalem,[2] no particular area of the Græco-Roman world was regarded officially as Paul's own preserve and the Jerusalem Church was prepared to work both in and beyond the district in which Paul had elected to labour.

We have already remarked upon the extraordinary silence both in Paul's writings and in the Acts with regard to the origin or the existence of Christianity in the regions to the south of Palestine, and especially in the great city of Alexandria. Here we shall limit ourselves to commenting upon the significance of Paul's silence in this respect. The actual fact that Paul's writings contain no reference to a Christian community in Alexandria is certainly not particularly remarkable in itself, and it may well be explained as due merely to the fact that in his surviving Letters he never had occasion to mention the subject. An interesting question in this connection, however, is raised by his references to Apollos.[3] Although he says nothing of the antecedents of Apollos, it is obvious from Paul's remarks in the first Corinthian Letter that he was a person of considerable importance in the Church at Corinth, apparently one who could be reasonably associated with Cephas and Paul as a pre-eminent Christian leader. This prominence would agree with that accorded to the Alexandrian Apollos in the narrative of the Acts, for his mention there surely indicates that an Apollos was known to have been a notable figure in the apostolic generation of the Church.[4] If, therefore, the Apollos of the Corinthian Epistle may reasonably be identified with the celebrated Alexandrian of the Acts,[5] then the fact that he was known, either willingly or unwillingly, as the leader of a party in the Corinthian Church, the members of which obviously regarded themselves as differing from those who followed Paul, is significant. Clearly there must have been some commonly recognized difference

[1] 1 Cor. 1. 12; 3. 22; see below, pp. 139–140.
[2] Gal. 2. 6–9.
[3] 1 Cor. 1. 12; 3. 4 ff., 21–23; 4. 6.
[4] Acts 18. 24 ff.
[5] Cf. *B.C.*, vol. iv, p. 232, n. on v. 24.

between either the teaching of Paul and Apollos, or the interests which they represented, to afford an effective basis for such party differentiation. What Paul says of himself and Apollos is curious.   From his metaphors of planting and watering and building [1] it would seem that a situation is envisaged at Corinth in which Apollos was working on Paul's converts, and obviously in a way which caused a distinction to be drawn between the doctrines of the two men.   Of Paul's attitude towards Apollos there is much ground for doubt.   His assertion that he and Apollos were God's fellow-workers and his final note about him at the end of the first Corinthian Letter [2] have reasonably led many scholars to believe that the personal relations between the two men were excellent.   However, if Paul's caustic remarks about the divine test to which the quality of each man's work would be submitted [3] contain a reference to Apollos, and their context would fairly indicate that they do,[4] then the apparent cordiality of the previous remarks may reasonably be understood as a diplomatic attempt to show that the brilliant teacher really could not add anything essential to the foundations which Paul had laid.   However that may be, the fact does remain sure and significant that Apollos was designated the head of a party in contradistinction to Paul, which fact can only be adequately explained on the ground that his teaching differed notably from that of Paul, and so, if this Apollos is to be identified with the Alexandrian teacher of Acts, it would appear reasonable to suppose that the doctrine of the Alexandrian Church was similarly different from the Pauline interpretation.[5]

The Pauline Epistles thus provide us with a picture of the new faith as active in various cities of the eastern Mediterranean countries, from Rome in the north-west to, probably, Alexandria in the south.   The area covered is considerable and includes a variety of races, which was undoubtedly reflected in the converts.   However, despite this racial difference and the length and uncertainty of communications, the writings of Paul manifest a consciousness of the fundamental unity of the movement. Although he was accustomed to talk of different churches and was fully aware of their distinctive characteristics, Paul was uncompromising in his assumption of the underlying unity of the Church as a whole, and he naturally supposed that the same idea was held by the readers of his Epistles.[6]   His unwavering loyalty to this concept of unity as axiomatic is the more remarkable when we consider, as we shall do at length below, the seriousness of the controversies in which the Apostle found himself

---

[1] 1 Cor. 3. 6–15.

[2] 1 Cor. 3. 5; cf. 4. 1, 6; 16. 12.   In this last reference it is possible that the addition of τοῦ ἀδελφοῦ is meant to distinguish this Christian from the celebrated Alexandrian teacher.

[3] 1 Cor. 3. 10–15.

[4] It is significant that A. S. Peake, *Commentary*, p. 835b, is so sufficiently conscious of the evidence of the context that, while clearly not wishing to accept the reference as being to Apollos, he supposes that it is to the leader of either the Apollos or the Cephas party.

[5] Klausner, op. cit., p. 389, n. 8, suggests that Apollos by his opposition to Paul's teaching prevented the latter from preaching in Egypt.

[6] E.g. Rom. 12. 5; 1 Cor. 12. 12, 13; Col. 3. 11.

involved, for, even in his most vehement protestations of his spiritual independence and the validity of his authority, he never contemplates a secession from the Church and the organizing of a body of Christians completely conformable to his own views.

To Paul this unity was clearly inherent in his conception of the Christ, but as a working reality, for such it undoubtedly was, certain essentials of organization were naturally entailed. Paul had no occasion to give a formal account of these, but something of the form in which they found practical expression may be extracted from his writings. Foremost and clearest stands the fact of the centrality of Jerusalem. The Church there is the unchallenged centre of the movement, and even Paul thinks of his mission as beginning from there.[1] This unique status of Jerusalem would appear to be the natural consequence of the fact that Christian tradition agrees in locating there practically all the most crucial events of the Passion of Jesus, and probably also of the fact that the metropolis was the divinely appointed religious centre for all devout Jews.[2] Of these factors Paul says nothing, but in his Galatian Letter he reveals a more significant reason for this position of Jerusalem. In this Letter he is clearly at pains to prove to his converts his essential independence in matters of authority and knowledge, but the very *raison d'être* of his attempt confirms that the Church at Jerusalem was generally regarded as holding a unique position in these matters. Indeed, Paul's assertion of independence is of independence from Jerusalem, and even though he can make out a case that in his conversion he owed nothing to the Church there, he subsequently makes tacit acknowledgement of its essential authority in matters of faith and practice by submitting to the judgement of its leading members the gospel which he had been preaching among the Gentiles—"lest by any means I should be running, or had run, in vain".[3]

From Paul's various remarks and *obiter dicta* in the Galatian Epistle we may learn much about the personal constitution of the Jerusalem Church. Intent on preserving the integrity of his own claims to apostolic status, Paul carefully refers to the effective members of the Jerusalem community generally as "them which were apostles before me",[4] and the context clearly indicates that these men were commonly recognized as the original authorities on the faith. How many of these primitive apostles there were, or what exactly was their position, Paul does not tell, but from subsequent statements in this Letter it may reasonably be inferred that their significance was very subordinate to that of the

---

[1] Rom. 15. 19; cf. Gal. 1. 17 ff.; 1 Cor. 16. 3.
[2] According to the Lukan tradition, Acts 1. 4; Luke 24. 47, 49, 52, the choice of Jerusalem as the birthplace of the Church was due to a divine command. Luke preserves a tradition that all the post-Resurrection appearances took place in Jerusalem and its environs. Cf. Harnack, *Die Mission und Ausbreitung des Christentums*, I, p. 38; Lietzmann, *Geschichte der alten Kirche*, I, p. 53; Guignebert, *Le Christ*, pp. 60–4.
[3] Gal. 2. 2. Cf. Goguel, *L'Église Primitive*, p. 32, n. 2.
[4] Gal. 1. 17.

three leaders with whose relations with himself Paul displays the most lively concern. As we have already noticed, these three men, named as James, Cephas, and John, are described as "pillars" ($\sigma\tau\hat{v}\lambda o\iota$),[1] and, by the fact of Paul's profession of indifference towards their reputation, they clearly appear as supreme authorities in matters affecting the faith and practice of the Church, so that even Paul is eager to emphasize whatever degree of recognition he felt that they had accorded to him and his work.[2] Of these three leaders James is obviously regarded as pre-eminent; he enjoys the unique designation of the Lord's brother ('Ιάκωβον τὸν ἀδελφὸν τοῦ κυρίου),[3] his name is given precedence over those of the others when they are mentioned together, and to the reproof of his emissaries at Antioch Peter, without apparent protest, submits.[4] As we have already seen, this pre-eminence of James raises several important questions, but at this stage of our study they are better left for later consideration, and we shall more conveniently pursue here our investigation of the Pauline evidence relative to the organization of the Church.

The controlling influence of both James and the Jerusalem Church is variously illustrated in Paul's writings. We have just noted the Antioch incident, which clearly indicates that James exercised a decisive control on a Church situate well beyond the frontiers of Palestine and containing a notable body of Gentile believers—a control, moreover, which was apparently accepted as normal. Next, from the celebrated credal passage of the first Corinthian Epistle we see that a tradition, which seems already to have attained that preciseness of form which comes from liturgical recitation, proclaimed the unique status of Cephas and James as Resurrection-witnesses.[5] Furthermore, the same document reveals that Cephas was so sufficiently well known, undoubtedly through personal contact, to the Christians at Corinth that he could inspire the formation of a party bearing his name in the Church of that city.[6] Then we may also note that among Paul's converts there operated Judaizing Christians whose authority the Apostle never questions, although he strives passionately to combat their influence.[7] While the inference must

---

[1] Gal. 2. 9. The metaphorical use of στῦλος to describe a person has one other N.T. example, namely Rev. 3. 12: ὁ νικῶν, ποιήσω αὐτὸν στῦλον ἐν τῷ ναῷ τοῦ θεοῦ μου. Jeremiah is set forth by God וּלְעַמּוּד בַּרְזֶל (Jer. 1. 18). An interesting use of the metaphor is found in an epigram attributed to Leonidas of Tarentum (*Anthology*, vii. 648), in which the establishment of a family is recommended—ζωὴν στυλώσαιτο· κακὸς δ' ἄστυλος ἰδέσθαι οἶκος. Cf. Euripides, *Iph. in Tauris*, 57. Cf. Lightfoot, *Galatians*, p. 109 loc. cit. "Höchst bezeichnenderweise hängt aber auch die Vorstellung von der Schlüsselgewalt des Erwählten mit der Symbolik vom 'Zeltpfahl' (jathed) aufs engste zusammen: Jesaiah 22, 20 ff. heisst es", Eisler, *IHΣOYΣ ΒΑΣΙΛΕΥΣ*, Bd. ii, p. 289; cf. p. 788 zu 39.

[2] Ibid.

[3] Gal. 1. 19. Evidence has been produced by L. Cerfaux to show that the vizier of the Nabatæan kings regularly bore the title of ἀδελφὸς βασιλέως; see Eisler, op. cit., Bd. ii, p. 175, n. 5, p. 541, n. 1.

[4] Gal. 2. 9, 11, 12. Cf. Sieffert, *Der Brief an die Galater*, p. 118.

[5] 1 Cor. 15. 5, 7. Cf. *Gospel according to the Hebrews*, apud Jerome, *Vir. Ill.* 2 (*Apocrypha II, Gospels*, ed. E. Klostermann, 19).

[6] 1 Cor. 1. 12.

[7] 2 Cor. 11. 1 ff.; Gal. 1. 6 ff.

certainly be more adequately justified later, it does seem that these men are likely to have been emissaries of the Church of Jerusalem. Lastly, there is the evidence of the collection of alms throughout the Gentile churches for the community at Jerusalem. This duty Paul admits was enjoined on him by the three Jerusalem leaders, and he accepted it without demur, and his writings eloquently witness to the zeal with which he laboured for its fulfilment.[1]

The picture which the Pauline documents, therefore, present of the constitution and organization of the Church is sufficiently clear in the major outlines. The various communities, whether Jewish or Gentile in racial origin, are regarded as forming a unity, which has its centre at Jerusalem with the original community of believers. In practical effect this unity expresses itself through the decisive control exercised by the Jerusalem community in matters of faith and practice. James, the brother of the Lord, is in fact the head of the Church and his views are represented in distant communities by special emissaries. Another practical, and undoubtedly a very effective, symbol of the subservience of other churches to the Mother Church of Jerusalem is a monetary contribution to the personal support of "the saints" (οἱ ἅγιοι) there.[2] The unique position which Jerusalem thus held was certainly due to the residence there of persons of primary authority for the new faith, but it may fairly be interpreted also as a natural consequence of the prevalence of the Jewish *Weltanschauung*, which instinctively regarded the city as the divinely appointed centre of the earth.

The composite character of the Church racially, as it is revealed in his writings, implies a relative situation of which Paul also similarly provides abundant illustrative evidence. Christianity was essentially a product of Judaism, and it was primarily carried to the Gentiles by men who were by birth and upbringing Jews, generally of a very zealous type. Their whole interpretation and presentation of the new faith was essentially based upon Jewish concepts and permeated by the influence of Jewish practice and outlook. Paul himself supplies significant illustration of this. Although he is so vividly conscious of his role of Apostle to the Uncircumcision and although his Letters are clearly addressed to communities which are predominantly Gentile, he uses with an apparently unthinking familiarity concepts and examples which are thoroughly Jewish. In striking contrast to the later Gospel writers, he seeks to instruct, or exhort, or to demonstrate a point to his readers, by some quotation from the Old Testament, employed in a thoroughly rabbinical manner, without any kind of explanation.[3] The Law and Circumcision he continually refers to as to concepts of general currency; he expects his Gentile readers to know that Christ had come, died, and risen again according

---

[1] Gal. 2. 10; 1 Cor. 16. 1–6; 2 Cor. 9. 1–15; Rom. 15. 25–27.

[2] Cf. Leitzmann, op. cit., I, p. 68; cf. Schonfield, *Hist. of Jew. Christianity*, pp. 25 *seq.* On the meaning of "the saints", see Lohmeyer, *Galiläa und Jerusalem*, p. 65.

[3] See examples given by Klausner, *From Jesus to Paul*, pp. 453–8.

to the foretelling of the Jewish Scriptures; [1] he assumes that they will appreciate the significance of the examples of Abraham [2] and Isaac,[3] of Sarah and Hagar,[4] and, even more remarkable, that they will understand such recondite Judaistic ideas as the Spiritual Rock,[5] the Mosaic Tablets of Stone [6] and the Covenant,[7] the Sin of Adam,[8] and the Stumbling Stone and Rock of Offence.[9]   Indeed we may take Paul's evaluation of the Jewish Scriptures in his Epistle to the Roman Christians as a succinct summary of his instinctive ascription of a Jewish education to his Gentile readers: "For whatsoever things were written aforetime were written for our learning, that through patience and through comfort of the scriptures we might have hope." [10]

This Pauline evidence, so eloquently testifying to the natural inability of the supreme protagonist of Gentile freedom to present his teaching in concepts and terms completely dissociated from the ethos of Judaism, is symptomatic of the fundamental dependence of Gentile Christianity on the Judaistic origins of its faith.   Whatever may have been the antecedents of the Gentile Christians before their conversion, whether they had been proselytes or God-fearers or completely heathen, their entrance into the Christian Church brought them at once within the ambit of Jewish theology.   They were introduced by their preceptors to a well-established and impressive corpus of belief and practice, which demanded their reverence and respect.   Their teachers could not, even had they been conscious of any such need, divorce themselves from the traditional values, concepts, and modes of expression with which they had been intimately familiar from childhood and which now formed the natural background of their mind and emotions.   The consequences arising from such a situation appear to be obvious and of very great significance. It would have been inevitable that the Gentile Christians should be impressed by a sense of both the essentiality and the majesty of Judaism, and they must accordingly have been keenly conscious of their own inferiority *vis-à-vis* the Jewish members of their faith.   Hence the Jew who was an expert in his native religion, the one who, like the Apollos of the Acts, was mighty in the scriptures,[11] must certainly have seemed to the average Gentile convert to Christianity a very oracle of divine law and wisdom.   We may rightly conclude, therefore, that the Gentile Christians were thoroughly dominated in all essential matters of the faith by their Jewish brethren, and that even in the case of those who had been converted by Paul and his companions there was a natural predisposition to subservience to Judaistic influence.

There is an interesting corollary to this predominance of the Jewish

---

[1] Rom. 1. 2; 1 Cor. 15. 3.
[2] Rom. 4. 2, 3; Gal. 3. 6 ff.
[3] Gal. 4. 28.
[4] Gal. 4. 21–31.
[5] 1 Cor. 10. 4.   Cf. Knox, *Gentiles*, p. 123.
[6] 2 Cor. 3. 2, 3.

[7] 2 Cor. 3. 6.
[8] Rom. 5. 14.
[9] Rom. 9. 32, 33.
[10] Rom. 15. 4.
[11] Acts 18. 24—ἀνὴρ λόγιος . . . δυνατὸς ὢν ἐν ταῖς γραφαῖς.

element in the primitive Christian Church. The logic of Paul's emphasis upon spiritual regeneration through faith in Christ led him inevitably to conceive of the Christians as forming a distinct body or nation apart from both the Jews and the Gentiles; for him the incorporation into Christ nullified all former distinctions of race, culture, and social class.[1] But it would appear that Paul was practically alone in his advocacy of this very exalted concept, and his several assertions of the impeccable character of his own national status eloquently point to the prestige which the Jewish Christian party claimed among the Gentile converts.[2] Clearly Jewish nationality was still being effectively accounted a factor of primary importance within the Christian Church.

This Pauline picture of the Church in its various aspects has now to be compared with that presented by the Acts of the Apostles. A proper appreciation of the significance of the testimony of this latter document must await the elucidation of the circumstances of its production, which can only be adequately attempted in this essay when conclusions have been reached about other matters which appear likely to have had a conditioning effect upon those circumstances. However, at this stage we can usefully employ two conclusions about its nature on which there is a general consensus of critical opinion. The first is that the Acts is at least forty years later in production than the genuine writings of Paul,[3] and it consequently represents a view of Christian Origins current in the Church some time after the destruction of Jerusalem. The second conclusion is that a definitely apologetical purpose informs the work, which has been aptly described as an attempt to show, perhaps to certain imperial patrons, the way in which the Christian Faith developed from a small and despised sect in the Jewish metropolis until it was preached publicly at Rome, "with none forbidding".[4] The interests of this apologetical theme may thus reasonably be expected to have coloured its presentation of the story of the beginning and early expansion of the Church, and must, therefore, be regarded as constituting an important factor which must be duly reckoned with in any evaluation of the evidence of the Acts in comparison with that of Paul.

We have already noticed that the Acts is in agreement with the writings of Paul in representing the geographical expansion of Christianity as a movement northwards and then north-westwards from Jerusalem, adding in its narrative of the missionary labours of Philip and Peter, of Barnabas and Paul, the names of other places within the area in which the new faith was preached and converts made. The agreement of Acts in this

---

[1] Rom. 4. 16–25; 9. 22–33; 10. 11, 12; 1 Cor. 1. 22–24; 10. 32; Gal. 3. 26–29; Col. 3. 10, 11.
[2] 2 Cor. 11. 21, 22; Phil. 3. 4–6; Rom. 11. 1; cf. 9. 4, 5; 11. 13–24.
[3] Cf. Moffatt, *Intro. to N.T.*, pp. 311–13; *B.C.*, vol. ii, pp. 358–9; Guignebert, *Le Christ*, pp. 55–7.
[4] Cf. Streeter, *Four Gospels*, pp. 531 *seq.*, *Camb. Anc. Hist.*, vol. xi, p. 258; J. Weiss, *Urchristentum.*, p. 525; *B.C.*, vol. ii, pp. 175 *seq.*; Lake, *Landmarks in Hist. of Early Christianity*, pp. 59 *seq.*; McNeile, *Intro. N.T.*, pp. 79 *seq.*; Moffatt, op. cit., pp. 284–5; Klausner, op. cit., pp. 228–9; Guignebert, op. cit., pp. 58–9.

respect is the more remarkable, since it constitutes a complete silence, as we have seen, about any spread of the Church southwards from Palestine, especially to Egypt. But the silence is not quite complete as to the existence of Christians in Alexandria, the great Egyptian metropolis. An account is given of an Alexandrian who was clearly an important personage in the primitive Church, namely Apollos, who, as we have seen, is probably to be identified with the Apollos of the First Corinthian Epistle.

What the author of the Acts has to tell of this Alexandrian is certainly curious. He is described as having entered the Pauline mission-field at Ephesus, where he proceeded to teach "the things concerning Jesus carefully" (ἀκριβῶς τὰ περὶ τοῦ Ἰησοῦ).[1] However, despite the fact that he was "mighty in the scriptures", "fervent in spirit", and "instructed in the way of the Lord" (κατηχημένος τὴν ὁδὸν τοῦ κυρίου), he only knew the baptism of John (ἐπιστάμενος μόνον τὸ βάπτισμα Ἰωάννου), and it was necessary that two of Paul's friends "expounded unto him the way of God more carefully" (ἀκριβέστερον αὐτῷ ἐξέθεντο τὴν τοῦ θεοῦ ὁδόν).[2] The whole situation as it is recounted here in the Acts is most extraordinary and hard to comprehend, the terminology which is employed being in particular both inexplicable and contradictory. It might fairly be asked how this Apollos could be described as κατηχημένος τὴν ὁδὸν τοῦ κυρίου and as teaching carefully τὰ περὶ τοῦ Ἰησοῦ and yet be depicted as ἐπιστάμενος μόνον τὸ βάπτισμα Ἰωάννου. Throughout the Acts, "the Way" (ἡ ὁδός) is a characteristic summary expression for full Christian faith and practice,[3] so that presumably to be κατηχημένος τὴν ὁδὸν τοῦ κυρίου should normally have described a fully instructed Christian. Further, it is a matter for legitimate astonishment that a man could carefully teach "the things concerning Jesus" and yet only know the baptism of John. According to the Lukan Gospel the baptism of John was but a weak prototype of the baptism in the Holy Spirit and fire, which would be effected by Jesus, and John in his teaching had merely pointed to the coming of one mightier than himself.[4] Certainly a form of Christian teaching given by one who was κατηχημένος τὴν ὁδὸν τοῦ κυρίου, but which

---

[1] Acts. 18. 25. The force of ἀκριβῶς for Luke is seen in Luke 1. 3. Cf. the use of the comparative in Acts. 18. 26; 23. 15, 20; 24. 22.

[2] Acts 18. 25, 26. See the non-committal conclusion to the note in *B.C.*, vol. iv, pp. 233–4, on the contrast between the uses of the word "accurately" here.

[3] Cf. Acts 9. 2; 16. 17; 18. 26; 19. 9, 23; 22. 4; 24. 14, 22; cf. John 14. 4-6. (Cf. *B.C.*, vol. iv, p. 100—"the Way".) In the passage in question there seems to be no reason to suppose that Luke intends to contrast τὴν ὁδὸν τοῦ κυρίου and τὴν τοῦ θεοῦ ὁδὸν (see *B.C.*, vol. iii, p. 178, for MS. authority for omitting the qualifying genitive τοῦ θεοῦ after τὴν ὁδὸν in v. 26). There appears to be no justification for the suggestion in *B.C.*, vol. iv, p. 233, that κατηχημένος means "hearsay" knowledge, thereby implying a measure of imperfection. Although the verb probably had not yet acquired its later technical connotation, its use in Luke 1. 4; Rom. 2. 18; 1 Cor. 14. 19; Gal. 6. 6 sufficiently attests its currency at this period as an accepted expression for normal religious instruction—an expression which was certainly not used in a comparative sense. Cf. Guignebert, op. cit., p. 290.

[4] Luke 3. 15-17.

expounded τὰ περὶ τοῦ 'Ιησοῦ carefully as far as the baptism of John, is inconceivable in terms of all that we otherwise know of the primitive Christian Faith.[1] The problem is further deepened by the sequel to the narrative of the Acts here. Paul subsequently meets at Ephesus twelve disciples who had presumably been baptized by Apollos, apparently before the time of his fuller instruction at the hands of Priscilla and Aquila.[2] To Paul's significant question concerning their possession of the Holy Ghost they reply professing ignorance of its existence [3] and stating that they were baptized into John's baptism. Paul is then described as having to explain to them the limitations of John's baptism, and his witness to Jesus. The amazing conclusion, therefore, follows that Apollos, despite his careful teaching of "the things concerning Jesus", did not even know or teach that John had borne witness to the unique vocation of Jesus.

On a fair analysis, then, the statements which the writer of the Acts makes about the Alexandrian Apollos are demonstrably preposterous both in their substance and in their mutual contradiction. The question therefore arises of the author's intention in including this account of Apollos, which is not apparently necessary to the development of his narrative and which has caused him to flounder so hopelessly in self-contradiction. The most probable solution seems to be suggested by a consideration of two facts which have already been noticed. The first is that Apollos is specially described as an Alexandrian Jew, who had presumably acquired his knowledge of Christianity in his native city.[4] Secondly, as we have seen in our examination of the Pauline evidence, an Apollos had operated at Corinth in such a way that certain of Paul's converts there were led to form themselves into a party under the name of Apollos and in contradistinction to that of Paul. From these two facts we may reasonably infer that an Alexandrian Christian of considerable personal prestige had taught among Paul's converts an interpretation of the Christian faith which was notably different from that expounded

[1] See the statement of W. Manson, *Jesus the Messiah*, p. 166, that the apparently contradictory elements in the Apollos passage are not to be explained as due to a conflation of diverse sources, since such an explanation ignores "the possible complexities of Christian history in the apostolic age". Loisy, *Le Origini del Cristianesimo*, p. 165, suggests that Apollos was perhaps the founder of the Christian community at Ephesus, a fact which Luke does not wish to make known. Lietzmann, *Geschichte der alten Kirche*, I, p. 56, pertinently observes that, according to the Lukan account, Apollos "*der auch nur die johanneische Taufe empfangen hat, aber doch bereits vom Geist getrieben als christlicher Missionar auftritt*". Guignebert, op. cit., p. 293, makes the interesting comment, "*Je crois qu'il faut voir en Apollos un bon type d'apôtre indépendant du Tarsiote, mais conduit, par une formation analogue et aussi par l'influence du milieu dans lequel il agit, à poser les mêmes postulates.*" But he also, significantly, observes that, "*C'est que, sans doute, il a, lui aussi, son Évangile, qui n'est pas tout à fait celui de Paul, ou qu'il pense autrement que lui sur la conduite à tenir à l'égard des judaïsants. Nous ne savons pas.*" Cf. Klausner, *From Jesus to Paul*, p. 387.
[2] Acts 19. 1–7. [3] Cf. *B.C.*, vol. iv, p. 237, n. on v. 2.
[4] Acts 18. 24: 'Αλεξανδρεὺς τῷ γένει. Codex Bezæ adds: ὃς ἦν κατηχημένος ἐν τῇ πατρίδι τὸν λόγον τοῦ κυρίου. Lietzmann, op. cit., I, p. 134, comments, "*ob er dort (Alexandria) oder anderswo zum Christentum bekehrt ist, erfahren wir nicht*". On the actual evidence this observation is true, but value must be given to the fact that in the tradition utilized by Luke Apollos was specially distinguished as an Alexandrian by race, which must surely mean that the fact had more than a racial significance.

by Paul. The knowledge of this situation would appear to have established itself in the tradition of the Church and the author of the Acts
had to reckon with it. The line which he adopted is clear in its intention,
but, as we have just seen, singularly unhappy in its execution. Two
points seem to stand out distinctly in his handling of the subject. Quite
obviously Apollos' status as an instructed Christian could not formally
be denied, since it was a fact of common tradition. This clearly embar-
rasses the author, who is certainly intent on depreciating the religious
antecedents of the celebrated Alexandrian and describing the limitations
of his teaching. Hence we have his series of contradictory statements
about the quality of Apollos' knowledge and his assertion that the
Alexandrian could only be commended to the Pauline churches after
he had received necessary instruction from two eminent supporters of
Paul. The conclusion which we reach, therefore, from this lengthy
examination of the Apollos passage is that the author of the Acts, who
agrees with the Pauline evidence in representing the important geographical
movement of the Christian faith as that with which Paul was essentially
associated, also agrees in showing a dislike for the teaching of Apollos
and goes further in representing it as defective to the extent of absurd
caricature. Since, then, in this work Apollos is specially described as
an Alexandrian Jew, the evidence of the Acts may thus be reasonably
interpreted as indicating that the Christianity of Alexandria was regarded
as seriously different from that identified as Pauline, and was judged as
being defective in comparison with it.[1]

Although he makes no formal statement thereon, the author of the
Acts agrees with Paul in recognizing that the Church is essentially a
unity, with its centre at Jerusalem. His narrative, which is designed
to set forth the consequent stages of the progress of the new faith, is
constant in showing that at each of the more crucial of these stages the
decision, by way of either initiation or confirmation, was taken by the
Church of Jerusalem. The regulating of the new situation caused by
the evangelization of the Samaritans is dealt with by a special apostolic
commission;[2] the problem involved in the Gentile conversion at Cæsarea
is decisively debated in the metropolitan Church;[3] another commission
is dispatched from there to inquire into the position at Antioch occasioned
by the deliberate evangelization of the Gentiles,[4] and it is in formal council
at Jerusalem that the question of the terms on which the Gentiles are
to be admitted into the Church is finally decided.[5] The Pauline saga,
moreover, represents the Apostle as being generally in close touch with
the Mother Church,[6] and the climax of its drama is really constituted

---

[1] The fact that this Apollos passage may reflect the view which Luke had of Alexandrian
Christianity was recognized by R. B. Rackham, *The Acts of the Apostles*, p. 342, though his
attempt to account for it seems rather naive.

[2] Acts 8. 14 ff.

[3] Acts 11. 1–18.

[4] Acts 11. 22, 23.

[5] Acts 15. 6–29.

[6] Acts 9. 27–30; 11. 25, 26, 30; 15. 2 ff.; 18. 22.

by his final visit to Jerusalem, the purpose of which is significantly depicted as that of reporting on his work.[1]　Thus, although the author of the Acts is clearly concerned with showing the evolution of Christianity as a religion of universal validity, and is, therefore, the more interested in its fortunes in the world of Græco-Roman culture, he is, nevertheless, governed by a tradition which knows that the Church during the period concerned was decisively controlled from its original centre at Jerusalem.

The Acts shows a similar casual agreement with the evidence of the Pauline documents with regard to the unique position of James.　Its first reference to him is certainly remarkable.[2]　Peter, who had to this point in the narrative been clearly represented as the leader of the community of the disciples at Jerusalem, is described as directing, before his departure to "another place" consequent on his escape from the Herodian captivity, the inmates of the house of John Mark's mother to "tell these things unto James, and to the brethren".　This first unqualified reference to James is surely significant, and it must undoubtedly be interpreted as indicating that the author was so conscious of the fame of James that he naturally assumed that his readers would immediately understand his unheralded and unexplained appearance here as a pre-eminent personage in the primitive community.[3]　His second mention of James occurs in the account of the so-called Council of Jerusalem and is equally significant.[4]　Here James definitely appears as the leader or chairman of the assembly.　Peter, and then Barnabas and Paul, are represented as making their statements before the assembled Apostles and elders; they are heard in silence, and when they end no comment is made until James sums up the matter and makes his proposals, which apparently are accepted without debate.[5]　The third reference to James is similarly eloquent of his unique position in the Jerusalem Church. On the occasion of his last visit to Jerusalem Paul is significantly described as going in "unto James; and all the elders were present".[6]　The picture thus given of James as the essential head of the Mother Church, attended by the elders,[7] must certainly be a natural expression of the author's

---

[1] Acts 21. 18, 19.　　　　　　　　　[2] Acts 12. 17.

[3] Klausner, op. cit., p. 215, thinks that the sudden appearance of James as an authoritative person indicates that the author of Acts draws here upon a source in which James' identity had been previously explained.　If this were the case, it would still mean that Luke must have felt that James was sufficiently well known to his readers, unless he were guilty of a peculiarly bad piece of literary workmanship.　Meyer, *Ursprung und Anfänge des Christentums*, III, p. 223, comments on Acts 1. 14 (the first reference, by implication, of James' adherence to Christianity), "*konstatiert nur die Tatsache*"; cf. Lohmeyer, *Galiläa und Jerusalem*, pp. 56–57.

[4] Acts 15. 13–21.

[5] See *B.C.*, vol. iv, p. 177 ("I decree").　The objection of Knox, *Jerusalem*, p. 233, n. 38, that James cannot be considered as a president of the Council whose ruling was definitive, seems to be based on his belief that the Lukan account is authentic and that the Council is to be regarded as pursuing Sanhedrin procedure, a supposition which, of course, fails to evaluate the account as representative of Luke's idea of what a Church Council should be in terms of his apologetic purpose.

[6] Acts 21. 18.

[7] "James is obviously the chief, and the presbyters are only assessors . . ." (*B.C.*, vol. iv, p. 270).

conception of the organization of authority in the apostolic community, a conception which by virtue of its tacit inclusion in the narrative must surely be regarded as representative of common knowledge in contemporary Christian circles.

The evidence of the Acts on the subject of the racial constitution of the Church is also given unconsciously, and it is generally in agreement with the testimony of Paul's writings. It represents the movement of evangelization as consistently a movement from the Jewish centre outwards to the Gentile periphery, whether it be on the geographical plane, as from Jerusalem out into the Roman Empire, or locally, as from the synagogue, where the Christian message is always at first given, out to the Gentiles beyond its pale. Thus in each local Church it would appear that there was an original nucleus of Jewish believers, and the attention of the Gentiles to the new faith was usually attracted in the first instance through the controversy caused in the synagogue by the Christian exegesis of the Jewish scriptures to prove the unique status and vocation of Jesus.[1] The picture which the narrative of the Acts gives, therefore, of the beginnings of Christianity in the Pauline mission-field shows the faith as generally germinating in an essentially Judaistic ethos, and the reputation which Apollos enjoyed as a man "mighty in the scriptures" is symptomatic of the prestige acquired, in lesser degrees perhaps, by other Jewish Christians, whether of Paul's following or not. Consistent also with this aspect of Christian Origins is the fact that those of Paul's lieutenants and friends whose work was deemed noteworthy in the tradition were without exception Jews.[2]

In this connection we shall do well to notice also that the author of the Acts in his presentation of the tradition of Christian Origins never gives any indication that the numbers of the Gentile converts were large,[3] while he makes several statements about the considerable numerical strength of the Jewish Christians in Palestine,[4] which, even when due recognition is made of their probable exaggeration, must fairly be interpreted as genuine indications of the comparative situation. More

---

[1] E.g. Acts 13. 43–48; 14. 1–4; 17. 10–12; 18. 5–8.

[2] E.g. Silas, Timothy, Aquila and Priscilla. On Paul's own showing Titus is the obvious exception, e.g. Gal. 2. 3; 2 Cor. 2. 13; 7. 6, 13. However, no memory of him seems to have reached Luke or was thought worthy of preserving by him; the ascription of one of the Pastoral Epistles to Titus sufficiently attests the fact that outside Lukan circles the memory of this efficient Gentile companion of Paul remained strong.

[3] Acts 14. 21 ($\mu\alpha\theta\eta\tau\epsilon\acute{\upsilon}\sigma\alpha\nu\tau\epsilon\varsigma$ $\acute{\iota}\kappa\alpha\nuο\acute{\upsilon}\varsigma$); 16. 40; 17. 4 ($\pi\omicron\lambda\grave{\upsilon}$ $\pi\lambda\widehat{\eta}\theta\omicron\varsigma$ surely balances $\gamma\upsilon\nu\alpha\iota\kappa\widehat{\omega}\nu$ $\tau\epsilon$ $\tau\widehat{\omega}\nu$ $\pi\rho\acute{\omega}\tau\omega\nu$ $\omicron\grave{\upsilon}\kappa$ $\grave{\omicron}\lambda\acute{\iota}\gamma\alpha\iota$); 17. 12, 34; 20. 6–8 (a peculiarly significant passage in this respect, since it shows that the Church at Troas could be gathered in one single upper-room). The $\lambda\alpha\acute{ο}\varsigma$ . . . $\pi\omicron\lambda\grave{\upsilon}\varsigma$ claimed by the Lord in a vision (Acts 18. 10) is notably at Corinth, one of Paul's greatest centres. Hoennicke, *Das Judenchristentum im ersten und zweiten Jahrhundert*, p. 175, produces no convincing evidence in support of his opinion that the Gentile outnumbered the Jewish Christians. The number of the Jewish Christians to that of their unbelieving countrymen may have been "*verhältnismässig gering*", but not to that of the Gentile Christians.

[4] Acts 2. 41, 47; 4. 4; 6. 1, 7; 9. 31; 21. 20. Paul's reference to the five hundred "eye-witnesses" would seem to be derived from Palestinian tradition (1 Cor. 15. 6) and may well represent the round number of a body of persons claiming special prestige in the Palestinian Church in Paul's time.

important still are his statements and allusions with regard to the essential orthodoxy of the Jewish Christians in Palestine in terms of Judaism, and the reputation which they enjoyed among their countrymen. The Temple continues to be their place of worship,[1] they remain true to the laws of ritual purity,[2] they come to include many priests and Pharisees among their ranks,[3] and they merit the description of being "zealous for the law" (ζηλωταὶ τοῦ νόμου).[4] Ritual acts of a supererogatory character are practised by them,[5] and they significantly demand of Paul that he should demonstrate his Jewish orthodoxy by participation in such an act, thus to rebut the alleged calumnies that he had betrayed the essential customs of Judaism in his teaching. Further in this connection it is to be noted that the author of the Acts knew that the outbreak of persecution occasioned by the activity of Stephen had not been directed against the Apostles at Jerusalem,[6] who were the recognized leaders of the Christian movement, and in his last general summary of the fortunes of the Palestinian Church he significantly states: "So the church throughout all Judæa and Galilee and Samaria had peace, being edified; and, walking in the fear of the Lord and in the comfort of the Holy Ghost, was multiplied." [7]

It appears, therefore, that despite their difference in the date, in the circumstances, and in the purpose of production, the writings of Paul and the Acts of the Apostles show a remarkable agreement, in both statement and sympathy, with regard to the position of the Church in the first three decades of its life. They agree in manifesting a sympathetic interest in the spread of the new faith in Asia Minor, Achaia, and Rome, and a corresponding dislike of the Christianity current at Alexandria. They witness equally to the fact that the Church was subject to the vigorous control of the Jerusalem *Urgemeinde*, and that this control was personified in James, the brother of the Lord. The inevitable consequence of the original preponderance of the Jewish element is likewise revealed in the continuing dependence of the new faith on Judaism and the essential domination of the Gentile converts by Judaic influences.

The evidence of Paul and the Acts is thus seen as attesting the situation of the Church at this time as one fraught with problems and possibilities for the future development of the Christian Faith—problems and possibilities, moreover, which urgently demand a tracing of their issue during the next few decades. However, before this task can be attempted, it

---

[1] Acts 2. 46; 3. 1; 5. 12, 42; 21. 23, 24, 26; cf. Luke 24. 53. Cf. Lietzmann, *Geschichte der alten Kirche*, I, p. 54; Guignebert, *Jesus*, p. 309, *Le Christ*, pp. 111–12.
[2] Acts 10. 14; 11. 2, 3; 15. 1; 21. 21–24.
[3] Acts 6. 7; 15. 5.
[4] Acts 21. 20.
[5] Acts 21. 23, 24. Cf. *B.C.*, vol. iv, p. 272; Knox, op. cit., p. 283, n. 49; Klausner, *From Jesus to Paul*, p. 398.
[6] Acts 8. 1.
[7] Acts 9. 31.

is necessary to remember that these two sources of evidence show a general sympathy of outlook on these matters, so that, even after making allowance for the fact that their relationship has yet to be explained, they must fairly be regarded as representing one distinctive side in a conflict of interests. That the other side, namely that of the Jewish Christians, should be known from its own witness, if we are to understand aright that aspect of the problem of Christian Origins which we have set ourselves to study here, is obvious. We have already seen that the matter is complicated by the complete absence of any certain authoritative documents representative of Jewish Christianity; it now remains to be seen whether from any other of the New Testament writings or from any other ancient source we can glean information about those features of the Church which are, as we have noted in this chapter, revealed from the point of view of their own peculiar interests by Paul and the author of the Acts.

3

The Church in Palestine according to the Evidence of the Synoptic Gospels and other Palestinian Sources

IT is a remarkable fact that the Mother Church of Christianity is known to us through no writing which can unhesitatingly be accepted as one of its own production. Although there is adequate reason to suppose that the Palestinian Christians were accustomed to give literary expression to certain forms of their teaching,[1] it is in documents designed for Greek-speaking communities living after the overthrow of Jewish national life that the traditions of the Palestinian Church have been preserved. This fact naturally creates a problem of peculiar seriousness for the study of the original Jewish Christianity, since it is obvious that difference of time and ethos alone are likely to have been conditioning factors of vital importance in the process of the transmission and expression of the initial Palestinian *Weltanschauung*. But this is not the full extent of the problem, for we have already seen signs, and more abundant evidence will soon have to be considered, of a deep cleavage of sympathy between the Jerusalem Church and the Gentile churches founded by Paul in the various cities of the Levant. Hence the very existence of Greek documents purporting to preserve Palestinian traditions, as has already been suggested, does itself constitute a major problem of Christian Origins. However, having carefully noted this basic difficulty, we can still regard the Synoptic Gospels as legitimate sources of information about Palestinian Christianity, because they are manifestly composed of original Palestinian material which must have once been the possession of the native believers. For instance, to quote just three obvious examples of this, their essential familiarity with Palestinian geography,[2] the evident interest displayed in controversy with various Jewish sects,[3] and the concern shown for certain Jewish institutions and customs[4] attest the existence, beneath later interests and applications, of a definite substratum of original tradition, which was born and shaped in the environment of

---

[1] Cf. Taylor, *Formation of Gospel Tradition*, pp. 44 *seq.*; Dodd, *History and the Gospel*, p. 82. 2 Cor. 3. 1 would seem to indicate that letters of commendation were issued by the Jerusalem Church to its emissaries; these may well have touched on theological matters, as did the letters of Paul.

[2] K. and S. Lake, *Intro. N.T.*, Appendix B.

[3] E.g. Mark 2. 16–18; 3. 6; 7. 1–8; 9. 11–13; 11. 27–33; 12. 13–27, 35–40.

[4] E.g. Mark 1. 44; 2. 16, 18–20; 2. 23–3. 6; 3. 22–30; 7. 1–5, 8–23, 24–28; 10. 2–12; 11. 7–10, 15–17, 27–33; 12. 13–27, 35–41; 13. 1, 2; Luke 1. 5–11; 2. 22–25; 3. 23–38; 4. 16–20; 10. 13–15; Matt. 1. 1–17; 5. 17–24, 33–35; 17. 24–27; 23. 1–39. Cf. Bultmann, *Die Geschichte der synoptischen Tradition*, pp. 25, 34, 146–7.

Palestinian Christianity.　But, while it is accordingly justifiable to turn to the Synoptic Gospels for evidence of the primitive Jewish Church, their utilization for this end obviously and inevitably entails many complicated problems of literary and historical criticism, so that the extraction of any particular passage as a pertinent datum will require separate justification.

Beyond the Synoptic Gospels and in this connection the earlier chapters of the Acts of the Apostles, as will be indicated later, there is no other source of evidence having even their degree of reliability for Palestinian Christianity.　There does exist, however, certain material which demands the attention of any scholar who sets himself the task of investigating this aspect of the problem of Christian Origins.　It is well known that the contemporary Jewish historian, Josephus, in the extant Greek version of his works makes only two references to the Christian movement and that the authenticity of both passages has been subject to long debate, in which the verdict has generally been, in the case of the passage about Jesus, of a condemnatory character; the account of the death of his brother James in the other passage has usually been regarded with more favour, and its evidence relative to our present subject must, therefore, duly be discussed.[1]

The publication in recent years of a Slavonic version of what is claimed to be Josephus' original work on the Capture of Jerusalem (the *Halosis*), and the amazing interpretation of it propounded by Dr. Robert Eisler in a work of truly monumental proportions, have raised several new and very complicated issues with regard to the original nature of the Christian movement.　But since the primary question involved concerns the genesis of Christianity as a particular expression of nationalist agitation in contemporary Jewish political life, the problem which the Slavonic version constitutes will be more properly discussed later when we come to consider Palestinian Christianity in relation to the movement and the events which eventually led to the Jewish revolt against Rome in A.D. 66.[2]

The remaining material to claim our attention as a possible source of information about Palestinian Christianity comprises certain fragments of the writings of Hegesippus preserved by Eusebius and Epiphanius, either in the form of direct quotation or in that of summarized reference.[3] The validity of the testimony of this second-century member of the Church of Aelia Capitolina for Palestinian Christianity in the first century has been the subject of the diverse opinions of many scholars.[4]

[1] The problems relative to the evidence of Josephus are discussed at length in Chapter Six, pp. 95 *seq;* 110 *seq.*
[2] See Chapter Six, pp. 114 *seq.*, and Appendix I.
[3] The fragments of, or references to, the writings of Hegesippus will be indicated when utilized.　On the subject generally see H. J. Lawlor, *Eusebiana*, Essay I; Hort, *Judaistic Christianity*, pp. 164–80; B. F. Westcott, *Canon of the N.T.*, pp. 185–90; E. Schwartz, *Z.N.T.W.* (1903), *Zu Eusebius Kirchengeschichte, I. Das Martyrium Jakobus des Gerechten.*
[4] E.g. J. Weiss, *Urchristentum*, p. 553, writes of the accounts of Hegesippus: "*Diese tragen den Stempel judenchristlicher Legende und sind als solche für die Anschauungen der späteren judenchristlichen Gemeinde allerdings ein höchst wertvolles Zeugnis*".　E. Meyer's comment, *Ursprung und Anfänge*

The soundest view of the matter appears to be that which recognizes
Hegesippus as having recorded certain ecclesiastical traditions current in
Palestine in his day, which, while obviously inclined to elaborate un-
critically the prestige of the original centre of the Christian Faith, did,
however, preserve some genuine memories of the first-century community.
It is obvious that if it is evaluated in this way, the evidence of Hegesippus
can only be regarded as a secondary source, the use of which must be
limited to confirming and illustrating conclusions which have been drawn
from the study of more reliable documents.

It is now our task to endeavour to extract, from this problematical
Palestinian material, information about the original Jewish Christianity
of the land, and particularly information referring to those relevant
parts of the Christian movement which are depicted in the writings of
Paul and the Acts of the Apostles, and which we noted in the last chapter.
We shall accordingly commence by investigating the Palestinian data
for evidence of the attitude of the native Christians towards the extension
of the faith to the Gentiles.

Of primary importance among the material relevant to this subject
is the episode of the Syro-Phœnician woman, which is recorded in the
Markan Gospel and reproduced, without any substantial alteration, by
Matthew, but significantly omitted by Luke.[1] The authenticity of the
passage as a piece of original Palestinian tradition is attested by its
obvious unpalatableness to Gentile Christian taste, for such a story could
not conceivably have arisen gratuitously in a Gentile environment.[2] If,
therefore, it may reasonably be regarded as a fragment of genuine
Palestinian tradition, the significance of its testimony is supreme. It
means that the Jewish Christians in Palestine were accustomed to tell a
story about the attitude of Jesus to a Gentile in which an authoritative
pronouncement was made on the relative claims of the Jews and Gentiles
to the benefits of the Master's mission. The Gentile claim is not
absolutely refused, but it is contemptuously relegated to a secondary place:
"Let the children first be filled: for it is not meet to take the children's
bread and to cast it to the dogs." [3] Thus the Gentile claim to participation in the faith is grudgingly admitted and the occasion exploited to the
fullest to exalt the natural privilege of the Jews at the expense of the
Gentiles. The passage truly breathes the spirit of national intolerance

des Christentums, III, p. 73, n. 2, is scornful: "*eine phantastische Legende ohne jeden geschichtlichen
Wert*". Lietzmann, *Geschichte der alten Kirche*, I, p. 58, designates them "*Gemeindelegende*";
cf. G. Kittel, *Z.N.T.W.* (1931), p. 145. For other opinions, qualifiedly favourable to the
value of Hegesippus' record, see Streeter, *Primitive Church*, pp. 20, 38 *seq.*; Schürer, *G.J.V.*, I,
p. 582, n. 46; J. B. Lightfoot, *Galatians*, p. 278 ; *Supernatural Religion*, pp. 268 *seq.*; Eisler, *Messiah
Jesus*, pp. 519, n. 4, 541; Burkitt, *Christian Beginnings*, pp. 60–1; Guignebert, *Le Christ*, p. 19.
[1] Mark 7. 24–30; Matt. 15. 21–28. Cf. Streeter, *Four Gospels*, p. 221, n. 1.
[2] Cf. Goguel, *Jesus*, pp. 321–2; Guignebert, *Jesus*, p. 317; Taylor, *Formation of Gospel Tradition*,
pp. 75–6.
[3] Cf. C. H. Turner, *New Com. N.T.*, p. 76a; Strack und Billerbeck, *Kommentar*, I, pp. 724–5.

and religious exclusiveness, and must, by virtue of its very brutality, be a true reflection of Jewish Christian sentiment. It must, moreover, be regarded as connoting the definitive official attitude of the Jewish Church, for it is obvious that even Mark, writing outside Palestine for a Gentile public, was so conscious of its authority that he felt obliged to record it, despite its blatant insult to Gentile feelings and despite the apologetic nature of his work, which we shall discuss later. Matthew also, writing after Mark, witnesses to its significance, but he makes additions to the Markan version which are characteristically indicative of his essentially Jewish outlook.[1] The question of the original use of the story in the Palestinian Church is more difficult to answer.[2] Two interpretations appear to be possible, namely either that it was invoked first by the Jewish Christians to justify isolated admissions of Gentiles to a qualified membership of the Church and later gained currency as an established ruling, or that it was originally employed to express disapproval of the extension of Christian privileges to the heathen. In the light of the fact that the story has been preserved in Mark it would seem that the former interpretation may be the more probable,[3] since it would be reasonable to suppose that what was once enunciated as a grudging permission for Gentile admission into the Church was quickly invoked in favour of subsequent Gentile converts until it came, despite its inherent uncongeniality, to be regarded as the precious charter of Gentile right to participation in the benefits of the new faith.

The spirit of contemptuous condescension and national intolerance which permeates the story of the Syro-Phœnician woman is strikingly consistent with that implicit in the attitude displayed by the Jerusalem Christians in the incident at Antioch which Paul has recorded in his Galatian Epistle,[4] and it may indeed be argued that it is not substantially different from that spirit of nationalist superiority which the Apostle himself betrays when he likens his non-Jewish converts to a wild olive, grafted, contrary to its nature and without any apparent merit, into the stock of the good olive tree. [5]

That this story which Mark has preserved is not a unique specimen of Jewish Christian tradition in this respect is further proved by other passages from the Gospel records. The two which we have now to consider are peculiar to Matthew and are typical of that writer's essentially Jewish outlook; however, although the determination of the *raison d'être* of the First Gospel constitutes one of the major problems of the study of Christian Origins, which we shall only be able profitably to discuss at a

---

[1] Cf. Streeter, op. cit., pp. 260, 425, 514.
[2] Cf. Taylor, op. cit., p. 76.
[3] Cf. Taylor, op. cit., p. 148. M. Werner, *Der Einfluss paulinischer Theologie im Markus-evangelium*, p. 201, is certainly right in thinking that the original incident cannot be interpreted as laying down the principle of universalism, but he fails to consider Mark's purpose in preserving the memory of such an incident in his record.
[4] Gal. 2. 11–13.
[5] Rom. 11. 13–24.

much later stage, these passages may fairly be judged as representative of a true continuity of thought from the primitive Palestinian community.

The first passage takes the form of a dual admonition of Jesus to the disciples not to cast what is holy (τὸ ἅγιον) to dogs, nor their pearls before swine, lest the latter trample the pearls under their feet and then turn to rend their benefactors.[1] That the allusion intended here under the figures of dogs and swine is to the Gentiles appears to be generally accepted,[2] and, even though the picture of the Gentile reaction may reasonably be thought to correspond more exactly to a situation which was probable after A.D. 70, the general tenor of the passage is so consistent with the other evidence already noticed that there is no clear ground for supposing that it represents a change in the normal attitude of the Jewish Church in Palestine. The other passage comes in the injunction which the author places in the mouth of Jesus on the occasion of the sending out of the Twelve Apostles on their first evangelizing mission.[3] They are specially charged, "Go not into any way of the Gentiles, and enter not into any city of the Samaritans". The Matthean account here appears to be a conflation of Markan and *Q* material, but it is impossible to tell whether the strict limitation of the mission to the Jews was derived from the latter source or whether it was originally a characteristic addition of the First Evangelist.[4] On *a priori* grounds it would seem to have been added specially by Matthew, since it is very difficult to believe that the evangelization of the Gentiles could ever have been initiated and permitted to continue if there had existed in the original tradition of the teaching of Jesus an express command to confine the Gospel to Israel. If this interpretation be valid, the Matthean passage here remains nevertheless pertinent, for it significantly reveals the temper of Jewish Christianity in that even after A.D. 70 a Jewish Christian writer had the confidence to expect that his Jewish Christian readers would be prepared to accept such a statement as part of the authentic tradition.[5]

A further series of passages in Matthew and Luke next demands attention because of their application to the status of the Gentiles. The first to be considered is that which records the Healing of the Centurion's Servant, which is common to the two Gospels and was probably derived by each writer from *Q*.[6] The faith shown by the Centurion, who is evidently intended to be a Gentile, calls forth from Jesus the declaration,

[1] Matt. 7. 6.
[2] Cf. Strack und Billerbeck, op. cit., I, pp. 449–50. In rabbinical literature "swine" is especially used as a term of reference to Rome, i.e. the non-Israelite world. Cf. A. J. Grieve, *Peake's Commentary*, p. 707a. On the question of the interpretation of τὸ ἅγιον and "pearls" in connection with the Law, see M. Black, *An Aramaic Approach to the Gospels and Acts*, pp. 146–8.
[3] Matt. 10. 5, 6.
[4] Streeter, op. cit., pp. 255 *seq.*, thinks that the passage represents a short Judaistic charge which Matthew has conflated with the versions given by Mark and *Q*. Cf. Moffatt, *Intro. to N.T.*, pp. 246–7; *New Com. N.T.*, p. 150b; T. W. Manson, *The Teaching of Jesus*, p. 222.
[5] Cf. Weiss, *Urchristentum*, p. 124; Goguel, op cit., pp. 321–2; Guignebert, op. cit., pp. 317–8; Streeter, *Camb. Anc. Hist.*, vol. xi, p. 269.
[6] Matt. 8. 5–13; Luke 7. 2–10. Cf. Streeter, *Four Gospels*, pp. 253, 256; Taylor, op. cit., p. 75.

"I say unto you, I have not found so great faith, no, not in Israel". If this story goes back to Q, we have again a valuable indication of the attitude of the Palestinian Christians to the Gentile question. It means that there was current among them a story that the Master had been willing to have dealings with a certain distinguished Gentile and had actually praised his faith in contrast to the obduracy of his own countrymen. Two motives, probably of a complementary nature, seem to lie behind the preservation of this story. It would clearly have been gratifying to be able to record that the Master had been appealed to by a Gentile official of standing [1] and the fact would have constituted a good precedent for a benevolent attitude on the part of the Church towards certain Gentiles of substance who showed themselves to be sympathetically interested in the new faith. It is possible, therefore, that we have here a clue to the original policy of the Jewish Christians towards isolated cases of Gentile converts in Palestine, a policy probably of an *ad hoc* character, which did not foresee its future consequences when developed by Paul into a definitive mission for the general conversion of the Gentiles.

The Lukan parable of the Good Samaritan does not appear to be pertinent evidence here, because, like the story of the grateful Samaritan leper, it was probably derived from a cycle of tradition once current in Christian communities in Samaria,[2] and consequently is not to be regarded as representative of the outlook of the Jewish Church. The parable of the Wedding Feast presents a more complicated problem. The Lukan and Matthean versions generally resemble each other, but the latter contains an elaboration of a very divergent character.[3] However, on comparison it would appear that in essential structure the two versions are identical, so that it is reasonable to suppose that they are derived from a common source.[4] If this is correct, then we have a further piece of relevant evidence showing that, faced with the fact of the persistent unbelief of their own countrymen, the Jewish Christians sought thereby to justify the inclusion into the Church of those who, they agreed, had no natural right to the privilege of membership. Interpreted thus, the parable has a peculiar significance in that it tacitly reveals that the Jewish Christians regarded the accident of their compatriots' obduracy as causing a change in the divine intention, which had originally excluded the Gentiles from participation as being those who were beyond the pale of divine providence in this respect.[5] The elaborations of Matthew clearly show that the writer was intent on interpreting the parable in the light of the destruction of Jerusalem, and his addition of the parable

---

[1] It is instructive to note how pleased Josephus is to record the conversion of notable personages to Judaism; see *Ant.*, xviii. 3. 82, xx. 2. 17 *seq.*; cf. Schürer, *G.J.V.*, III, p. 119.
[2] Cf. Streeter, op. cit., pp. 218 *seq.*; Creed, *St. Luke*, p. lxx.
[3] Matt. 22. 1–14; Luke 14. 16–24.
[4] Streeter, op. cit., p. 516, thinks that Luke preserves the original form of the parable.
[5] Matt. 22. 3, 8. The Jews are clearly οἱ δὲ κεκλημένοι.

of the Wedding Garment to the original version was similarly prompted by contemporary factors, and it will accordingly require separate treatment at a later stage of our study.[1]

The evidence which we have surveyed is found, therefore, to be quite consistent with the verdict of Paul's writings in witnessing to the general superciliousness of the Jewish Christians towards the Gentiles and their grudging acceptance of the right of the Gentile converts to participate in the privilege of membership in the faith. There would appear, moreover, to be grounds for believing that the extension beyond Israel of at least some of the benefits of the new faith was made in the first instance where certain Gentiles of standing and resident in Palestine had shown signs of interest and sympathy. These concessions were isolated and did not represent a definitive policy, but they had naturally the effect of affording precedents which could not very well be disavowed later, although no hesitation was shown in making known the general attitude of disapproval which was felt towards the admittance of Gentiles to the peculiar privileges of Israel.[2]

The centrality of Jerusalem for nascent Christianity in all matters of faith and discipline, which is attested by the evidence of Paul and the Acts, is not formally demonstrated in the Synoptic writings; this fact is not surprising, considering the theme of the Gospels, but much incidental evidence is given by them which confirms the fact of the unique prestige enjoyed by the Jewish metropolis in the primitive tradition.

The preservation, in the tradition, of the account of the Cleansing of the Temple is significant.[3] Although the incident is represented by Mark as constituting a powerful cause for the hatred of the Jewish authorities and a stimulus to their resolve to destroy Jesus,[4] the record naturally presupposes an ethos in which the Temple is the accepted House of God and any practice which sullied its unique status as such was a matter for the deepest concern. It is a story which could only have had its origin and gained currency in a society such as that depicted by the author of Acts as "day by day, continuing steadfastly with one accord in the temple".[5] Similar witness to the venerated position which the Temple had in the Jewish Christian mind and to familiarity with its customs is afforded by the Matthean denunciation of swearing by the Gold of the Temple and by the Markan story of the Widow's Mite.[6] The ascription to Jesus of a prophecy foretelling the destruction of the great Jewish sanctuary,[7] however, seems to contradict this view and to suggest that a certain antipathy towards the national shrine was current in Jewish Christian circles. The problem which is involved here

1 See below, pp. 230–1.
2 The memory of this is surely preserved in Acts 10. 1–48; 11. 1–21; 15. 1–35.
3 Mark 11. 15–17; Matt. 21. 12, 13; Luke 19. 45, 46; John 2. 13–17.
4 Mark 11. 18.
5 Acts 2. 46. Cf. Luke 24. 52, 53.
6 Matt. 23. 16, 17; Mark 12. 42.
7 Mark 13. 1–4; Matt. 24. 1–3; Luke 21. 5–7.

is a very complicated one and its elucidation will demand the anticipation
of certain conclusions which will only properly be reached later.

The Markan evidence for Christ's prophecy of the destruction of the
Temple is found on analysis to contain some remarkable discrepancies.
According to the verses which introduce the Little Apocalypse, Jesus
clearly foretold the calamity, which was so completely realized in A.D. 70.
However, in the account of the Trial before the Sanhedrin the charge
that Jesus had declared that he would destroy the Temple, "made
with hands" (τὸν χειροποίητον), and after three days build another,
"made without hands" (ἄλλον ἀχειροποίητον), is imputed to false
witnesses (τινες . . . ἐψευδομαρτύρουν), and it is stated to have failed
through lack of mutual corroboration.[1]   Then further on, in the record
of the Crucifixion, the bystanders are described as taunting Jesus with the
same prophecy,[2] which in the light of his former statement must mean
that Mark intended his readers to understand that again his enemies
maliciously imputed to Jesus words which he had never uttered.   We
have then in Mark's account of the Trial and Crucifixion a clear and
definitive repudiation of the suggestion that Jesus had announced that
he himself would destroy the Temple, with the corollary that such a
suggestion had been the invention of his enemies.   Now this fact raises
a problem of peculiar seriousness.   The substance of the statement which
Mark places in the mouth of the false witnesses appears in a saying which
John attributes to Jesus,[3] namely, "Destroy (λύσατε) this temple, and
in three days I will raise it up".   The Johannine record adds an interpretation: "But he spake of the temple of his body", thus clearly identifying the statement as a prophecy of the Resurrection.   The fact that
John so interprets the saying, besides assigning it to a different place
in the Gospel narrative, would seem to indicate that, even if he knew
the Markan version, he deliberately chose to follow a different tradition.
Moreover, it must be noted that Mark's own use of the adjectives χειροποίητον and ἀχειροποίητον and the allusion to the three days would seem
to point to some Christian usage of the saying which he attributes to the
false witnesses.   Consideration of these facts, therefore, suggests both
that there was already current in Christian circles, when Mark wrote,
the belief that Jesus had in some form predicted the destruction of the
Jewish Temple, and also that some parallelism was worked out between
that coming event and his Resurrection.

With this conclusion we accordingly reach a curious situation where
the Markan Passion Narrative repudiates as a Jewish calumny a prophecy
which was treasured by some Christians as a precious utterance of Jesus.
The question naturally follows here of the source of the Markan Passion
Narrative, whether it is the free composition of the Evangelist or whether

---

[1] Mark 14. 57–59.   Cf. Matt. 26. 59–61.
[2] Mark 15. 29.   Cf. Matt. 27. 39, 40.
[3] John 2. 19–22.

it had already acquired the prestige of a traditional structure and as such was incorporated as a whole by Mark into his Gospel. The general opinion of New Testament scholars would appear to confirm the latter view,[1] thus tending to attribute to the Markan Passion Narrative, with a few minor qualifications, the authority of the Jerusalem Church. This conclusion would seem to be probable, although, as we shall endeavour to show later, a far greater allowance must be made for the influence of Mark's peculiar apologetics on this part of his narrative. There is, however, a fact of more pertinent significance to be considered. Mark, as we have already noted, has prefaced the Little Apocalypse with a definite prophecy by Jesus of the destruction of the Temple. In the light of his representation of the similar prophecy in the Passion Narrative as a Jewish calumny, this fact at first sight appears very surprising. But despite the general similarity of the two versions of the prophecy, on comparison an important distinction is at once obvious. In the version which prefaces the Little Apocalypse, Jesus does not state that he is to be the agent of the coming destruction of the national sanctuary, whereas in the two versions in the Passion Narrative the prophecy definitely takes the form of a threat couched in the first person singular. The distinction may reasonably be judged to be one which was consciously made by the Evangelist, who, while obliged by loyalty to the tradition of the Passion Narrative to record a definitive repudiation of the suggestion that Jesus had himself threatened to destroy the Temple, yet in the light of the catastrophe of A.D. 70, which, as we shall see later, provided the impetus for his writing the Gospel, felt the need of showing that the Lord had foreseen this tremendous event.

This analysis of the Markan evidence will now afford us a valuable insight into the attitude of the Jewish Christians towards the national sanctuary and all for which it stood in the mind of Judaism. It appears that the Jewish Christians would not accept the suggestion that Jesus had pronounced the doom of the Temple and claimed that he would accomplish it, and they represented such a suggestion in their official tradition as a lying calumny perpetrated by his enemies. Now the fact that the prophecy is depicted as a charge preferred against Jesus at his trial is significant. It looks as though there was current in Palestine an account of the trial of Jesus in which it was recorded that he had been condemned for threatening with destruction the very citadel of Israel's faith. What was the original substance of this charge it is now impossible to tell, but it would seem that some saying of Jesus was known which could with apparent reason be interpreted as against the Temple.[2] Moreover, if the record of the Acts with regard to Stephen may be accepted as preserving an authentic memory of Palestinian Christianity,

---

[1] Cf. Taylor, *Formation of Gospel Tradition*, pp. 44–50, 57–9; Dodd, *History and the Gospel*, p. 82; Dibelius, *From Tradition to Gospel*, pp. 47–8.

[2] Cf. Dodd, *Parables of the Kingdom*, p. 73: "Nor, in spite of Mark's aspersions upon the witnesses, is there good reason to deny the substantial authenticity of the saying."

we have further evidence pointing in the same direction in that one notable member of the Palestinian Church could be described by his enemies as a man who "ceaseth not to speak words against this holy place, and the law: for we have heard him say, that this Jesus of Nazareth shall destroy this place, and shall change the customs which Moses delivered unto us"—a charge which was substantially confirmed by the martyr's subsequent speech before the Sanhedrin.[1]

In the light of this evidence we may, therefore, construct a reasonable interpretation of the attitude of the Jewish Christians in this matter. It would accordingly appear that some saying of Jesus about the fate of the Temple had been made part of the charge on which he had been condemned.[2] How far this saying had been maliciously distorted by his enemies we have no means of knowing, but in some form, perhaps with a reference to the Resurrection, it was later propagated in Palestine by certain Christians who were at least critical of the whole structure of the Jewish cultus as it was exemplified in the Temple. The situation which consequently ensued was painful and embarrassing for the original community of believers, who had remained strictly loyal to their national faith and who by no means felt that their new belief must cause them to repudiate the cherished institutions of their people. Faced, therefore, not only with the charge made by their admitted opponents that their Master had spoken words of treason against the national shrine, but also with the ready acceptance and propagation of such a charge by members of their own faith, they saw no other line of defence than that of stigmatizing the offending saying as a malicious calumny of the false witnesses at the trial of Jesus. Such a view then, we may note in conclusion, well accords with the evidence of Paul and the Acts that the Jerusalem Christians continued faithful to the cultus of Judaism and that the Temple was their accustomed place of worship.

The Lament over Jerusalem, which has been preserved in different contexts by Matthew and Luke,[3] would appear to constitute another objection to the view that the Jewish metropolis and Temple formed the venerated home and centre of the primitive Church, and as such it must be examined. It may be maintained that the passage shows that another prophecy of the destruction of the vital foci of Israel's life and faith was current in the traditions of the original Christian community. This objection, however, is found on analysis to be difficult to substantiate, for several facts seem to indicate that the saying was originally composed

---

[1] Acts 6. 13, 14. Although the charge here is also described as a calumny (ἔστησάν τε μάρτυρας ψευδεῖς λέγοντας), Stephen's own words (7. 47–51) indicate that the charge was not without substance. Cf. Meyer, *Ursprung und Anfänge des Christentums*, III, p. 159; Weiss, *Urchristentum*, pp. 122–3; Knox, *Jerusalem*, p. 50, n. 10; Loisy, *Le Origini del Cristianesimo*, p. 113. Goguel, *La Naissance du Christianisme*, p. 195, thinks that the charge was ascribed to false witnesses because it seemed too daring to the primitive Christians.

[2] Cf. Eisler, *Messiah Jesus*, pp. 494–500; Goguel, *Jesus*, pp. 419–20; Guignebert, *Jesus*, p. 310; Loisy, op. cit., p. 86; Dodd, op. cit., p. 61.

[3] Matt. 23. 37–39; Luke 13. 34, 35.

to meet the situation consequent on the Jewish disaster of A.D. 70. Apart
from its general incompatibility with the evidence already surveyed and
the unlikelihood that the Jewish Christians should have treasured a
condemnation of their Holy City, the passage presupposes the accomplishment of Jerusalem's overthrow after the elapse of a period of time sufficiently long to give point to the words "how often (ποσάκις) would I
have gathered thy children together". Since the Synoptic tradition
only records one visit of Jesus to Jerusalem,[1] it would seem, therefore,
that the saying here rather expresses the mind of his followers, who had
continued for many years without notable success his work of evangelizing
the inhabitants of the Holy City. Moreover we may note that, if Matthew
is correct in placing the Lament here in direct sequence to the passage
condemning the Jews for their shedding of righteous blood from the time
of Abel to that of Zachariah, son of Barachiah, the true nature of the passage
as apologetic to meet the situation created in the Church by the events
of A.D. 70 becomes apparent,[2] as we shall endeavour to show more fully
later. Having disposed thus of an interpretation which might be thought
to constitute an objection to our view of the attitude of the Jewish Church
towards the citadel of Judaism, we may now invoke the testimony of
the passage in support of that view. As we have noted above, the words
"how often would I have gathered thy children together" presuppose
an extended period of evangelization in the city. The prominence
thus given to the fate of Jerusalem from this point of view significantly
witnesses to the deep concern shown by the Christians of that city
to win its inhabitants to the faith, and in this way it eloquently
confirms the picture provided by the other material which we have
surveyed.

The Gospels afford no explicit information about the Christian communities in other parts of Palestine to which Paul and the author of
Acts make reference. There are, however, certain features of the Synoptic record which constitute a curious problem with regard to the relations
possibly existing between the Church at Jerusalem and the churches in
other parts of the country, particularly in Galilee.

The chief evidence comes from the divergence of tradition with regard
to the locality of the appearances of the Risen Lord. Matthew, obviously
following the only tradition of which Mark shows knowledge, places
the crucial Resurrection Appearance to the disciples, and the Ascension,

---

[1] The theme of the Synoptic narrative clearly only permits of one visit to Jerusalem; if
Jesus did visit the city on other occasions, which is likely, the tradition has certainly preserved
nothing notable in connection with them. The Gospel evidence is obviously insufficient to
enable us to reconstruct any itinerary of the Ministry. Cf. Guignebert, op. cit., pp. 223–30.

[2] Streeter, *Four Gospels*, pp. 254, 283, thinks that Luke preserves a far more original context,
presuming the Lament passage comes from Q. This is a matter of opinion, but it would
seem more probable that the Lament had originally a Jerusalem and not a Galilæan setting.
However that may be, the passage appears to have had no inextricable context in the
tradition, since either Matthew or Luke felt justified in placing it in a different setting. This
fact would seem to confirm the impression that it was an unattached logion of apologetic
currency.

in Galilee.[1]　This seems certainly to have been the original tradition, and it has been thought, with considerable reason, that the Johannine account was specially designed to reconcile this Galilæan tradition with another, which located the appearances exclusively at Jerusalem and its environs.[2]　This latter tradition is preserved in the Lukan Gospel and Acts,[3] in which there also appears to be evidence of some embarrassment over the existence of a contradictory record.[4]

The exact significance of this conflict of tradition over so vital a matter cannot certainly be determined,[5] but several valuable inferences may reasonably be drawn.　It would seem to be unlikely on *a priori* grounds, in view of the decisive prestige of the Jerusalem Church in matters of faith, that claims would have been subsequently advanced in favour of locating the Resurrection Appearances far outside the Holy City, if the original tradition had clearly placed them within its environs.　Hence, as has already been suggested, the tradition of a Galilæan location must surely be older.　As a corollary to this inference we may be led further to assume that the metropolitan Church, in a natural desire to increase its prestige, had wrongly claimed that the vital post-Resurrection events had been exclusively enacted within its own local confines.　But this conclusion, although reasonable, may possibly not be quite the true explanation.　Luke's testimony is several decades subsequent to the destruction of Jerusalem and the disappearance of the original Christian community there.　Consequently it is very questionable whether Luke could have had direct knowledge of the teaching of the Jerusalem Church in this matter of the locality of the Resurrection Appearances.　Other evidence supports this doubt.　In the Lukan record of the Acts of the Apostles an account is given of the death of Judas Iscariot, which notably differs from that provided by Matthew.[6]　The Lukan version as a statement of fact appears to be the more improbable, and its fabulous character seems apparent in the explanation which it gives of what is asserted to be a Jerusalem place-name.　It is scarcely credible that the inhabitants of Jerusalem should have commemorated the death of an erstwhile follower of Jesus of Nazareth by the assigning of a special name to the field where he met his death, or, if they had done so, that Matthew, with all his love of giving allusions to matters of peculiarly Jewish interest, should have failed to have placed on record so interesting an incident as this.　On reflection, therefore, it would rather appear that Luke's version here has been partly prompted by the fact that there was at Jerusalem a

---

[1] Matt. 28. 10, 16–20 (the Ascension is, of course, implied); Mark 14. 28; 16. 7.

[2] John 20–21.　Cf. Streeter, op. cit., pp. 351 *seq.*; Guignebert, op. cit. p. 504; Gardner Smith, *Narratives of the Resurrection*, pp. 87–9; Goguel, *La Naissance du Christianisme*, p. 74.

[3] Luke 24; Acts 1. 1–12.

[4] Luke 24. 49 (ὑμεῖς δὲ καθίσατε ἐν τῇ πόλει ἕως οὗ ἐνδύσησθε ἐξ ὕψους δύναμιν); Acts 1. 4 (παρήγγειλεν αὐτοῖς ἀπὸ Ἱεροσολύμων μὴ χωρίζεσθαι).　Cf. B.C., vol. iv, p. 6, vol. v, n. ii.

[5] See below, pp. 197–8, for notice of the views of Lohmeyer, *Galiläa und Jerusalem*, and R. H. Lightfoot, *Locality and Doctrine in the Gospels*.

[6] Acts 1. 16–20; Matt. 27. 3–10.　Cf. Bacon, *Studies in Matthew*, p. 252.

place with the suggestive title of *Akeldama*.[1] If, as some scholars have thought, the author of Luke–Acts derived much of his material from the Church at Cæsarea,[2] a reasonable explanation of the origin of his version of the end of Judas, and also of the Jerusalem Appearances of the Risen Lord, is accordingly forthcoming. The Church at Cæsarea after A.D. 70 would probably have been the chief centre of Christianity in Palestine, being composed mainly of Gentiles, who would certainly have constituted the more influential party after the Jewish national disaster. As such the Cæsarean Church is likely to have inherited certain traditions of the original Jerusalem Church and a considerable respect for its memory. Many of these traditions were probably held in a rather garbled form, and their presentation was undoubtedly coloured by the natural tendency to assign all important events to Jerusalem as the original centre of the faith. Consequently, in the case of the story of the death of Judas, it would seem that some vague knowledge of the topography of Jerusalem, such as we might reasonably expect members of the Cæsarean community to have, had led to an explanation of the end of the traitor-disciple in terms of a Jerusalem place-name. Similarly it is probable that, while the Jerusalem Church had shown the first signs of the later characteristic ecclesiastical tendency to claim the prestige which accrues from the possession of sacred sites, the Cæsarean Christians, some two or three decades after the disappearance of the Mother Church, naturally limited the post-Resurrection events entirely to the locality of Jerusalem, adopting in consequence an antagonistic attitude towards the older Galilæan tradition.

From a consideration of these facts and the inferences which may accordingly be made from them we may justifiably conclude that, although the Gospel evidence not only points to Galilee as being the original centre of the movement initiated by Jesus of Nazareth, but also shows that the most crucial of the post-Resurrection events also happened there, the prestige of Jerusalem was such that it rapidly became the unchallenged home of the new faith. Whether this decision to settle at Jerusalem, despite the fact that the city was only linked in the earliest tradition with the memory of the culminating tragedy, was due to some remembered saying of Jesus, which was interpreted as commanding it, or whether it was the outcome of the shrewd appraisal of the first disciples of the superior value of Israel's holy city as the centre of their movement, remains unknown,[3] but it is certain that the reason, whatever it may

[1] See *B.C.*, vol. iv, p. 13 (Akeldama). It is, of course, probable that Matthew is also concerned to explain a local place-name, but, if Klostermann's reasonable suggestion be accepted that the word in its original form meant "the field of sleep", i.e. κοιμητήριον, then it would be likely that Matthew reveals a more intimate acquaintance with Jerusalem topography. Cf. Dibelius, *Die Formgeschichte des Evangeliums*, p. 113. In a letter to the author Dr. Eisler maintains that *Akel damah* was the local name of the "*Schindanger*", where corpses of criminals, etc., were thrown.

[2] Cf. Streeter, op. cit., pp. 218–9, 232; Creed, *St. Luke*, p. lxx; Moffatt, *Intro. to N.T.*, pp. 276, 293; Taylor, *Formation of Gospel Tradition*, pp. 185–6.

[3] Cf. Harnack, *Die Mission und Ausbreitung des Christentums*, I, p. 38 and n. 2.

have been, was sufficiently compelling to override the original claims of Galilee.

The preservation by Mark and Matthew of the tradition which locates the post-Resurrection events in Galilee may attest the strength of the original memory even in the Jerusalem Church, or it may indicate the existence of a vigorous Christian community in Galilee, which treasured and upheld the precious tradition.[1] That such a Galilæan Church should have existed is very probable, and it would be consonant with the fact of the Galilæan origin of Jesus and of the majority of his disciples, which appears to have been a well-established tradition throughout the whole Church.[2] Of the nature of the relations obtaining between this Galilæan Church and the Church of Jerusalem, as our foregoing survey has shown, we have no certain information. However, in default of any evidence to the contrary, we may justly deduce from the fact that Mark and Matthew have preserved the tradition of the Galilæan Appearances, and also from the fact of the Galilæan antecedents of the leaders at Jerusalem, that the relations between the two churches were quite harmonious and the precedence of the metropolis undisputed.[3]

We may note, to complete our survey of Gospel data relative to the constitution of the Church in Palestine, that the Lukan documents also indicate, by their inclusion of several passages in which distinct interest and sympathy are shown for the Samaritans, that a Christian community flourished in Samaria.[4] This evidence in its extant form, like that for Christianity at Cæsarea, would properly be representative of a situation obtaining several decades after the destruction of Jerusalem, but there would seem to be no necessary reason for doubting that the account which is given in Acts of the conversion of the Samaritans and its careful regulation by the Jerusalem Church may preserve an authentic tradition.

From this survey of the incidental evidence, relative to the situation of the Church in Palestine, which is afforded by the Synoptic Gospels we may legitimately conclude therefore that the unique supremacy of the Jerusalem Church, which is attested by the writings of Paul and illustrated in the later narrative of the Acts, is completely substantiated by material which may reasonably be identified as coming from a Palestinian provenance and ultimately reflecting the tradition of the original Christian communities there.

What may be interpreted as the testimony of the Synoptic Gospels

[1] Cf. Lohmeyer's comment, op. cit., p. 52, on the omission of Galilee in Acts 1. 8: "*Die Wortwahl lässt also nur den Schluss zu, dass Galiläa absichtlich nicht genannt ist; und es wird nicht genannt, weil es gerade nach diesem Wort schon eine terra christiana ist.*"

[2] Cf. L. Clarke, *New Test. Problems*, pp. 132 seq.

[3] "*Wenn also faktisch Jerusalem das Übergewicht hat, so ist damit noch nichts über die gläubige Anschauung, sei es Jerusalems oder Galiläas gesagt; anderseits wenn Galiläa dogmatisch das Land des Evangeliums heisst, so wäre damit noch nichts über seine faktische Bedeutung erkannt.*" (Lohmeyer, op. cit., p. 60.)

[4] Luke 10. 33–37; 17. 16, 17; cf. 9. 51–55; Acts 1. 8; 8. 1, 5–25. Cf. Streeter, *Primitive Church,* pp. 56–7.

relative to the matter of leadership in the Palestinian Church appears to conflict absolutely with the evidence of Paul's writings and of the later chapters of the Acts of the Apostles. As we have seen, Paul's references in his Galatian Epistle show that authority in the Church at Jerusalem was vested generally in the Apostles and particularly in a trio which comprised James, Cephas, and John; the mention of the Twelve in the First Corinthian Epistle as a special group among the Resurrection-witnesses would also indicate that a body thus designated was of particular repute in the Church. The James whom Paul especially describes as the Lord's brother was, as we have also already noticed, the virtual head of the Church and to his direction even Cephas was submissive.

This Pauline picture receives no confirmation from the Synoptic Gospels, except in the matter of the Twelve, whose appointment is specially recorded by all three Evangelists, although disagreement is shown in the names of the constituent members.[1] The Synoptic writers do, however, preserve the tradition of a select trio among the Twelve, who were favoured by Jesus to be the sole witnesses of his actions and experiences on certain crucial occasions.[2] This trio curiously comprises the same names as the Pauline trio, but with the essential difference that the James is the son of Zebedee and the brother of John. Again with striking parallelism to the Pauline series, but with also a radical distinction, Peter is represented as the leader of the Synoptic triumvirate, and in the Matthean Gospel he is actually described as being commissioned by Jesus with binding authority both in this world and in heaven.[3] With regard to James, the brother of the Lord, nothing is said or implied about his supremacy in the Church, but rather to the contrary he is included by inference among the members of Jesus' family who are described as being so far incredulous of his unique vocation that they endeavour to restrain him as one who is insane.[4]

This conflict of evidence clearly raises a problem of radical import for our understanding of Christian Origins. At this particular stage of our study we are not well placed to undertake a complete discussion of the matter, since a vital factor of the issue is obviously that of the date of the Gospel material. Considering the priority of the Galatian Epistle in time of production and the nature of its subject matter, its evidence in this respect must surely be regarded as unquestionable. The Gospels, on the other hand, were all produced after the Jerusalem Church had ceased to be the effective centre of the Christian movement, so that it would appear highly probable that the validity of their testimony in such a matter, especially in view of its divergence from that of the earlier

---

[1] Mark 3. 13–19; Matt. 10. 1–4; Luke 6. 13–16. Cf. Acts 1. 13. Cf. Guignebert, *Jesus*, pp. 219–23; *B.C.*, vol. v, pp. 37–46.
[2] Mark 5. 37; 9. 2; 13. 3; 14. 33; Matt. 17. 1; 26. 37; Luke 8. 51; 9. 28. Cf. Goguel, *Jesus*, pp. 342–3.
[3] Matt. 16. 17–19.
[4] Mark 3. 21, 31–35. Cf. Klostermann, *Das Markusevangelium*, pp. 42, 44; Turner, *New Com. N.T.*, p. 62, loc. cit.; Klausner, *From Jesus to Paul*, p. 266.

document, is conditioned by the circumstances of their production, which can only be determined at a later stage of our investigation here. However that may be, certain observations may be made now which are pertinent to the particular subject under consideration and will contribute towards the later solution of the larger problem.

We may note that in the earlier chapters of the Acts, which appear to be based on Jerusalem tradition as current in the Church of Cæsarea in the later decades of the first century, Peter and John are associated as the heroes of two different episodes.[1] The second of these episodes is of particular significance, for in it the two Apostles appear as the special representatives of the Jerusalem Church to inquire into the momentous situation created for the new faith by the conversion of the Samaritans. From these accounts, therefore, it would seem that there was some tradition that Peter and John exercised a position of leadership in the first days of the Church. Now it is to be noticed also that in these chapters there is a curious silence about James, who in the Synoptic record always appears with his brother John. The author of Acts does make one special mention of this James, namely the record of his death at the hands of Herod.[2] The fact of the bare reference to this incident is certainly strange, and it provides legitimate ground for wonder, especially when it is remembered that ample space is given in the narrative to describing the circumstances of the death of Stephen and Peter's escape from death. For what reason, it may be asked, did the author of Acts mention the death of James and yet not trouble to give his readers an adequate account of that notable martyrdom? The apparent reason seems to be that the author sought thus to prepare his readers for the introduction into his narrative of James, "the brother of the Lord", whom he did not wish, for reasons yet to be determined, to designate by that unique title, which, as Paul shows, was current in the Church for him.

The situation which is, therefore, indicated by our documents assumes the following significant proportions. The record of the Acts shows that tradition preserved the memory that Peter and John acted together as leaders in the earliest days of the Church, a tradition which, so far as these two Apostles are concerned, is confirmed by the evidence of Paul in the Galatian Epistle. The absence of James, the brother of the Lord, from effective association with Peter and John in the Acts is rendered the more remarkable by his sudden unexplained appearance in the narrative as the paramount leader of the Jerusalem Church.[3] That this curiously clumsy handling of this phase of the story of Christian Origins was due to Luke's ignorance of the antecedents of James' rise to power

---

[1] Acts 3. 1–4, 23; 8. 14–25.

[2] Acts 12. 2. Cf. *B.C.*, vol. iv, p. 133 (James). The attempt of Eisler, *Enigma of Fourth Gospel*, pp. 81–3, to identify the James of Gal. 2. 9 with James the Apostle has only the strength of the tenuous web of allusions and peculiarities which he has woven from chance variant readings in some relevant MSS. and from Irenaeus, *Elenchus* III, 12, 15.

[3] Acts 12. 17; see Chapter Two, p. 27, n. 3.

is unlikely, since Paul's special inclusion of James among the Resurrection-witnesses [1] must surely signify that James was intimately connected with the movement during the vital period of the Resurrection experiences and that in Paul's time he enjoyed equal status with Peter as a specially designated Resurrection-witness; indeed it may be noted that in a general statement Luke himself testifies to the fact that the brethren of Jesus were among the very first believers after the Ascension.[2] The conclusion, therefore, seems to be justified that Luke, although unable by the very weight of fact to exclude all mention of James' paramount position in the Church or of Peter's willing co-operation with him, to which Paul witnesses, was so far embarrassed by the fact of James' unique prestige that, except for one significant remark, he says nothing of his relations with Peter and John and maintains a complete silence about his entry into the Church and emergence to a position of so great authority therein.

The embarrassment thus revealed in Luke's handling of the subject of James, the brother of the Lord, appears to be connected also with the curious manner in which he treats the death of James, the brother of John. The notable fact of the martyrdom had clearly been preserved in the tradition which had reached Luke, but whether it was with a full account of its attendant circumstances we do not know. It would, however, seem improbable that, whereas the tradition preserved the details of Peter's escape from death and of Stephen's martyrdom, no similar information had been handed on about the way in which so distinguished a disciple had died for his faith. It has already been suggested above that the Acts seems to have made this brief reference to the death of James in order to avoid any confusion due to the unexplained introduction of another James, shortly after, into its narrative. But a further question of similar and great pertinence raises itself. If the author of Acts thus felt it necessary to make such a reference to James, the brother of John, why should he limit himself to so bald a statement? Certain observations may be made on the issue apparently involved here which are likely to indicate the answer.

To have given James the prominence of a detailed account of his martyrdom would necessarily have linked him with his brother John as a leading member of the primitive Church, and this in turn would have had the effect of bringing into the narrative of the Acts the semblance of a triumvirate of Apostles. The striking resemblance of the names of the members of this triumvirate to those attested by Paul, of which some recollection must surely also have survived elsewhere in the Church, must obviously have led to confusion in the narrative, unless the author had given a full explanation of the antecedents of James, the brother of the Lord, which he apparently, as his extant text shows, was bent on avoiding—hence his brief reference to the martyrdom of James to

[1] 1 Cor. 15. 7.   [2] Acts 1. 14.

distinguish him from his namesake, whom he had then to introduce into his narrative, and hence also his curious changing round of the names of James and John in the Acts' version of the Twelve Apostles,[1] which is a small, but in this context a significant, index to the desire to minimize the importance of James, the son of Zebedee.

We have now to consider the fact of the Gospels' emphasis on the triumvirate of Peter and the sons of Zebedee, of their witness to the primacy of Peter, and of their hostile attitude to James, the brother of the Lord, all of which clearly run counter to the evidence of Paul and the Acts.

The problem is greatly simplified by the fact that the emphasis on the triumvirate is Markan, and is derived by Matthew and Luke from this source. This means in effect that we are faced with the question of why Mark has in this matter diverged from what must be the authentic record preserved by Paul and the Acts. This question is essentially bound up with that of the hostility shown by the same Evangelist towards the family of Jesus, which must, of course, have included James. An adequate answer involves the prior determination of the factors which prompted the production of the Markan Gospel, and this of necessity cannot be done at this stage of our study. However, we may again make certain preliminary observations, as we did above, which may profitably serve our present discussion and establish certain points on the way to the ultimate solution.

It is evident from the fact that their conversion is specially recorded [2] and that they had the significant name of Boanerges that the brothers James and John were two of the three best-known of the disciples of Jesus.[3] Luke's special story of their desire to destroy a village of obdurate Samaritans, together with the evidence of Acts which we have been considering,[4] also points to the existence of a cycle of stories about them. Indeed they, and Peter, are the only Apostles about whom the Synoptic writers appear to have any detailed information, the rest being, with the possible exception of Judas Iscariot, mere lay figures in the story of Jesus.[5] This means in effect that Mark gave prominence in his Gospel to the only three Apostles about whom any real knowledge survived, so that their apparent pre-eminence above the other nine may be due to the simple fact that they were either the only Apostles of whom tradition had retained any detailed memory or the only effective Apostles during the earliest period——or, indeed, both.

Whatever may have been the true cause and nature of the apparent pre-eminence of Peter and the sons of Zebedee among the original

---

[1] Ἰωάννης καὶ Ἰάκωβος, Acts I. 13.

[2] Mark I. 19, 20.

[3] Mark 3. 17. It is interesting to note that, although Andrew is associated with Peter in the Markan account of the calling of the first disciples, nothing further is told of him as an individual.

[4] Luke 9. 51–55.

[5] Cf. Guignebert, *Jesus*, p. 221.

disciples of Jesus according to the tradition, the question still remains of the origin of the association of James, the Lord's brother, with the new faith. According to the record of the Acts, although he was presumably already a believer, James was not even considered as a likely candidate for election into the ranks of the Twelve after the defection of Judas.[1] This must mean that the tradition was quite clear that James was not a member of the Twelve. However, this fact cannot necessarily be interpreted as certain proof of the relative lateness of James' association with the movement, because, in view of the confusion in the Synoptic accounts about the names of the Twelve and the fact that only three Apostles emerge from the names as personalities, the historical reality of the Twelve is open to doubt.[2] It is indeed true that in the extant text of the First Corinthian Epistle Paul mentions the Twelve in his list of Resurrection-witnesses,[3] but it must be noted that, according to his phraseology here, if we had not the Synoptic evidence for the inclusion of Cephas in the Twelve, we should be naturally led to think that Paul had specially distinguished him from its membership. This difficulty, however, at once disappears, if the words εἶτα τοῖς δώδεκα are regarded as an early addition to harmonize the Pauline list at this point with the Synoptic tradition,[4] and complete consistency is thereby secured for the other Pauline evidence relative to the organization of authority in the Church, for in the crucial passage in the Galatian Epistle reference is made only to "them which were apostles before me" and to the triumvirate of James, Cephas, and John, the first of whom incidentally is described as an Apostle.[5]

If the existence of the Twelve as an historical fact of the pre-Crucifixion period may, therefore, be regarded as extremely doubtful, and is perhaps to be more reasonably interpreted, in terms of the tradition which lies behind Luke 22. 29–30 and Matt. 19. 28, as an ideal apostolate necessitated by the number of the tribes of Israel,[6] then we may regard the Synoptic Gospels as agreeing with Paul in witnessing to an original triumvirate of leaders, although they differ from him in identifying James as the son of Zebedee and the brother of John.

The position which we have accordingly reached in this matter is a curious one. The Pauline evidence shows us a triumvirate of James, Peter, and John, of which James, the Lord's brother, is clearly the dominant member; and with this picture the inferential evidence of

[1] Acts 1. 14, 23–26.
[2] Cf. Guignebert, op. cit., p. 223; Goguel, *Jesus*, pp. 340–1. Guignebert, *Le Christ*, pp. 67 *seq.*, thinks that the Twelve was a creation which was called forth to meet the situation of the primitive community when it was realized that their original hopes of the immediate accomplishment of the Parousia had failed.
[3] 1 Cor. 15. 5.
[4] It would appear that it was early noted that "the twelve" would necessarily include Judas Iscariot, who had died, apparently, before the Crucifixion. Hence in a number of MSS. δώδεκα has been changed to ἕνδεκα; see critical note in *Novum Test. Graece*, ed. A. Souter.
[5] Gal. 1. 17–19; 2. 9.
[6] Cf. Goguel, op. cit., pp. 340–1; Guignebert, op. cit., p. 69, n. 1.

Acts is in agreement. The Synoptic Gospels, on the other hand, also witness to a triumvirate of Peter, James, and John, of which Peter is certainly the leader, and James is the brother of John. Moreover, the Synoptic writers have preserved fragments of a tradition which represents the sons of Zebedee as being men of vigorous personality, and they are once significantly described as asking for the chief places in the coming Kingdom of their Master.[1] Of the antecedents of James, the brother of the Lord, who was indubitably the effective head of the Church throughout the period of Paul's activity, all our records tell nothing. This last fact possibly holds the key to at least a partial solution of the problem here.

Eduard Meyer, the eminent authority on ancient history, in his monumental study of Christian Origins suggested that the rise of James to power in the Church was due to the supreme fact of his blood relationship with Jesus and that in the primitive Christian movement there were the beginnings of a caliphate, founded in the Prophet's own family, such as developed to mature proportions in Islam, the other great Semitic world religion.[2] There seems to be strong reason for believing that this suggestion is sound. But, while we may thus regard the dynastic factor as the effective cause of James' precedence, the question of the time of his original entry into the apostolic band still remains to be answered. It has been suggested that James was converted by the vision of the Risen Lord which is referred to by Paul and described in some detail in the *Gospel according to the Hebrews*.[3] This, however, is unlikely, since the tradition is unanimous in limiting the witnesses of the Risen Lord to those who already believed in him. The conclusion, therefore, necessarily follows that on analysis the sources provide no definitive evidence against the natural supposition that James was sympathetically associated with his brother's mission before the Crucifixion. The antagonism shown towards the family of Jesus, which must have included James, by Mark does not appear to have been an original feature of the movement, and,

---

[1] Mark 10. 35–45; Matt. 20. 20–28. Cf. Mark 3. 17.

[2] Op. cit., III, pp. 224–5; cf. Streeter, *Primitive Church*, pp. 39–40, *Camb. Anc. Hist.*, vol. xi, p. 272; Harnack, *Die Mission und Ausbreitung des Christentums*, II, p. 77; Lohmeyer, *Galiläa und Jerusalem*, p. 53. A strict analogy with the Islamic Caliphate must not, however, be too greatly emphasized, for, as Carra de Vaux has shown in his article on "King (Muslim)" in Hastings, *Encycl. of Religion and Ethics*, vol. vii, p. 723b, "the first successors of Muhammed called themselves lieutenants (Kalif). In practice they preserved their sovereignty in the military order; but in the religious and judicial orders the Qur'an, which is regarded as perfect, had fixed the law, at least in all its most important points. . . . The legitimacy of the Kalif does not exactly depend upon the manner of his election or on a law of succession; it is derived from the proclamation of the people." Of course, in the first century there was no corpus of Christian tradition which had reached such a state of concreteness or enjoyed such universal recognition as the Qur'an, but there was the great controlling power of the Jewish Law. Cf. art. on "Brother" by K. Kohler, *Jew. Encycl.*, vol. iii, p. 396; Eisler, *ΙΗΣΟΥΣ ΒΑΣΙΛΕΥΣ*, Bd. ii, p. 541, n. 1; Goguel, *La Naissance du Christianisme*, pp. 130–3.

[3] I Cor. 15. 7; *Gospel according to the Hebrews (Apocrypha II*, ed. E. Klostermann, pp. 6–7); see also Eusebius, *Eccl. Hist.*, II. i. 4. Cf. Lightfoot, *Galatians*, pp. 265, 274, 364; Knox, *Jerusalem*, p. 80; Klausner, *From Jesus to Paul*, p. 266. Goguel, op. cit., p. 57, makes the interesting comment on this passage: "*Nous sommes en présence d'un récit créé dans le milieu du Christianisme dynastique* ad majorem Jacobi gloriam, *sur la base de la simple mention de l'épître aux Corinthiens.*"

as we shall attempt to show later, it is susceptible of quite a different interpretation, and one, moreover, which is entirely in accord with the definite apologetical theme of the Second Gospel.

The evidence of the Synoptic Gospels and that of Paul and the Acts point together, therefore, to the existence of four effective leaders in the primitive Church, namely James, the Lord's brother, Peter, and the two sons of Zebedee. As to how far their mutual relationships were harmonious or to what extent the primacy of James was allowed to develop unchallenged by the others, we have but one certain fragment of information. Early tradition has preserved the memory of some bid on the part of the sons of Zebedee for supremacy. In the Markan version it takes the form of a request made directly by the brothers to Jesus for the chief seats in His kingdom; in the later Matthean account the petition is put into the mouth of the mother of the two disciples.[1] The reply of Jesus is significant. Although James and John are promised a share in their Master's experiences, possibly signifying their martyrdom,[2] their petition is refused, and they are told that the places which they seek are already reserved for others. The account then goes on to describe the not unnatural reaction of the other Apostles; they are moved with indignation against those who had thus sought precedence over them. According to Mark this was not the only occasion on which the question of supremacy had come up, for at an earlier point in the narrative the Twelve had disputed the matter among themselves.[3] This admission of strife on such a subject and the special association therewith of James and John must surely reflect an historical situation, and it may possibly be not over subtle to see in the declaration of Jesus that the chief places were reserved for certain others unspecified, but presumably outside the circle of the Twelve, some allusion to the accession of the other James to primacy in the Church.

The primacy which the Synoptic Gospels, especially Matthew's Gospel, attribute to Peter, when compared with the evidence of Paul and Acts that such a position was held by James, appears to indicate that Peter must subsequently have been replaced by the Lord's brother. In some way this may have been so, but other factors are involved here which can only be properly elucidated at a later stage of our study. However, at this point, we may fairly conclude our investigation of the problem of leadership in the apostolic Church by remarking that, whatever may have been the nature of James' original entry into the faith, and powerful though his claim of blood-relationship undoubtedly was, when we con-

---

[1] Mark 10. 35–45; Matt. 20. 20–28. Cf. Weiss, *Urchristentum*, p. 559.

[2] Cf. Meyer, *Ursprung und Anfänge des Christentums*, III, p. 174; Dibelius, *From Tradition to Gospel*, p. 60; Eisler, *Enigma of Fourth Gospel*, pp. 59 *seq.*; Streeter, op. cit., p. 32.

[3] Mark 9. 33–37; Matt. 18. 1–3; Luke 9. 46–48. Mark 10. 42–45; Matt. 20. 25–28; Luke 22. 24–30. Eusebius, op. cit., II. i. 3, gives an interesting quotation from the 6th book of Clement's Hypotyposes: Πέτρον γὰρ φησιν καὶ Ἰάκωβον καὶ Ἰωάννην μετὰ τὴν ἀνάληψιν τοῦ σωτῆρος, ὡς ἂν καὶ ὑπὸ τοῦ σωτῆρος προτετιμημένους, μὴ ἐπιδικάζεσθαι δόξης, ἀλλὰ Ἰάκωβον τὸν δίκαιον ἐπίσκοπον τῶν Ἱεροσολύμων ἐλέσθαι.

sider the vigorous personalities of Peter and the sons of Zebedee as they
clearly emerge from the various strata of the tradition, we have to recognize that James, the Lord's brother, must have been a man of resolute
and dynamic character to have maintained his position, or rather perhaps
in the first instance to have won it, with such competitors; and with this
view of James the evidence of Paul and the Acts fully concurs.

Before concluding this chapter on the Palestinian sources of evidence
about the primitive Church it remains for us to notice the fragments of
relevant information preserved in the writings of Josephus and Hegesippus.

In the extant Greek text of the Jewish historian there is a short
passage in which the death of James (τὸν ἀδελφὸν Ἰησοῦ τοῦ λεγομένου
Χριστοῦ) at the instigation of Ananus, the Sadducean High Priest, during
an interregnum of the Roman procuratorial government, is recorded.[1]
This passage, like those referring to Jesus and to John the Baptist, remains
a storm-centre of Josephean studies.[2]   However, although the wider
significance of the passage must be considered in detail later when we
come to study the attitude of the Jewish Christians to the cause of Jewish
nationalism,[3] we can at this point utilize this testimony of Josephus to
the importance of James.   Whether the present Greek passage stood in
the original text of Josephus, or whether Origen's witness to the currency
in his day of a different version[4] indicates the action of a vigorous Christian
censorship of passages of Josephus bearing on Christian Origins, we may
in either case reasonably conclude that the Jewish historian had made
some allusion to James, which fact provides testimony external to Christian
circles of the prominence of the brother of Jesus among the Christians
in Palestine.

The accounts of Hegesippus about James, which have been preserved
by Eusebius and Epiphanius, are of an extremely laudatory type and
are in many respects palpably false.[5]   As was suggested above, Hegesippus

[1] *Ant.*, xx. 9. 1.   [2] Cf. F. Jackson, *Josephus and the Jews*, pp. 89, 279.
[3] See Chapter Six below.
[4] *Ad Matt.*, x. 17; *Contra Celsum*, i. 47, ii. 13.   The problem involved here is discussed in
Chapter Six, pp. 110 *seq.*
[5] Eusebius, op. cit., II. i. 2–5, xxiii; Epiphanius, *Haer.* xxix (*Pat. Gr.* t. 41, p. 396), *Haer.*
lxxviii, 6–7 (*Pat. Gr.*, t. 42, p. 721).   The former passage of Epiphanius (*Haer.* xxix, 3–4) merits
quotation in full in view of its extraordinary statement: Ἔτι δὲ καὶ ἱερατεύσαντα αὐτὸν κατὰ
τὴν παλαιὰν ἱερωσύνην εὕρομεν. Διὸ καὶ ἠφίετο αὐτῷ ἅπαξ τοῦ ἐνιαυτοῦ εἰς τὰ Ἅγια τῶν ἁγίων εἰσιέναι,
ὡς τοῖς ἀρχιερεῦσιν ἐκέλευσεν ὁ νόμος, κατὰ τὸ γεγραμμένον. Οὕτω γὰρ ἱστόρησαν πολλοὶ πρὸ ἡμῶν
περὶ αὐτοῦ, Εὐσέβιός τε καὶ Κλήμης, καὶ ἄλλοι. Ἀλλὰ καὶ τὸ πέταλον ἐπὶ τῆς κεφαλῆς ἐξῆν αὐτῷ
φέρειν, καθὼς οἱ προειρημένοι ἀξιόπιστοι ἄνδρες ἐν τοῖς ὑπ' αὐτῶν ὑπομνηματισμοῖς ἐμαρτύρησαν.
Whether Epiphanius derived his account from Hegesippus is unknown, but his statement
about James' sacerdotal status seems to be alluded to by Eusebius, op. cit., II. xxiii. 6, who
states that he is quoting Hegesippus—τούτῳ (James) μόνῳ ἐξῆν εἰς τὰ ἅγια εἰσιέναι.
The amazing claim here that James exercised the functions and privileges of the High Priest
has been explained by Eisler, *Messiah Jesus*, pp. 540 *seq.* as proving his theory that the nationalist
party maintained a rival priesthood to that of the pro-Roman Sadducees; cf. Eisler, op. cit.,
pp. 36 *seq.*; cf. Lightfoot, *Galatians*, p. 366, n. 1.   It is instructive to note that a modern
Jewish scholar, Klausner (op. cit., p. 279), ignores the problem here by translating the τὰ ἅγια
of Eusebius as "the Temple"; he does not notice the more definitive description of Epiphanius
on this point.   On the curious reference of Julius Africanus to the δεσπόσυνοι (*apud* Eusebius,
op. cit., I. vii. 14) see Eisler, *ΙΗΣΟΥΣ ΒΑΣΙΛΕΥΣ*, Bd. i, pp. 353–4, Bd. ii, pp. 175–6; also
Goguel, op. cit., pp. 133, n. 3, 134, n. 1.

appears to have retailed legends current in the Church of Aelia Capitolina about its aboriginal predecessor in the Jewish metropolis, legends which set out to enhance the glory and prestige of the Jerusalem Church in the natural hope that something of its unique reputation might redound to the advantage of its insignificant successor.[1] However, after we have made adequate allowance for this factor of exaggeration, the record of Hegesippus does also testify to the unique predominance of James among the Jerusalem Christians, which is so clearly indicated upon examination, as we have seen, in the earlier sources. Moreover, although it may perhaps be fairly considered as an *argumentum a silentio*, it is significant to note that the hagiography of the Church of Aelia Capitolina apparently concentrated on the figure of James and not on that of Peter.

We may, therefore, conclude this chapter with the summary observation that the extant Palestinian data for primitive Christianity, although they are of a most varied nature and value, are found on examination to agree with the testimony of Paul's writings and the Acts of the Apostles. In particular, while many points remain for further elucidation, the fact of the supremacy of the Jerusalem Church and its essentially Jewish outlook emerges clear of serious doubt, and so also does the unique leadership of James, the brother of the Lord.

[1] In the fourth and fifth centuries the Church of Aelia Capitolina, the Gentile city which replaced the older Jerusalem, strove hard and successfully to win for itself a place of unique honour as the ancient centre of Christianity; cf. W. Bright, *The Age of the Fathers* (London, 1903), vol. ii, pp. 319, 534–5; Kidd, *Hist. of the Church*, vol. ii, pp. 330–2; Streeter, op. cit., pp. 41–3; Burkitt, *Christian Beginnings*, pp. 63–71, and his ref. to C. H. Turner's art. in *Journ. Theol. Studies*, i, p. 550. Meyer, op. cit., III, p. 601, says of the community at Aelia: "*Sie gibt sich aus für die Nachfolgerin der Urgemeinde des Jakobus und der zwölf Apostel, aber in Wirklichkeit ist sie eine Neuschöpfung, die Verbindung war völlig unterbrochen.*" It may well have been a "*Neuschöpfung*", but it is questionable whether its connection with the *Urgemeinde* had been so completely interrupted. The *Clementine Homilies*, with their exaltation of James, seem to have originated, at least in their final form, either in Palestine or in the near vicinity; cf. Hort, *Clementine Recognitions*, p. 89; Bartlet, "Clementine Literature", art. in *Encycl. Brit.* (xi. ed.), vol. vi, p. 492b; C. Schmidt, *Studien zu den Pseudo-Clementinen*, pp. 292–3; Cullmann, *Le Problème littéraire et historique du Roman Pseudo-Clémentin*, pp. 98–9.

4

The Pauline Interpretation of Christianity

A CURIOUS tension shows itself throughout the major part of Paul's writings, but it is not, as might have been expected, a tension between Christianity and heathenism. It is an internal tension, a disharmony, amounting at times to overt strife, between two parties and their modes of interpretation within the Church itself. Evidence of this situation is found particularly in three different Letters of Paul, and it shows a remarkable consistency of expression.

In his Epistle to the Galatians Paul professes surprise that they had so quickly deserted his teaching for another gospel (ἕτερον εὐαγγέλιον). However, he goes on to say that this was not really another (ἄλλο) gospel, but a perversion (μεταστρέψαι, or παρ᾽ ὃ εὐηγγελισάμεθα) of the gospel of Christ, which had been preached to them by himself and his companions.[1] Paul considers the act so pernicious that he states twice his opinion that the man who was responsible for it should be anathema.[2] Similarly in his Second Epistle to the Corinthians the Apostle writes that he fears that his converts have been beguiled from their original faith in Christ by one who has preached "another Jesus, whom we did not preach", that they have received a different spirit from that which they received at the first, and likewise a different gospel (εὐαγγέλιον ἕτερον)[3]. A reminiscence of this apparent tension between two different gospels or interpretations is also to be found in a curious passage in Paul's Letter to the Roman Christians.[4] After saying that he is desirous of preaching the gospel to them, the Apostle goes on to declare that he is not ashamed of the gospel, because it is "the power of God unto salvation to every one that believeth; to the Jew first, and also to the Greek. For therein is revealed a righteousness of God by faith unto faith: as it is written, But the righteous shall live by faith." Now, when considered fairly as a statement, this passage indicates a truly remarkable situation. The Roman Christians should naturally have been already familiar with the gospel, and yet Paul alleges as the reason for his desire to preach the gospel to them the fact that he was

---

[1] Gal. I. 6, 7. Lightfoot, op. cit., p. 76, after a survey of the comparative meanings of ἄλλος and ἕτερος concludes, "Thus while ἄλλος is generally confined to a negative of identity, ἕτερος sometimes implies the negation of resemblance." Cf. Lake, *Earlier Epistles*, p. 267, n. 1.

[2] Gal. I. 8, 9. Cf. Sieffert, *Der Brief an die Galater*, p. 304.

[3] 2 Cor. I. 3, 4. Cf. Lightfoot, ibid.

[4] Rom. I. 15–17.

not ashamed of it. The embarrassment evident here must naturally prompt the question why Paul should have felt it necessary to write to the Roman Christians in this way. The situation implied seems to have only one adequate explanation, namely that the Christians at Rome, who were not his converts, had been acquainted with some other interpretation of Christianity and that Paul, conscious of this, now desired to present to them his gospel, which he knew had acquired a notorious reputation among them and of which he felt it well to proclaim himself boldly as still the champion.[1]

This Pauline evidence of the existence of two rival gospels is certain, but, as we have just seen, it is of an inferential nature. The issue involved was clearly one which deeply stirred the Apostle, but since all his references to it are contained in controversial polemic or apologia, we are afforded no systematic exposition of either his own gospel or that of his antagonists. However, the issue being thus so evidently serious, it is necessary to attempt some appreciation of the essential contents of these gospels, as far as they may be legitimately elucidated from the data at our disposal.

In his letter to the Corinthian Christians Paul finds occasion to describe the nature of his teaching as a whole to his converts. The language which he uses is very significant. He states that he, and presumably his companions, speak an other-worldly wisdom ($\sigma o\phi\acute{\iota}a\nu$) among the perfect. This wisdom they pass on in a mystery ($\acute{\epsilon}\nu\ \mu\nu\sigma\tau\eta\rho\acute{\iota}\wp$), for it had been hidden by the divine providence before the aeons, so that in some unexplained way it might now redound to their glory.[2] After describing how none of the rulers of this aeon knew this mystery and how consequently they had crucified the Lord of glory ($\tau\grave{o}\nu\ \kappa\acute{\upsilon}\rho\iota o\nu\ \tau\hat{\eta}s\ \delta\acute{o}\xi\eta s$), Paul then goes on to state that the revelation of this mystery had been made to them by the Spirit, and that, therefore, their teaching was not presented in terms of human wisdom.[3]

This idea of the Spirit-given origin of his own particular teaching is fervently maintained by Paul in other passages of his writings. In his great apologia to the Galatians he boldly claims that the Gospel which he preached had no human source ($o\grave{\upsilon}\kappa\ \acute{\epsilon}\sigma\tau\iota\ \kappa\alpha\tau\grave{\alpha}\ \acute{\alpha}\nu\theta\rho\omega\pi o\nu$), that it had not been mediated to him through any human agency, but that he had received it by the special revelation of Jesus Christ;[4] any suggestion which might have been made that some vital part of his knowledge had been derived by him from the Apostles of the Jerusalem community is significantly repudiated at length.[5] A further illuminating passage of similar import is found in 2 Corinthians 5. 12–19, and it appears also

---

[1] For a further exposition of this interpretation see below, pp. 145 *seq.*
[2] 1 Cor. 2. 6, 7.
[3] 1 Cor. 2. 8–16. Cf. Knox, *Gentiles*, p. 115 and Notes iv and v; Guignebert, *Le Christ*, pp. 346 *seq.*
[4] Gal. 1. 11, 12.
[5] Gal. 1. 15–17. Cf. Lightfoot, op. cit., p. 82 (note on 15–17); Nock, *St. Paul*, p. 67; Guignebert, op. cit., pp. 329–30.

to throw some light on the content of this Pauline gospel. Here Paul states his intention of providing his converts with an apologia on his behalf, so that they may have something to oppose to the pretensions of certain men who boast about the outward appearance and not about the inner, essential reality (ἐν προσώπῳ . . . μὴ ἐν καρδίᾳ). Then the Apostle significantly adds a remark of no apparent relevancy to the context of what he had written, but which is clearly very pertinent to his thought at this point. He states that, even if he and his companions are out of their mind (ἐξέστημεν),[1] this state is only due to the fact that their minds are orientated towards God, whereas towards their converts they maintain a normal state of mental balance. This piece of gratuitous and laboured apologia here must surely indicate that the subject of the derivation of his own peculiar teaching was one of extraordinarily great moment to Paul and that he was so keenly conscious of the usual malicious explanation advanced for it by his opponents that he must betray his agitation by adverting to it in this manner. Quite clearly it would seem that his claim to a special spiritual revelation was rejected and its content dismissed by the counter-assertion of his lack of mental soundness. Owing to the strength of the reaction which the recollection of this calumny induced in him, Paul becomes rather confused in the logical sequence of his argument from this point. It is, however, reasonable to suppose that, after this disturbing digression, he returns to his proper theme of giving his converts something with which to meet those who are described as guilty of that particular form of boasting. To this end he alleges that, constrained by the love of Christ, he and his companions have reached a decision or interpretation regarding the meaning of the death of Christ, namely, "that one died for all, therefore all died", so that the living should no longer live unto themselves, but unto him who had died on their behalf and rose again. The consequence of this Paul then asserts to be a cessation of knowledge on their part of anyone κατὰ σάρκα, with the further issue that whatever former knowledge they may have had of Christ κατὰ σάρκα was henceforth to be completely discounted. The final result of this process is then described as the transforming of every man into a new creature, the old order thus giving way to the new. As we have noticed, it is extremely difficult to be certain of the logic of Paul's argument here, for, like so many another of crucial significance, this passage is packed full with pregnant thoughts, which seem to have very little apparent logical connection the one with the other. However, the general meaning of the Apostle can fairly be made out. He is obviously in conflict with certain Christian teachers who base their position on what he chooses to call outward appearance.[2] The anti-thesis which Paul sets forth here between ἐν προσώπῳ and ἐν καρδίᾳ is shown in the sequel to be no mere rhetorical contrast of emphasis

---

[1] Cf. Knox, op. cit., p. 143.
[2] Cf. Lietzmann, *An die Korinther*, I, II, pp. 124–5.

upon some abstract idea of what is essential, and what is not, to the faith. The subsequent repudiation of knowledge of Christ κατὰ σάρκα, and the supersession of the old order which it implied, surely reveal that Paul was basing his interpretation of the faith not on what would now be described as the Jesus of History, and would then have been the Jesus of Tradition, but on the Christ who is spiritually apprehended.[1]

The claim which Paul so fervently makes in his Galatian Epistle to complete originality for his gospel would appear to be contradicted by his own words in 1 Corinthian 15. 1 ff. There he states that in his evangelizing of the Corinthians he had included in his exposition of the primary principles of the faith a certain credal affirmation, which he himself had also received (ὃ καὶ παρέλαβον). This credo sets forth a soteriological interpretation of the death of Christ and an assertion of his Resurrection from the dead, which is supported by a catena of references to experiences of the Risen Lord ascribed to certain well-known persons in the Church. Although this statement is tantamount to a denial of that absolute originality to which Paul laid claim, the problem which it thus constitutes is more apparent than real, for quite clearly Paul's acknowledgement of the source of his teaching here is a kind of *obiter dictum* and was obviously made without any reference to that logical consistency which would have been demanded of him if this Letter were addressed instead to the Galatians. However that may be, the passage has a great value here in revealing to us both more information on the nature of the basis of Paul's authority and also the inherent weakness of his position in this respect. It is to be noted that to the classic list of Resurrection-witnesses Paul adds himself, thus equalizing his experience with that of the Apostles, from whose number he thereby unwittingly excludes himself. Moreover, he seems at once aware of his temerity in making his claim and he seeks to qualify it by likening himself to an abortion.[2] But of much greater consequence to our purpose here is the fact that this passage reveals that Paul, despite the essential emphasis which he laid upon his spiritually apprehended doctrine of the Christ,

---

[1] The interpretation of the crucial verse, 2 Cor. 5. 16, has been a matter for great debate: H. Windisch, *Der zweite Korinthbrief*, pp. 186–8, describes six different interpretations. This fact may prove that there is an ineluctable element of ambiguity in the verse, but it may also be the result of certain scholars not liking to accept a view of Paul's teaching which would seem to represent him as one who consciously discounted the Gospel presentation of the tradition. If the presupposition of the existence of a single harmonious tradition of interpretation be abandoned, the problem here is correspondingly reduced and Paul's teaching in this passage can easily be understood in terms of his general position; cf. Streeter, *Camb. Anc. Hist.*, vol. xi, pp. 274–5. On the subject cf. Windisch, op. cit., p. 188; Nock, op. cit., p. 243; Deissmann, *St. Paul*, p. 195; Klausner, *From Jesus to Paul*, pp. 413–17, 436–7, 477; Schweitzer, *Mysticism of Paul*, pp. 114, 266; Loisy, *Les Mystères Païens et le Mystère Chrétien*, pp. 242, 243; Guignebert, *Jesus*, pp. 25–6, 55, 74, 232; *Peake's Commentary*, p. 853a, added note by A. J. Grieve (in connection with which cf. Rom. 9. 4, 5); Martinetti, *Jésus Christ et le Christianisme*, p. 224; Goguel, *Jesus*, p. 118. It is interesting to note that Knox, op. cit., p. 181, describes 2 Cor. 5. 16 as "the incautious outburst". Goguel, *La Naissance du Christianisme*, pp. 112–16, 254, also thinks that, except for the short Christophany period, the Christianity of Jerusalem was not pneumatic.

[2] Cf. A. S. Peake, *Peake's Commentary*, p. 846a, and also Moffatt, *First Corinthians*, pp. 238–9.

was ultimately dependent upon the tradition of the historical Jesus.
There was obviously a substructure of traditional narrative about the life
and death of Jesus of Nazareth which constituted the original rationale
of the faith, and which, though it might be subsequently overlaid with
ideas of a highly mystical character, remained the real intellectual basis
of those beliefs which gave to Christianity its. own proper individual
form and content.[1] To this particular point we shall have to return
later.[2]

The position which we reach then is that Paul is the exponent of an
interpretation of the Christian faith which he himself regards as differing
essentially from the interpretation which may tentatively be best described
as the traditional or historical one. Now, when regard is paid to Paul's
relative closeness in time to the life of Jesus of Nazareth, the question
must naturally arise of the cause of this remarkable departure from what
presumably was the traditional interpretation, at so early a period in the
evolution of Christian thought. Surely, it might be asked, the very
strength of personal recollection of the historical Jesus at such a time
must have been a sufficient guarantee against any serious movement
to propound an interpretation which ran counter to the traditional
one?

The answer to such questions certainly lies in the' psychology of Paul's
faith. Paul, as he himself clearly tells us, was not converted by the logic
or the example of those who were Christians before him—indeed to the
contrary, for we have his own testimony that he was an exceedingly
zealous promoter of his national faith and actually persecuted the Church;
his conversion, he vehemently maintains, was due to no human agency,
but to the direct intervention of God.[3] The exact nature of this event,
of course, defies our analysis. Paul's own statement, as we have already
noticed, is that God directly interposed in the course of his life in a sudden
manner, and that he received what he calls the gospel which he had
preached to the Galatians through the revelation of Jesus Christ. In
accepting this statement of Paul's (and we have no other of equal
authority) we are clearly in the absolute realm of personal experience
of a highly mystical order.[4] We may note, however, that there was
later current in the Church an account of Paul's conversion which shows
remarkable agreement with these biographical references in Galatians,
and which also does not appear to have been derived therefrom. [5]

It is obvious, of course, that the very interest in the new faith which

---

[1] Cf. Guignebert, *Jesus*, pp. 502–3, *Le Christ*, pp. 350–1; Lightfoot, *Locality and Doctrine
in the Gospels*, p. 27, n. 1; A. D. Nock, *Early Gentile Christianity*, p. 49; Goguel, *R.H.P.R.*, t. xxviii,
pp. 19–25.

[2] See below, pp. 73, 149.

[3] Gal. 1. 1, 11–17; cf. Phil. 3. 6.

[4] See generally Schweitzer, op. cit.; cf. his *Paul and his Interpreters*, pp. 226, 245–6; cf. Nock,
St. Paul, pp. 239 *seq.*; Cave, *Gospel of St. Paul*, pp. 31 *seq.*; Klausner, op.cit., pp. 311–30;
Deissmann, op. cit., p. 191; Guignebert, *Le Christ*, chap. vi.

[5] Acts 9. 1-19; 22. 3–16; 26. 9–20; cf. *B.C.*, vol. v, n. xv.

his fierce animus against it reveals must have meant that Paul was fairly well acquainted with its chief tenets before his conversion, but it is equally obvious that he had found nothing attractive in its presentation by the Palestinian Christians. Perhaps, if Romans 7 is to be considered auto-biographical,[1] a spiritual conflict had been going on within Paul's mind about the possibility of obeying the Law, but we have no grounds, as we shall presently see, for believing that the new faith in its Palestinian form could have accentuated this conflict and precipitated the crisis which resulted in his conversion. We shall have cause later to study the problem of the nature of primitive Palestinian Christianity, but it is necessary here to anticipate one of its essential features, namely its pro-clamation of the Resurrection of Jesus from the dead, which is strikingly attested by the well-constituted list of Resurrection-witnesses in 1 Cor-inthians 15. 3–7. When we consider the essentially personal character of the experiences which he describes in 1 Corinthians 15. 8 and Galatians 1. 12, and which are remarkably confirmed by the conversion narratives in Acts, it would seem to be a reasonable assumption that Paul had been so powerfully attracted by the concept of the Risen Jesus that, when at last the crisis of personal experience came, his resistance to the new faith collapsed and he submitted himself completely to the appeal of him around whom it centred. However, it would appear that this fact of conversion on these essentially personal grounds had not neces-sarily implied Paul's acceptance of the interpretation of the vocation of Jesus which was propounded by the Palestinian Christians. Indeed, as we have already seen, in his Galatian Epistle Paul was at great pains to show that during the crucial period of his conversion he was completely independent of the Jerusalem Church and only visited it and made con-tact with its two leading members, Cephas and James, after the space of some three years.

Paul had his own explanation of the purpose of the signal act of divine intervention which had resulted in his conversion, and it should be care-fully noted: "It was the good pleasure of God . . . to reveal his Son in me, that I might preach him among the Gentiles." [2] The phrase "to reveal his Son in me" is admittedly a curious one, but it clearly has a high significance for our understanding of Paul's own interpretation of God's purpose for him, so that its elucidation here is important. When care-fully considered as a statement of fact, the words really constitute a tremendous, indeed a preposterous, claim for any man to make, and more especially a man of Paul's antecedents. They mean literally that in the person of Paul God had revealed his Son to the end that Paul might "evangelize" him among the Gentiles.[3] Considering Paul's faculty for highly mystical thinking, it is tempting to connect these words with his

---

[1] Cf. Dodd, *Romans*, pp. 104–8; Sanday and Headlam, *Romans*, p. 186.
[2] Gal. 1. 15, 16.
[3] See Lightfoot's note on ἐν ἐμοί, *Galatians*, p. 83.

statement at the end of this same Epistle about his bearing in his body
the stigmata of the Lord Jesus; [1] however, from the context it is unlikely
that some such Passion-mysticism has inspired these words, and it would
seem more reasonable to interpret them as meaning that Paul believed
God had intended through Paul's instrumentality to reveal the true
nature of his Son to the Gentiles. The logical implications of the words
must also be noted. God's action, Paul's statement implied, was a new
unveiling of his Son, so that there was afforded an apprehension of Jesus
which was hitherto unknown in the Church. Thus in effect Paul maintains
that the singular nature of his own conversion was a consequence of
God's action of making a new revelation of his Son specifically for
propagation among the Gentiles,[2] and the unique nature of this revelation is attested, according to the logic of his argument, by his complete
independence of the Jerusalem community during the vital period of his
conversion.

That Paul was conscious of the serious problem involved in his claim
to a special revelation of the true nature of Jesus Christ is evident from
many of his remarks in this Galatian Epistle. His curious statement in
I. 6, 7, that his Galatian converts had changed over to a different
(εἰς ἕτερον) gospel, which was not, however, another (ἄλλο) gospel,
seems only to be explicable as an attempt to draw a subtle distinction between his own interpretation of Christ and that of his
antagonists—a distinction which was vital to him, but which he felt
could not safely be drawn in such a way as to imply condemnation of the
other interpretation by attributing to it an alien source; indeed, despite
all his hostility towards it, Paul clearly recognizes that its authority has to
be respected, that it is derived from a common source, and that at the
most it can only politicly be described as a kind of different version from
his own. Paul's consciousness of embarrassment over professing to have
his own gospel is further illustrated in a more significant way in the
second chapter of this same Epistle. In verse 2 we find him defining
his gospel, which he felt obliged to submit to certain leaders of the Jerusalem Church, as "the gospel which I preach among the Gentiles".
A little further on (vv. 7–9) Paul fully reveals the line of explanation
which he had taken in the matter, relative to the Jerusalem Church.
Here he describes his gospel as "the gospel of the uncircumcision" in
contradistinction to that of which Peter is regarded as the special protagonist, namely "the gospel of the circumcision". How far Paul was
aware of the logical implications of the distinction which he thus draws
remains an important subject for our future study, and here it will
suffice to note that the Apostle could acknowledge to his converts that

---

[1] Gal. 6. 17; cf. Schweitzer, *Mysticism of Paul*, p. 143.
[2] Schweitzer, op. cit., p. 181, while recognizing the importance of this verse, seems to miss
the significance of ἀποκαλύψαι τὸν υἱὸν αὐτοῦ ἐν ἐμοί through his preoccupation with the eschatological issue.

he was teaching a different gospel from that which was taught by the Church of Jerusalem.[1]

For our understanding of Paul's position relative both to Jewish Christianity and to the general development of Christian thought this distinction which he makes between the two gospels is of fundamental importance. The fact of the distinction, moreover, indicates the operation of two factors, the appreciation of which should also greatly help in elucidating the long-debated question of the relation of Paul's teaching to contemporary Judaistic and Hellenistic concepts and expression.

One of these factors is Paul's belief that he was expounding an interpretation of the new faith which was specially designed by God for the Gentiles, and which, therefore, must have been intelligible to them. Quite obviously his distinction between a "gospel of the circumcision" and a "gospel of the uncircumcision" means that he was conscious that the interpretation presented to the Jews was not suitable for presentation to the Gentiles. And this unsuitability clearly did not lie only in the Gentile distaste for the practice of circumcision, for the references in the Second Corinthian Epistle to "another Jesus" and "another spirit" conclusively show that a more profound issue was involved here than that of the practical question of submitting to an obnoxious custom. If then Paul believed that his gospel was thus specially suited to Gentile needs, it is legitimate to infer that that gospel was set forth in concepts and terms which would be readily comprehensible to those nurtured in the culture of the Græco-Roman world. And it would follow in turn from this inference that the Apostle was himself acquainted with aspects of this culture and so far sympathetically disposed towards them that he was ready to use their ideas and terminology to mediate a revelation which had originated in Israel.[2]

We come then to the second factor involved in the fact of the currency of these two gospels in the Church. It is that Paul must have had some predisposition to sympathy with the Gentiles. What was the cause

---

[1] It would seem that the seriousness of the evidence of these verses for the traditional view of Christian Origins was clearly recognized by Lightfoot, op. cit., p. 109, who sought to anticipate its discussion by the statement that the gospel of the circumcision "denotes a distinction of sphere and not a difference of type", quoting Tertullian, *Praescr. Haer.* 23, in support. He ignores the witness of τὸ εὐαγγέλιον ὃ κηρύσσω ἐν τοῖς ἔθνεσι in Gal. 2. 2. Cf. Lake, *Earlier Epistles*, p. 267. The distinction was apparently significant to Marcion; see Harnack, *Marcion*, p. 36. Cf. Cullmann, *Le Problème littéraire et historique du Roman Pseudo-Clémentin*, pp. 244–50.

[2] Knox, *Some Hellenistic Elements*, pp. 30 *seq.*, has produced evidence showing that even in Palestine certain of the rabbis were alive to the need of presenting Judaism in a form which would be appreciated by those nurtured in the traditions of Græco-Roman culture. G. Ricciotti, *Flavio Giuseppe*, pp. 128 *seq.*, throws some interesting light on Jewish activity in this connection in explaining Josephus' parade of Greek learning. Compilations of extracts from Greek writers, mixed together with Old Testament material, were used for apologetical purposes—"*così il lettore pagano era servito con astuto appropriatezza, giacchè gli si offriva un cibo che odorava di erudizione greca ma la cui sostanza era essenzialmente guidaica*". Guignebert, *Le Christ*, pp. 233–9, is surely right when he suggests that, while Paul would undoubtedly have refused to unroll a hermetic book or deliberately concern himself with a mystery cult, he could not have remained insulated from the influences of the *milieu* of Græco-Roman culture in which he had been born and for long years had lived.

6

of this we can only surmise. Paul tells us little of his antecedents, but the emphasis which he lays upon his Judaistic orthodoxy in his Letter to the Galatians [1] may well be interpreted as the fervent assertion of a Jew of the Diaspora who was peculiarly sensitive to the suspicions which the Palestinian Jews entertained towards those who had not been born and bred in the Holy Land.[2] Such an exhibition of embarrassment would also well accord with the tradition preserved in the Acts that Paul was a native of the city of Tarsus in Cilicia.[3] However, the fact of having lived the early years of his life in a Gentile environment would not, of course, necessarily have meant that a Jew would become naturally sympathetic towards the Gentiles, and there is much evidence to show that often close acquaintanceship with Græco-Roman culture led to a thorough revulsion of feeling, causing the Jew to hate and despise the heathen and to cling more fanatically to his own exclusive creed.[4] Paul certainly does not seem to have been moved by any such reactions,[5] but to the contrary his intimacy with the Gentiles appears to have stimulated in him such a measure of sympathy that on his conversion to Christianity he was inspired to think of his new faith particularly in terms of its applicability to the spiritual needs of the Gentile world.

Much labour and ingenuity have been devoted to the task of trying to determine the nature of Paul's knowledge of the religious beliefs of the Græco-Roman world and the degree to which he was influenced by them in his exposition of Christianity. Much of this research seems to have been made on the assumption that the case in one direction or another would be adequately proved by showing from the extant documents illustrative of the many aspects of Græco-Roman religion that Paul either knew or did not know certain specific features. It is obvious, however, on reflection that such a method is scarcely likely to be conclusive, for two reasons. The first is that the corpus of material relative to the religious cults of the Hellenistic world of the first century of the present era is very meagre and the selection of its contents has been determined by the chance of circumstances of many varying kinds. The second is constituted by the fact of Paul's own great genius. It is indeed strange how often scholars, while readily acknowledging the power of Paul's intellect and the profundity of his spiritual insight, have apparently expected the writings of the Apostle to reveal obvious pieces of unassimilated theology from the mystery cults as proof of the influence

---

[1] Gal. 1. 13, 14; cf. 2 Cor. 11. 22; Phil. 3. 4–6.
[2] On the greater tendency of the Diaspora Jews to lapse from orthodoxy see Klausner, *From Jesus to Paul*, pp. 35 *seq.*; Schürer, *G.J.V.*, III, p. 90–102; Guignebert, *Le Monde Juif*, pp. 307–10.
[3] Acts 9. 11, 30; 11. 25; 21. 39; 22. 3.
[4] See A. Peretti, *La Sibilla babilonese nella Propaganda ellenistica*, pp. 23 *seq.*; Klausner, op. cit., chap. II. Even Josephus could publish a polemic against Gentile religion and morals; see *Contra Apionem*, II, 236 *seq.*
[5] Rom. 1. 18–32 shows that Paul was alive to the moral failings of Græco-Roman society, but, as the sequel proves, the Jews were not excepted, and the conclusion of general condemnation is reached: "There is none righteous, no, not one" (ib. 3. 9 ff.).

of his Græco-Roman environment. A more reasonable supposition, surely, is to credit Paul with at least the ability of his earlier contemporary, Philo, and to be prepared to expect that whatever he may have received from his acquaintanceship with heathen religious thought would have been thoroughly digested in his vigorous mind before it found expression in his teaching.

But more important than a due consideration of these very pertinent points is the recognition that in the long debate on the subject of Paul's relations with the religious culture of the Græco-Roman world the essential fact appears to have been persistently overlooked that in his differentiation of "the gospel of the uncircumcision" from "the gospel of the circumcision" the Apostle patently witnessed to his consciousness of the distinct needs of the Gentiles and of the special provision to meet them with which he had identified his own mission. That this consciousness and this response sprang from a sympathetic insight into the mind of the pagan Gentile, and an appreciation of where common ground could afford the best facilities of approach, would appear, as we have just seen, to be self-evident. Paul's "gospel of the uncircumcision" is thus clearly to be understood as an interpretation of Christianity purposely designed to commend itself to the Gentile mind, and the implications of the fact must accordingly be accepted.

Bearing carefully in mind these necessary qualifications with regard to Paul's genius and intention, we shall find it more profitable to note the chief features of his teaching than to attempt to identify therein concepts with which we have become fortuitously acquainted in the texts of various oriental cults current in the Levant at this period. Moreover, it must be remembered also that in his Letters Paul's statements of his teaching are essentially *ad hoc* statements and are consequently rarely carefully conceived expositions; again, there is much reason for believing that Paul was not a systematic thinker and that not only did his thoughts develop in the process of time, but he was liable to elaborate a theme which his imagination suggested on the strength of some association of ideas.[1]

From a study of his writings the following appear to be the main lineaments of Paul's gospel. A summary philosophy of history illustrates the workings of God's providence for mankind.[2] From the creation God had provided in the natural world sufficient evidence of his power, so that men might glorify him and give him thanks. But human wisdom proved perverse, so that man turned from the worship of God to various and revolting forms of man and animal worship. The consequence of this perversion was ethical degradation, which manifested itself in the most vicious and abandoned ways. This philosophy of history, which

---

[1] E.g. 1 Cor. 5. 6–8. Cf. Nock, *St. Paul*, pp. 234 *seq.*
[2] Rom. 1. 16–3. 31, also 9. 1–11. 36. Cf. Sanday and Headlam, *Romans*, pp. 342–7; Dodd, *History and the Gospel*, pp. 144–5.

is expounded in the Roman Epistle, is not developed beyond the point that such wickedness merited death; however, a passage from the Letter to the Galatians supplies what would appear to be the next consequent stage in this line of thought.[1] It is that the Gentiles, not knowing God, were held in bondage to the elements of the world until the fulness of time came. Much discussion has been caused by Paul's use of the term τὰ στοιχεῖα τοῦ κόσμου here, but whether the Apostle is thereby elaborating an identification between the angels and these cosmic entities, as Schweitzer has suggested,[2] or whether he has in mind some piece of astral belief,[3] it is certain that he represented the Gentiles as being in the power of dæmonic forces, from which their redemption had eventually been effected by God. The exact mode of this redemption is obscure, but it certainly occasioned the sending of God's Son into the world, where he was incarnated through the process of a human birth.[4] This incarnated Son of God was by race a Jew, a fact for which Paul seems to give two explanations, namely that thereby ancient prophecies were fulfilled and that thereby the redemption of the Jews might be accomplished;[5] it may be noted that neither of these explanations provides an adequate reason for the Jewish nationality of this divine person, which fact indicates something of the difficulties which Paul encountered in trying to square his new interpretation with the original tradition of Jesus of Nazareth. The identity of this Son of God is one of the great mysteries of Paul's teaching. From Paul's many varied, and not always consistent, references it would appear that he conceived of this divine being as pre-existent,[6] as the image of God (εἰκὼν τοῦ θεοῦ),[7] as being in the form of God (ὃς ἐν μορφῇ θεοῦ ὑπάρχων), and in a position to grasp at equality with God (οὐχ ἁρπαγμὸν ἡγήσατο τὸ εἶναι ἶσα θεῷ).[8] In this divine being, moreover, the whole fulness of God bodily dwells (ἐν αὐτῷ κακοικεῖ πᾶν τὸ πλήρωμα τῆς θεότητος σωματικῶς),[9] while through him and unto him (δι' αὐτοῦ καὶ εἰς αὐτὸν) all things have been created and in him they consist (τὰ πάντα ἐν αὐτῷ συνέστηκε), and he is the head of all principalities and powers.[10] He is especially designated both Lord (κύριος)[11] and Christ. The former appellation is clearly one of crucial significance, although its exact connotation eludes our analysis, and it appears to have been conferred on the Son of Man

---

[1] Gal. 4. 1–9.

[2] *Mysticism of Paul*, pp. 70–1, 198–9; cf. Clarke, *New Test. Problems*, pp. 153–6.

[3] Cf. Knox, *Gentiles*, pp. 103–10; Angus, *Religious Quests of the Graeco-Roman World*, pp. 254 *seq.*; Lietzmann, *An die Galater*, pp. 24–5.

[4] E.g. Rom. 1. 3; 8. 3; Gal. 4. 4; Phil. 2. 5–8; Col. 1. 15.

[5] E.g. Rom. 1. 2, 3; 9. 5; 10. 4; 15. 8–12; Gal. 3. 16; 4. 4.

[6] Phil. 2. 6; Col. 1. 16, 17; cf. Gal. 4. 4.

[7] 2 Cor. 4. 4; Col. 1. 15. Cf. Knox, op. cit., p. 159, n. 2; Nock, *Early Gentile Christianity*, p. 101, n. 1; Lightfoot, *Colossians and Philemon*, pp. 210 *seq.* (εἰκὼν).

[8] Phil. 2. 6. Cf. Knox, op. cit., p. 180; A. A. T. Ehrhardt, *Journal of Theological Studies*, vol. xlvi, No. 181–2, pp. 45–51. See below for further discussion of this passage, pp. 82–3.

[9] Col. 2. 9; 1. 19. Cf. Knox, op. cit., pp. 154–6; Lightfoot, op. cit, pp. 224–5, 247–8, 323 *seq.*

[10] Col. 1. 16, 17.

[11] Phil. 2. 11; cf. Rom. 14. 9; 1 Cor. 8. 5, 6.

at his triumphal exaltation after his incarnate life.[1] The title Christ, which must certainly originate from Jewish Messianic beliefs, appears to have acquired both the currency of a personal name [2] and that of a theological concept; in its latter form it is used by Paul in some very curious ways, for example, as an equation of the Spiritual Rock which is related to have followed the Israelites in the wilderness,[3] and in the quaint interpretation of Deuteronomy 30. 11–14 in the Epistle to the Romans.[4] This divine being, whose various attributes logically rendered him a veritable δεύτερος θεός, is in his incarnate state identified by Paul with Jesus.[5] This identification is implicit in many references, but, as we have already seen, the incarnate life of the Son of God in the person of the historical Jesus has very little interest for Paul, and he even betrays an impatience towards any vital emphasis upon its significance. Two facts only about this incarnated phase appear to be of fundamental concern to the Apostle, namely those of the Death and of the Resurrection.[6] The Death is clearly identified with the historical death of Jesus by crucifixion, but it is completely divorced from the historical circumstances which, on the evidence of the Gospels and pagan testimony, occasioned it.[7] According to Paul's most explicit statement in this connection, the Death was accomplished by dæmonic powers and was to be regarded as a mystery of God (τὸ μυστήριον τοῦ θεοῦ).[8] The Death had a vital soteriological significance and its validity was universal. The way in which the Death acquired this character and its mode of operation in securing the salvation of individual persons are matters about which there must for ever be doubt, since Paul has used such a variety of concepts in his soteriological statements and references

---

[1] Phil. 2. 5–11; Rom. 14. 9. Cf. Nock, op. cit., pp. 84–7; Klausner, *From Jesus to Paul*, pp. 484–5; Guignebert, *Le Christ*, pp. 195–9.

[2] E.g. its unexplained use in the opening of Paul's Letters; cf. Klausner, op. cit., p. 478.

[3] 1 Cor. 10. 4.

[4] Rom. 10. 6, 7. Cf. Knox, op. cit., p. 222 (4); Sanday and Headlam, *Romans*, p. 287.

[5] Cf. Klausner, op. cit., pp. 479–81; Loisy, *Les Origines du Noveau Testament*, p. 282; Nock, op. cit., pp. 99–102; K. E. Kirk in *Essays on Trinity and Incarnation*, ed. A. E. J. Rawlinson, pp. 191, 195–8.

[6] E.g. 1 Thess. 4. 14a; 1 Cor. 1. 18 ff.; 11. 24–27; 15. 1 ff.; 2 Cor. 4. 14; Rom. 3. 25; 5. 6; 6. 3–11; 14. 9; Phil. 2. 8, 9; Col. 1. 18–20.

[7] The only clear reference to the Jews' part in the Crucifixion is 1 Thess. 2. 15, which occurs in a passage of which the authenticity is suspect; see below, pp. 92–3. Of the meaning of Χριστὸν ἐσταυρωμένον (1 Cor. 1. 23) there is ground for doubt: "*Man streitet, ob man übersetzen soll: 'einen gekreuzigten Messias' . . . oder 'Christus als Gekreuzigten'*" (J. Weiss, *Der erste Korintbrief*, p. 32 loc. cit.). Cf. Deissmann, *St. Paul*, pp. 197–8. The many references to the "blood of Christ" are probably no more than natural references readily occurring to one to whom the significance of the blood of the sacrificial victim was a familiar concept, and they are not likely to mean that Paul actually witnessed the Crucifixion, as Anderson Scott, *Christianity according to St. Paul*, p. 11, suggests; cf. Guignebert, *Jesus*, p. 447. The phrase προσηλώσας αὐτὸ τῷ σταυρῷ of Col. 2. 14 is similarly an imaginative illustration rather than an allusion to an actual detail of the Crucifixion; cf. Lightfoot, *Colossians and Philemon*, p. 255.

[8] 1 Cor. 2. 8. "*Die ἄρχοντες sind also nicht irdische Machthaber, deren Charackteristikum doch nicht gerade die Verbreitung von σοφία ist, sondern die Engelmächte.*" (Leitzmann, *An die Korinther, I, II*, pp. 11–12.) Cf. Knox, op. cit., pp. 220–1; Goguel, *Jesus*, p. 112, n. 3; Guignebert, *Le Christ*, p. 357 and n. 2. Cullmann, *Christus und die Zeit*, p. 173, suggests that the "*Engelmächte*" were conceived as standing behind the *irdische Machthaber*.

that it is fairly evident that he had thought out no consistent theory and interpretation of this crucial part of his gospel.[1]   The Death was essentially connected with the Resurrection.   This latter event in Paul's extant writings, with one significant exception, appears to have no practical association with the tradition of the Resurrection of the historical Jesus, it never being linked by the Apostle with any of the circumstances which were later recorded in the Gospels.[2]   The Resurrection was certainly effected by God and it apparently had a cosmic efficacy, in that the dæmonic forces were notably vanquished by it.[3]   The nature of the salvation which this divine action secured for men is obscure. There is evidence in Paul's writings for regarding it severally as a deliverance from dæmonic powers,[4] from the curse of the Jewish Law,[5] from death (usually depicted in a hypostasized form),[6] from sin,[7] or sometimes from a combination of some of these forces, which are then represented as a consequential series.   On the other hand, in certain passages Paul seems to regard salvation as delivery from the Divine Wrath or, conversely, a process of reconciliation to God.[8]   One positive, and clearly the most important, consequence of this salvation was the gift of eternal life to the convert, although the nature and currency of this gift are also matters which are inherently obscure.   There is evidence, however, of the essentiality of two factors, namely faith[9] and baptism,[10] in the process of securing to the individual the fruits of Christ's work.   The former was, in the form in which he expounded its significance, a peculiarity of Paul's gospel, as we shall have occasion presently to see, and its logic set at nought all Jewish pretensions to exclusive spiritual privileges and consequently became the immediate cause of offence to his countrymen, whether Christian or not.

The most vital question in this matter of Paul's teaching is that of the degree of his originality, first in the identification of the pre-existent Son of God with the historical Jesus, and secondly in the interpretation of the Crucifixion of Jesus as a divine action with soteriological intent and of cosmic significance.   Unfortunately the determination of the issue depends upon data which are both meagre and ill-balanced, so that it is hopeless to look for any conclusions, except those of a very general kind.

---

[1] E.g. Rom. 5. 6–21; 6. 4–11, 16–23; 8. 1–11, 31–39; 14. 7–9, 15; 1 Cor. 11. 23–30; 15. 3, 4, 12–28, 56, 57; 2 Cor. 4. 7–18; 5. 1–10, 14–19; Gal. 1. 4; 2. 20, 21; 3. 13, 14; 5. 24; 6. 14. 15; Phil. 2. 7–11; 3. 10–12, 20, 21; Col. 1. 14, 18, 20–23; 2. 12–15; 1 Thess. 4. 13–18.

[2] Cf. Guignebert, *Jesus*, pp. 524–6.

[3] Col. 2. 15; Rom. 8. 37–39. Cf. Goguel, op. cit., p. 111; Eisler, *ΙΗΣΟΥΣ ΒΑΣΙΛΕΥΣ*, Bd. ii, pp. 616, 755.

[4] E.g. Gal. 4. 3, 8, 9; Rom. 8. 38, 39; Col. 2. 14, 15.

[5] E.g. Rom. 5. 20, 21; 7. 1–8. 4; Gal. 3. 10–22; 1 Cor. 15. 56. Cf. Knox, op. cit., p. 109; Klausner, op. cit., pp. 501–2.

[6] E.g. Rom. 5. 12–17; 1 Cor. 15. 26, 55; 2 Cor. 4. 11, 12.

[7] E.g. Rom. 5. 21; 6. 6–11; 7. 9, 10; 8. 2; 1 Cor. 15. 56.

[8] E.g. Rom. 5. 10, 11; 2 Cor. 5. 18–20; Col. 1. 21.

[9] E.g. Rom. 3. 28; 4. 16; Gal. 2. 16; 3. 7, 8, 23–25.

[10] Rom. 6. 3, 4; Col. 2. 12.

Viewed as an historical phenomenon, the teaching contained in Paul's writings appears quite inexplicable in terms of the evolution of Jewish religious thought, varied as the latter is now known to have been.[1] It is indeed true that there is some evidence that in certain Jewish circles a divine force, such as Wisdom, could be thought of in a hypostasized form, so that it might fairly be regarded as a kind of separate divine being.[2] But such a belief cannot be held as at all representative of normal Jewish theological thinking, and it is significantly the product of the Hellenistic Diaspora of Israel. Moreover, this unique departure from the strict monotheism of orthodox Judaism was only made in connection with an entity which was essentially a divine attribute, whereas Paul's fundamental postulate of a Son of God who was unique in this filial relationship to the Deity, and whose attributes were such that he was truly a δεύτερος θεός, is completely unknown in all other extant records of Jewish thought at this period or in those of the century immediately antecedent to it.[3] The concept can be most obviously paralleled in Græco-Roman religious thought and, although it is hopeless to expect to be able to identify the exact source of the Pauline idea, it is probable that Hellenistic influences were the more potent factor in its formulation.[4]

It is evident, as we have seen, that Paul identified this pre-existent Son of God with the Messiah of Jewish apocalyptic hopes, but, in significant contrast to the Synoptic writers, he shows practically no interest in the exercise or significance of the role; indeed the title *Christos* appears to be used by Paul as a conventional title of little relevancy for his own particular interpretation. Of far greater moment, however, is Paul's identification of the historical Jesus as the incarnated form of the Son of God. Here again we meet an idea which is essentially un-Jewish, for it runs counter to the peculiar genius of Judaism, which placed a gulf of absolute difference between God and man,[5] and it is completely without parallel in all our extant records of Jewish religious thought. The concept of the incarnation of a divine being in human form does, of course, frequently appear in the various pagan cults, Greek, Egyptian, and oriental, which were current in Paul's day in the Near East, and once more we must conclude that it was undoubtedly such environmental

---

[1] Cf. Guignebert, *Le Monde Juif*, pp. 119–28; Klausner, op. cit., p. 441.

[2] Cf. Knox, op. cit., chap. III; Guignebert, op. cit. p. 124.

[3] Even if *Enoch* xxxvii–lxxi could be certainly dated for the period before the rise of Christianity, the concept of the Son of Man therein in no way approximates to Paul's interpretation of the status and function of Jesus Christ. Cf. Guignebert, *Jesus*, p. 272 and n. 4; Charles, *Between the Old and New Test.*, pp. 85–7; Manson, *Jesus the Messiah*, p. 176.

[4] "It was therefore an easy matter for Paul in writing his first letter to Corinth to transfer the person of the historical Jesus from the category of the heavenly Messiah of Palestinian Judaism and Christianity into that of the divine Wisdom which was the centre of Hellenistic-Jewish speculation, where the term Logos had not yet ousted it under the influence of Philo" (Knox, op. cit., p. 114; cf. p. 115). Cf. Klausner, op. cit., pp. 470–85; Nock, *Early Gentile Christianity*, pp. 99–102; Loisy, *Le Origini del Cristianesimo*, pp. 239–40; Deissmann, *St. Paul*, pp. 191–2; Martinetti, *Jésus Christ et le Christianisme*, pp. 247 *seq.*; Streeter, *Camb. Anc. Hist.*, vol. xi, p. 280; Guignebert, *Le Christ*, pp. 194–200.

[5] Cf. Guignebert, *Le Monde Juif*, pp. 119–22; A. Lods, *Les Prophètes d'Israël et les Débuts du Judaïsme*, pp. 364–5, 398–9.

influences which predisposed the Apostle to think in terms of incarnation in interpreting his new faith to pagan peoples.[1]

We have already noticed that, despite this momentous identification of the pre-existent Son of God with the historical Jesus, Paul appears to find scarcely anything of real significance in the events of the incarnated life, except in the Crucifixion, which he interprets in a context far removed from its historical circumstances. His statement in his Second Epistle to the Corinthians, repudiating knowledge of a Christ κατὰ σάρκα in favour of the Christ conceived as a supernatural being, may justly be regarded as an apt summary of the orientation of his faith in this respect.[2] This indifference of Paul's towards the life of the incarnated Son of God, amounting thus to a veritable disavowal of interest in what we should now term the Jesus of History, obviously constitutes a most fundamental problem, both of Pauline theology and with regard to the relevant situation in the Church generally, and we shall return to its discussion again below.[3]

The soteriological interpretation of the death of Jesus, with the concomitant assertion of its universal validity in this respect, is essentially connected with Paul's evaluation of the person of Jesus; but again we are faced with the problem of the origin of such an idea. That Paul did not derive it from a Jewish *milieu* seems to be certain, for, despite the most thorough investigations, no passage has been found in the relevant Jewish literature which contains or makes reference to the idea of an incarnated saviour of mankind who redeems by virtue of his own sacrificial death.[4] The obvious consequential question of a Jewish Christian ethos for the formulation of such a belief is a much more complex matter for discussion. As we shall have occasion to notice at length presently, in the Synoptic writings and in Acts there is evidence that the Jewish Christians saw in the Passion and Death of Jesus the fulfilment of Isaiah's prophecy of the Suffering Servant of God. But this interpretation of Jesus curiously finds no place in Paul's theology, which fact has reasonably been thought to mean that the Apostle had some special reason for refraining from its use.[5] To this point we shall also return later, but

---

[1] Cf. Macchioro, *Zagreus*, pp. 486 *seq.*; Gernet et Boulanger, *Le Génie Grec dans la Religion* pp. 255–7; Gressmann, *Die orientalischen Religionen im hellenistisch-römischen Zeitalter*, p. 96; A. Erman, *Die Religion der Aegypter*, pp. 68–9; S. H. Langdon, *Tammuz and Ishtar* (Oxford, 1914), pp. 344, 347; Klausner, op. cit., pp. 103–7; Nock, op. cit., pp. 97, 99–102, *Conversion*, pp. 236–7 (Nock here suggests that the idea of a god taking human flesh and experiencing birth and death was unpalatable to the Greek mind. Stated in this form, it probably was, but it must be remembered that Paul is ever occupied with the work of the pre-existent Son of God and not with the historical Jesus; he lays no emphasis upon the fact of his human birth, and his death, as we have seen, is regarded as an event of which the real significance far transcended its historical circumstances); Guignebert, *Le Christ.* pp. 172, 174; Murray, *Five Stages of Greek Religion*, pp. 152–65.

[2] 2 Cor. 5. 14–17; see above, pp. 55–7 and notes.   [3] Pp. 74 *seq.*

[4] Cf. Klausner, op. cit., pp. 139–40; Lods, op. cit., pp. 275–80; Guignebert, *Le Monde Juif*, pp. 191–8, *Jesus*, p. 289; Schürer, *G.J.V.*, II, pp. 553–6; Manson, *Jesus the Messiah*, p. 7 and Appendix B; Moore, *Judaism*, vol. i, pp. 551–2; Brierre-Narbonne, *Le Messie Souffrant dans la Littérature Rabbinique*, pp. 1–2.

[5] Cf. Knox, *Jerusalem*, p. 3, n. 23.

for the present we must consider the significance of the apparently un-Jewish origin of Paul's soteriological teaching. Saviour gods who rescue the initiates of their mysteries from some dreaded fate, usually death, were, as is well known, familiar objects in the religious thought of the Græco-Roman world. Numerous attempts, generally manifesting indifference to the obvious fact of Paul's great genius, have been made to find some exact or very close counterpart among these saviour gods to the Apostle's concept of the Redeemer. It is not surprising that these attempts have failed in attaining their immediate object and that orthodox scholars have been able to show that there are certain unique features in the Pauline soteriology which mark it off as essentially different from the *mythoi* of the various pagan saviours. But these investigations have had their value, for they have shown what was the spiritual or psychological atmosphere of the peoples of the Levant in the first century and how a widespread hunger for the assurance of individual immortality was met by a number of cults which promised such an assurance through some form of ritual assimilation to a god or hero who had the power to confer the boon through his own triumph over death.[1] It is likely that, born and nurtured in such an atmosphere and familiar with the concept of a divine being who saves by virtue of his own death (although with what organized form of this idea he was acquainted we cannot tell), Paul was accordingly sensitive to the peculiar needs of this pagan society, and in the formulation of his special gospel for its members he naturally utilized concepts which his own genius and experience revealed to him as having been wonderfully fulfilled in the Death and Resurrection of Jesus.

After this survey we are now in consequence brought to the point where we must consider a very important aspect of the evolution of Paul's theology. This point may perhaps best be expressed in the form of a twofold question. If Paul had at first so fiercely opposed Christianity, as he himself tells us he did, what was the cause of this particularly vehement antipathy and how was that cause removed or overcome, so that he preached in time so complex and so un-Jewish an interpretation of Christianity?

A clue in answer to the first part of the question appears to be given in Paul's attitude towards the Death of Christ. In his First Epistle to the Corinthians we find him proclaiming the significance of the Crucifixion with a vehemence which must surely reflect a deeply rooted personal conviction. He writes: "Seeing that Jews ask for signs, and Greeks seek after wisdom: but we preach Christ crucified, unto Jews a stumbling-block, and unto Gentiles foolishness."[2] It would seem reasonable to

---

[1] Cf. Angus, *Mystery-Religions and Christianity*, pp. 149–234, *Religious Quests of the Graeco-Roman World*, pp. 19–46; Halliday, *Pagan Background of Early Christianity*, lecture vii; Gernet et Boulanger, op. cit., pp. 408 *seq.*; Macchioro, *Zagreus*, pp. 444 *seq.*; Nock, *Camb. Anc. Hist.*, vol. x, pp. 504, 506–9, vol. xii, pp. 418–9, 445; R. Eisler, *Orphische-dionysische Mysteriengedanken*, *passim*; Cumont, *Les Religions Orientales*, pp. 38–41.
[2] 1 Cor. 1. 22, 23.

suppose that the mental background of this verse is autobiographical, for before his conversion it is likely that Paul, as Jew and Hellenist, felt that the Christians' proclamation of the crucified Jesus as the Messiah was both an offence to the divine providence and an insult to man's intelligence.[1] Then we have his rabbinical argument in the Galatian Epistle to demonstrate the Christian's emancipation from the Law.[2] This argument was surely not based upon an original discovery of the Deuteronomic condemnation, "Cursed is every one that hangeth on a tree", but it appears rather to be a paradoxical interpretation of a text which he had hitherto used as a divine refutation of the Christian pretension.

If we are, therefore, justified in thinking that the Christian exaltation of the crucified Jesus as the Messiah was peculiarly offensive to Paul before his conversion, and that it probably constituted his chief objection to the new faith, the second part of the question formulated above becomes consequently more urgent, namely, how this fundamental objection was removed or overcome for him.

As we have already had occasion several times to note, Paul vigorously asserts that his conversion was due to the direct intervention of God, and he carefully shows that during the decisive period of this change he was quite independent of the Jerusalem Christians. In other words, Paul maintained that he had not become convinced of the truth of the new faith by the arguments of the Jewish Christians, but that he had been led to accept it by some introspective process, which he naturally interpreted as a divine act of revelation. The point is significant, because it means that for the erstwhile sceptic his chief objections had been overcome by some means other than the logic of Jewish Christianity and that he professed that his apprehension of the true meaning of Jesus was acquired independently of those who had known the historical Jesus. Now since, as we have seen, the judicial execution of Jesus by crucifixion had constituted for Paul the essential offence of the proclamation of Jesus as the Messiah, and since, moreover, we find him never invoking in his writings the conception of Jesus as the fulfilment of Isaiah's Suffering Servant, it is reasonable to suppose that he had discovered some means of overcoming the scandal of the Crucifixion without resort to the Jewish Christian apologetic, which explained the Passion in terms of the Isaianic prophecy.[3] What these means were may be fairly inferred. While it is impossible to know exactly what was the nature of that experience of conversion to which Paul obscurely refers in his Galatian Epistle and which is so vividly described as happening on the Damascus road in the later narrative of the Acts, it is certain that Paul became convinced that the crucified Jesus had been raised to life and had manifested himself

---

[1] Cf. Deissmann, *St. Paul*, p. 200; Goguel, *Jesus*, p. 116.
[2] Gal. 3. 10-13. Cf. Goguel, *La Naissance du Christianisme*, pp. 99-100.
[3] See pp. 76-7 below.

dynamically in his own life. From this conviction it would appear that the whole of Paul's theology subsequently sprang. If Jesus was indeed alive again in a supernatural sense, then clearly his death must be understood in the light of that tremendous fact. The traditional interpretation of the Jewish Christians that the death of Jesus was an accident, which had strangely fulfilled Isaiah's curious prophecy,[1] Paul had not accepted before his conversion and after that event he still found it inadequate. To him the reality of the Resurrection had demonstrated the divine nature of Jesus, so that inevitably for him the Death must have a significance consonant with the status of him who suffered it. And here undoubtedly the influence of his earlier Hellenistic environment and his own genius became the determinative factors which led him to see in the Death and Resurrection of Jesus a divine mystery of cosmic significance. Hence the Death was not merely a particularly shocking judicial murder accomplished by the Roman and Jewish authorities in Jerusalem in some particular year, but it was an event preordained before the foundation of the world and which in the wisdom of God had been effected, unwittingly to their cost, by the dæmonic powers.[2] The Death, moreover, had for mankind a supreme soteriological value, and, as such, it was to be exalted and placed in the forefront of the gospel. Hence was derived Paul's emphasis (in contradistinction to that of the Jewish Christians, as we shall see) upon the Cross of Christ, and hence also his fierce denunciation of his Judaizing opponents as enemies of the Cross of Christ.[3]

The exponent, therefore, of a faith which was based upon divine action of cosmic significance and of which the benefit extended to the whole of humanity, Paul was inevitably led in his thought, his words, and his actions to transcend the barriers of Judaism's national privilege. But herein lay a problem of fatal seriousness both for the Apostle himself and for the future of Christianity as a whole. As we have already seen partly and shall see later at greater length, the Jewish Christians instinctively regarded their new faith as but a further expression of their national religion; the Temple continued to be the central shrine at which they worshipped and many of their members became distinguished for their zealous observance of the Law. To such men the tradition of Israel's unique status with God was a matter of fervent belief, and we have seen something of the grudging and qualified consent which they gave to the admittance of certain favoured Gentiles to participation in the privileges of their new faith. By national instinct Paul must have shared in this belief, and in his Letters there are several passages which attest his pride in his Jewish birth and his natural assumption of Israel's spiritual superiority over the Gentiles.[4] Moreover, considerations of policy with

---

[1] See below, pp. 75–7. [2] 1 Cor. 2. 6–9; Col. 1. 12–23.
[3] Gal 6. 12–14; Phil. 3. 18. Cf. Schweitzer, *Mysticism of Paul*, p. 49; Goguel, *R.H.P.R.*, t. xxviii, pp. 23, 24–5.
[4] Rom. 9. 1–5; 11. 13–24; 2 Cor. 11. 21; Phil. 3. 4, 5.

regard to his relations with the Jerusalem Church would have demanded that he provided no gratuitous offence to Jewish susceptibilities in this respect, and there is much evidence in both the Epistles and the Acts that Paul strove diligently in formal act and statement to prove himself a zealous and orthodox Jew.[1]

Paul's continuing to affirm Israel's unique spiritual status, although undoubtedly sincere, was fundamentally incompatible with the logic of his own gospel. Although he may have been able to distinguish in his own mind some subtle nuance of Jewish privilege in the economy of God's providence, his teaching, as it has been preserved to us in his extant writings, shows such an absolute emphasis on faith as the only essential qualification for membership in Christ that all national and cultural differences are effaced, so that, in his own statement, "there cannot be Greek and Jew, circumcision and uncircumcision, barbarian, Scythian, bondman, freeman: but Christ is all, and in all".[2] Thus, whatever may have been the extent of Paul's own personal conformity to the requirements of orthodox Judaism, the very principles of his gospel negated the Jewish claim to unique favour with God. Whether Paul himself realized the essential illogicality of his position is not known; but that he was aware of its difficulty there can be no doubt, for, as we have seen, a deep embarrassment is implicit in his attempt to distinguish the two gospels current in the Church. But whether Paul fully faced the consequences of his teaching or not, the Jewish Christians certainly did, and they rightly saw in it the negation of most of what they held dear in their national faith.[3]

The nature and extent of the Jewish Christan reaction to Paul and his teaching will be the subject of our detailed investigation later;[4] here it will suffice to state summarily that this reaction principally took the form of repudiating Paul's claim to be an Apostle, an accredited exponent of Christianity, on the ground that he was a late-comer to the faith, that he had not been an eye-witness of the life of Jesus, and that he did not know accurately the original tradition concerning the person and teaching of Jesus. This form of attack is important, for it accordingly conditioned the nature of Paul's reaction and constituted a vital contributive factor in the formulation of his peculiar Christology.

Faced with an attack on his authority, an attack which was based on the assumption of the absolute worth of actual physical acquaintance-ship with the historical Jesus, Paul clearly had but one line of effective defence, and it was the line which his own spiritual experience would naturally suggest. It was to repudiate the historical experience as a factor of essential value in the life of a Christian, and consequently as a factor conferring a status of unique authority on those who could claim

---

[1] Rom. 3. 31; 7. 12; 1 Cor. 9. 20; Acts 18. 18; 20. 16; 21. 26.
[2] Col. 3. 11; cf. Rom. 10 . 12; 1 Cor. 12. 13; Gal. 3. 28; 5. 6.
[3] Acts 21. 20, 21; cf. Matt. 5. 17–19.
[4] See Chapter Seven.

to have participated in it. Knowledge of the Risen Christ, as Paul was fervently aware from his own experience, was decisive, and so he could assert, as we have already noted: "Wherefore we henceforth know no man after the flesh: even though we have known Christ after the flesh, yet now we know him so no more. Wherefore if any man is in Christ, he is a new creature: the old things are passed away; behold, they are become new."[1]

Hence Paul, besides distinguishing between two gospels, in order to maintain his position was led in effect to repudiate an interpretation of the new faith which based its authority upon the historical reality of the events of the life of Jesus. But this position contained an inherent weakness, which we have already noticed in Paul's citation of the list of Resurrection-witnesses in his First Corinthian Epistle, because the morphology of the *mythos* which he sought to expound was decisively conditioned by certain key facts of the life of the historical Jesus. Although reality for Paul lay in his spiritual experience and not in the factual accuracy of the historical tradition, he could not, however, avoid such reference to that tradition as belied the integrity and independence of his own position. The consequences of this defect in the maintenance and furtherance of Paul's interpretation of Christianity will be matters for our detailed study later, since our next immediate task is to examine the nature and source of what Paul chose to designate the gospel of the Circumcision and to inquire into the formulation and exposition of the tradition of the historical Jesus.

[1] See pp. 55–7 and notes.

5

Christianity according to the Church of Jerusalem

WE have seen that it is in the Synoptic Gospels that we have to look for our chief source of information about the thought and practice of Palestinian Christianity. As evidence in this respect these documents are very unsatisfactory, and it is only after the most careful analysis that any specific passage may be fairly regarded as preserving a genuine piece of primitive Palestinian tradition. The main reason for this, as we have also noted, is the fact that all three documents are compositions designed for Greek-speaking publics, resident outside Palestine, and that they date from after A.D. 70, when the Church of Jerusalem had ceased to exist. However, despite the truth of this general qualification, for our purpose in this chapter the Gospel of Mark in particular does contain some evidence of very high significance.

This evidence is constituted in the first place by the fact of the remarkable disproportions of the Markan Gospel when considered primarily as a biographical narrative of the career of Jesus of Nazareth. This fact, which means in effect that about one third of the Gospel is devoted to describing the last week of the life of Jesus, would appear to correspond to a similar concentration of interest in the tradition which Mark had received and which he accordingly felt obliged to perpetuate in his own writing. The feeling of compulsion must have been strong for Mark, for it overrode any desire that he may have had to present a more balanced narrative and to satisfy the natural curiosity to have more details of the life of the Lord, a desire which, as the Gospels of Matthew and Luke show, became very effective in the next few decades. Seen in this light, this concentration of interest on the events which immediately led to the Crucifixion, being embodied as it would seem to be in a well-constituted narrative, indicates that the subject was one of paramount concern to the Palestinian Christians. This fact may appear quite natural, especially when regarded in terms of the subsequent soteriological interpretations,[1] but on examination it will be seen that the concern was motivated by very different factors from those operative in the later developments of Christian theology.

There is in the Gospel of Mark an apologetic purpose which it will be our task to study in detail later. This purpose makes itself particularly

---

[1] Cf. Taylor, *Formation of Gospel Tradition*, pp. 49 *seq.*

obvious in the account of the Trial and Death of Jesus, where it takes the form of imputing to the Jewish authorities the guilt of planning and accomplishing the Crucifixion.[1]   But, in thus seeking to blame the Jews and consequently exculpate the Romans, Mark could scarcely have invented the part played in the drama by the Jewish leaders, for had he done so, we should be faced with the inevitable conclusion that Jesus was condemned and executed solely on the initiative of the Roman authorities, which conclusion would demand a drastic revision of the view of the origins of Christianity which has been almost universally held.   Therefore it appears to be certain that the leaders of the Jewish nation had a decisive part in the condemnation of Jesus.   Now this fact must have been a source of great embarrassment to the Jewish Christians.   If their Master had been done to death by the Romans alone, they could well have proclaimed him as a martyr worthy of Jewish veneration, but for him to have been condemned by the legitimate religious and civil authorities of their nation constituted a problem of peculiar seriousness.   How could they reasonably proclaim Jesus as the long-hoped-for Messiah if he had been condemned to death on a charge of blasphemy by the High Priest and the Sanhedrin?   Moreover, the mode of his death was peculiarly offensive to Jewish religious scruples, for the Law explicitly stated: "he that is hanged (on a tree) is accursed of God."[2]

The difficulties, therefore, which faced a Jew who was still convinced of the validity of his people's religion, and who was intent himself on continuing loyally in the observance of its precepts, in accepting Jesus as the Messiah, or at least as a divinely inspired teacher, were immense. Their immensity is indeed an index to the strength of the conviction of the reality of his Resurrection on the part of those Jews who thus accepted him.   However, although in their individual cases personal conviction overcame the logic of the fact that Jesus had been put to death as a blasphemer at the instigation of the High Priest and the Sanhedrin, that logic had still to be met if Christianity was to be presented to the Jewish people with any hope of success.   It was accordingly necessary to compose an apologia which would explain the Crucifixion in such a way as would set at rest the minds of those who were sensitive to the significance of the fact of the condemnation of Jesus by the Jewish national leaders. This would be most naturally and easily done by depicting the event as a tragic accident, for the causing of which the Roman procurator and the unpopular Sadducean sacerdotal aristocracy were to blame, although therein even these may have acted blindly; indeed a reminiscence of this primitive view seems to be preserved in one of the early speeches in Acts, where Peter is described as saying to his countrymen with reference

---

[1] Cf. Meyer, *Ursprung und Anfänge des Christentums*, I, p. 202; Guignebert, *Jesus*, p. 465; Dodd, *History and the Gospel*, p. 83.

[2] Deut. 21. 23.   Cf. Knox, *Gentiles*, p. 108; Klausner, *From Jesus to Paul*, p. 291; Manson, *Jesus the Messiah*, pp. 5, 116.

to the Crucifixion, "And now, brethren, I wot that in ignorance ye did it, as did also your rulers." [1]

To explain away in this manner the problem of the condemnation pronounced by the High Priest and the Sanhedrin did not, however, reduce the other, and perhaps more serious, problem of the death of Jesus, if he were indeed the Messiah. The concept of a Suffering Messiah, as has so often been pointed out, was not current in contemporary Jewish apocalyptic thought,[2] and so those who proclaimed the crucified Jesus as the long-expected redeemer of Israel had to show some creditable authority for their daring claim, if they were to secure even the least sympathetic attention of their fellow Jews. That such authority should be sought in the sacred Scriptures of the nation is obvious, and we have Paul's confirmation of the fact in his credal affirmation in 1 Corinthians 15, where he states that he had "received" the teaching that Christ died for our sins "according to the scriptures" ($\kappa\alpha\tau\grave{\alpha}$ $\tau\grave{\alpha}\varsigma$ $\gamma\rho\alpha\phi\acute{\alpha}\varsigma$), while it would appear likely that Luke in his story of the manifestation of the Risen Lord on the road to Emmaus has preserved a genuine memory of the line taken by Jewish Christian apologetic in this respect in the words, "Behoved it not the Christ to suffer these things, and to enter into his glory?" [3]

The scriptural warranty for this interpretation of the death of Jesus was obvious and of striking appositeness, although it would appear that the passage in which it was contained had singularly failed to excite the imagination of Israel before this time. Indeed it would seem that the dialogue of Philip and the Ethiopian Eunuch in Acts has preserved something of the original sense of novelty in this apologetic exegesis.[4] The Evangelist's question and the Eunuch's reply surely summarize the position of the Jewish Christian apologist in his exposition of the Servant Sagas of Isaiah—"Understandest thou what thou readest? And he said, How can I, except some one shall guide me?" And then the sequence which gives the classic identification—"I pray thee, of whom speakest the prophet this? of himself, or of some other? And Philip opened his mouth, and beginning from this scripture, preached unto him Jesus."

Apposite as the concept of Isaiah's Suffering Servant undoubtedly was to the case of the crucified Jesus, it would appear that the Jewish Christians continued to use it only for the sake of its apologetical value in providing scriptural authority for the proposition of a Suffering Messiah.

---

[1] Acts 3. 17. Cf. Knox, op. cit., p. 221, "some such explanation of the conduct of the rulers of the Jews was necessary as long as there was any hope of avoiding a final breach with the synagogue . . ."; cf. Klausner, op. cit., p. 439; Parkes, *Conflict of Church and Synagogue*, p. 47.

[2] See above, p. 68, n. 4.

[3] Luke 24. 26. Cf. Guignebert, op. cit, pp. 412–13; Loisy, *Le Origini del Cristianesimo*, p. 78; Dibelius, *From Tradition to Gospel*, pp. 47–8; Martinetti, *Jésus Christ et le Christianisme*, p. 200.

[4] Acts 8. 26–39. Cf. Burkitt, *Christian Beginnings*, p. 38; Goguel, *La Naissance du Christianisme*, p. 206.

The soteriological possibilities of the idea remained unexplored, and, so far as the relevant material goes, no interest seems to have been directed towards understanding the deeper significance of these convenient prophecies in the economy of the divine purpose; they were merely invoked, as were many other passages from the earlier Scriptures, as proofs that the career of Jesus of Nazareth was quite consistent with what had been foretold of the Messiah.[1]

One reason for this apparent lack of interest is obvious. Although for apologetical purposes the attention of the Palestinian Christians was necessarily centred on the problem of the death of Jesus and despite the fact that in the Isaianic prophecies of the Suffering Servant they found a peculiarly appropriate apologia, it was obviously not to their advantage to emphasize the tragedy more than the requirements of the defence and propagation of their faith demanded. Even if they could reasonably show that the condemnation of Jesus was largely due to the failure of the nation's leaders to realize their Master's true character and vocation, continued and emphatic reference to his death was not calculated to win the coveted sympathy and interest of such an influential class as the Pharisees.[2] Consequently it would appear that, beyond equipping themselves with a well-developed apologetic, which mainly consisted of a circumstantial narrative of the events immediately leading to the Crucifixion and a series of scriptural texts attesting the necessity of the suffering of the Messiah, the Jewish Christians were content to leave the possible theological significance of the tragedy largely unexplored, and, beyond the passing reference to its fulfilment of prophecy, the death of Jesus thus assumed no essential place in their exposition of the new faith which they professed.[3]

To Paul this interpretation of the death of Jesus Christ must have seemed seriously inadequate. Although he may have been content at

---

[1] The Editors of *B.C.*, vol. i, pp. 384–91, show that the clearest identification of Jesus with the Suffering Servant is found in the Lukan documents. It is accordingly interesting to note their comment on p. 391: "In Acts the Passion of Jesus is identified with the suffering of the Servant, but nowhere is described as giving salvation to men." That the original currency of the identification was Jewish, although in its clearest form it is found in the writings of Luke, is obvious in view of the fact that such an O.T. concept could have had no significance for Gentile believers independently of their introduction to it by their Jewish brethren; the episode of the Ethiopian Eunuch is cogent evidence in this connection. On the failure of the Jewish Christians to relate their concepts logically and to work out their theological implications, see Streeter, *Camb. Anc. Hist.*, vol. xi, pp. 265–6.

[2] See pp. 29, 85, and Chapter Seven. It is significant that W. D. Davies, *Paul and Rabbinic Judaism*, p. 274, finds the chief evidence, as he sees it, of Paul's familiarity with the Servant-concept in the celebrated Christological passage of Phil. 2, which was perhaps derived from a Jewish Christian source (see below, p. 82).

[3] Cf. Dodd, *Apostolic Preaching*, pp. 21–6. The statement in 1 Cor. 15. 3 that Christ "died for our sins according to the scriptures", even if it is certain that Paul is here strictly limiting himself to a résumé of the traditional teaching and not intermixing some of his own interpretation, only witnesses to the fact that the Jerusalem Christians had naturally ascribed to Jesus, in identifying him with the Suffering Servant, the vicarious function of the latter; Matt. 8. 17 probably shows the way in which this attribute was understood among the Jewish Christians. The idea of substitutive suffering did have some currency in Jewish pietistic thought (cf. Eppel, *Le Piétisme Juif dans les Testaments des Douze Patriarchs*, pp. 141–2), but it never appears to have been developed beyond a pious suggestion.

7

times to remind his converts of the essentials of the traditional *kērygma*, according to which Christ died κατὰ τὰς γραφάς, it is significant that in the whole of his extant writings he neither uses nor makes reference to the concept of the Suffering Servant in soteriological exegesis.[1] While an argument from silence may generally be regarded as unsound, in this particular case, considering the fact that the identification of the Suffering Servant with the crucified Jesus was a well-established feature of the teaching of the Jerusalem Church and that Paul was so intently interested in the soteriological aspect of the Crucifixion, it would appear that his neglect to mention or to use the Isaianic concept was intentional and that it was undoubtedly connected with his disapproval of the Jewish Christian interpretation in this matter.

If Paul, with his apprehension and exposition of the soteriological significance of the death of Jesus, which he considered to be an essential part of the supreme *mystērion* of God, felt the Jewish Christian interpretation thereof to be fatally inadequate, to the Jewish Christians Paul's soteriological doctrine must have been equally a source of great embarrassment. His declared intention to preach Christ crucified [2] drew attention blatantly to an aspect of their *raison d'être* which it would have been more politic to have left unemphasized. Hence in attacking the policy by which, as we shall see presently, the Jewish Christians sought to reconcile Pharisaic feeling, Paul believed himself justified in making the accusation before the Galatian converts: "They compel you to be circumcised; only that they may not be persecuted for the cross of Christ." [3]

The nature of the Jewish Christian Christology is even more obscure than that of their soteriology. It is obvious, of course, that behind the various concepts which find expression in the Synoptic Gospels there have been Jewish Christian originals, but in the form in which they have reached us they are clearly employed to represent the more developed and syncretistic beliefs of Greek-speaking and predominantly Gentile congregations, living outside the environment of the original Palestinian Church. It would consequently appear the sounder policy to approach the subject of Jewish Christian Christology by first considering certain general principles which are likely to have been operative in the formulation of belief about the nature and mission of Jesus of Nazareth.

The essential fact of Jewish monotheism must have served as an impregnable barrier to the conscious ascription on the part of any orthodox Jew of attributes or character which would have changed the human status of an individual, no matter how highly honoured, to that of divinity. Already Hebrew history contained the record of great heroes who were deeply reverenced and proudly remembered by their descendants, but even though, as Abraham, they were named "the friend of God", or, as Moses, were related to have conversed familiarly with Yahweh, or,

---

[1] See pp. 68, 70–1 above.   [2] 1 Cor. 1. 23.   [3] Gal. 6. 12.

as Elijah, had been miraculously assumed into heaven, the absolute gulf which marked off human from divine was never transgressed in the veneration which was paid to their memories. It may accordingly be fairly concluded that those Jews who had learned to reverence Jesus of Nazareth but who also continued faithful to their national religion would have instinctively preserved that essential demarcation between human and divine in the conscious formulation of their belief about their Master's true vocation and more especially in their exposition of that belief to their countrymen.[1]

To this general *a priori* presumption there may be added another which also points to the fundamental improbability of the conscious deification of Jesus by the Jewish Christians in Palestine. We have already noted the documentary evidence for believing that the Jerusalem Christians succeeded in establishing such good relations with the Pharisees that they actually came to number among themselves certain members of this influential party of orthodox Judaism.[2] Now it would appear to be extremely unlikely that such a *rapprochement* could have been effected if the followers of Jesus of Nazareth were known to be so outrageously heretical as to ascribe the status of divinity to their crucified Master.

There is one other point to be considered in this connection. It is that the figure of the Messiah of Jewish apocalyptic hopes, although extremely various and incapable of coherent definition, was never conceived of as divine in such a sense as to constitute a kind of "second god". However, it is useful also to note that the indefiniteness of the concept afforded a fruitful field for its development in the direction of deification when current in an ethos congenial to such thinking.

Having noted these points of general inference, we may now turn our attention to an examination of the documentary material. First, the most obvious feature of the Christology therein revealed is the identification of Jesus of Nazareth with the Messiah. The Pauline evidence is most striking in this connection. As we have already noticed, Paul used the words "Jesus Christ", or "Christ Jesus", as though they were well established as a personal name, while he almost entirely neglects to expound the significance of their Messianic character. It would seem to be certain, therefore, that the identification of Jesus with the Messiah was already by the time of Paul's missionary activity so customary that the title *Christos* had become intimately associated with the personal name of Jesus to such a degree that the combination of the two was the current form of address and reference in Gentile circles, where the essentially Jewish connotation of "the Christ" would surely have been regarded as strange and of little relevancy.

The maturity of its development thus presupposed in Paul's writings

---

[1] Klausner, *From Jesus to Paul*, p. 473; W. O. E. Oesterley, *New Com. N.T.*, p. 10a. The Talmud gives no indication that the Messiah might be a divine being; see A. Cohen, *Il Talmud*, p. 412; cf. Festugière, *La Révélation d'Hermès Trismégiste*, II, pp. 583-5.

[2] See p. 29.

surely indicates that this identification was achieved in the Palestinian
Church, and the inference is well supported by the evidence of the
Synoptic Gospels. The Confession at Cæsarea Philippi is undoubtedly
the *locus classicus* of Palestinian tradition in this respect.[1] The choice
of alternative identifications for Jesus therein set forth, namely, John the
Baptist, Elias, or one of the prophets, is significant in that the range is
strictly limited to the Jewish prophetic succession, with special emphasis
on him who was popularly regarded as the immediate forerunner of the
Messiah.[2] The arrangement of the series would appear to be intentional,
and it very probably reflects a certain line of Jewish Christian apologetic
in which the evidential data were arranged in a logical sequence to culminate in the identification of Jesus with the Messiah.[3]

This great act of faith, which the identification of the crucified Jesus
with the long-hoped-for Messiah certainly was, opened to the Jewish
Christians a rich field for theological speculation, but it would appear
that it was not exploited beyond the point of the immediate needs of the
faith in the formulation of a coherent teaching and apologetic. One
aspect of this we have already noticed, namely the identification of the
Messiah with the Suffering Servant of Isaiah. It is possible that a
reminiscence of this identification and an illustration of its corresponding
Christology is to be found in the speeches of the Christian leaders in the
early chapters of Acts.[4] For example God is invoked to intervene on
behalf of the faithful in the significant words: "stretching forth thine
hand to heal; and that signs and wonders may be done by the name of
thy holy child (παῖς) Jesus"; [5] while the Jews are called upon to note:
"Jesus of Nazareth, a man approved of God among you by miracles and
wonders and signs, which God did by him in the midst of you, as ye
yourselves also know", after being betrayed "by the determinate counsel
and foreknowledge of God" and slain, was resurrected by God, thus
fulfilling a prophecy of David, with the result, "Therefore let all the
house of Israel know assuredly, that God hath made that same Jesus,
whom ye have crucified, both Lord and Christ." [6] In this primitive
use of the word παῖς as a description of Jesus of Nazareth we may well
have, as has been suggested, the clue to the later Gentile belief in Jesus
as the Son of God, the fact that παῖς originally translated *ebed* (slave)
being either forgotten or not known and the humbler term being naturally
changed to the nobler form of υἱός.[7]

---

[1] Mark 8. 27–33; Matt. 16. 13–23; Luke 9. 18–22.
[2] Cf. Mark 9. 11, 12.
[3] On the probable course of the process of identifying Jesus with the Messiah, see Guignebert,
Jesus, pp. 287–95.
[4] Cf. Dodd, *Apostolic Preaching*, pp. 20 *seq.*, 73; *B.C.*, vol. i, p. 391.
[5] Acts 4. 30.　　　　　　　　　　　　　[6] Acts 2. 22–36.
[7] Cf. Guignebert, op. cit., pp. 259–68. See the discussion of παῖς as a title of Jesus by H. J.
Cadbury, *B.C.*, vol. v, pp. 364–70. The interpretation of the use of the Suffering Servant
concept in Jewish Christian circles put forth above would meet the objection which Cadbury
sees in the limitation of the use of the "vicarious" phrases in the Synoptic Gospels. Cf. Goguel,
La Naissance du Christianisme, pp. 116–22.

The other concept which appears to have been characteristic of Jewish Christian theology was that of Jesus as the Son of Man. The origin of this concept has become a matter about which there is a considerable conflict of expert opinion. However, leaving aside the problem of whether Jesus had originally applied the expression to himself, we may safely regard it as connoting a certain evaluation notably current among the Palestinian Christians, since otherwise its essentially Hebrew construction would be inexplicable in a Gentile ethos. But what that evaluation was exactly is a more difficult question. It is obvious that, despite its possibly original use by Jesus as a kind of self-effacing personal pronoun, it was soon used as a distinctive title for him and so is likely to have had an essential reference to some definitive and well-known application of the term.[1] This being so, the title would clearly appear to have referred to the mysterious personage described in the book of Daniel [2] as "one like unto a son of man", and possibly also to the similar figure depicted in the book of Enoch.[3] The concept, set in this context, is clearly pregnant with suggestion calculated to implement a process, if not of deification, at least of what might fairly be termed the supernaturalization of the historical Jesus of Nazareth. However, it would appear that the evaluation therein implied was really more proleptic in its significance, for not only is the Danielic Son of Man presented in an essentially eschatological setting, but the use of the concept in our earliest stratum of the Synoptic record has invariably an eschatological reference.[4]

From our survey of this evidence it would accordingly be reasonable to conclude that the Jewish Christians formulated a Christology which, while inherently rich in possibilities of future development, did in fact remain static. This failure to advance to concepts of more complete and fundamental theological import was undoubtedly due to the circumstances of their situation in the social and religious environment. Monotheists by instinct and upbringing and resident at the very centre of their nation's monotheistic faith, it was logically impossible for them ever consciously to regard their Master in any way which annihilated the absolute gulf between the human and the divine. Consequently, although they believed that God had raised up Jesus from the dead to be the Messiah and although they found it congenial to think of him at his hoped-for *Parousia* in terms of the mysterious and supernatural figure of Daniel's Son of Man, to them, however, he remained essentially

---

[1] Cf. Guignebert, op. cit., p. 274; Campbell, "The Origin and Meaning of the Term Son of Man", article in *J.T.S.*, vol. xlviii (1947), pp. 150–5.

[2] Dan. 7. 13, 14. Cf. Guignebert, op. cit., pp. 271–2. For the astral background of the concept and the consequent idea of *Weltherrschaft* see Eisler, *ΙΗΣΟΥΣ ΒΑΣΙΛΕΥΣ*, Bd. II, pp. 667–70.

[3] *Enoch* xxxvii–lxxi. Cf. Manson, *Jesus the Messiah*, p. 176; but see also Campbell, op. cit., pp. 145–8.

[4] Cf. Guignebert, op. cit., pp. 275–9, *Le Christ*, p. 199; R. Otto, *Kingdom of God and the Son of Man*, p. 161; Manson, op. cit., p. 102; Lohmeyer, *Galiläa und Jerusalem*, pp. 69, 72, 73–4.

distinct from the Deity.   Moreover, it is to be noted that the role which they attributed to him, namely that of the Messiah, was primarily one of Judaistic significance and conformed to Jewish nationalist aspirations.

Before passing on from this subject of the Christology of the Palestinian Church we must consider the possible significance for our conclusions of a certain interpretation of the famous Christological passage in Paul's Epistle to the Philippians.   Some years ago the suggestion was made that the passage might reasonably be regarded as a quotation made by Paul from a Christian hymn.[1]   The immense importance which would be conferred on the passage, if this hypothesis were justified, was further increased by a subsequent suggestion that the supposed hymn might be a Greek translation of an Aramaic original, thus affording us direct access to the Christology of the Palestinian Christians, for from them such a hymn must undoubtedly have come.[2]   Such basing of hypothesis on hypothesis rarely carries conviction, and in an instance such as this corroborating evidence is never likely to be forthcoming.   However, the second hypothesis is really a logical corollary to the first; for, if Paul at this point is quoting from a hymn, it would mean that there was already current in the Greek-speaking churches a well-articulated doctrinal statement, adapted for liturgical use, and the fact of its apparent independence of Paul's authorship would demand its ultimate ascription to some primary authority in the Church, and the evidence at our disposal indicates no other than that of the Jewish Christians.

If we accept the possibility that Paul thus quotes from a hymn, certain interesting inferences relative to our subject in this chapter follow and warrant noting, even though their value is essentially qualified by the hypothetical nature of their original basis.

After the problematical description of "being in the form of God" (ἐν μορφῇ θεοῦ ὑπάρχων), we have the surprising assertion that Jesus did not reckon equality with God (τὸ εἶναι ἴσα θεῷ) a thing to be grasped at (ἁρπαγμὸν).[3]   This statement is truly surprising, for, considering the passionate Jewish emphasis upon the uniqueness of God, it is very strange to find Jewish Christians obviously regarding it as necessary to make such a repudiation about their Master and to make it so definitively that it had already received a kind of liturgical crystallization.   There would accordingly appear to be only one adequate explanation of so extraordinary a fact, namely, that the Jewish Christians had felt an urgent need to reject in this way a doctrine which in some form asserted,

---

[1] Lohmeyer, *Philipper, Kolosser, und Philemon*, pp. 90 *seq.*   Cf. Moffatt, *Intro. to N.T.*, pp. 167–8; Loisy, *Les Origines du N.T.*, p. 282.

[2] Clarke, *New Test. Problems*, pp. 146–8; cf. Streeter, *Camb. Anc. Hist.*, vol. xi, p. 285; Hunter, *Paul and his Predecessors*, pp. 45–51.

[3] Phil. 2. 6.   Clarke, op. cit., p. 144, gives reasons for regarding ἁρπαγμός in Hellenistic Greek as being a term almost equivalent to εὕρημα (lucky find).   Cf. Nock, *St. Paul*, p. 224, *Early Gentile Christianity*, p. 99; Ehrhardt, "Jesus Christ and Alexander the Great", *J.T.S.*, vol. xlvi, pp. 45–50.   It is interesting to compare the laborious disquisition of Lightfoot, *Philippians*, pp. 131–5, on the meaning of the expression.   On "equality with God" see Lohmeyer, op. cit., p. 92; Ehrhardt, op. cit., pp. 47–50.

or was thought to assert, that Jesus had attained to a status of equality with God.   Thus it would follow that, whatever dignity was ascribed to Jesus by the Jewish Christians, there was no intention on their part to deify him, and so certain was their attitude that when they became conscious that such deification was either a possible danger to themselves or an actual imputation of their critics, they sought to meet it by so unequivocal a refutation.

Two other points in the passage call for comment.   The statement that Christ Jesus "made himself of no reputation, and took upon him the form of a servant, and was made in the likeness of men", would very well represent an explication of Jesus in terms of the Isaianic Servant, which, while assigning to him a unique spiritual status, implying particularly his pre-existence, conveniently describes a role divorced from any suggestion of deification.   Then there is the apparent climax in the universal recognition of Jesus Christ as Lord to the glory of God the Father.   The use of the Aramaic watchword *Maranatha* shows that the title *Maran* (our Lord) was current among the Aramaic-speaking Christians for Jesus.[1]   But the ascription of the title here clearly differentiates its bearer from God, and it is undoubtedly to be understood as an honorific title of the highest order short of deity; perhaps its meaning for Jews can best be seen in the derisory use made of the term by the Alexandrians in their elaborately staged insult to Agrippa, the Jewish king, which Philo has recorded.[2]

It can be seen, then, that if this passage is truly a quotation from a hymn of Jewish Christian origin, it may be regarded as a particularly significant expression of that Christology which we have found indicated in various indirect and negative ways in the Gospels and the early speeches of Acts.   However, it would be unwise to invoke the passage as definite evidence in this connection, owing to the essentially hypothetical character of the case for its being a quotation made by Paul from some such source.[3]   Nevertheless it is well that the point should be made that it can be shown that, should the passage have this high evidential worth for our understanding of Jewish Christian Christology, its testimony illustrates and confirms in a very remarkable way the conclusions which we have independently reached by our study of other evidence.

From the sparse and complicated data at our disposal it would appear, therefore, that the faith of the Jewish Christians had its original and essential basis in a conviction that Jesus of Nazareth had a unique spiritual status and mission.   That this conviction had survived the

---

[1] Cf. Nock, *Early Gentile Christianity*, p. 85; Dalman, *Jesus-Jeshua*, p. 13.
[2] Philo, *In Flaccum*, 5–6; cf. Schürer, *G.J.V.*, I, p. 497; see below, pp. 223–4.
[3] A. A. T. Ehrhardt's "Jesus Christ and Alexander the Great" (*J. T. S.*, vol. xlvi) has recently provided interesting evidence that Paul was herein drawing on some pre-Roman Hellenistic model from which Plutarch also drew in his *Alex. Virt. s. Fort.*, i. 8 fin.   For other possible sources of derivation see Moffatt, op. cit., pp. 171–2.

scandal of his Crucifixion must surely indicate that the post-Crucifixion experiences of the disciples had been so profound in character that every objection of logic, creed, and custom was ignored or overwhelmed by the power of its inspiration. But these personal experiences of the original recipients had to be expressed in intelligible concepts, especially since they were felt to be evidence of divine action of at least nation-wide significance. Moreover, the expression of these experiences in certain specifically Jewish concepts, such as that of the Messiahship, was instinctive to men who were Jews. However, as we have seen, the propagation of such an interpretation had necessarily to encounter many objections based on facts which were often of a peculiarly embarrassing kind. The result was the formulation of a Christology which adroitly invoked the support of certain concepts, which in turn were suggestive of great theological development. But in the situation of the Jewish Christians there were strong reasons against such development, so that we find proof of a kind of embarrassed and illogical suspension of doctrinal inference in the Church of Jerusalem, which was strongly, though guardedly, condemned by Paul. This failure to develop the implications of their Christology would appear necessarily to have operated also to restrict the Jewish Christian *Weltanschauung* to a very limited and unsatisfactory horizon.

The subsequent propagation of Christianity among non-Jewish peoples outside Palestine, unrestricted as it was by any kind of racial preference or prejudice, has caused the general impression to be formed that the outlook of the primitive community of Jewish believers must from the beginning have contained an essential element of universalism. But the evidence of Paul's controversial writings necessarily leads to much challenging of this impression, and, as we have already seen, there are certain indications in the Synoptic Gospels that a narrow particularism once characterized the attitude of the Palestinian Christians towards the Gentiles. We have now to consider other evidence that the outlook of the Jerusalem Church remained essentially nationalistic.

In the Matthean Gospel (19. 28) Jesus is depicted as promising his disciples that "in the regeneration when the Son of man shall sit on the throne of his glory" they would sit upon twelve thrones, judging the twelve tribes of Israel. The inferred number of twelve for the company of the Apostles and the eschatological reference suggest some maturity of theological concept, which would well correspond to the situation obtaining in the community in which this Gospel originated,[1] as we shall later see. However that may be, there is other evidence from an independent source which suggests that this limitation of eschatological interest to the nation of Israel was primitive. The author of Acts at the beginning of his work, in which part he appears to be using some primitive material,

---

[1] Cf. p. 49, n. 6. Cf. Schürer, op. cit., II, pp. 544–6. On the Jewish origin of the eschatological ref., see Strack und Billerbeck, I, pp. 974–5.

represents the disciples as asking the Risen Jesus the revealing question: "Lord, wilt thou at this time restore again the kingdom to Israel?" [1] Thus it would seem that the hopes of the original Palestinian community were centred about some form of national restoration which would be consequent on the *Parousia* of their Master; it was indeed a belief which would be natural to those nurtured in the atmosphere of Messianic eschatology, but it is notable for its apparent unconcern for the future of the Gentile peoples.

Further indications of the *Weltanschauung* of Jewish Christianity which are consistent with this interpretation are forthcoming. For example we have a significant revelation, made unconsciously, of the mind of the Jewish Christian in the words which are attributed to Jesus in comment on the faith of the Gentile Centurion. Such faith is regarded as a matter for wonderment and, although it is accepted as the typical justification of Gentile entry into the Church, it is the Israelite who is instinctively looked upon as the true and proper son of the Kingdom.[2] The same attitude of mind is even shown by Paul. Although absolutely devoted to the truth of his own universalist outlook, he clearly felt to the full the problem which it involved. To him the Jew was the true and original object of God's interest; hence the urgency of the problem both of Israel's obduracy and rejection and of the consequent acceptance of the Gentiles. When Paul writes to the Roman community "Hath God cast away his people?", he is certainly anticipating the question which he knew that his interpretation must at once involve for any Jewish adherent to the new faith.[3] But the question was the making of the logic of Paul's theology, and he and those Jews who believed him had to face the fact of its outrage on Jewish patriotism. To the Jewish Christians of Palestine, however, who were accustomed to worship in the Temple, to pay the Temple tax,[4] to accept the authority of the scribes and Pharisees,[5] and to reverence the ideal of the well-instructed scribe,[6] such thinking, when it became known to them, was truly a terrible outrage on all which they held sacred, and as such it was repudiated with horror and hatred.[7]

We have not the means of knowing whether the Jerusalem Christians held any clearly defined *Weltanschauung*. It is unlikely that they did so, and more probable that their attitude was inspired by the traditional ideal of Jewish patriotism and qualified unconsciously and illogically by their new faith in the character and mission of Jesus. As we shall have occasion

---

[1] Acts 1. 6. Cf. *B.C.*, vol. iv, p. 8, loc. cit.; Guignebert, *Le Christ*, pp. 62 *seq.*; Goguel, *La Naissance du Christianisme*, pp. 137–8, *L'Église Primitive*, p. 30, n. 1.

[2] Matt. 8. 10–12; Luke 7. 9. The material used here would seem to have come from *Q*, although Matthew adroitly appends to the account of the Healing of the Centurion's Servant the logion about the gathering of the faithful from the four corners of the world which Luke gives in 13. 28, 29 in a different context, a context which Streeter, *Four Gospels*, p. 514, believes to be the original one.

[3] Rom. 11. 1.

[4] Matt. 17. 24–27. Cf. Bultmann, *Die Gesch. der synopt. Trad.*, pp. 34–5.

[5] Matt. 23. 1–3.

[6] Matt. 13. 52.

[7] Cf. Klausner, *From Jesus to Paul*, pp. 534–6.

to notice more carefully later, their view of the future was undoubtedly foreshortened by their belief in the imminent return of their Master and the catastrophic end of the contemporary world. The chance conversion of certain Gentiles committed them unwittingly to an extension of their faith beyond the confines of Jewry. But it would appear probable that they were conscious of no need to adjust their traditional *Weltanschauung* to include this new contingency, ready certainly as they were to exploit its advantages; with the example of their nation's proselytizing activity before them, they doubtless thought of their Gentile converts in terms of this activity, but, so soon as they realized the existence of more revolutionary possibilities, their reaction was violent and decisive, as we shall have occasion to study at length.

In the matter of the policy of evangelization consciously directed by the Church of Jerusalem, as we have already seen in our study of the Lament over Jerusalem,[1] there is evidence of an attempt extending over a considerable period to win the city to an acceptance of Jesus. There is some evidence in the Gospel tradition for believing also that much energy and concern were given to evangelizing the Jewish inhabitants of the other parts of Palestine. The disciples are commissioned to limit their efforts strictly to the Israelites,[2] and, although much activity seems to have manifested itself in Galilee, the original home of the movement, certain cities remained notoriously unresponsive,[3] and it is probable that such parables as that of the Sower and the obvious apologetical use of Isaiah 6. 9 represent the explanations advanced by the Jewish Christians to account for their meagre success.[4] In this connection also we may note that the account of the missionary technique of Paul and his companions, as described in Acts,[5] may be based on a genuine tradition of the methods of the primitive Jewish Christians. In the passages concerned we find a regular pattern of action depicted wherein the Gospel is always presented first, and apparently exclusively, to the Jews and is only made available to the Gentiles when the Chosen People reject it; indeed, therein is ground for the interesting speculation whether the Gospel would ever have been presented to the non-Jewish races if the Jews had shown themselves from the beginning sympathetically disposed to receive its message.

The evidence which we have reviewed in this chapter is of a very fragmentary character and, it must be admitted, often patient of a different interpretation, but it does appear to bear consistent witness to the fact that the Jewish Christians interpreted their new faith in the

---

[1] Pp. 40–1.
[2] Matt. 10. 5, 6. Cf. Streeter, op. cit., p. 255; Guignebert, *Jesus*, pp. 317–8.
[3] Matt. 11. 20–24; Luke 10. 13–15. That the situation envisaged here refers to a time later than the Ministry of Jesus seems a necessary inference, unless we are to conclude that the Galilæan period was much longer than is indicated in the Synoptic Gospels. Cf. Luce, *St. Luke*, p. 110 loc. cit.
[4] Mark 4. 11, 12.
[5] Acts 13. 14–48; 14. 1; 17. 1–4, 10–12, 16, 17; 18. 1–6; 19. 8–10.

Messiahship of Jesus as being in no wise contradictory to their loyalty to their ancestral religion; indeed to the contrary, the significance of this faith was only valid and intelligible to them within the *ethos* of contemporary Judaism. That in seeking to express their beliefs in terms of concepts current or permissible within their national faith, or in making certain *ad hoc* concessions to a few favoured Gentiles, the Jewish Christians of Palestine created possibilities of theological development, of a very revolutionary kind, was truly incidental; they did it unconsciously. For their own part these Jewish Christians continued by instinct and by conscious conviction, in so far as any question to the contrary was apparent to them, as loyal and devout Jews, and their rejection of any idea of secession or fundamental difference from Judaism was immediate and vigorous so soon as any such issue presented itself.

In our survey so far of the life and thought of the Palestinian Christians we have had occasion frequently to notice evidence of their attachment to the national religion of Israel. The nationalist character of this religion was notoriously narrow and capable of generating the fiercest passions of a fanatical devotion. In the period under consideration these passions were inflamed by Israel's contemporary political situation, and, as we shall see, they were destined ultimately to produce the fatal revolt against the Roman suzerainty in A.D. 66. It accordingly becomes our task to seek to understand to what degree the Jewish Christians of Palestine were affected by these sentiments; for clearly herein lies a vital factor in the determination of their fate during the disastrous years of war for Israel's freedom from the yoke of heathen Rome.

6

The Jewish Christians and their Nation's Cause against Rome

THE Acts of the Apostles by the uniqueness of its implicit claim to describe the origins of the Christian Church has inevitably come to exercise a most profound and far-reaching influence upon all thought about the genesis and early evolution of Christianity. That its evidence is not altogether sound we have had occasion already to note; it now becomes our task to inquire how far it is trustworthy in its presentation of Christianity as a movement originating in Palestine and developing there during its first crucial years.

The general impression which the Acts gives of the nascent faith is that of its virtual insulation from contemporary Palestinian social and political life. By a number of direct statements and allusions it represents the infant Church as standing well in the estimation of the general population; [1] a certain initial hostility, which appears to originate with the Sadducean sacerdotal aristocracy, has little effectiveness and quickly ceases when the celebrated Pharisee doctor, Gamaliel, counsels that the followers of the crucified Jesus be left in peace.[2] This instance of Pharisaic sympathy is not isolated, and, as we have seen, evidence is given that an effective number of Pharisees joined the new movement, the members of which could be described as "zealous for the law".

The consistency of this picture of the pacific development of the Church in Palestine is broken by two accounts of persecution. However, besides the patent incompatibility of such incidents with the general picture, the accounts of each of these instances of persecution contain features which cause serious doubt with regard to their accuracy or authenticity.

The first of these acts of violent suppression is that of which Stephen was the central figure. We shall have occasion later to examine the account of this event from the point of view of its internal significance in the evolution of primitive Christianity; here it will suffice to note certain obvious discrepancies in the record as constituting an index to its credibility. The first of these is found in the fact that, although Stephen and his six colleagues are specifically appointed to "serve tables", Stephen's most notable subsequent activity is disputation in support of the faith with certain bodies of Hellenistic Jews.[3] It would, therefore, appear that the record of

---

[1] Acts 2. 37–47; 4. 4; 5. 12–16, 26, 42; 6. 7; 9. 31.
[2] Acts 4. 1, 2, 5–21; 5. 17–40. Cf. Meyer, *Ursprung und Anfänge des Christentums*, III, p. 75; Goguel, *La Naissance du Christianisme*, pp. 491–6.
[3] Acts 6. 1–6, 8 ff. Cf. Meyer, op. cit., pp. 154–5; Goguel, op. cit., p. 193.

the Acts here is not adequate on the antecedents or exact status of Stephen. Secondly, it is to be noted that the speech which is put into the mouth of Stephen at his trial is really a bitter polemic against the Jews, culminating in a denunciation of the Temple cultus.[1] Such sentiments ill accord with the other evidence of Acts, which we have examined, of the Jewish Christians' essential attachment to both the faith and the practice of Judaism. As we shall see later, the story of Stephen is used by Luke to serve his theme of tracing the course of Christianity from Jerusalem out into the world of Græco-Roman culture; hence, when this factor is considered, together with the discrepancies just noted, there is good reason for regarding the whole episode, as presented in Acts, with suspicion as being vitiated by tendentious distortion. However that may be, it is even more important for our purpose here to note that Luke specially excepts, without explanation, the Apostles from the persecution which, he says,[2] arose against the Jerusalem Church in consequence of the activity of Stephen and resulted in its being scattered abroad throughout Judæa and Samaria. It would surely be a strange measure of suppression which operated against the ordinary members of an organization but exempted its leaders, who apparently had no special immunity conferred by rank or other social privilege.

It would consequently appear that the movement of which Stephen was the most notable champion was one which was distinctly separate from that of the original community and its followers, and was even distinguished by a certain measure of hostility to Jewish Christianity, with its continuing attachment to the national cultus. What was the exact significance of the new movement it is impossible to determine on the evidence available,[3] but it should be noted that Paul in all his disputes with the Jewish Christians, so far as they have been recorded in his extant writings, never once invokes the example of Stephen in support of his own cause. This fact is capable of two interpretations, neither of which can be decisively proved: either the martyrdom of Stephen was not sufficiently known among the Pauline churches for its significance to be appreciated, or Paul did not find it convenient to his purpose to cite the memory of this antagonist of Judaism.

The second instance of persecution is that contained in the brief reference to the death of the Apostle James and the story of the imprisonment of Peter.[4] According to the record of the Acts, this repressive action was undertaken by "Herod the king". It is generally accepted that this monarch is to be identified with Agrippa I, who received the

---

[1] Acts 7. 1–53. Cf. Knox, *Jerusalem*, p. 50, n. 10; Goguel, op. cit., pp. 496–9.
[2] Acts 8. 1. Codex Bezæ adds after ἀποστόλων the note: οἳ ἔμειναν ἐν Ἱερουσαλήμ— "which is doubtless a correct interpretation" (*B.C.*, vol. iv, p. 87). There seems to be no warranty for Knox's statement (*Jerusalem*, p. 45) that the Twelve went into hiding, "refusing to desert their posts, for the Church had no existence outside the city, . . .". Cf. Weiss, *Urchristentum*, p. 123.
[3] Cf. *B.C.*, vol. v, pp. 150–1; Guignebert, *Le Christ*, pp. 75 *seq.*
[4] Acts 12. 1–19.

addition of Judæa and Samaria to his kingdom from Claudius after that emperor's accession in A.D. 41.[1]   If this identification be sound, the policy pursued by Agrippa of ingratiating himself with his new subjects, especially by appealing to their religious susceptibilities,[2] would well accord with his undertaking an action to suppress some odious religious heretics. However, as we have repeatedly seen, there is no evidence for believing that the leaders of the Jerusalem Church were regarded in such a light by their countrymen.   Moreover, according to the statement of the Acts itself, King Agrippa executed James for no apparent motive, and only proceeded against Peter when he found that his first act "pleased the Jews".   This last expression seems to provide the clue to the real nature of the story here.   It could obviously have been written only by one who was separated by a considerable distance in racial sympathy, and probably also in time, from the situation which he claims to describe. Further, in this connection it has to be noticed that there is a strong body of learned opinion in favour of thinking that the two sons of Zebedee perished together, despite the fact that the death of John is not recorded in the Acts; [3] moreover, we have also seen that there is reason for believing that Luke has handled the matter of the death of James with a certain feeling of embarrassment.   When there is added to these considerations the significance of certain details which forcibly present themselves when the story is critically examined, namely the miraculous circumstances of Peter's escape, then his sudden disappearance from the narrative in which he had hitherto held the leading place, and the strange end of Herod the king,[4] the conclusion appears to be inevitable that this account of persecution cannot be accepted as accurate.   Whether it does contain any authentic elements is a more difficult question to answer.   The safest inference would seem to be that a tradition connected the death of one, or possibly both, of the Boanerges with the action of a Jewish king, who was vaguely designated by the dynastic name of the Jewish royal house.   What motive prompted the king to this action and what were the circumstances of the Apostle's death cannot be recovered from the narrative.

On examination it accordingly appears that the general picture given by the Acts of the fortunes of the Jerusalem Church is not to be regarded as effectively contradicted by the two accounts of persecution.   But what is probably sounder evidence of the general freedom of the Palestinian Christians from official molestation is the fact that the author of Acts shows the Jerusalem Church at various points in his narrative as settled and flourishing; he gives no hint whatsoever that its existence was ever

[1] Cf. Schürer, *G.J.V.*, I, p. 553.
[2] Cf. Schürer, op. cit., pp. 556 *seq.*; Derenbourg, *Essai sur l'Histoire et la Géographie de la Palestine*, p. 217; Graetz, *Hist. of the Jews*, vol. ii, pp. 192 *seq.*
[3] Cf. *B.C.*, vol. iv, pp. 133–4; Eisler, *Enigma of Fourth Gospel*, pp. 59 *seq.*, 86–9; Howard, *Fourth Gospel*, pp. 247–51; Meyer, op. cit., p. 174; Goguel, op. cit., pp. 126, 503, n. 3.
[4] Acts 12. 20–23.   Cf. *B.C.*, vol. iv, p. 139 loc. cit.

seriously jeopardized by official repressive action on the part of either the Jewish or the Roman authorities.

With this Lukan picture the evidence of Paul's Epistles seems to agree, except in two instances. We may briefly notice the general testimony of these documents first. The most striking feature is that Paul can visit the Jerusalem Church at widely separated times and find there an obvious stability of life and organization; [1] then in all his care to collect an impressive sum from his converts for "the saints" at Jerusalem he never uses as an incentive to their generosity the fact of any notable sufferings endured by "the saints" in defence of the faith.

The statements which seem to contradict this view are contained in the Epistles to the Galatians and the Philippians and the First Epistle to the Thessalonians. In effect they group themselves into two separate references to two distinct instances of persecution. The first two references are really part of the personal confession of Paul: in the Galatian passage he asserts that he "persecuted the church of God, and made havoc of it", [2] while in Philippians the same fact is even more briefly stated in the words, "as touching zeal, persecuting the church".[3]

It is hard to read these statements without at once associating them with the graphic narrative of Paul's conversion in the Acts, but, as we shall see later, this tendency must be resisted and Paul's words considered quite independently as his own record of his past. Now, while these statements are quite explicit that Paul acknowledged himself to have been formerly a persecutor of Christians and their testimony to the fact must accordingly be accepted, it must also be recognized that they are the statements of a convert about his past, made on occasions when he wanted to emphasize his former zeal for his national faith in order to bring out the contrast effected by his conversion; consequently it is not unreasonable to feel that there may be in them a certain natural exaggeration of the violence of his persecuting activity. But of far greater importance for our purpose here is the fact that these statements afford no clue to the time and place of the persecution which they imply. However, a subsequent remark in the Galatian Epistle provides some indication of locality. In the passage concerned [4] Paul states that some three years after his conversion he was not known by face to the churches of Judæa. Now this is Paul's own statement of his past and as such it must be considered without any reference to the much later record in the Acts of his career as a persecutor of the Church in Palestine. Quite clearly then on Paul's testimony he could not have been a known persecutor of the Christians of Judæa; and Judæa here undoubtedly means the area of procuratorial administration, which comprised Judæa, Samaria, and Galilee.[5] Where was the scene of his persecuting activity

---

[1] Gal. 1. 18 ff.; 2. 1 ff.   [2] Gal. 1. 13.   [3] Phil. 3. 6.

[4] Gal. 1. 18–23. Cf. Lietzmann, *An die Galater*, p. 9 loc. cit.

[5] Judæa, Samaria, and Galilee, which had formed part of the kingdom of Agrippa I, were placed under direct Roman administration after the death of the Jewish king in A.D. 44,

remains a matter for speculation, but it would be reasonable to look for
it in some region where it would have been natural for Paul, after his
conversion, to go away into Arabia and return "again to Damascus".[1]
And there is another fact still to be considered. After saying that he
was unknown to the Christian community of Judæa, Paul states that the
only information which its members had of him was a report that, "He
that once persecuted us now preacheth the faith of which he once made
havoc." The particle ὅτι used here seems clearly to introduce a quotation,[2] which fact from the context must mean that the Judæan churches
first heard of Paul in terms of a report which reached them from some
other Church, which had suffered from his persecuting zeal. Consequently it is possible that the tradition, preserved in Acts,[3] which places
the effective scene of Paul's conversion in Damascus may also be interpreted as indicating that in this locality was also the scene of his activity
as a persecutor of Christians and that it was from the Christian community of Damascus that the Jerusalem Church first heard of Paul.
In turn this would also mean that the depicting of Paul as a persecutor
of the Palestinian Christians in Acts is a later attempt made to connect
Paul with the proto-martyr Stephen,[4] and was probably made in ignorance
of the direct contradiction it thus constituted to Paul's own explicit
statement in the Galatian Epistle that he was unknown personally to
the Palestinian Christians until some three years after his conversion.

There is now the reference to persecution in the First Thessalonian
Epistle to be considered.[5] In this Paul draws a parallel between the
sufferings of his converts at the hands of their compatriots and those of
the members of the Judæan churches at the hands of the Jews. This
statement and its immediate sequel, in which, after making some condemnatory observations about the persecuting activity of the Jews, he
includes himself, or his party, among the objects of this persecution,
would clearly constitute evidence for believing that the Jewish Christians
in Palestine notably suffered for their faith at the hands of their countrymen. But there are serious grounds for doubting the authenticity of the
passage which comprises verses 14–16, for not only is there no obvious
connection between this passage and the verses which precede it, but it
expresses a fierce animosity towards the Jews such as is without parallel
in Paul's other writings and which strangely contradicts the sentiments

according to Jos., *Ant.*, xix. 9. 2, *Wars*, ii. 11. 6; cf. Tacitus, *Ann.*, xii. 23. Cf. Meyer, *Ursprung
und Anfänge des Christentums*, III, pp. 42 *seq.*; Schürer, *G.J.V.*, I, p. 564. Goguel, *La Naissance
du Christianisme*, pp. 499–501, tries to remove the evidence of Paul's statement here by suggesting
that the Christian communities in Judæa were so small and isolated that there was no direct
contact with all the persecutors of the Church at this time.
[1] Gal. 1. 17.
[2] Cf. Lightfoot, *Galatians*, p. 86. Lietzmann, op. cit., p. 8, translates 1. 23, 24: "*nur
vernommen hatten sie durch Hörensagen: der uns einst verfolgte, der verkündigt jetzt den Glauben, den er
einst vertilgen wollte, und sie priesen an mir Gott.*"
[3] Acts 9. 1–22; 22. 5–16; 26. 12–20.
[4] Cf. Nock, *St. Paul*, p. 32; Guignebert, *Le Christ*, pp. 248–9.
[5] 1 Thess. 2. 14–16. Goguel, op. cit., pp. 143, 502, thinks that Paul here has the persecution of the Hellenists in mind.

which he displays towards his nation in Romans 9. 3; 10. 1. Moderate critical opinion has indeed recognized this to the extent of suggesting that verse 16b is an addition made by some anti-Jewish scribe shortly after the destruction of Jerusalem in A.D. 70.[1] But such an admission is illogical in its limitation of the interpolation to these few words, for, in addition, the unsympathetic way in which the words τῶν Ἰουδαίων are used, and the assertion that the Jews "please not God, and are contrary to all men", express a depth of anti-Semitic feeling which would be quite understandable from the pen of a Gentile, but which contradicts all that we otherwise know of Paul and his attitude towards his own people. The passage would consequently be far more comprehensible if it were regarded as an interpolation made by some Gentile Christian, with an anti-Semitic bias, such as Marcion, in whose collection of Paul's writings this Epistle to the Thessalonians appears to have held an unchallenged place.

It may accordingly be concluded that the evidence of Paul's Epistles agrees with that of the Acts in representing the Christian Church in Palestine as living its life over some decades untroubled by any official action aimed at its suppression. Before accepting this conclusion as final, we have to notice some references to persecution in the Gospels which may conceivably reflect something of the experiences of the Palestinian Christians.

The passage which seems to contain the clearest evidence of persecution suffered by the Jewish Christians occurs in the Gospel of Matthew.[2] Herein Jesus is depicted as telling the Twelve as he commissions them for their evangelistic work: "when they persecute you in this city, flee into the next: for verily I say unto you, Ye shall not have gone through the cities of Israel, till the Son of man be come." The picture here suggested of the Jewish Christians is that of an itinerant band, continuously pursued from one city to another and thus without any centre of stable life. Such a view is, of course, quite contrary to that given by Paul in his Galatian Epistle, as we have seen. There we find that Jerusalem is the established centre of the Church, where its leaders are generally found, and this state of things enjoys such a measure of stability that Paul can return there after fourteen years to find no great change has taken place. And this continuity of settled life is naturally to be inferred also from the later narrative of the Acts. Consequently it would appear that the Matthean passage cannot reflect with any degree of accuracy the general situation of the Jewish Christians in Palestine, but that it is rather to be regarded as expressive of some period of intense crisis, and we shall have cause to

---

[1] Cf. Moffatt, *Intro. to N.T.*, pp. 72–3.

[2] Matt. 10. 17–23. The passage seems to be a conflation of different sources; see Streeter, *Four Gospels*, pp. 254–5, 263. Cf. pp. 174–6 below. G. D. Kilpatrick, *The Origins of the Gospel according to St. Matthew*, p. 119, writes: "If we can interpret the phrase τὰς πόλεις τοῦ Ἰσραὴλ as meaning cities in which Jewish communities are to be found, the restrictive implication of the verse disappears. We must remember, too, that the Gospel was probably written outside Palestine." Cf. ibid., p. 125.

note later that there is much reason for dating it for the terrible years immediately preceding and following the destruction of Jerusalem in A.D. 70.

A similar judgement must be passed on the Matthean version of the denunciatory record of the Jewish rejection and persecution of God's messengers from Abel to Zacharias, which comes at the end of the Woes against the Pharisees.[1] There seems to be good reason for regarding the milder Lukan parallel to this section as preserving more accurately the Q original,[2] so that Luke's interesting editorial note in introducing his version of the passage, namely, "Therefore also said the wisdom of God (διὰ τοῦτο καὶ ἡ σοφία τοῦ θεοῦ εἶπεν)", has a special significance here. It means that Luke was conscious that he was quoting here from some earlier oracle, and this appears to have been a Jewish Christian polemical writing against the Pharisees in which the vices of the sect are viewed in terms of the cause which brought destruction on the nation. In the Matthean version the greater passion of the invective surely indicates the writing of one who felt the significance of Israel's disaster more nearly, undoubtedly because he himself, or those with whom he was connected, had suffered some measure of persecution during the days of national tension and distress. Hence the additions which he makes to the acts of violence committed against the messengers of God, namely scourging in the synagogues and pursuing from city to city, express what he feels is his brethren's share in the persecution of which the Jewish leaders were guilty and which had such terrible consequences for his generation; but it should be noted that the sufferings which he here particularizes are mild and insignificant in comparison with those of which the historic prophets and wise men and scribes had been the victims.

A passage of the Markan Gospel which occurs in the so-called Little Apocalypse, and which is given in Luke in a similar context, but by Matthew in quite a different setting, presupposes a considerable measure of persecution.[3] But the question of its date and origin is uncertain. The passage seems in verse 9 to break the sequence of the theme of political and cosmic catastrophe with a quite different orientation of interest, and the former theme appears to be resumed again in verse 14, i.e. at the end of this digression on persecution. The suggestion has consequently been reasonably made that the author of Mark here interpolated the apocalyptical writing which he had decided to insert in this part of his Gospel, with some verses commemorating the recent experiences of the Christians, probably at Rome during the Neronian persecution, with perhaps some reference to a pattern of suffering experienced by some well-known witness, possibly Paul.[4]

---

[1] Matt. 23. 29–36.   [2] Luke 11. 47–51.   Cf. Streeter, op. cit., pp. 253–4.
[3] Mark 13. 9–13; Luke 21. 12–19; Matt. 10. 17–21.
[4] Streeter, op. cit., p. 494. Meyer, op. cit., I, p. 130, thinks that the persecution mentioned here was Jewish, not Roman; but it is difficult to believe that βασιλέων is a reference to Agrippa I only, and Christian tradition contains no account of persecution at the hands of

A similar uncertainty about date, but with an indication of its comparative lateness,[1] is also involved in the reference to persecution in the explanation of the Parable of the Sower, while the allusions to persecution in the Beatitudes,[2] a series of sayings which appear to be derived from *Q*, really show that the suffering involved amounted to no more than a deep unpopularity and social ostracism.

The Gospel evidence, therefore, on analysis seems to provide no serious contradiction to that inferred from Paul's writings and the Acts, namely, that the Jewish Christians in Palestine were not notably molested by their countrymen for their profession of a new faith, or rather a new interpretation of certain parts of their national faith. This absence of any tradition of notable persecution suffered by these Christians, and especially the failure to commemorate the martyrdom of any leader except James the Apostle, consequently confirms the general impression given by Paul and the Acts that the Jerusalem Church and the other Jewish Christian communities in Palestine enjoyed an effective measure of security and stability of life among their compatriots.

There remains some evidence, of secondary value, of the persecution suffered by the Christians of Palestine, which we must notice before finally accepting the conclusion indicated by our survey so far. This evidence concerns the death of James, the brother of the Lord, who was surnamed "the Just", and some companions, which event is recorded in the extant texts of Josephus and Hegesippus, and appears to be reflected in the writing known as the *Clementine Recognitions*.

The more simple and straightforward account is that given in Josephus' *Antiquities of the Jews*.[3] Herein we are told that, during an interregnum of procuratorial rule caused by the death of Festus, the High Priest Ananus took the opportunity (νομίσας ἔχειν καιρὸν ἐπιτήδειον) to convene a Sanhedrin (συνέδριον κριτῶν), before which he brought James (described as τὸν ἀδελφὸν Ἰησοῦ, τοῦ λεγομένου Χριστοῦ) and some others (τινας ἑτέρους) on a charge of breaking the Law (ὡς παρανομησάντων κατηγορίαν ποιησάμενος). How the trial was conducted and on what evidence the accused were found guilty is not recorded, for the narrative continues immediately to the statement that Ananus delivered them to be stoned (παρέδωκε λευσθησομένους). Then follows the significant remark that all those who in Jerusalem were reputed to be men of good sense and strict in their observance of the Law (ὅσοι δὲ ἐδόκουν ἐπιεικέστατοι τῶν κατὰ τὴν πόλιν εἶναι καὶ τὰ περὶ τοὺς νόμους ἀκριβεῖς) were so far

any other Jewish king—in fact there could only be one other, namely Agrippa II, who might conceivably, but inaccurately, be regarded as a Jewish king. But a more serious objection to Meyer's suggestion is that he appears to accept the testimony of the Acts at its face value in this matter. The objection raised here with regard to βασιλέων applies also to the interpretation of Mark 13. 9b advanced by Burkitt, *Christian Beginnings*, pp. 145–7. Cf. Moffatt, op. cit., pp. 323 *seq.*

[1] Cf. Taylor, *Formation of Gospel Tradition*, p. 103.
[2] Matt. 5. 10–12; Luke 6. 22, 23.
[3] *Ant.*, xx. 9. It is given in full by Eusebius, *Eccl. Hist.*, II. xxiii. Cf. Goguel, *La Naissance du Christianisme*, pp. 144–8, 151–2.

angered at the deed that they actually sent a secret report to the Emperor, begging him to restrain Ananus from his unlawful actions; some among them were even moved to go to meet the new procurator, Albinus, on his way from Alexandria, to complain especially that Ananus had no right to assemble a Sanhedrin without the Roman governor's permission.

The authenticity of this passage from the *Antiquities*, like that of the other so-called *Testimonia Flaviana*, has been the subject of long and unceasing controversy. The famous passage about Jesus is to be discussed later, and with the question of its genuineness the present passage is necessarily connected, but here it will suffice to observe that what the extant Greek text tells of the death of James bears an air of verisimilitude; indeed, if this passage were to be considered a later Christian forgery, it would be an incredibly clever one for so early a period, because the restraint shown both in the reference to Jesus and in the description of the circumstances which led to the death of James is not to be expected from a forgery, of which the purpose would be apologetical and edificatory. It has particularly to be noted that, while the facts leading to the condemnation of James are concisely described, no details whatever are given of the execution; indeed its occurrence is only to be inferred from the sentence pronounced by Ananus ($\pi\alpha\rho\acute{\epsilon}\delta\omega\kappa\epsilon$ $\lambda\epsilon\upsilon\sigma\theta\eta\sigma\omega\mu\acute{\epsilon}\nu\upsilon\varsigma$). It is surely beyond expectation that a Christian scribe who had felt it worth while to tamper here with the text of Josephus should have been content to leave so notable a martyrdom a matter of inference and have given none of the graphic details which are usual to hagiography. Again it is surprising, if the passage be a forgery, that the scribe responsible limited himself to referring to James' companions in martyrdom, who would accordingly have been heroes of the faith, by the vague words $\tau\iota\nu\alpha\varsigma$ $\acute{\epsilon}\tau\acute{\epsilon}\rho\upsilon\varsigma$.

In view of these considerations, therefore, although complete certainty cannot from the nature of the material be forthcoming, this passage about James which stands in our present texts of Josephus may be regarded as authentic. This being so, special notice must now be given to whatever information it may afford on the nature of the persecution which was then suffered by the Jerusalem Christians. Accordingly it must first be pointed out that the execution of James and his companions is primarily related as the supreme example of the high-handed action of Ananus, the High Priest, during the procuratorial interregnum. Secondly, there is the very significant fact that those who stood high in repute and who were distinguished for their observance of the Law are described as being unanimous in their condemnation of the act and so strongly moved about it that they undertook hostile action against the High Priest in ways which must have caused them much trouble and possibly danger.

In the light of this information, therefore, the death of James and his companions must be seen as an untoward act of personal spite on the part of the High Priest Ananus. Far from its being a popular measure, it was effectively condemned by a body of men whose description must surely indicate that they were Pharisees.[1]   Moreover, it is also certain that the accusation of antinomianism preferred against the Christians is to be regarded as a trumped-up charge, for it is impossible to believe that the Pharisees would have compromised themselves and their principles by condemning the action of a High Priest, if he were indeed suppressing certain notorious despisers of the Law.

Eusebius claims to give in his *Ecclesiastical History* an account of the death of James the Just which is taken from the writings of Hegesippus.[2] This account, which is very much longer than that of Josephus, presents a quite different version of the antecedent circumstances and the death of James.   From the point of view of our interest in this chapter the following points of difference have to be noted.   The chain of events which culminate in the martyrdom commences when James, who is depicted as a Jewish ascetic of great reputation among the people for his holiness and one who enjoyed some curious religious privileges, is asked by what seems to be a religious party (τινὲς οὖν τῶν ἑπτὰ αἱρέσεων τῶν ἐν τῷ λαῷ) what was the "gate of Jesus" (θύρα τοῦ 'Ιησοῦ).   What was the original meaning of this curious expression has never been satisfactorily explained;[3] possibly it is a corruption of some Aramaic concept.   The answer given by James is that Jesus was the Saviour (εἶναι τὸν σωτῆρα). The use of this Greek word to describe Jesus at once suggests a maturity of soteriological speculation which, as we have already seen, there is reason to believe was not attained in the Palestinian Church at the time. The narrative now becomes more involved and illogical.   James' answer is stated, surprisingly, to have caused some to believe that Jesus is the Christ.   The identity of the inquirers is then indicated by the statement that they did not believe in a resurrection or a final judgement, which fact from our other information would lead us to recognize them as Sadducees.   Since those converted by James included many of the rulers (τῶν ἀρχόντων), there was a tumult of "the Jews, and the Scribes and Pharisees", who believed that the whole people were in danger of looking for Jesus as the Christ ('Ιησοῦν τὸν Χριστὸν προσδοκᾶν).   The differentiation of the Jews from the Scribes and Pharisees here must surely indicate a writer with little exact knowledge of Jewish society in Palestine in the first century; however, since "the Jews" do not appear again in the other two places where the Scribes and the Pharisees are mentioned in the rest of the narrative, it is possible that the words are a later addition to the text.   Faced with such a danger, the Scribes and the Pharisees

---

[1] Cf. G. Kittel, *Z.N.T.W.* (1931), p. 146; Lietzmann, *Gesch. der alt. Kirche*, I, p. 185.

[2] *Eccl. Hist.*, II. xxiii. 1–19; cf. Goguel, op. cit., pp. 148–51.

[3] K. Kohler, *Jew. Encycl.*, vol. 7, p. 68, suggests that Hegesippus gave the original Jewish question: "What is the gate of salvation?" (*sha'ar ha-yeshu 'ah*), which possibly contained a reference to Ps. 118. 20, and that this was later erroneously copied as "*sha'ar Yeshua*" ("the gate of Jesus").   Eisler's explanation, *Messiah Jesus*, pp. 518 *seq.*, deserves to be noted for its ingenuity.   Cf. K. Lake, Loeb *Eusebius*, vol. i, p. 173; Burkitt, op. cit., p. 64; Lohmeyer, *Galiläa und Jerusalem*, p. 71; Eisler, *ΙΗΣΟΥΣ ΒΑΣΙΛΕΥΣ*, II, pp. 537–9.

have recourse to a most extraordinary, and, as far as can be judged, a most unlikely, line of action. They actually appeal to James himself to help them in persuading the crowd assembled in Jerusalem at the Passover "not to err concerning Jesus" (περὶ 'Ιησοῦ μὴ πλανᾶσθαι). The reason given is even more amazing: because of James' great reputation for righteousness, "the whole people and all of us trust you" (πᾶς ὁ λαὸς καὶ πάντες πειθόμεθά σοι), say the Scribes and the Pharisees. For the demonstration James, who apparently undertakes it willingly, is given a place of vantage in the Temple, from which he is questioned by the Scribes and Pharisees. Their question deserves to be given in full: "O just one, whom we all are obliged to trust (πείθεσθαι ὀφείλομεν), announce unto us what is the gate of Jesus." James answers with a question which has no apparent logical connection with the question of the Scribes and Pharisees, and then he immediately follows with a *confessio fidei*, which seems to refer to the eschatological content of the expression "Son of Man"—"Why do ye inquire of me concerning the Son of Man? He himself is sitting in heaven at the right hand of the great power, and is about to come on the clouds of heaven." This declaration of faith, which presupposes a common knowledge of the identification of Jesus with the eschatological Son of Man, causes a great impression and converts many people, who, significantly, respond with the Messianic greeting, "Hosanna to the Son of David". The Scribes and Pharisees are dismayed at the result of their strange plan and vent their wrath on James by casting him down, apparently from the pinnacle of the Temple on which he had been placed, and stoning him. He is finally killed by a blow from the club of a laundryman, who rather curiously appears to be in the vicinity of the Temple with the implement of his trade. After noting that James had been buried on the spot, near the Temple, and that his grave-stone still survived, the excerpt from Hegesippus closes with the observation that Vespasian immediately after began the siege of Jerusalem (εὐθὺς Οὐεσπασιανὸς πολιορκεῖ αὐτούς).

Our former estimate of the value of the testimony of Hegesippus needs no emendation in this matter of his account of the martyrdom of James. The whole narrative, as we have noted, bristles with difficulties in the form of mutual inconsistencies, historical errors, and impossible situations. How, it must inevitably be asked, could the Scribes and the Pharisees have chosen the leader of the Christian community itself to give such public instruction as would lead the people away from a view of Jesus which they (the Scribes and Pharisees) regarded as dangerous? What did the Scribes and Pharisees mean in their statement about their obligation, and that of the people, to obey James? Why did James undertake such a commission from those who are depicted as the enemies of the Christian movement? Why did his answer to the question of the Scribes and Pharisees about "the gate of Jesus" differ from the answer which he made to the same question when put to him by the Sadducees? Unless the answer to these questions is the obvious and simple one that no complete reliance can be placed on this account of Hegesippus, the impossible alternative must be faced that the record presupposes a situation in regard to Palestinian Christianity which is quite unattested in our other and earlier sources, and some such ingenious hypothesis as that of Dr. R. Eisler [1] will be needed to explain it.

However, it would be an unscientific judgement which would, because of these obvious discrepancies, reject the whole tale as completely a fabrication. There are certain features therein which it seems difficult to believe are only the inventions of a later writer: for example, the curious expression "the gate of Jesus" and the title *Oblias* given to James are unlikely to have been deliberately coined by such a person as Hegesippus seems to have been, unless contrary to all other indications he was a creator of bogus archaisms, subtle beyond our imagining.

There is another fact, small but of real significance, still to be considered. In the curious pious romance known as the *Clementine Recognitions* there is an account,[2] remarkably similar in some respects to that of Hegesippus, in which James undertakes a public demonstration in the Temple of the true doctrine about Jesus, with Gamaliel and Caiaphas as his interrogators. The eloquence and logic of James are about to convert the people when an enemy (who is undoubtedly to be identified with Paul) interferes by stirring up a tumult, in the course of which James is thrown down a flight of steps and is left for dead, although later he recovers and is rescued by his supporters.

The origin and nature of the Clementine literature remains a matter for speculation.[3] The parallels between the account of Hegesippus of the martyrdom of James and that of the *Recognitions* have long been noted, and many years ago a particularly interesting suggestion was put forward to explain them.[4] However, although here again we have another case in which the nature of the material precludes any certainty of conclusion, it would seem a reasonable inference that both accounts have come, probably in a very distorted form, from some cycle of early Palestinian tradition in which there figured prominently a story that the assistance of James, as a revered personage in Jerusalem, had been enlisted by the Jewish religious authorities in order to prevent the popular development of some undesirable belief about Jesus, and that in some way the demonstration had resulted in the death of the Christian leader.

If the account of Hegesippus may thus reflect an ancient Palestinian Christian tradition concerning the death of James, we have then to

---

[1] *Messiah Jesus*, pp. 540–6: that James was one of the High Priests set up by the Zealots in opposition to the pro-Roman Boethusean and Sadducean High Priests. Cf. *ΙΗΣΟΥΣ ΒΑΣΙΛΕΥΣ*, II, pp. 580–8.

[2] Chapters 66–70 (trans. *Ante-Nicene Christian Library*, vol. iii).

[3] Cf. C. Schmidt, *Studien zu den Pseudo-Clementinen*, pp. 7, 292–3, 296–7; Bartlet, "Clementine Literature" in *Encycl. Brit.* (ed. xi), vol. vi, pp. 491 *seq.*; Hort, *Notes Introductory to Study of Clem. Recognitions*, pp. 81 *seq.*; Streeter, *Primitive Church*, pp. 7 *seq.*; Lietzmann, op. cit., I, p. 197; *Supernatural Religion*, pp. 299–320. See below, pp. 262–4.

[4] Lightfoot, *Galatians*, p. 367, n. 1; cf. p. 330.

reckon with its representation of the Scribes and Pharisees as being responsible for engineering the crime, for such a fact, if authentic, would seriously contradict all that we otherwise know of Palestinian Christianity in its relationships with the leading religious party of Judaism. Indeed, in view of this contradiction and as his account contradicts that of Josephus, there would seem to be the most cogent reason for rejecting *a priori* Hegesippus' testimony on this particular point. However, it is fortunately not necessary to resort to this drastic solution, since it has convincingly been shown by Eduard Schwartz [1] that in the original version of Hegesippus the slayers of James were the Sadducees, but that their name had been replaced by the names of the Scribes and Pharisees, as being the better known New Testament adversaries, by a later writer, who thus unintelligently sought to emend the ancient text.

From our examination of the records of Josephus and Hegesippus it would accordingly appear that the death of James was the outcome of a piece of high-handed action on the part of the Sadducean aristocracy, led by the High Priest Ananus, and that the crime was effectively condemned by the Pharisees.[2] Consequently, from these two sources outside the New Testament, corroboration comes of the evidence of the relevant New Testament documents that the Palestinian Christians stood well in the estimation of their fellow countrymen and were subjected to no concerted persecution by the popular leaders and the people.

.   .   .

Having thus determined that the Palestinian Christians were not an outcast body from the national life of Israel, but rather that they enjoyed a certain measure of sympathy from the Pharisees, we must now proceed to inquire how far the testimony of the Acts is to be accepted in representing the Church in Palestine as living in idyllic insulation from contemporary social and political life. It is true that this testimony is mainly an *argumentum a silentio*, but it must be accepted as valid here, because our other evidence shows that the life of the Jewish people in Palestine during this period was agitated by political events, one of which was of the most serious import, and yet no reference whatsoever is made to them or to their repercussions on the life of the Church in the narrative of the Acts.

That the picture which the Acts thus gives of the apparent indifference of Palestinian Christianity to its contemporary *milieu* is justly suspect emerges at once from a preliminary consideration of some of the issues necessarily involved in such a presentation. We have seen, partly on the evidence of the Acts itself, that the Jewish Christians remained firmly attached to their national faith and worshipped regularly in the Temple. Consequently, it becomes difficult to believe that they would have remained undisturbed by the dynamic passions of Jewish nationalism, which was

---

[1] *Z.N.T.W.* (1903), pp. 59 *seq.*
[2] For a further discussion of this Josephean passage see below, pp. 110–14.

practically synonymous with Judaism, and especially on the occasion of
the sacrilegious attempt of the Emperor Gaius to place his statue in the
Temple, the threat of which Philo and Josephus tell us convulsed the life
of the nation.[1]   The question, therefore, arises whether this representation of the Palestinian Church as immune from the agitation of contemporary political life was due either to a lack of interest on the part of
Luke in the historical context of the events which he relates or to a lack
of information about such matters in the sources which he used, or whether
it was the result of the operation of some more serious factor in the general
situation of primitive Christianity.

That lack of interest in the historical significance of its theme is responsible for Acts' picture of the insulation of Palestinian Christianity from
contemporary circumstance can quickly be dismissed as unlikely, when
it is recalled that the Lukan Gospel is distinguished among the New Testament writings for the interest displayed therein in recording synchronizations of events of the sacred history with secular affairs.[2]   It is true that
the Acts does not contain any example of such elaborate synchronizations,
but in at least four different instances a real interest in the historical
context is shown.[3]

The possibility that lack of historical reference in the sources used has
resulted in the production of the curious picture of Palestinian Christianity
under consideration is partly answered by the facts cited in evidence
against the validity of the first possibility.   Luke must have found among
his material sufficient data to enable him to make such synchronizations
and references to secular events, and to the instances just noted can be
added a number of others which convincingly attest that in the sources
of information at the disposal of the Lukan writer there was a considerable
amount of reference to the historical context of the events therein
recorded.[4]

Accordingly we find ourselves still faced with the question of the cause,
or causes, which led the author of Acts to present Palestinian Christianity
as pursuing its way in serene unconcern for its political environment.
To provide an answer to this question will necessitate the prior determination of the existence of factors calculated to render such a picture intelligible in terms of a specific situation prevailing in the Christian Church
of the first century.   To this end a survey must be made of all data which
might conceivably be regarded as relevant.

We shall best begin by noting a fact of supreme significance in this
connection—indeed of a significance truly supreme but so familiar in
its dramatic context that it is extremely difficult to evaluate it as a hard
piece of historical fact.   This fact is the mutual agreement of the primary
Christian records that Jesus of Nazareth was sentenced to death and

[1] See below, pp. 107–9. Cf. Kennard, *Politique et Religion chez les Juifs* , p. 12.
[2] E.g. Luke 1. 5; 2. 1, 2; 3. 1, 2, 23. Cf. Knox, *Some Hellenistic Elements*, p. 21.
[3] Acts 5. 34–37; 11. 27–30; 18. 12; 21. 38. Cf. 18. 2; 24. 24, 27.
[4] E.g. Luke 8. 3; 13. 1–4; 23. 6–12.

executed by the Roman governmental authorities as a rebel against the Roman suzerainty in Palestine.[1]   In the Gospel narratives there is clear evidence of a tendency to shift the responsibility from the Romans to the Jews by representing the destruction of Jesus as initially the work of the Jewish leaders and its ultimate accomplishment as only achieved by their criminal overbearing of the resistance of Pilate to what he knew would be an outrage upon justice.[2]   However, despite this tendency, and indeed the more significant because of it, the crucial fact remains uncontested that the fatal sentence was pronounced by the Roman governor and its execution carried out by Roman officials.

The Christian tradition is strong that Jesus carefully eschewed any involvement with the political issues then at stake in Palestine, and the significance of that tradition must be respected, although its origins need to be closely investigated.[3]   Nevertheless, whatever may have been the degree to which Jesus had become involved in the cause of Jewish freedom, it is certain that the movement connected with him had at least sufficient semblance of sedition to cause the Roman authorities both to regard him as a possible revolutionary and, after trial, to execute him as guilty on such a charge.

The supreme witness of this fact is not an isolated phenomenon in the New Testament documents, for there are other items of various kinds which indubitably point in a similar direction.   The most remarkable of these is constituted by the evangelical account of the arrest of Jesus in Gethsemane.   To begin with we must notice that Luke specially tells us [4] that the disciples were already armed and that before going to Gethsemane Jesus issued definite instructions that they should arm themselves: "And he said unto them, But now, he that hath a purse, let him take it, and likewise a wallet: and he that hath none, let him sell his cloak, and buy a sword ($\mu\acute{a}\chi a\iota\rho a\nu$). . . .   And they said, Lord, behold, here are two

---

[1] Mark 15. 1–15, 18, 26; Matt. 27. 11–13, 26, 29–31, 37; Luke 23. 1–5, 24, 38. Cf. John 18. 33; 19. 2, 3, 12–16, 19; 1 Tim. 6. 13.   The earliest pagan testimony is quite explicit on the point. Tacitus, *Ann.*, xv. 44: "*Auctor nominis eius Christus Tiberio imperitante per procuratorem Pontium Pilatum supplicio adfectatus erat.*"   The much disputed *Testimonium Flavianum* (Josephus, *Ant.*, xviii. 3. 5) reads: καὶ αὐτὸν ἐνδείξει τῶν πρώτων ἀνδρῶν παρ' ἡμῖν σταυρῷ ἐπιτετιμηκότος Πιλάτου.   Cf. Guignebert, *Jesus*, p. 468; Klausner, *From Jesus to Paul*, p. 438; Ginsburg, *Rome et la Judée*, p. 134.

[2] E.g. Mark 14. 1, 2, 10, 11, 43, 53–65; 15. 1, 6–15; Matt. 27. 20–26, 62–66; 28. 11–15; Luke 23. 6–25.   Guignebert, op. cit., pp. 465, 467–8, 470, 477; Dodd, *History and the Gospel*, p. 83; Martinetti, *Jésus Christ et le Christianisme*, pp. 206–7, 210.

[3] Mark 12. 13–17; Matt. 22. 15–22; Luke 20. 20–26 (note v. 20 giving the motives of the Jewish leaders: "that they might take hold of his speech, so as to deliver him to the rule and to the authority of the governor"). See below, pp. 188, 191–2, for discussion of the significance of this passage.

[4] Luke 22. 35–38. It is significant that Creed, *St. Luke*, p. 270, after discussing the difficulties inherent in this passage, could only suggest that the most satisfying solution is that v. 36 is to be interpreted as a warning of coming disaster.   Martinetti, op. cit., p. 207, thinks that the passage does not prove that Jesus intended to lead an armed revolt, "*mais se défendre d'une embûche que les prêtres du temple pourraient lui tendre*"; he admits that even this design was not in harmony with the traditional view of the teaching of Jesus. Cf. Klostermann, *Das Lukasevangelium*, p. 214: "*und verweisen auf zwei vorhandene Schwerter—schwerlich sind hier μάχαιραι dolchartige Messer zur Schlachtung des Pascha-lammes, trotz Chrysostomus, Hofmann, Zahn*".   The perplexity here of Windisch, *Der messianische Krieg*, pp. 47–9, is significant.

swords. And he said unto them, It is enough ('Ικανόν ἐστι)."[1] Luke attempts to explain away the incident by quoting the prophecy of Isaiah 52. 12; but to represent the matter as a deliberately planned fulfilment of prophecy by Jesus is neither convincing nor edifying; moreover, even if the disciples only mustered two swords among them, for what were they enough? However that may be, the even more significant fact has still to be considered that all the Evangelists agree on three essential points, namely that the disciples in Gethsemane were armed, that the Roman or Jewish officials sent to effect the arrest were heavily armed, obviously in anticipation of violent resistance, and that armed resistance was offered by the disciples, even if only to the extent of wounding one of the police officers.[2]

The two facts already mentioned sufficiently attest the presence of a political aspect of some kind, at least during Jesus' last fatal days in Jerusalem, and there are others which further reinforce and illustrate their evidence. For example, the synoptic Gospels agree in representing the entry of Jesus into the Holy City as a specially prepared demonstration, which caused an outburst of popular excitement, in which Jesus was significantly hailed in terms of political Messianism as the harbinger of the Davidic sovereignty.[3] And this politically significant act is quickly followed by another of similar import. Jesus is recorded to have attacked the commercial and banking activities of the Temple, which were the profitable privilege of the Sadducean sacerdotal aristocracy, then popularly hated for its rapacity and pro-Roman policy.[4] The Gospel narrative depicts the event as effected by the personal authority of Jesus, which the merchants and bankers did not attempt to resist. However, a little reflection on the excitability and fierce passions of an oriental people naturally causes speculation on whether the expulsion could thus have been so pacific, or whether it was not rather accomplished, under the leadership of the Prophet of Nazareth, by the violent action of his followers and the crowd, stirred as they were to a high pitch of revolutionary

---

[1] "*Die Jünger haben bezeichnenderweise die Aufforderung Jesu nicht abgewartet. Sie antworten, indem sie ihm,—jeder von ihnen natürlich!—zwei Schwerter vorweisen*" (Eisler, *ΙΗΣΟΥΣ ΒΑΣΙΛΕΥΣ*, II, p. 268; see also ib. n. 2). Cf. Klostermann, op. cit., pp. 214–15, for a survey of the various interpretations advanced by the commentators for the words. See also Eisler, *Flavius Josephus-Studien I*, n. 104 to p. 45.

[2] Mark 14. 43, 47, 48; Matt. 26. 47, 51–55; Luke 22. 49–52. Cf. John 18. 3, 10. It is not without significance in this connection that, according to Mark, the servant of the High Priest says of Peter, "This man is one of them (ἐξ αὐτῶν ἐστιν)"; cf. M. Goguel, *Harvard Theological Review*, vol. xxv, p. 7.

[3] Mark 11. 1–10; Matt. 21. 1–11, 15, 16; Luke 19. 28–38; John 12. 12–19. Note should be taken of Matthew's significant words: καὶ εἰσελθόντος αὐτοῦ εἰς Ἱεροσόλυμα ἐσείσθη πᾶσα ἡ πόλις λέγουσα, Τίς ἐστιν οὗτος; Eisler, *ΙΗΣΟΥΣ ΒΑΣΙΛΕΥΣ*, II, pp. 462–3, writes with great justification: "*Es darf als bekannt vorausgesetzt werden, dass kein Kommentator je erklären konnte was für ein Aufruhr ἡ στάσις und was für Aufrührer οἱ στασιασταί sind, einfach weil man sich nicht klar machen konnte oder wollte, dass die Ausrufung des 'Davidschen Königtums' in der bestehenden aristokratischen bzw. hierokratischen Klientelrepublik in den Augen eines in Rom unter Vespasian oder Titus . . . schreibenden Verfasser (Josephus) nichts anderes darstellen konnte, als eine στάσις, eine seditio.*" See also his note 7, ib., p. 462. Cf. A. von Gall, *ΒΑΣΙΛΕΙΑ ΤΟΥ ΘΕΟΥ*, p. 375.

[4] Mark 11. 15–18; Matt. 21. 12–16; Luke 19. 45, 46. Cf. John 2. 13–17. Cf. Eisler, op. cit., II, p. 499; Martinetti, op. cit., p. 192; Olmstead, *Jesus in the Light of History*, pp. 91–3.

fervour by the excitation of their Messianic hopes by the triumphal entry into the city. It would therefore appear certain that the presence of Jesus in Jerusalem was marked by a notable demonstration of Messianic enthusiasm, which the authorities, both Roman and Jewish, must inevitably have regarded as a dangerous expression of revolutionary feeling, and in this connection it is particularly interesting to note that in some curious way in the early tradition the fate of Jesus became associated with that of a certain Barabbas, who was "bound with them that had made insurrection (μετὰ τῶν στασιαστῶν), men who in the insurrection (ἐν τῇ στάσει) had committed murder".[1]

It is not without significance here that according to the Markan narrative, which has been closely followed on the point by Matthew and Luke,[2] during the last days at Jerusalem Jesus was actually asked by the representatives of two parties of the Jewish state, one of which was probably pro-Roman,[3] about his attitude towards the burning question of the Jews' obligation to pay tribute to Rome. The answer of Jesus is really an evasion of the point at issue,[4] and we shall have occasion later to consider the significance of the recording of the incident by Mark in his Gospel; here it will suffice to note that primitive Christian tradition preserved a consciousness of the fact that the attitude of Jesus towards the national cause of Israel had been called in question and that it was only possible to provide an answer in this ambiguous way.

Another fact which must be noticed for its pertinence to our subject here is that tradition recorded that Jesus included among the inner band of disciples, known as the Twelve, one Simon, who was specially designated "the Zealot" (τὸν καλούμενον Ζηλωτήν or ὁ Ζηλωτής).[5] If this title merely indicated this disciple's special zeal,[6] or if it only signified that he had formerly been a member of the Zealot faction but had abjured its principles on his conversion,[7] it would be hardly credible that such a compromising title should have been still given to a disciple

[1] Mark 5. 6–11; Matt. 27. 15–26; Luke 23. 18–25; John 18. 34–40. Cf. Eisler, op. cit., II, pp. 463 *seq.*; Kennard, *Politique et Religion chez les Juifs*, pp. 60–2.

[2] See p. 102, n. 3 above. "*Kaum ist Jesu Wort v. 17 einmal isoliert überliefert gewesen. Vielmehr liegt ein einheitlich konzipiertes und ausgezeichnet geformtes Apophthegma vor, bei dem man nur in v. 13 mit der redaktionellen Arbeit des Mk zu rechnen hat*" (Bultmann, *Die Gesch. der synopt. Trad.*, p. 25).

[3] Rowley, "The Herodians", *J.T.S.*, vol. xli, p. 27.

[4] "*Jesus entzieht sich trotz seines Mutes und seiner vermutlich antirömischen Gesinnung dem Dilemma mit einer Antwort, die sich gleich weit von der relativen Staatsfreundlichkeit des römischen Bürgers Paulus . . . wie von revolutionärem Zelotetum hält*" (Klostermann, *Das Markusevangelium*, p. 139). Such a comment as that of Turner, *New Com. N.T.*, p. 97b, that "the purpose of Christ was to draw a sharp distinction between the *civitas Dei* and the *civitas terrena*", fails, when taking the reply to be the *verba ipsissima Christi*, to discern that the real point at issue for the Jews was that of whether Yahweh's Holy Land constituted one of the things of Cæsar. Loewe, *Render unto Caesar*, p. 110, emphasizes the fairness of the question, but he seems to avoid a decision on its historical consequences. Cf. Weinel, *Die Stellung des Urchristentums zum Staat*, pp. 8–9.

[5] Luke 6. 15; Acts 1. 13. Cf. Mark 3. 18; Matt. 10. 4. Cf. E. Bevan, *New Com.*, Apoc., p. 15b.

[6] E.g. *B.C.*, vol. i, p. 425; Olmstead, op. cit., p. 111. It would indeed be strange, if Simon was thus distinguished by his zeal among the other disciples, that he should have left no deeper impress on Christian memory than that of the mere recollection of his name.

[7] E.g. Klostermann, op. cit., p. 41; Turner, *New Com. N.T.*, p. 62a.

after the disastrous part played by the Zealots in leading their country-men to revolt against Rome; these explanations are therefore inadequate.[1] Moreover, there is the decisive evidence that Mark realized the in-criminating nature of the Greek title and replaced it by "the Cananæan".[2] Consequently full weight must be given to the significance of this fact that a member of the extreme nationalist party of contemporary Jewish life was a close supporter of Jesus of Nazareth and that he continued to be known for his profession of Zealot principles, which would seem to imply that he found nothing incompatible in holding both loyalties together.

The significance of the presence of a Zealot in the inner band of dis-ciples naturally helps to interpret the strange silence preserved in the New Testament about the attitude of Jesus towards the Zealots. It is remarkable that, whereas Jesus is shown in decisive contact not only with the Sadducees and the Pharisees, but also with the Herodians, the memory of whom was otherwise so quickly lost,[3] of the Zealots nothing is said either in praise or in condemnation. Now as these patriots were extremely active, especially in Galilee,[4] and did not withdraw into closed com-munities as did the Essenes,[5] it would be most improbable that Jesus

---

[1] See Jos., *Ant.*, xviii. 1. 16, xx. 5. 2; *Wars*, ii. 8. 1 (117–18), 17. 8 (433–40), iv. 3. 9 (158–61); cf. Acts 5. 37. Cf. Schlatter, *Geschichte Israels*, pp. 261, 322–6; Schürer, *G.J.V.*, I, pp. 486, n. 138, 573–6, 617 *seq.*; T. Momigliano, *Camb. Anc. Hist.*, vol. x, p. 852; Eisler, *IHΣOYΣ ΒΑΣIΛEYΣ*, II, *passim*; Guignebert, *Le Monde Juif*, pp. 220–2; Graetz, *Hist. of the Jews*, vol. ii, pp. 130, 131; Derenbourg, *Essai sur l'Histoire et la Géographie de la Palestine*, p. 193, n. 2; Klausner, *Jesus of Nazareth*, pp. 156, 203–6. The editors of *B.C.*, vol. i, App. A, and F. Jackson, *Josephus and the Jews*, pp. 262–5, have endeavoured to discount the influence of Zealotism before A.D. 66. Against the validity of their view there would seem to be three fatal objections: (1) Josephus, ib., clearly associates the movement of Judas of Galilee with the politico-religious fanaticism which goaded the nation into war, and this was certainly the dynamic of Zealotism. (2) The action of Judas must clearly have gone further than mere seditious teaching, since Josephus and Luke looked back to it as a memorable event. (3) The inclusion of a Zealot in the apostolic band would indicate the existence of Zealotism long before A.D. 66, for, even granted the artificial nature of the tradition of the Twelve, there must have been some factual justification for setting forth certain names as those of men uniquely associated with Jesus of Nazareth. See also the Preface to the *Halosis* as given in the Slavonic version: Eisler, op. cit., I, p. 427. If there is any reference to a rejection of Zealotism in Matt. 23. 35; Luke 11. 51, as Goguel, *La Naissance du Christianisme*, p. 153, thinks, it would clearly be a *damnatio ex eventu*.

[2] "*Es ist nicht ein* קַנְעֲנִי—*das wäre Χαναναῖος, auch nicht einer* de uico Chana Galilaeae, ubi aquam dominus uertit in uinum, Hieronymus—*das wäre Καναῖος, sondern ein* קַנְאָן *d.h. ein (ehema-liger) Angehöriger der Zelotenpartei unter den Pharisäern*" (Klostermann, op. cit., p. 41). Cf. Schürer, *G.J.V.*, I, p. 486, n. 138; G. Dalman, *Jesus-Jeshua*, p. 12; Eisler, op. cit., II, p. 68, n. 3; Strack und Billerbeck, *Kommentar*, I, p. 537. The editors of *B.C.*, vol. i, p. 425, declare that the use of קַנְאִים is not found before the *Aboth* of R. Nathan, which is a post-Talmudic work. However, the point is not important, since Luke's translation by ὁ Ζηλωτής sufficiently witnesses to the first-century connotation, especially in Christian circles, of the term.

[3] Prof. H. H. Rowley has shown in a recent article in the *J.T.S.* (see p. 104 n. 3 above) the extent of Christian ignorance of the true identity of the Herodians, which fact fairly answers the con-tention of K. Lake, *Landmarks of Early Christianity*, pp. 30–2, that the evangelical silence about the Zealots is to be explained as due to their having ceased to exist as a party when the Gospels were written; for quite the reverse would seem to have been the case, namely that so strong was the tradition about some original Christian connection with Zealotism that even an apologetic document such as Mark was obliged to make some recognition of it. The later ignorance about the identity of the Herodians indicates how quickly certain historical details of the life of Jesus faded from the Christian memory.

[4] Cf. Klausner, op. cit., p. 162; Schlatter, op. cit., pp. 262–4, 322.

[5] See Jos. *Wars*, ii. 8. 2–13 (119–61); cf. *Life*, i. 2.

should have been completely indifferent to them. Accordingly it would seem reasonable to regard this silence as the result of the suppression of the records of the dealings of Jesus with his nation's patriotic party, and so the fact that he did include a Zealot among his more intimate followers may be interpreted as the one surviving piece of evidence about his true attitude towards its members and their ideals. As a pendant to this question of the sympathy of Jesus for Zealotism it should be noted that two of the leading disciples were given the significant title of *Boanerges*, which is interpreted as "Sons of thunder",[1] and that there is a tradition that they met with a violent death, although, as we have seen, the fact has not been adequately recorded in the New Testament documents.

Another fragment of what appears to be primitive tradition about the relations of Jesus with contemporary secular events is preserved in Luke in the curious reference to the Galilæans "whose blood Pilate had mingled with their sacrifices" and the eighteen (Galilæans?) who had perished in the catastrophic fall of a tower in Siloam.[2] According to Luke, the fate of the unfortunate men was held up by Jesus as a warning to his informants that, unless they repented, they would similarly perish. It would seem that Luke intended that the word "repent" should have a spiritual connotation, but it may be questioned whether that was the original meaning.[3] The Galilæans who were slain by Pilate must clearly have been involved in some situation which called for repressive action by the procurator, and, although the nature of the Siloam incident is not explained, it is probable from the context that those who lost their lives there were not just the victims of an unforeseen accident, but were in some way deserving of their fate. In other words, violent death is asserted to be the consequence of a certain line of action, and Jesus warns those who inform him of the incident(s) that, unless they change their conduct, such will be their end. Now two points in particular call for special notice. The first is that there were certain persons who had deemed it necessary to inform Jesus specially about the slaughter of the Galilæans. The second is that according to the text of Luke the reply of Jesus was addressed to these particular persons. The inferences which we may legitimately draw therefrom are necessarily meagre, but they are of value in the light of our observations above. They are that Jesus was regarded as one who should be specially informed of some act of political

---

[1] Mark 3. 17. Cf. Dalman, op. cit., p. 12; Olmstead, *Jesus in the Light of History*, p. 110; Eisler, *Enigma of Fourth Gospel*, pp. 86–9. If von Gall, *ΒΑΣΙΛΕΙΑ ΤΟΥ ΘΕΟΥ*, p. 353, is right in thinking that the βιασταὶ of Matt. 11. 12 are the Zealots, the fact of their anonymity is significant. See Eisler's interpretation of *Iskariotes* in *ΙΗΣΟΥΣ ΒΑΣΙΛΕΥΣ*, II, p. 528, n. 5.

[2] Luke 13. 1–5. See Eisler's interpretation of the passage (*Messiah Jesus*, pp. 500–10). The possibility that some political reference is involved here is recognized but explained away on conservative lines by Luce, *St. Luke*, p. 144; Creed, *St. Luke*, p. 180; Olmstead, op. cit., p. 149; Dodd, *Parables of the Kingdom*, p. 65. There seems little to justify Wellhausen's suggestion that the slaughter here referred to is that of the Samaritans on Mt. Gerizim, described by Jos., *Ant.*, xviii. 4. 1. Cf. Eisler, *ΙΗΣΟΥΣ ΒΑΣΙΛΕΥΣ*, II, pp. 516–25.

[3] But see Klostermann, *Das Lukasevangelium*, p. 143 (2).

violence and that he counselled that such a course should not be persisted in; it must remain a matter for speculation whether the counsel was limited to some particularly rash expression of patriotic fervour or was a general warning against the danger of precipitating events by undisciplined acts of violence.

The data which we have so far surveyed have been primarily expressive of the tradition concerning Jesus, although, of course, they also afford invaluable evidence of the mind of those among whom the tradition was preserved and developed. We come now to consider a fragment of the tradition which appears to reflect the attitude of the Palestinian Christians on an occasion of great national tension.

A considerable number of New Testament scholars have expressed the opinion that the thirteenth chapter of the Markan Gospel, which is generally known as the Little Apocalypse, incorporates, to some degree of completeness, a Jewish Christian apocalypse, or a Jewish apocalypse which had gained an effective currency in Jewish Christian circles.[1] As such this document must antedate the Gospel which incorporates it, but no unanimity of opinion has been shown with regard to its probable date. Nevertheless, it is obvious that the writing must have been produced originally in response to some specific crisis in Jewish life in Palestine, and it is here suggested that there are cogent reasons for regarding it as an expression of the Jewish Christian mind when the sanctity of the Temple was threatened by the sacrilegious project of the Emperor Gaius to erect his statue therein in A.D. 39–41.[2]

If the passage contained in verses 14–20 is taken in its sequence, a remarkable series of allusions to what may reasonably be regarded as features of the contemporary situation can be made out. First there is the cabalistic reference to the Abomination of Desolation. The striking parallelism between Antiochus Epiphanes' act of desecration and that which was threatened by Caligula must have been as apparent to the Jew of the first century as it is to us, so that no more fitting identification of the Abomination of Desolation can be found prior to A.D. 70 than that of the image which the Roman tyrant planned to place in the sanctuary of the Temple. Then the time element in the situation described in verses 14–20 is significant. The verbal construction of verses 14–19 indicates that the presence of the Abomination is a future contingency and so likewise the advice and observations which follow apply to future action. But in verse 20 the verb changes to the historic tense and the intervention of God is depicted as having stopped a process of disaster. Now it is interesting to note that in the accounts of Philo and Josephus the threat of the desecration of the Temple overhung the Jews for about

---

[1] Cf. Streeter, *Four Gospels*, pp. 491 *seq.*; Moffatt, *Intro. to N.T.*, pp. 207–9; Meyer, *Ursprung und Anfänge des Christentums*, I, p. 129; Bultmann, *Die Gesch. der synopt. Trad.*, p. 129; Dibelius, *From Tradition to Gospel*, p. 65; Klostermann, *Das Markusevangelium*, p. 147.

[2] Cf. Jerome, *Com. Matt.*, xxiv; Goudge and Levertoff, *New Com. N.T.*, p. 191b; Weiss, *Urchristentum*, p. 233; Loisy, *Les Origines du N.T.*, p. 104; Piganiol, *Histoire de Rome*, pp. 258, 269.

a year, because of the strength of their own demonstrations and the consequent procrastinations of Petronius, the legate of Syria who was commissioned to execute the imperial decree, but who clearly realized the folly and danger of it.[1] What would have eventually happened if the death of Gaius had not unexpectedly caused the cancellation of the project is not doubtful, for the temper which the Jews had already shown towards the measure, which they knew was deliberately calculated to strike at the very centre of what they held most sacred, must inevitably have led to a nation-wide uprising against the hated domination of the heathen tyrant.[2] The situation presupposed in verses 14–20 of the Little Apocalypse can be seen on comparison to correspond most strikingly to that which must accordingly have obtained for the Jews of Palestine during this time. The threat of the terrible sacrilege becomes more imminent; it is recognized in terms of the historic Abomination of Desolation; memories of the glorious Maccabæan resistance inspire the mind to emulate the celebrated deeds of those heroic ancestors. Mattathias and his sons and followers rather than blaspheme their God in submitting to the heathen's command had fled into the mountains, there to maintain themselves and their beliefs by force of arms.[3] Thus, when their descendants were faced with the Roman Emperor's impiety, similar counsels prevailed, and in Judæa flight into the mountains was anticipated and, consequently, armed resistance to the heathen overlord. The hardships of such a flight are vividly realized, perhaps from the experiences of those Jews who are recorded to have left their homes in the winter of 39 to petition Petronius at Ptolemais.[4] The sudden news of the death of Caligula must have seemed a veritable act of mercy on the part of Yahweh for the sake of his own people, for thus the threatened calamity was stayed.[5]

The calamity was stayed, but the impression of the threat upon Jewish minds was deep and lasting. The sacred Temple had been threatened, Israel had remained faithful, ready to suffer in its resistance to the heathen,

---

[1] Philo, *Leg. ad Caium*, xxix–xliii; Jos., *Ant.*, xviii. 8. 1–9, *Wars*, ii. 10. 1–5 (184–203); cf. Tacitus, *Hist.*, v. 9. Cf. Schürer. *G.J.V.*, I, pp. 503–7; Oesterley, *Hist. of Israel*, vol. ii, pp. 396–7; Jones, *Herods of Judaea*, pp. 196–203; T. Lewin, *Fasti Sacri*, secs. 1553–1606; M. P. Charlesworth, *Camb. Anc. Hist.*, vol. x, pp. 662–3; Ferrero e Barbagallo, *Roma Antica*, vol. ii, pp. 248–9.

[2] Tacitus, ibid., states that the Jews did resort to arms: "*dein iussi a Gaio Caesare effigiem eius in templo locare arma potius sumpsere, quem motum Caesaris mors deremit.*" The Jewish writers are intent on stressing the remarkable forbearance of the Jews under the threat. Cf. E. R. Goodenough, *Politics of Philo Judaeus*, pp. 9–20.

[3] 1 Macc. 2. 23 ff. Strack and Billerbeck, *Kommentar*, I, pp. 951–2, cite a rabbinic ruling that flight should be made to Upper Galilee in the troublous times preceding the coming of the Messiah.

[4] According to Jos., *Ant.*, xviii. 8. 2, with which Philo, *Leg. ad Caium*, xxxii, would seem to agree. There is some difference of opinion about the true timing of the course of events (cf. Schürer, op. cit., pp. 333, 503, n. 179, 506, n. 187; Ricciotti, *La Guerra giudaica*, vol. ii, p. 264, n. 199; Charlesworth, *Camb. Anc. Hist.*, vol. x, p. 662, n. 2); however, it appears certain from the accounts of both Philo and Josephus that a demonstration was made by the Jews at either Ptolemais or Tiberias at a time of year when the weather is likely to have been bad; see especially Jos., *Ant.*, xviii. 8. 6.

[5] According to the rabbinic tractate *Megillat Taanit*, the day of Caligula's death was noted as one of rejoicing; see Derenbourg, *Essai sur l'Histoire et la Géographie de la Palestine*, pp. 207 seq.

but Yahweh had justified the trust of his elect and had saved them in destroying their persecutor. Profoundly moving must this experience have been to all Jews in Palestine, and that the Jewish Christians had fully participated in the national agitation is surely testified by the preservation of this apocalyptic writing in the primitive Christian tradition. And full weight must be given to its testimony. It means in effect that at this moment of supreme crisis in the nation's life even those who believed that the crucified Jesus of Nazareth was the Messiah were united with their compatriots in their reaction to the impending sacrilege and were prepared to abandon their homes and resist the impious demand.

The result of this investigation of the relevant New Testament material has been to afford a body of evidence which, though diverse in nature, shows remarkable agreement of testimony to the fact that Palestinian Christianity from its origins was closely associated with the nationalist aspirations of Israel. Of the exact details or proportions of this association we cannot know, owing to the paucity of the data and their fragmentary character; anyhow, certain features do stand out clear and certain. These are, namely, that the profession of Zealotism was not incompatible with allegiance to Jesus of Nazareth, that the arrest of Jesus was accompanied by some armed resistance by his followers, that the charge on which Jesus was tried before the procurator Pontius Pilate was that of sedition, and that the fatal sentence was given and its execution carried out on Roman authority. Further, the Palestinian Christians are seen to be devoted to the practice and maintenance of their national faith, and to enjoy a certain reputation for their zeal with the Pharisees. That persons who were thus so far loyal in their attachment to Judaism should have been profoundly moved by any threat to the citadel of their faith is a natural inference, and that the reactions of the Jewish Christians were of such an order when the Roman Emperor Gaius threatened the sanctity of the Temple is attested by the survival of a fragment of an apocalypse, expressive of their fears and hopes during the period of this crisis.

The significance of these conclusions for our understanding of the situation of the Christian Church in Palestine as the Jewish people moved towards the tragedy of A.D. 70 is supreme, and their importance in estimating the effect of the overthrow of Israel upon that Church is obvious. But here we may briefly note one of its consequences for a problem raised earlier in this chapter, namely that of the reason for the patently erroneous picture given in the Acts of the idyllic insulation of the Palestinian Church from contemporary political circumstance. Our investigation has sufficiently shown that there was in the primitive tradition much information about the involvement of the first disciples in the cause of Jewish nationalism. That the fact seems to appear only incidentally in the Gospels is a matter which we shall have to investigate in due course. That it scarcely appears at all in the Acts, which professes to be a record

9

of the fortunes of the infant Church, can surely have no other explanation than that to Luke the presentation of such information would have been detrimental to his theme of illustrating the course of the divinely guided progress of Christianity from Jerusalem to Rome.

Before concluding this chapter on the attitude of the Palestinian Christians to their nation's cause against Rome, we have still to consider the possibility that some information is to be derived from certain non-Christian sources, a possibility which, if fulfilled, would afford an invaluable means of comparison for judging the evidence of the Christian data.

The chief of these potential sources is constituted by the works of Josephus. The three references to matters concerning the New Testament presentation of Christian Origins, the so-called *Testimonia Flaviana*, in the Jewish historian's great work on the history of his people, have for centuries engaged the interest of scholars and have provoked an unceasing debate about their authenticity.[1]   In more recent years this controversy has been made immensely more complex and the issue involved therein rendered most profound by the discovery of what purports to be a Slavonic version of Josephus' account of the Jewish War against Rome and by its utilization in an amazing interpretation of Christian Origins by Dr. Robert Eisler.[2]   Into this hotly disputed field of debate we may perhaps most safely enter by considering first, in the light of our present subject, the two passages about Jesus and James in the extant Greek text of the *Antiquities*; the passage about John the Baptist does not particularly concern us here.[3]

Our earliest witness to the present Greek text of these two passages is Eusebius, the famous fourth-century Bishop of Cæsarea and ecclesiastical historian.[4]   As we have seen, the passage concerning James in its extant form contains nothing which it would have been impossible for a non-Christian Jew, such as Josephus seems to have been, conceivably to have written.   The position is very different in regard to the other passage. As it now stands, it could only have been written by one who held so high an estimate of the character and ability of Jesus—one who recognized his Messiahship, and who believed in his resurrection from the dead—that he must have been a Christian by virtue of this acceptance of the

---

[1]   An interesting survey of the evolution of opinion about the *Testimonium Flavianum* concerning Jesus is given by Eisler, with his own ingenious reconstruction, in *Messiah Jesus*, pp. 36–62.   W. Whiston gives a valuable catena of writers who mention Josephus' testimony in Dissertation I, appended to his translation.   Cf. Schürer, op. cit., pp. 544–9; Thackeray, art. on Josephus in Hastings, *Dictionary of the Bible*, extra vol., p. 472, *Josephus: the Man and the Historian*, pp. 136–49; Barnes, *Testimony of Josephus to Jesus Christ*; Bentwich, *Josephus*, pp. 241–4; Leclercq, art. on Josephus in *Dict. d'Archéologie Chrétienne et de Liturgie*; Klausner, *Jesus of Nazareth*, pp. 55–60; Ricciotti, *Flavio Giuseppe*, pp. 173–85; Meyer, *Ursprung und Anfänge des Christentums*, I, pp. 206–9; F. Jackson, *Josephus and the Jews*, pp. 279–80; V. Burch, *Jesus Christ and His Revelation*, pp. 174 seq.; Guignebert, *Jesus*, pp. 16–19; Goguel, *Jesus*, pp. 77–82; Eisler, *ΙΗΣΟΥΣ ΒΑΣΙΛΕΥΣ*, I, pp. 3–45.
[2] See below, pp. 114 *seq.*
[3] They are respectively *Ant.*, xviii. 3. 3, xx. 9. 1, xviii. 5. 2.
[4] Eusebius, *Eccl. Hist.*, I. xi. 7–8; II. xi, xii; *Dem. Evang.*, III. v.

essentials of the faith. Consequently it is not strange that this passage has become the centre of so much speculation and controversy. There is, however, one fact which decisively proves that the passage which now stands in our Greek text of Josephus was not to be found in some versions prior to Eusebius' attestation, which must in turn mean that it was not contained in the original.

In two different places in his writings the celebrated Alexandrian scholar, Origen, states that, while acknowledging the righteousness of James, Josephus did not believe that Jesus was the Christ (καὶ τὸ θαυμαστόν ἐστιν, ὅτι τὸν Ἰησοῦν ἡμῶν οὐ καταδεξάμενος εἶναι Χριστόν, *Ad Matt.* x. 17; Ὁ δ'αὐτὸς (Josephus) καίτοι γε ἀπιστῶν τῷ Ἰησοῦ ὡς Χριστῷ, *C. Cels.* i. 47). Origen makes these observations when specifically referring to the passage about James in the twentieth book of the *Antiquities* and that about John the Baptist in the eighteenth book of the same work. Now it is obvious that he could not have made such a statement about Josephus' rejection of the Messiahship of Jesus if in the eighteenth book of the *Antiquities* he had read our present passage about Jesus, containing the categorical affirmation that Jesus was Christ (ὁ Χριστὸς οὗτος (Jesus) ἦν). The word "rejection" has been advisedly used here, since the expressions employed by Origen, namely οὐ καταδεξάμενος and ἀπιστῶν, clearly imply an active element and cannot be interpreted as indicating only that Josephus had not recognized the Messiahship of Jesus in any explicit statement. Consequently, the conclusion would seem to be inevitable that Origen, instead of reading in his copy of the *Antiquities* the extant passage about Jesus, had found one in which the Messiahship of Jesus had been definitely repudiated. And, since Origen antedates Eusebius by about one century, it would seem a necessary deduction that this represents the original statement of his attitude on this matter by Josephus himself.

However, these statements of Origen involve a more complicated problem. In both of the statements fully, and in another briefly,[1] the Alexandrian philologist asserts that Josephus explained the overthrow of the Jewish nation by the Romans in terms of God's vengeance for the murder of the righteous James. Now, since the extant passage about the death of James contains no such statement by Josephus and since the account of Hegesippus of the same subject does end with a sentence which seems to interpret the death of James as the cause of the siege of Jerusalem (καὶ εὐθὺς Οὐεσπασιανὸς πολιορκεῖ αὐτούς),[2] it has been thought that Origen made the mistake of ascribing to Josephus what he had read in Hegesippus.[3] But such an explanation means convicting the great Egyptian scholar of the incredible blunder, made not once but twice, of rightly quoting the title and the particular books of the *Antiquities*

---

[1] *Contra Celsum*, ii. 13.
[2] *Apud* Eusebius, *Eccl. Hist.*, II. xxiii. 18. Cf. Eisler, op. cit., pp. 148–50.
[3] E.g. Thackeray, *Josephus: the Man and the Historian*, p. 135; Barnes, *Testimony of Josephus to Jesus Christ*, p. 19; Ricciotti, *Flavio Giuseppe*, pp. 175–6.

in which occur the passages with which he was dealing, and yet of meaning
Hegesippus when he wrote Flavius Josephus. Nor would that be the
full extent of his confusion, because the very *raison d'être* of his citation
was the significance of the fact that Josephus acknowledged the righteousness of James, while repudiating the Messiahship of Jesus; whereas, on
the other hand, it would have been known that Hegesippus was a Christian
writer, who had lived only about one generation before the time of
Origen and whose testimony in this connection would have had no force
whatsoever.

Due consideration of these factors, therefore, surely indicates that
Origen's assertion that Josephus attributed the Jews' sufferings to the
murder of James is not to be explained so easily in terms of misquotation.
Thus the problem which that assertion constituted has still to be faced.
Although in view of the paucity of the material available a sure conclusion
about it cannot be expected, there are some points which call for special
notice here. The first is that, according to Origen, Josephus had praised
James to the extent of recognizing his righteousness,[1] while he had
repudiated Jesus' Messiahship, which act must necessarily have involved
a degree of condemnation. Secondly, it would be difficult to maintain
that the extant Greek account of James' death constitutes a clear
acknowledgement of his righteousness, although, as we have seen, it
may reasonably be inferred from the reaction of the Pharisees. The
third point is that Origen knew a version of the *Antiquities* in which there
was ground for the assertion that Josephus admitted a causal connection
between the murder of James and the overthrow of the Jewish nation
in the war of A.D. 66–70.

We may now at this point conveniently draw some inferences which
our analysis so far would seem to justify. The most important is that in
the time of Origen there existed a version of Josephus' *Antiquities* which
differed from the surviving Greek version in that an uncomplimentary
account of Jesus was given and a favourable one of James, with some
suggestion that his murder was regarded as the cause of the Jewish national
disaster. This inference necessarily leads to another, namely that
between the times of Origen and Eusebius the uncomplimentary account
of Jesus had been replaced in some way by that which now appears in
the extant text;[2] it is possible that the criticism of Origen had imple-
mented this replacement. Of the nature of the version of Josephus used
by Origen we are not in a position to know beyond the fact that he knew
it as "the Jewish Archæology" (τὴν Ἰουδαϊκὴν ἀρχαιολογίαν), which
is the usual ancient title of the work known in English as the *Antiquities
of the Jews*. That this version contained an account of the death of James
in which the destruction of Jerusalem was regarded as an act of divine

---

[1] οὐδὲν ἧττον Ἰακώβῳ δικαιοσύνην ἐμαρτύρησε (Josephus) τοσαύτην, *Ad Matt.* x. 17. φησὶ ταῦτα
συμβεβηκέναι τοῖς Ἰουδαίοις κατ' ἐκδίκησιν Ἰακώβου τοῦ δικαίου . . . ἐπειδήπερ δικαιότατον αὐτὸν
ὄντα ἀπέκτειναν, *C. Celsum*, i. 47.
[2] Cf. Meyer, op. cit., I, p. 206.

vengeance for the crime would suggest that it too had already been subjected to some interpolation in the Christian interest, for it would *a priori* appear improbable that Josephus should have entertained such an idea. But there is a fact which makes this conclusion by no means certain. It is that in the same version, as we have seen, there was an uncomplimentary account of Jesus, so that it would be most unlikely that a Christian interpolator would have emended the passage about James in the interests of his faith and yet have left the far more shocking statement concerning Jesus quite untouched. Consequently, it would seem that there were in circulation in the time of Origen manuscripts of Josephus which differed seriously in the tenor of their accounts of Jesus and James, and that some of these manuscripts preserved the genuine text of the Jewish historian.

Now that we have thus established the fact that the *Antiquities* must originally have contained an account of Jesus which was offensive to Christian feeling, it naturally becomes a matter of great interest to know what Josephus did write. Several scholars have offered reconstructions of the original passage, but it would seem to be certain from the above considerations that something like the reconstruction made by Dr. Eisler [1] would be necessary to fit the requirements demanded by Origen's remarks and what we otherwise know of Josephus. However, in view of the nature of the available data all such attempts have to be regarded as essentially speculative, and only on one point, but to us a particularly valuable one, can there be anything like certainty. It is that we have the twice-repeated statement of Origen that Josephus did not recognize Jesus as Christ. Now if the original form of the Jesus passage contained an explicit repudiation of the Messianic claims of Jesus, it must necessarily follow that Josephus had regarded Jesus as a claimant to Messiahship, which accordingly means that there must have been certain aspects of the mission of Jesus and of Palestinian Christianity which caused him to view Jesus in this light. And, if we wish to know what was Josephus' concept of the Messiahship, there is a particularly instructive passage on the subject in his *Wars of the Jews*.[2] Therein he states that the Jews were led on to their fatal resistance to Rome, above all, by their belief in an ambiguous oracle (χρησμὸς ἀμφίβολος) [3] in their sacred scriptures which foretold that at that time (κατὰ τὸν καιρὸν ἐκεῖνον) a man from Palestine (ἀπὸ τῆς χώρας αὐτῶν) would become the ruler of the world (ἄρξει τῆς οἰκουμένης). The Jews interpreted this prophecy as meaning that a member of their own race would gain this supreme position, and many of their wise men were deceived therein, because, according to Josephus, the person really meant was Vespasian, who was proclaimed Emperor while on Jewish soil. It is obvious, of course, that

---

[1] *Messiah Jesus*, pp. 61–2; *ΙΗΣΟΥΣ ΒΑΣΙΛΕΥΣ*, I, pp. 87–8.
[2] *Wars*, vi. 5. 4 (310–315).
[3] Cf. Eisler, *Messiah Jesus*, pp. 544 *seq.*; *ΙΗΣΟΥΣ ΒΑΣΙΛΕΥΣ*, II, pp. 591–9.

the historian in his service to the Flavii felt obliged thus to interpret a notorious prophecy which had been productive of so much hatred and suffering, but it is also obvious that Josephus instinctively thought of the Messianic hope of his people in political terms.   Hence he would have tended to recognize a candidate for Messiahship in any popular leader whose conduct, or whose followers' conduct, had a political aspect.   It would accordingly be reasonable to suppose from Origen's remarks that Josephus had viewed Jesus and those who followed him as exponents of political Messianism and similar to many others whose fate he records.[1]

That Josephus should have written comparatively favourably of James, the brother of Jesus, does not necessarily contradict this view, since it must be noted that Origen says in one of the relevant passages [2] that, although Josephus recognized the righteousness of James and in his murder a cause of the Jewish overthrow, he did so "as it were unwillingly" (ὥσπερ ἄκων).   It is quite feasible from what we have seen of the sympathy of the Pharisees for the Jerusalem Christians that in popular Pharisaic circles the murder of so distinguished an observer of the Law as James was spoken of as a cause of the sufferings which shortly afterwards afflicted the Jews, perhaps in a manner similar to that in which certain Jews attributed the destruction of the army of Herod Antipas to a divine act of retribution for that monarch's slaying of John the Baptist.[3] Consequently in the original passage Josephus may have felt obliged to record this opinion, but he did so in such a way that Origen could justly describe his attitude as ἄκων.   Why such a passage, which apparently redounded so greatly to the credit of James, should not have been preserved by subsequent Christian scribes in their revision of the Josephean *Testimonia* is, of course, unknown, but it would be reasonable to think that in its original form it was so thoroughly offensive to Christian taste, perhaps by making a scandalous comparison between the legal righteousness of James and the Messianic pretensions of Jesus, that, to render it sufficiently decent for Christian reading, it was necessary to delete much that was creditable to James.   Indeed it may not be over subtle to suggest that Origen's remark[4] that Josephus ought to have said (δέον δ'αὐτὸν εἰπεῖν) that the national disaster which befell the Jews was caused by their slaying of Jesus, the prophesied Messiah, was instrumental in prompting the Christian censors to make a special point of removing a statement which was deemed to give greater honour to James than to Jesus.

We must now turn from this intricate problem of the *Testimonia Flaviana* in the extant Greek text of Josephus' *Antiquities* to consider what

---

[1] E.g. *Ant.*, xviii. 1. 1 ; 4. 1 ; xx. 5. 1 ; 8. 5–6.
[2] *C. Celsum*, i. 47.
[3] *Ant.*, xviii. 5. 1–2.
[4] Ibid.

are claimed by Dr. Eisler to be genuine accounts of Jesus and his followers as preserved in a Slavonic translation of either an Aramaic or a Greek prototype of the extant Greek version of Josephus' *Wars of the Jews*.[1] Eisler has chosen to designate this hypothetical work the *Halosis* (of Jerusalem).

With a few notable exceptions, Dr. Eisler's thesis has been vigorously repudiated by scholars of Christian, Jewish, and agnostic denomination.[2] Their attack has generally been directed against what is the most

---

[1] The fullest presentation of Eisler's thesis is found in his *ΙΗΣΟΥΣ ΒΑΣΙΛΕΥΣ ΟΥ ΒΑΣΙΛΕΥΣΑΣ* (Heidelberg, 1929-30, 2 *Bände*): the full title is explanatory and reads—"*Die messianische Unabhängigkeitsbewegung vom Auftreten Johannes des Täufers bis zum Untergang Jakob des Gerechten. Nach der neuerschlossenen Eroberung von Jerusalem des Flavius Josephus und den christlichen Quellen.*" The Slavonic version was first made known to the general world of scholarship by A. Berendts in *Texte und Untersuchungen*, Bd. xiv, Heft 4, 1906, under the title of "*Die Zeugnisse vom Christentum im slavischen 'De Bello Judaico' des Josephus*". In 1926-7 the *magnum opus* of Berendts was published posthumously under the supervision of K. Grass in *Eesti Varbariigi Tartu Ülikooli Toimetused*; the title is "*Flavius Josephus vom Jüdischen Kriege, Buch i–v, nach der slavischen Übersetzung*" (Dorpat).

[2] Eisler, *Messiah Jesus*, pp. 624-30, gives an interesting bibliographical review of the subject down to 1930. It is instructive to note that one of the greatest authorities on Josephean studies, the late Dr. St. John Thackeray, seemed prepared, at least tentatively, to accept the Slavonic version as representing some intermediate stage between the original Aramaic and the extant Greek text of Josephus' *Wars of the Jews*. He printed the parts which concerned Christianity, together with other interesting variants, in his edition of Josephus in the Loeb Classical Library, vol. iii, app. iii; cf. his book, *Josephus: the Man and the Historian*, p. 34; see also B. S. Easton, *Christ and the Gospels*, pp. 78-81. A distinguished convert to Eisler's views has been S. Reinach (see his *Orpheus*, pp. 247 *seq.*). It should also be noted that a scholar of the calibre of Dr. C. G. Montefiore considered himself unqualified to review Eisler's work (*Hibbert Journal*, Jan., 1932, p. 298). The following is a selection of more recent opinion on Eisler's thesis: A. Momigliano, *Camb. Anc. Hist.*, vol. x, p. 885, says that Eisler's thesis that the Slavonic version is a translation of a Greek text between the Aramaic original and the present Greek text has little to support it, but he does not give his reasons beyond citing articles by A. Goethals and J. M. Creed. Guignebert, *Jesus*, p. 19 and notes, similarly rejects Eisler's position, referring only to Goguel's article in *Revue Historique*, t. clxii, 1929; cf. Guignebert, *Le Mond Juif*, p. 27, n. 1. For Goguel's views see also his *Life of Jesus*, pp. 82-91. Streeter, in *Camb. Anc. Hist.*, vol. xi, p. 256, n. 2, referred to Creed's article (see below) as a sufficient refutation of Eisler's thesis. The article of J. M. Creed in *The Harvard Theological Review*, vol. xxv (1932), under the title of "The Slavonic Version of Josephus' History of the Jewish War", is a most valuable survey. However, Creed's concluding suggestion (pp. 318-19), that the passages about Christianity are the work of a Slavonic translator who, introducing Josephus "to a simple, half-barbarous, yet Christian people", decided that thus he would meet their desire to have "their new history-book" linked up with the familiar narrative of Scripture, is not convincing. These passages are so different from the traditional Christian view (e.g. in the *Wonder-worker* passage Pilate at first releases the *Wonder-worker*; of his subsequent death only the bare fact is mentioned) that it is difficult to see how any Christian writer could have inserted them to provide parallels to the Gospel narrative which would be useful to the Christian cause; these "parallels" appear strangely detached from the interests of both Jewish and Christian partizanship. Moreover, Creed does not give an adequate explanation of the existence of the passages dealing with secular affairs which are peculiar to the Slavonic version. The most comprehensive examination in English of Eisler's theory seems to be that of Dr. J. W. Jack in his *Historic Christ* (1933), a book of 278 pages. Dr. Jack makes some most valuable criticisms and exposes many of the impossibilities of Eisler's position, but he does not seem to appreciate the strength of the evidence for the existence of various versions of Josephus' *Wars* and the great contradictions to be found between the *Wars* and the *Life*. G. Ricciotti, *Flavio Giuseppe* (1937), vol. i, pp. 91-4, rejects Eisler's thesis on the ground of its improbability; he incidentally makes a novel and significant suggestion about the magnitude of the controversy caused by Eisler's work—"*Perchè, dunque, tanto chiasso attorno alla pubblicazione dell'Eisler? Certamente per ragioni non scientifiche ma di altro genere, e che quindi non ci riguardano più (ad esempio potrebbe darsi che, trattandosi di documenti russi, ne favorissero la diffusione le autorità dei Sovieti, supponiamo per mecenatismo nazionale, oppure per altre mire non speculative ma pragmatiche; ad ogni modo siamo sempre fuori del campo della pura scienza)*", p. 94. In a letter Dr. Eisler has informed the author that Dr. L. P. Jacks and Dr. Rendel Harris expressed considerable appreciation of his work. See also below, p. 261.

fundamental premise of the thesis, namely that the extant Slavonic version is to be regarded as preserving in an authentic form an earlier edition of the *Wars of the Jews*, which had escaped the revisions of later Christian censors to which the existing Greek versions have been subjected. An adequate criticism of Eisler's work demands a rare combination of intimacy with Josephean studies, New Testament research, and Slavonic scholarship, and it would generally appear that his critics, possibly because they lack his amazing width of erudition, although they have exposed some weaknesses and absurdities of his theories, have not succeeded in providing a convincing alternative explanation of the Slavonic *Halosis*. This is a point of fundamental importance and it requires elucidation.

The opponents of Eisler's thesis generally regard the Slavonic *Halosis* as an anti-Christian Jewish forgery, based on Josephus' *Wars of the Jews*. But if this were so, it would be necessary to view it as one of the most laboriously senseless compositions known in the whole field of literary creation, for it would mean that some writer had set himself the enormous and tedious task of producing a revision of the whole of Josephus' *Wars of the Jews*, in order, at the most, to work in two short and very vague passages about Jesus and his followers. For these passages are indeed vague both in their reference to Jesus and in their presentation of his actions and those of his followers. In the first [1] Jesus is referred to only as "a man" and "the Wonder-worker"; he uses his miraculous power to perform many healings, and is briefly condemned for breaking the Law and violating the Sabbath, but it is also expressly stated that he did nothing shameful. His influence stirs many Jews to hope that he might be instrumental in freeing them from the Roman domination. He is consequently invited to lead an insurrection in Jerusalem to exterminate the Romans there. What was the nature of his response is not clearly stated; however, before any effective action is attempted, the Jewish (sacerdotal) leaders take alarm and warn Pilate, who takes strong repressive action, as a result of which the *Wonder-worker* is captured and finally condemned by the procurator as a rebel, desirous of kingship. The second passage [2] records how during the reign of Claudius many of the followers of the *Wonder-worker* excited the Jewish proletariat of Palestine by promising that their Master, whom they asserted to be alive, would free them from their bondage. The movement, however, was promptly suppressed by the Roman authorities.

It would, therefore, surely seem incredible that a Jewish scribe, intent on spreading anti-Christian propaganda, perhaps in South Russia, should have set himself so long and tedious a task of revising Josephus' *Wars of the Jews* in order to incorporate these two passages. It scarcely needs to

[1] See Appendix II (1) to this Chapter. An English translation of the passage is given in Eisler, *Messiah Jesus*, pp. 583–5; cf. Creed, op cit., pp. 309–11 ; cf. Eisler, *ΙΗΣΟΥΣ ΒΑΣΙΛΕΥΣ*, II, pp. 290–300.
[2] See Appendix II (2) to this Chapter. An English translation of the passage is given in Eisler, *Messiah Jesus*, pp. 528–9; cf. Creed, op. cit., pp. 311–12.

be said that such an opponent of Christianity could have found more effective ways of accomplishing his purpose.[1]

But there are other factors to consider, which still more strongly indicate that such a theory does not adequately explain the origin of the Slavonic *Halosis*. There are a number of passages on secular events in both Jewish and Roman history which cannot be paralleled in the extant Greek text.[2] One of the most significant of these is the account of a stratagem successfully employed by Vitellius against the troops of Otho in the battle of Bedriacum. It is the use of the *tribulum*, and the fact is not recorded by Dio Cassius, Plutarch, Suetonius, or Tacitus, who describe the action. Now the recording of such a matter, unsupported as it is by any known writer, has far more the appearance of being the work of a writer who had access to first-hand reports of the battle than of one who was primarily concerned to undermine Christianity.[3] And the testimony of the other passages, of course, points in a similar direction.

When these facts are considered, together with the evidence of Origen for the existence of a version of Josephus' *Antiquities* which notably differed in its references to Christianity from the extant Greek text, it is not unreasonable to suppose that the Slavonic *Halosis* may preserve an earlier version of a writing of Josephus which in a revised form is known to us as *The Wars of the Jews*. The issue is admittedly a balance of probabilities, and it would accordingly be rash to use any statement from the Slavonic *Halosis* as a primary evidential basis for a novel interpretation of Christian Origins, but its testimony has a real relevancy in a matter where research

---

[1] Jack, *Historic Christ*, pp. 77 *seq.*, attempts to controvert Eisler's theory that the Slavonic version was made by Judaizing sects in Russia by arguing that it was issued by the Orthodox Church to combat heresy; a sufficient answer to such a suggestion is surely the question *Cui bono?*, for the Slavonic *Halosis* would constitute the most extraordinary Christian propaganda, and it would be as hard to imagine the type of Christian mind which could have produced it as it is to conceive of the kind of convert it would have been designed to win. As has been noted in n. 2, p. 115 above, a similar view has been advanced by Creed. It is, of course, not without significance that two such diametrically opposed solutions as that of Eisler, on the one hand, and that of Jack and Creed, on the other, have been put forward to account for the origins of the same passages, in their extant form, in the Slavonic Josephus.

[2] English translations of the principal additional passages in the Slavonic version are given by Thackeray in the Appendix to his Loeb edition of Josephus, vol. iii; cf. Eisler, op. cit., chapter viii.

[3] See Thackeray, op. cit. (19), pp. 656–7; Eisler, op. cit., pp. 180–1. Jack, op. cit., p. 60, endeavours to belittle this piece of evidence. However, the hard fact remains that this is a valuable record of military tactics, which has been preserved only here. If it had been preserved in some document and thought worthy by some later scribe of inclusion in Josephus, the question inevitably arises of why it was not also interpolated in other relevant writings. Further, it must be remembered that Josephus did actually have, by virtue of his peculiar relationship with the Flavii, better opportunities for knowing such things than Tacitus or Suetonius. In n. 5 on the same page Jack thinks that Josephus could not have been so mentally dull as not to notice at first such a *faux pas* as the recording of a notable piece of their rival's military skill might have been to Vespasian and Titus. But it might well have happened that Josephus was particularly interested in the stratagem (indeed in the Greek text of the *Wars* he manifests a lively interest in the employment of various stratagems, e.g. at the siege of Jotapata); probably he was only given to understand later that its commemoration was not regarded favourably. The objection may well denote an idiosyncrasy of Vespasian, which Josephus did not know until he encountered it in this connection. Creed, op. cit., p. 284, significantly seeks to explain away the testimony of the passage in another way, namely by pointing out that in the Greek text Josephus shows that he knew that Vitellius was not present in person at the battle.

has shown that the existence of a certain situation is indubitably indicated by evidence of unquestionable value.

We may now consequently consider particularly the evidence of the Slavonic *Halosis* which concerns our subject in this chapter. The most striking feature of this is, of course, the fact that the chief significance of the career of the *Wonder-worker* and the subsequent activity of his followers is regarded as political. His work excites the popular desire for national emancipation from Rome, he is specially invited to lead an armed attempt to overthrow the Roman government, and he is finally executed as a rebel by Pilate after the forceful suppression of his followers. An effective number of his followers survive and continue to propagate his teaching, inspired by a belief in his return to life, and their movement reaches such proportions in the reign of Claudius, apparently mainly through their promise to the proletariat that their Master is able to free them from the Roman yoke, that the procurators have to take action to suppress them.

It is to be noted, however, that in both the passages concerned there is a curious lack of information about the attitude of the *Wonder-worker* himself to the political issue. The most explicit statement thereon seems to come in a sentence in which are described his reactions to the invitation to lead the insurrection at Jerusalem: Eisler translates the Slavonic here [1] as "*verachtete er uns nicht*" ("he did not disdain us"), and in his commentary on the words he interprets them to mean "as subjects: 'he did not disdain the kingship over us that was offered to him'".[2] Unfortunately this reading is by no means certain, and there is a variant of quite different import, namely, "*aber dieser beachtete (es) nicht*" ("he did not heed it"), which apparently has as good manuscript support as the reading preferred by Eisler.[3] Consequently the important question whether the *Wonder-worker* did or did not definitively commit himself to leading an armed revolt must remain undecided. But that his personality and his teaching stimulated nationalist fervour, and that his supporters did in consequence resort to arms against the Romans, there is no doubt.

From this rather involved discussion it would appear, therefore, that there is reason to think that Josephus regarded Christianity primarily as a revolutionary movement against the Roman domination of Palestine, akin to the many other similar movements which characterized Jewish national life during the period from the incorporation of Judæa into the Empire in A.D. 6 to the destruction of Jerusalem in A.D. 70. It may, of course, be objected that Josephus could not be expected to have given

---

[1] See Appendix II (1) (*c*) to this Chapter. Cf. Creed, *The Harvard Theological Review*, vol. xxv, p. 310. In a letter to the author Dr. Eisler cites parallel phrases in the *Monumentum Ancyranum* in which Augustus states that, in answer to some specific request, "I did not refuse", or "I did not neglect"—"obviously Roman rulers 'deigned' to do this or that". See also *Messiah Jesus*, p. 459, on a case of "*culpa lata*" ; *ΙΗΣΟΥΣ ΒΑΣΙΛΕΥΣ*, II, pp. 443, 447.

[2] *Messiah Jesus*, p. 458, n. 3.

[3] See Appendix II (1) (*b*) and (*c*). Cf. Eisler, op. cit., p. 117.

a fair account of Jesus and his followers, and there would be much reason in such an objection; but nevertheless for our purpose here there is very great significance in the fact that it is probable that the Jewish historian recognized Christianity primarily as a revolutionary movement against Rome, for it means that to an external and unsympathetic observer the new faith must have presented such features that he was led to depict it as political in inspiration and intent rather than under any other guise, and there are obviously several which could have been used effectively, if he had been concerned merely to malign Jesus and his followers.

There remain two fragments of possible evidence still to be considered. Taken chronologically, the former concerns the attitude of the Emperor Claudius to Christianity. In a recent study Professor Momigliano has given reason for believing that there can be discerned a progressive severity in the policy of Claudius towards the Jews, and that Christianity was the cause of the adoption of the harsher attitude; [1] to such a degree did the Emperor take cognizance of Christianity as a disturbing factor in the public peace that he published an edict designedly aimed against that movement in Palestine. Evidence of this Professor Momigliano finds in an inscription which was discovered at Nazareth in 1870 but which remained unknown until its publication by Fr. Cumont in 1930.[2] This διάταγμα decrees death as the penalty for the violation of tombs (τυμβωρυχία), thus evidently to prevent such acts from being repeated in that neighbourhood and, undoubtedly, elsewhere in the country. A measure against the violation of tombs in Palestine is naturally most suggestive, and Momigliano has interpreted it as evidence that Claudius, for whose reign he dates the inscription on grounds of internal evidence,[3] having heard in some form that Christianity was centred round a belief in the reappearance from the tomb of a dead man, in his policy of suppressing the new movement issued an edict in Palestine which was calculated, according to his view of the movement, to prevent any possibility of the recurrence of an act which, he believed, supplied its original impetus.

Such an interpretation in itself can obviously only be regarded as a particularly interesting suggestion. However, it is worth noting in connection with our present subject that the theory would provide very apt corroboration of the account of the revolutionary activity of the followers of the *Wonder-worker* in the Slavonic *Halosis*. There it is related, as we have seen, that in the time of Claudius the followers of the *Wonder-worker* had excited the Messianic expectations of the people by promising that

---

[1] *L'Opera dell'Imperatore Claudio*, pp. 66 *seq.*
[2] *L'Opera dell'Imperatore Claudio*, pp. 73–6. For the text of the inscription see Appendix III to this Chapter. A critical examination of the inscription is made by de Zulueta, *Journal of Roman Studies*, vol. xxii, pp. 184 *seq.* See the bibliography given by A. Piganiol, *Histoire de Rome*, p. 239.
[3] Op. cit., p. 73, n. 1. Cf. de Zulueta, *Journal of Roman Studies*, vol. xxii, pp. 186–7.

delivery would come to them from their Master, who "was alive, although he had been dead". It is not unreasonable, therefore, to suppose that one of the safeguarding measures taken by the Roman authorities, after their suppression of this threatening movement, was the edict (framed in terms of a vague knowledge of one of the sectaries' chief tenets) which aimed at preventing any recrudescence of a movement originating, as they might well have thought, in bogus allegations of a resurrection from the dead, consequent on some act of tomb violation.

The other piece of possible evidence is a passage in the fifth-century *Chronica* of Sulpicius Severus [1] in which it is related that, prior to the Roman assault on the Temple in the siege of A.D. 70, Titus, the Roman commander, called a staff conference to debate the fate of the Jewish sanctuary. Some members were of the opinion that the reputation of Rome would suffer if so celebrated an edifice were purposely destroyed, while others, including Titus, voted for its destruction on the ground that the Temple was the source of inspiration to both Judaism and Christianity. This account of the attitude of Titus decisively differs from the record of Josephus, who represents the prince as desirous of saving the sanctuary and as being shocked at its ultimate accidental burning.[2] Consequently there has been much debate about the source of the Christian chronicler's account here, and the suggestion has been strongly maintained that it was derived from the lost portion of the *Histories* of Tacitus.[3] Here again we have a problem which permits of no final solution until further documentary evidence is discovered. However, there are two factors in the problem, as it is at present placed, which suggest that the passage can aptly fit into the evidential pattern of Christian Origins which we have gradually been constructing.

When we remember the popularity of the works of Josephus with Christians, it is indeed strange to find a Christian writer giving an account of a secular event such as this of the deliberations of the Romans on the fate of the Jewish Temple, and flagrantly contradicting the long and emphasized record of the Jewish historian. It would accordingly be far more reasonable to think that this divergence from a standard authority is to be explained as being due to the chronicler's following of a completely independent source of information, and obviously one of considerable prestige in his eyes since he preferred it to that of Josephus. Then there is the significant fact that in the passage the Temple is regarded as an object of equal concern to both Jews and Christians, so that the religions

---

[1] In *Patr. Lat.*, ed. Migne, t. xx; see Appendix IV to this chapter. Cf. Orosius, *Hist.*, vii. 9 (*Patr. Lat.*, ed. Migne, t. xxxi, 479).

[2] Jos., *Wars*, vi. 4. 3, 5–7 (236–243, 250–266). Cf. Schlatter, *Geschichte Israels*, p. 334.

[3] See the account of the debate in Schürer, *G.J.V.*, I, p. 631, n. 115. Cf. Thackeray, *Josephus: the Man and the Historian*, p. 37; Loeb, *Josephus*, vol. ii, p. xxv; Ramsay, *Church in the Roman Empire*, pp. 254–5; Milman, *Hist. of the Jews*, vol. ii, p. 90, n. 1; Morrison, *Jews under Roman Rule*, p. 176, n. 1; Mommsen, *Provinces of Roman Empire*, vol. ii, p. 217, n. 1; Momigliano, *Camb. Anc. Hist.*, vol. x, p. 862, n. 1; Streeter, *Camb. Anc. Hist.*, vol. xi, pp. 254–5; Eisler, *Messiah Jesus*, pp. 552, 554; Ricciotti, *Flavio Giuseppe*, vol. i, pp. 86–8.

of both would be equally adversely affected by its destruction.[1]   Now in view of the prominence which is given in the Gospels to Christ's prophecy of the destruction of the Temple, it is scarcely believable that a Christian writer of the fifth century should have been so unmindful of this that he invented an account in which the preservation of the Temple was represented as being of essential concern to Christianity.

In consideration of these facts it would seem that any attempt to explain the passage as solely a Christian composition is not adequate, and that it is necessary to predicate some non-Christian source of sufficient reputation to commend itself to an author who was writing for an educated public.[2] Hence we have reason for seeing here a further possible item of evidence of the involvement of Jewish Christianity in the cause of Jewish nationalism.   Titus, clearly regarding Christianity as of Jewish origin, as did Tacitus, saw it also as a movement of political significance in Palestine, and he thought that it would suffer equally with the parent faith of Judaism, if the Temple were overthrown.

We therefore emerge finally from this complicated study of the attitude of the Palestinian Christians to the cause of Israel's freedom from the yoke of heathen Rome with the conviction that the extant literary evidence unmistakably shows that that attitude was generally one of very close and sometimes active sympathy, and so the appreciation of it accordingly constitutes a factor of the utmost importance in our understanding of the nature of Christian Origins.

APPENDIX I

On the alleged references to the revolutionary activity of the primitive Jewish Christians in the Hebrew Josippon

Dr. Eisler has claimed that in the mediæval Hebrew translation of Josephus, known as the *Josippon*, there are several important references to the revolutionary activity of the followers of Jesus in Palestine.[3]   The case upon which the claim is advanced is briefly as follows.   From the Latin translation of Josephus, made about 370 by Hilarius or Gaudentius, a converted Jew, some centuries later another converted Jew made a Hebrew translation.   In the ninth century this Hebrew translation, the *Josippon*, was worked over by some Jews in the interests of Judaism.   In this revision they used a Greek MS. of Josephus, which had apparently escaped the Christian censorship which has falsified all the existing Greek versions, thus presumably rendering the *Josippon* nearer the unexpurgated original.   However, the various mediæval versions of this revised *Josippon* were sought out by the ecclesiastical censors and their offending passages deleted to a more or less complete degree.   But a failure

---

[1] It is interesting to compare the statement of Tacitus, *Ann.*, xv. 44, about Christianity: "*rursum erumpebat, non modo per Judaeam, originem eius mali,* . . ." with the words of Sulpicius Severus that "*Christianos ex Judaeis exstitisse*".   The tendency to place an essential emphasis upon the Jewish origin of Christianity is clear.

[2] Cf. P. de Labriolle, *History and Literature of Christianity*, p. 382.

[3] *Messiah Jesus*, chap. vi ; *ΙΗΣΟΥΣ ΒΑΣΙΛΕΥΣ*, I, pp. 461–519.

to be absolutely thorough on the part of some censors in three different manuscripts permits of the reconstruction of a passage in which the followers of Jesus are described as the "robbers of our people" and are depicted as fighting against the Pharisees during the time of the Emperor Gaius. This apparent identification of the followers of Jesus then enables another to be made, by "a transparent allusion (in the usual rabbinical way) to the prophecy of Daniel 11. 14: 'and in those days many shall stand up against the king of the South, also the children of the bandits among thy people (*pārişej 'amekha*) shall rebel in order to realize the vision, but they shall stumble'". Eisler interprets "the king of the South" to mean Agrippa, who was descended from the Idumæan Herod, and in "the transparent allusion" to the prophecy of Daniel 11. 14 he sees evidence that the Danielic prophecy of "the abomination of desolation" was instrumental in causing a rising of the Christian Messianists against the sacrilegious attempt of Caligula to place his image in the Temple.

The series of consequential hypotheses involved here naturally renders such an interpretation essentially a speculation, interesting and ingenious, but clearly incapable of acceptance as a probability. The *Josippon* has, however, a certain relevancy for us here in that it is certain that Christian censors removed from it passages which they regarded as offensive to Christian doctrine, and some of those passages apparently contained accounts of the primitive Jewish Christians as political revolutionaries.[1] Consequently, considering the many various lines that Jewish anti-Christian propaganda could have taken, it is significant that the one chosen was that of presenting Christian Origins in the guise of a Jewish political movement against heathen Rome, which after all was also an object of deep hatred for orthodox Jews.

APPENDIX II

Relevant extracts from the Slavonic Josephus

(1) On the invitation made to the *Wonder-worker* to lead the insurrection at Jerusalem:

(*a*) From A. Berendts, *Die Zeugnisse vom Christentum im slavischen "De Bello Judaico" des Josephus*, p. 9:

"*Da sie aber sahen seine Macht, dass er alles, was er wolle, ausführe durchs Wort, so befahlen sie ihm, dass er einziehe in die Stadt und die römischen Krieger (Acad. alles Römische) und den Pilatus niederhaue und über sie (Syn. uns) herrsche. Aber jener verschmähte es.*" This translation was made from Cod. Mosqu. Acad. 651, f. 47 v., and Cod. Synod. 770, fol. 70 v *seq*.

(*b*) From A. Berendts und K. Grass, *Flavius Josephus vom Jüdischen Kriege, Buch i–iv*. This was the posthumous work of Berendts and was edited for publication by Grass in 1926. The extract is taken from p. 269:

---

[1] Eisler's theory rests upon his assumption that the words בן יוסף in the *editio princeps* of R. Abraham Conat (printed at Mantua *ante* 1470) refer to Jesus (*Messiah Jesus*, pp. 96 *seq*., Pl. ix). These words are followed by the abbreviation וכו' (= etc.), which indicates that something compromising has been omitted. Jack, *Historic Christ*, pp. 181–2, argues against this and cites another MS. of the *Josippon* in the Bibliothèque Nationale, Paris, dated for 1472 (see Eisler, op. cit., Pl. x), which in the parallel passage speaks of "Jeshua ben Pandara, the Nasoræan, who did great miracles in Israel"; this he believes is the earlier and preferable reading, and he explains that in the printed *editio princeps* as a corruption of this reading; hence he argues that the passage has no historical value, since it places Jesus in the reign of Caligula. But such a corruption is impossible when the two sets of words are compared in the Hebrew, and further the abbreviation וכו', followed by a blank, is significant. Cf. Eisler, *ΙΗΣΟΥΣ ΒΑΣΙΛΕΥΣ*, I, pp. 476 *seq*., Tafeln I, IA, LII.

"*Da sie aber seine Kraft sahen, dass er alles, so viel er wolle, durch(s) Wort vollbringe, und da sie ihm ihren Wille kundtaten, dass er in die Stadt hereinkomme und niedermache die römischen Truppen und den Pilatus und herrsche über uns, verachtete er uns nicht(?).*" Note 14, giving the authority for the reading adopted in the last clause, reads: "*Acad. Sy.* 770, 991. *Kas: 'aber dieser beachtete (es) nicht'.*"

(*c*) Eisler gives the crucial sentence as follows in his *ΙΗΣΟΥΣ ΒΑΣΙΛΕΥΣ ΟΥ ΒΑΣΙΛΕΥΣΑΣ*, Bd. ii, p. 298:

"*dass er in die Stadt einziehe und niedermache die römischen Truppen und den Pilatus und herrsche über uns, verachtete er uns nicht . . .*" Note 13, giving the authority for the reading preferred in the last clause, reads: "*Acad. Sy.* 770, 991. *Kas: 'aber dieser beachtete (es) nicht'. nt. h.* οὐ κατεφρόνησεν ἡμᾶς = *nas' ne nebreza. Rumän. 'sein Sinn war aber nicht darauf gerichtet'.*"

(2) On the revolutionary activity of the followers of the *Wonder-worker* in the time of Claudius: Berendts und Grass, op. cit., p. 279:

"*Und da zur Zeit jener viele Anhänger des vorherbeschriebenen Wundertäters erschienen waren und zu dem Volk redeten von ihrem Meister . . . 'Der wird euch von der Knechtschaft befreien'. Diese edlen Prokuratoren aber, da sie die Abwendung des Volkes sahen, beschlossen zusammen mit den Schriftgelehrten (sie) zu ergreifen und zu töten, damit das Kleine nicht klein sei, wenn es sich im Grossen vollendet hat. . . . Darnach aber, von ihnen veranlasst (?), entliessen sie sie, die einen zum Kaiser, die andern aber nach Antiochien, andere über in ferne Länder, zur Erprobung der Sache.*"

APPENDIX III

The presumed edict of Claudius against the violation of tombs in Palestine

The text as given by M. P. Charlesworth, *Documents illustrating the Reigns of Claudius and Nero* (Cambridge University Press, 1939), p. 15, No. 17:

Διάταγμα Καίσαρος.

Ἀρέσκει μοι τάφους τύμβους τε, οἵτινες εἰς θρησκείαν προγόνων ἐποίησαν ἢ τέκνων ἢ οἰκείων, τούτους μένειν ἀμετακινήτους τὸν αἰῶνα. ἐὰν δέ τις ἐπιδείξῃ τινὰ ἢ καταλελυκότα ἢ ἄλλῳ τινὶ τρόπῳ τοὺς κεκηδευμένους ἐξερριφότα ἢ εἰς ἑτέρους τόπους δόλῳ πονηρῷ μετατεθεικότα ἐπ' ἀδικίᾳ τῇ τῶν κεκηδευμένων ἢ κατόχους ἢ λίθους μετατεθεικότα, κατὰ τοῦ τοιούτου κριτήριον ἐγὼ κελεύω γενέσθαι καθάπερ περὶ θεῶν εἰς τὰς τῶν ἀνθρώπων θρησκείας· πολὺ γὰρ μᾶλλον δεήσει τοὺς κεκηδευμένους τιμᾶν. καθόλου μηδενὶ ἐξέστω μετακινῆσαι· εἰ δὲ μή, τοῦτον ἐγὼ κεφαλῆς κατάκριτον ὀνόματι τυμβωρυχίας θέλω γενέσθαι.

"*Dalle de marbre envoyée de Nazareth en 1878.*" Published by Fr. Cumont in *Rev. Hist.*, clxiii, 1930, pp. 241 ff.

APPENDIX IV

Sulpicius Severus on the destruction of the Temple

Chronica or *Historia Sacra*, Lib. ii, c. xxx, in *Patrologia Latina*, ed. Migne, t. xx:

"*Fertur Titus adhibito consilio prius deliberasse, an templum tanti operis everteret: etenim nonnullis videbatur, aedem sacratam, ultra omnia mortalia illustrem, non debere deleri: quae servata modestiae Romanae testimonium, diruta perennem crudelitatis notam praeberet. At contra alii, et Titus ipse, evertendum templum in primis censebant, quo plenius Judaeorum et Christianorum religio tolleretur, quippe has religiones, licet contrarias sibi, iisdem tamen auctoribus profectas; Christianos ex Judaeis exstitisse; radice sublata stirpem facile perituram.*"

APPENDIX V

The Johannine evidence of a political element in Christian Origins

Critical opinion about the Fourth Gospel and its sources still continues to be conflicting, so that it would be unwise to seek to use Johannine testimony as a primary source of information on a specifically historical problem such as that of the attitude of Jesus and the first Christians to the nationalist cause. However, the Johannine material has a real historical value in showing what views were current about Christian Origins in the sub-Apostolic age, for such views are likely to have been conditioned either by a known tradition or by theological interests.

There are two passages in the Gospel of John which, considered in this light, have a great significance for our present subject.   The first is the statement in 6. 15 that, in consequence of the great impression made upon the people by his miracles, "Jesus therefore perceiving that they were about to come and take him by force, to make him king, withdrew again into the mountain himself alone".   The parallel which this passage constitutes to that of the Slavonic *Halosis* about the *Wonder-worker* is most striking.   In both cases the miraculous deeds stir the people to a state of great excitement, which has an essentially political aspect.   In the Johannine account the use of ἁρπάζειν and the consequent action of Jesus clearly show that he did not wish to become involved in such an issue.   However, the significance of the occasion abides, namely that according to this passage in John's Gospel the career of Jesus provoked political excitement which obviously expressed itself in terms of the current Messianic expectations.

The second passage, 11. 47–51, is of similar import, but the political significance is even more clearly set forth.   Herein we are told that "The chief priests therefore and the Pharisees gathered a council, and said, What do we? for this man doeth many signs.   If we let him thus alone, all men will believe on him: and the Romans will come and take away both our place and our nation.   But a certain one of them, Caiaphas, being high priest that year, said unto them, Ye know nothing at all, nor do ye take account that it is expedient for you that one man should die for the people, and that the whole nation perish not.   Now this he said not of himself: but being high priest that year, he prophesied that Jesus should die for the nation; . . ."

Again the resemblance to certain points of the relevant account of the Slavonic *Halosis* is very remarkable.   Also the importance of the fact that a consciousness is here clearly revealed of the Sadducean aristocracy's view of the danger which Jesus constituted must be fully noted.   The effect of the deeds of Jesus is seen as having only a political relevancy, and nothing is said of his mission being a challenge to the moral prestige of the sacerdotal class, or of his claims being a blasphemous offence to the principles of Judaism. And with this presentation the Johannine account of the Trial of Jesus is in notable agreement (18. 19, 29, 30, 33, 34, 37).   The theme which runs throughout the examination of Jesus by Pilate is that of the kingship of Jesus, and in the Jewish argument to secure his condemnation from the procurator the quintessence of the issue is bluntly expressed: "every one that maketh himself a king speaketh against Cæsar"; with the corollary, which is also a comment on the Sadducean policy: "The chief priests answered, We have no king but Cæsar" (19. 12, 15, 16).

It has been stated above that the presentation of Christian Origins in the sub-Apostolic age is likely to have been conditioned either by tradition or by theological interest.   We have then to face the question which of these forces was probably operative in the composition of that part of the Johannine picture with which we are concerned here. The question has really only to be formulated for the answer to become at once apparent, namely that such a representation cannot have served any known theological purpose and must accordingly conform to some inherited tradition of Christian Origins.

We may conclude, therefore, that the part of the sub-Apostolic Church of which the Johannine writings are representative had inherited a tradition which shows remarkable agreement with the evidence we have deduced from the relevant New Testament documents and other sources to the effect that in its origins the movement which was initiated by Jesus of Nazareth was invested with an essentially political aspect, expressive of Jewish nationalist aspirations to be rid of the yoke of heathen Rome.[1]

[1] It may also be noted here that the interesting suggestion has been made by Knox, *Some Hellenistic Elements*, p. 26, n. 1, that the comparison made between Jesus and Joshua in the Epistle to the Hebrews may represent a feature of the very early Christology of the Jewish Church, which was abandoned owing to its awkward associations with the many false Christs of Jewish national life. That Jesus might thus have been regarded as a kind of Joshua *redivivus* would correspond well with the other evidence which has been examined in this chapter. In a letter to the author Dr. R. Eisler has drawn his attention to the possible political significance of "the originally pejorative Antiochene term 'Christianoi'" (Acts 11. 26), comparing it with such terms as "Herodianoi", "Cæsariani", "Antoniani", "Pompeiani". Cf. *B.C.*, vol. iv, p. 130 *sub voce*, vol. v, pp. 383–6; Eisler, *ΙΗΣΟΥΣ ΒΑΣΙΛΕΥΣ*, Bd. ii, p. 435, n. 1.

7

The Crisis of A.D. *55 to 66*

IT would appear that the author of the Acts of the Apostles was conscious of the proportions of the task which he had set himself in undertaking to relate the origins of the Christian Church—the task of explaining how what was at first essentially a Jewish movement in a very limited field became a religion of universal validity, established throughout one of the most important areas of the world of Græco-Roman culture. On *a priori* consideration such a process of metamorphosis clearly presupposes the operation of many diverse forces in thesis and antithesis until the final synthesis was achieved, and it is consequently reasonable to expect that much conflict of opinion and clash of personalities, perhaps involving some fundamental matters, ensued and constituted vital factors in influencing the course of this evolution. But similar preliminary reflection also raises the question of how far complete frankness and objective description can be expected from a Christian author who, many years after the events which he purports to describe, is writing for the instruction and edification of a Christian patron.[1] And if to the implied negative conclusion it be objected that reference to the actual work will provide a striking example of the author's frankness in his account of the quarrel which led to the separation of Paul and Barnabas,[2] it may be countered that his treatment of this very incident is suspect, if comparison be made with what Paul himself tells of the circumstances of his estrangement from Barnabas.[3] Consequently, in view of his didactic or apologetical purpose, it may fairly be inferred that the author of Acts is not likely to have gratuitously presented either his Christian readers with a painfully realistic account of bygone controversies between the now sainted dead, or his pagan readers, if there chanced to be any, with opportunities for derision. Moreover, on the other hand, the picture which he draws of the development of Christianity, in its various phases and details, may reasonably be taken to represent the most favourable aspect which he could give to the traditions with which he had to deal.

With these qualifications in mind, we must now turn to survey the account which the Acts gives of the progress of the Christian movement. One of the first most noticeable features is that the process of evolution

---

[1] Luke 1. 1–4; Acts 1. 1 ff. Cf. *B.C.*, vol. ii, pp. 507–10. If Theophilus was not a catechumen but an influential non-Christian, as Cadbury here suggests, the influence of the apologetic factor would, if anything, be even greater.
[2] Acts 15. 36–40.   [3] See below, p. 132.

clearly divides into two distinct stages, namely that of the expansion of
Christianity in Palestine and that of its subsequent extension throughout
the Levant. The record of the former is mainly made up of a series of
stories in which Peter figures as the hero; the inadequacy of this account,
especially in the matter of its serious failure to explain the emergence of
James to leadership of the Church, has been already noted and discussed.
The record of the second phase is equally unsatisfactory, since it comprises
almost entirely an account of the exploits and fortunes of Paul. Between
these two quite distinct stages, or rather cycles of stories, comes the account
of Stephen and his martyrdom, which the author obviously employs as
a bridge to carry over the continuity of his theme from the earlier to the
later phase.[1]

This means in effect that the author of the Acts saw the transition from
the Palestinian stage of the Christian movement to what might be termed
the universalist stage in the rise of a party at Jerusalem which was anti-
Judaic and from which subsequently came forth the first champions of
Christianity as a universal religion.[2] But this presentation of the course
of Christianity at what was clearly one of its most vital turning-points is
obviously inadequate and itself poses several very serious questions. The
first is prompted by the speech which is put into Stephen's mouth during
his trial before the Sanhedrin, and which may reasonably be regarded
as expressing what the Lukan writer held to be the characteristic teaching
of this new party.[3] In this speech a most virulent attack is made on the
Jewish people for what is regarded as their continual spiritual obduracy,
and the Temple is singled out for particular condemnation. Now in all
that we otherwise know from the earliest New Testament sources, as we
have already seen, there had been no repudiation of the Temple cultus
either by Jesus or by his original followers; indeed the evidence is all to
the contrary: the primitive community of disciples at Jerusalem remained
devout and zealous Jews, the Temple being their regular place of worship.
Consequently the question arises of the origin of this new anti-Judaic
attitude, of which Stephen is made the first distinguished representative.
For our understanding of Christian Origins, as they are presented in the
Acts, the answer to this question is of fundamental importance, but the
Lukan writer appears to be quite oblivious of it and offers not the slightest
piece of explanation. The unsatisfactory treatment of this particular
point is paralleled by a similar inadequacy on other related matters.
While the names of the seven Deacons are suggestive of the existence of
an extraneous element in the Palestinian Church, an obvious problem
lies in the fact that the two most notable of these new officers, namely
Stephen and Philip, are never described as fulfilling the duties of the
office to which they had been specifically appointed, but, strangely, they

---

[1] Cf. *B.C.*, vol. ii, pp. 122 *seq.*   [2] Acts 6. 1–8. 4; 11. 19–21.
[3] Acts 7. 1–53. Cf. Meyer, *Ursprung und Anfänge des Christentums*, III, pp. 159–61; *B.C.*, vol.
iv, pp. 69–70; Goguel, *La Naissance du Christianisme*, pp. 195–8.

occupy themselves effectively in the quite different work of evangelization, which, it is stated, was the function which the Apostles had specially
reserved to themselves.[1]   Then the information that the Apostles were
excepted from the persecution which was provoked against the Church
consequent on the martyrdom of Stephen raises several natural and
pertinent questions, to which no answer is provided by Luke.   These
omissions or inadequacies accordingly justify a feeling of serious doubt
about whether the whole episode of Stephen, if based on some original
substratum of fact, has not been so tendentiously fabricated by the Lukan
writer that we cannot safely place our confidence in its record beyond
concluding that he believed it to be necessary and plausible to trace
the origins of an interpretation of Christianity as a religion of universal
validity, with its concomitant anti-Judaic bias, to the Palestinian period
of the evolution of the faith.   However, a more positive inference can
also be made therefrom, namely that even the author of Acts admits
that the rise of the party which propagated these views originated in some
form of controversy with the original Hebrew community, that that
community remained at least aloof from the activity of the new party,
and that the members of that community were clearly recognized by
their fellow-countrymen as effectively different when efforts were made
to suppress the subversive teaching of Stephen and his followers.[2]

The unsatisfactory presentation of the Stephen episode is unfortunately
matched by the similar treatment given to the conversion of the Samaritans.[3]   The serious nature of the step taken in admitting the Samaritan
heretics to fellowship in the new faith must have been obvious and disturbing to all loyal Jews,[4] and Luke shows ample evidence in his Gospel that
he was alive to the significance of Jewish antipathy to the Samaritans.[5]
His failure, therefore, to comment upon so notable a precedent as that
of Philip's evangelization of Samaria is truly surprising, and it tends to
suggest that he did not find it convenient to draw the attention of his
readers to the nature of the issue involved, or to the way in which the
problem was solved.   However, it is to be noted that even so Luke was
obliged to record that Philip's work was investigated by two of the leaders
of the Jerusalem Church and that steps were taken by them to remedy
some defect which was still deemed to exist in the Samaritans' membership of the Church after their baptism by Philip.

According to the record of the Acts, the logic of the events initiated by
the career of Stephen ended in the preaching of the gospel to the Gentiles
by some of his followers.[6]   But before this culminating act is reached the

---

[1] Acts 6. 1–6, 8, 9; 8. 5–40.   Cf. Meyer, op. cit., III, p. 154–5; Guignebert, *Le Christ*, pp.
76–81; Goguel, op. cit., p. 193.
[2] See Chapter Six , p. 89, n. 2.   [3] Acts 8. 4–25.
[4] Cf. Jos., *Wars*, ii. 12. 3–4 (232–5), *Ant.*, xviii. 2. 2, xx. 6. 1–3; Matt. 10. 5; John 4. 9, 20–22;
8. 48.   Cf. M. Gaster, *The Samaritans*, pp. 36–7; Klausner, *From Jesus to Paul*, p. 295; Knox,
Jerusalem, p. 68.
[5] Luke 9. 52, 53; 10. 33–36; 17. 11–19.
[6] Acts 11. 19, 20.

story of Peter's missionary exploits is inserted.[1] This Petrine episode ends with the great Apostle's acceptance of the Gentile Cornelius and his friends into the Church and his consequent defence, when his action was hotly contested at Jerusalem by them "that were of the circumcision", that he was led to this departure from the established policy by divine prompting. This presentation of the course of events by the author of Acts means that Peter is accordingly depicted as the apostolic authority who created the far-reaching precedent of admitting Gentiles into the privileges of the Church. Whether or not the story of Cornelius' conversion is a record of fact, and in view of Peter's earlier conduct at Antioch according to Paul [2] it may well be substantially true, its real significance for us lies in the fact that Luke, in thus using it as a prelude to the subsequent evangelization of the Gentiles at Antioch, was well aware of the crucial nature of the latter event and realized that it did constitute a very serious departure from what had been the policy of the primitive community of believers. Moreover, full weight must be given to the fact that it had to be recorded that even Peter, with all the prestige of his reputation, was strongly challenged in his action by at least some of the Christians of Jerusalem.

The Palestinian stage of the Church's development is thus shown to end with the emergence of a party which, instead of being a natural product of the original disciples' faith and experience, appears to be distinct to such a degree that even the persecutors of Stephen, in all the fury of their fanaticism, did not fail to distinguish it from the community of the primitive disciples. Further, it is evident that from the beginning there was antagonism between these two bodies of Christians and that it continued to be accentuated by the liberalizing policy adopted by the one and the reaction thereto of the other, which at first condemned, and then later sought to control, the resulting admission of Gentiles into the Church.

The first strand of the theme of the second part of the narrative of Acts appears interwoven with the Stephen episode, which serves, as we have just noticed, to bridge the gap between the two distinct cycles of tradition from which Luke constructs his account of Christian Origins. This strand first appears in the depicting of Paul, as a young man, participating in the killing of Stephen.[3] The nature of Paul's participation is singularly passive and artificial, and, as we have seen, there is good reason for doubting its historicity. However, it has an important function in the narrative of the Acts, being clearly employed to introduce the portrait of Paul as the most notorious persecutor of the Church,[4] and thereby to render more dramatic his conversion on the road to Damascus —a presentation which, as we have also seen, can scarcely be accurate so far as its location of Paul's persecuting activity in Palestine is concerned.

---

[1] Acts 9. 32–11. 18.
[2] Gal. 2. 12.

[3] Acts 7. 58b; 8. 1.
[4] Acts 8. 3; 9. 1 ff.

From this point in the narrative the record of the progress of Christianity is almost completely unfolded in terms of a biography of Paul down to the time of his coming as a prisoner to Rome.

This remarkable feature of Acts, with its consequent neglect of the achievements of other Christian missionaries elsewhere in the Roman Empire, naturally provokes the question of its cause. That others had preceded Paul in carrying the gospel out into the Gentile world, most notably to Alexandria and Rome, is certain, so that the inference appears to be necessary that Paul's pre-eminence was not due to his priority in time in the Christian mission field, but to the significance of his personality and teaching, and to this indeed the survival of so much of his writings, in comparison with those of other leaders, eloquently witnesses.[1]

If the author of Acts was justified to this degree in presenting the story of the progress of Christianity outside Palestine in the form of a biography of Paul, he unfortunately fails to give us any specific explanation of the factors which led to his becoming the supreme champion of Gentile Christianity. He does indeed account for the origin of Paul's mission to the Gentiles in terms of a divine vision in the Temple,[2] but this scarcely appears satisfactory to the modern instinct to seek for psychological pre-dispositions, and the only, unconsciously given, clue in this direction is the casual statement that Paul was a native of Tarsus, which was an important centre of Hellenistic culture.[3] However, despite this failure to explain what in Paul's antecedents predisposed him on his conversion to direct his energies to the winning of the Gentiles to faith in Christ, the author of the Acts quite clearly believed that the effective progress of Christianity in the world of Græco-Roman culture was the work of one whose antecedents were notoriously different from those of the original Christian leaders and who stood apart from them by virtue of both his past history and his present activity.

This serious cleavage in the Church, which is apparent even through the apologetically inspired narrative of the Acts, soon produces an inevitable crisis. After the success of the mission of Paul and Barnabas in the provinces of Asia Minor, it is recorded that, first, at Antioch members of the Jerusalem Church arrived and began to assert that acceptance of Mosaic circumcision was an essential condition for salvation, and then in Jerusalem itself the delegation from the Antiochene Church, headed by Paul and Barnabas, which was sent to deal directly with the recognized authorities about the matter, encountered a similar contention from those who are described as "certain of the sect of the Pharisees who believed".[4] Luke then goes on to relate how this question was settled in a general council of "the apostles and elders", at which Paul and Barnabas were present, and over which, without any explanation, James is clearly represented as

---

[1] Cf. Meyer, *Ursprung und Anfänge des Christentums*, III, p. 583.
[2] Acts 22. 17–21. Cf. 26. 16–18; 9. 15.
[3] Acts 9. 11, 30; 11. 25; 21. 39; 22. 3.
[4] Acts 15. 1, 2, 4, 5. Cf. *B.C.*, vol. iv, p. 169 loc. cit.

presiding.[1]   The proceedings of the Council, on Luke's showing, were of
a most edifying character, for, after hearing first a speech from Peter in
which, alluding to his own action in the case of Cornelius, he propounded
a view which is indistinguishable from that expressed on the point at issue
in Paul's Epistles, and then a recital of the success of their Gentile mission
from Paul and Barnabas, James pronounced his judgement, which appears
to have been definitive for the rest of the Council.   According to this
judgement, and the letter in which it was subsequently embodied for
publication among the Gentiles, the latter were completely emancipated
from any requirement to observe the Mosaic Law, and there was only
demanded of them the keeping of certain rules concerning some elementary
moral principles and some specific dietary prohibitions.[2]   Moreover, the
action of those Jews who had originally raised the issue at Antioch is
specially condemned, and Paul and Barnabas are praised for their Christian
witness.[3]

Taken at its face value, Luke's record shows that there was a serious
crisis in the life of the Church over the question of the essentiality of the
observance of the Mosaic Law for Gentile converts to the faith and that
the issue was decisively solved in favour of Gentile freedom at a specially
convoked and amicably conducted council of the Church's leaders in
Jerusalem, the chief champions of the liberal policy, besides Paul and
Barnabas, being Peter and James ; moreover, the advocates of the Jewish
rigorist policy are represented as being merely a section of the Jerusalem
Christians, and as being specifically repudiated in the encyclical issued
by the Council.

As is well known, this Lukan record of the so-called Council of Jerusalem, by reason of its intractable discrepancies when compared with the
evidence of Paul's Epistles, has created a *locus classicus* of New Testament
debate.[4]   However justified or not may be the ingenious attempts of
certain scholars to reconcile Luke's account of the transactions at Jerusalem
with what Paul tells of his visits to the city in the Galatian Epistle, the
stubborn fact remains that nowhere in his writings does Paul appeal to
the decisions of such a Council, which were clearly so completely in his
favour, nor indeed does he ever appear in the slightest allusion or reference
to be conscious of their existence.   But for the moment we will leave the
problem of this conflict between Pauline and Lukan evidence and notice
certain discrepancies in Luke's own account.

The matter is first introduced by relating how certain men from Judæa

---

[1] Acts 15. 6–29.

[2] Cf. *B.C.*, vol. v, pp. 205–8; Lietzmann, *Gesch. der alt. Kirche*, I, p. 107; Nock, *St. Paul*,
pp. 116, 117.

[3] Acts 15. 24–26.

[4] See Note 16 in *B.C.*, vol. v.   The recent attempt of W. L. Knox, *The Acts of the Apostles*
(1948), pp. 40–53, to defend the historicity of the Council is necessarily founded upon his
assumptions that the famine-visit is to be identified with that recorded in Gal. 2. 1–14 and
that Peter was subsequently reconciled to Paul and supported him.   The weakness of these
assumptions is evident from our discussion in the text of the issues involved.

had come to Antioch and asserted the need of circumcision as an essential to salvation. And when the Antiochene delegates had reached Jerusalem and had made their first report of the success of their Gentile mission to the Apostles and Elders, they then encountered certain Christian Pharisees who similarly maintained the essentiality of circumcision and the observance of the Mosaic Law. However, in the encyclical embodying the Council's decisions, the representatives of the policy of subjecting the Gentile converts to the ritual requirements of Judaism are depicted as "certain which went out from us . . . to whom we gave no commandment", while the fact that a notable body of Pharisaic Christians existed in Jerusalem itself and had voiced the same demand is completely ignored. Moreover, it would appear that in the Council itself either these Pharisaic Christians were not represented or their statement of their case was dismissed by Luke as merely "much questioning". Then the decrees of the Council are rather curious, because, while the chief point at issue had been that of circumcision, in them no specific mention is made of it and they are concerned, after a slight general preamble, with regulations which might possibly be regarded as provisions to enable social intercourse to exist between the Jewish and Gentile members of the new faith,[1] although the two moral principles for which they demand observance are strangely elementary.

The sequel to the account of the Council is also rather curious, when reference is made to the Galatian Epistle on what appears to be the same, or at least a very similar, incident. According to Paul, after a joint visit of Barnabas and himself to Jerusalem, on their return to Antioch, a situation was caused there by emissaries of James, on the question of social intercourse between Jewish and Gentile Christians, which resulted in Barnabas' seceding from the Pauline position on this point.[2] Luke, on the other hand, tells of a break in this missionary partnership shortly after the return from Jerusalem to Antioch, owing to the violent dispute about taking John Mark on their next journey.[3] It has to be noted that, even though such a quarrel between the revered leaders must have been an unedifying spectacle for Luke's readers to contemplate, yet such a cause of the separation of Paul and Barnabas is far less serious than that which Paul himself gives for the latter's defection in his letter to the Galatian Christians.

Having thus shown how an issue which might conceivably have led to bitter controversy and have had serious repercussions for the stability of the Church had been so amicably and definitively settled, Luke then allows the fortunes of the Jerusalem Church to pass from the record of his narrative, and he concentrates his attention instead on Paul, with whom it seems that he now regarded the true life and destiny of the Church to rest from this point. The great Apostle appears to have no important

[1] Cf. G. Kittel, *Z.N.T.W.* (1931), pp. 147–8, 150.
[2] Gal. 2. 11–13.   [3] Acts 15. 36–40.

connections with the primitive source and centre of the movement, and only one apparently quite uneventful visit there by him is briefly recorded before his final visit,[1] which resulted in his arrest and imprisonment. It is in his record of this last visit that Luke again gives ground for very serious doubt about the true nature of the transactions which he purports to relate, and the impression which he gives is that of one who has awkward facts to recount, but does his best, without too overt distortion, to maintain the edifying theme of his work.

The first mention of the fatal journey is given when it is told that "Paul purposed in the spirit, when he had passed through Macedonia and Achaia, to go to Jerusalem, saying, After I have been there, I must also see Rome".[2] No motive is assigned to Paul's intention;[3] whether the reference to Rome is to be understood as a kind of prophecy in the light of the sequel, or expresses an original and natural desire of the Apostle is perhaps equally doubtful. The second mention of the proposed journey occurs in the curious statement that Paul was prevented from sailing, apparently directly, to Syria from Greece by a Jewish plot against him.[4] The narrative proper of the journey emerges with the strange note that Paul decided to by-pass Ephesus, because he was in haste to reach Jerusalem by Pentecost.[5] Then is related Paul's speech to the elders of the Ephesian Church, specially summoned to meet him at Miletus.[6] The significance of the statements of this speech is immense, especially when it is remembered that they are written by one who knew what had happened finally to Paul and his work. The first point to be noticed is the general apologetic tone of the speech; for some unexplained reason Paul is on the defensive, for, after asserting his zeal for the ministry, he makes the surprising attestation: "I testify unto you this day, that I am pure from the blood of all men. For I shrank not from declaring unto you the whole counsel of God." Then follows the highly suggestive warning that great personal vigilance is needed, because "I know that after my departing grievous wolves shall enter in among you, not sparing the flock; and from among your own selves shall men arise, speaking perverse things, to draw away the disciples after them". The third striking feature is the foreboding of ill: Paul is made to say, "And now, behold, I go bound in the spirit unto Jerusalem, not knowing the things that shall befall me there: save that the Holy Ghost testifieth unto me in every city, saying that bonds and afflictions abide me. But I hold not my life of any account, as dear unto myself, so that I may accomplish my course, and the ministry which I received from the Lord Jesus, to testify the gospel of the grace of God." We are thus in this speech presented with a truly amazing situation, to which Luke's account of Paul's fortunes up to this point fails to correspond. We see the great Apostle undertaking

---

[1] Acts 18. 22.   [2] Acts 19. 21.
[3] In his speech before Felix Paul is made to give as his reason for visiting Jerusalem the bringing of alms to his nation (Acts 27. 17); cf. Goguel, *La Naissance du Christianisme*, p. 536, n. 4.
[4] Acts 20. 3.   [5] Acts 20. 16.   [6] Acts 20. 17–38.

a journey to Jerusalem, despite the warning of the Holy Spirit, to whose admonitions he had been so attentive in the past, that suffering and even death awaited him there. His own outlook is most pessimistic, for he tells his converts that they would behold his face no more and foretells the troubles which are to come to them when his presence is removed. And yet so fully aware as he is of the perils of his proposed visit to the Jewish metropolis and of the ill consequences which will ensue for his converts, he still persists in going forward. Luke gives no reason for his journey, but all that he tells witnesses eloquently to its imperative character, which led the Apostle to undertake it in the face of such profound anticipation of ill.

The intimation of impending doom grows more urgent when Paul reaches Cæsarea and the prophet Agabus utters a prophecy of the Holy Spirit that Paul would be arrested by the Jews and handed over to the Gentiles.[1] But Paul still persists in his intention, despite this most vivid divine warning, and he at last reaches Jerusalem. Luke has still said nothing of Paul's purpose, but from what has been noted hitherto, and from the sequel, it is clear that he knew that this visit to Jerusalem had been a most crucial event in the career of the great Apostle, and it would appear that it had concerned matters and had results which were most inconvenient for the apologetical theme of his book. Hence it would seem to be a fair inference that what he does tell us of the happenings of this visit represents the best aspect which he could give to the matter in his record. Accordingly we may begin by noticing that, whatever may have been Paul's purpose in going to Jerusalem, he certainly made a report of his work to James, in the presence of the elders of the Church.[2] We are next told, after the edifying remark that Paul's audience "glorified God" on hearing his report, that their leader, who was undoubtedly James, proceeded forthwith to question Paul about his orthodoxy: "Thou seest, brother, how many thousands there are among the Jews of them which have believed; and they are all zealous for the law: and they have been informed concerning thee, that thou teachest all the Jews which are among the Gentiles to forsake Moses, telling them not to circumcise their children, neither to walk after the customs. What is it therefore? they will certainly hear that thou art come."[3] The significance of these verses is truly immense. On Luke's showing we see that there was in Jerusalem a considerable body of Jewish converts to Christianity who still professed a zealous allegiance to the Law. These Jewish Christians had been scandalized by reports of Paul's active disloyalty to Judaism among the communities of the Diaspora, and consequently their anger was to be expected to find expression against him on his coming to Jerusalem. It is to be particularly noted with regard to the charges made against Paul that, although neither Paul's own writings nor Luke's narrative afford explicit evidence of the truth of the charge

---

[1] Acts 21. 10–12. [2] Acts 21. 18, 19. [3] Acts 21. 20–22.

that he actually counselled Jews to neglect their religious customs and duties, there is abundant material in the Epistles to show that the Apostle propounded an interpretation of Christianity which logically made the peculiar religious status claimed by Judaism of absolutely no vital effect.[1] Moreover, full weight must also be given to the fact that, according to Luke's showing, in this meeting between Paul and the leaders of the Jerusalem Church the initiative was decisively with the latter: Paul made his report and then had to face the charge that his Jewish orthodoxy was suspect. A test was proposed which was most cleverly designed to show publicly that Paul was an orthodox Jew to the degree of observing a quaint and expensive Jewish ritual custom.[2] When it is recalled that Paul is described as being accompanied on his journey to Jerusalem by representatives of his Gentile converts,[3] it is obvious that the spectacle of his submission to this test, imposed upon him by the Jerusalem Church, must have been peculiarly harmful to his prestige in their eyes and disturbing to their understanding of his teaching about the unique essentiality of faith in Christ.

The sequel of Paul's detection and molestation by the Jewish mob in the Temple might reasonably have been expected, and the question naturally arises whether James and the elders might not also have anticipated the danger to which they were exposing the champion of Gentile Christianity in requiring him thus publicly to prove his orthodoxy. Moreover, it is not without significance that Luke tells us nothing of the reaction of the Jerusalem Christians to Paul's arrest and imprisonment, which fact contrasts strangely with what he tells earlier in his narrative of their concern for the safety of Peter when arrested and imprisoned by Agrippa I.[4]

The subsequent lengthy description of Paul's imprisonment and trials serves chiefly to illustrate the author's theme of Jewish intolerance and Roman sympathy for the great exponent of Christianity as a universal faith. The narrative ends with Paul's coming as a prisoner to Rome, where, despite the mention of his contact with the Christian community already there existing, he is depicted as the leading champion of Christianity in the metropolis of the Empire and as introducing the new faith to the Jewish community resident in the city, who surprisingly know of it only by hearsay;[5] then comes the final act, which symbolizes the theme of the whole work: the Jews repudiate the gospel and Paul proclaims that God's salvation is now given to the Gentiles, who will receive it.[6]

---

[1] See Chapter Four.

[2] Acts 21. 23, 24. Cf. Klausner, *From Jesus to Paul*, pp. 398, 399 and n. 6; Lohmeyer, *Galiläa und Jerusalem*, p. 64.

[3] Acts 20. 4; 21. 29. Cf. *B.C.*, vol. i, pp. 253–4; Loisy, *Le Origini del Christianesimo*, p. 171.

[4] Acts 12. 5. See the interesting suggestion of Harrison, *Problem of Pastoral Epistles*, pp. 121–2, that 2 Tim. 4. 16–18a (? 18b) may refer to this fact. Cf. Goguel, op. cit., pp. 333, 346.

[5] Acts 28. 21, 22.

[6] Acts 28. 23–28. Cf. Loisy, op. cit., p. 182; Goguel, op. cit., pp. 510–30, who thinks that it was the purpose of Acts to represent Christianity as the true form of Judaism, thus to secure its status as a *religio licita*.

Such then are the omissions, the misproportions, and the inconsistencies of Luke's tendentious narrative of Christian Origins which are apparent on internal examination. Except on one point, no comparison has been made in this chapter with the testimony of Paul's Epistles, and to that we must now turn.

To read any of Paul's Epistles, with the exception of his private note to Philemon, is at once to enter into an atmosphere of fierce controversy. The conflict is quickly found to centre round two subjects, namely the essentiality of circumcision for Christians and Paul's own authority. If we start our examination by taking what is probably the earliest, or one of the earliest, of Paul's extant writings, we find ourselves immediately introduced into a situation in which the Apostle is putting forth all his power to defend himself to his Galatian readers and to counter the teaching of certain adversaries. Paul quickly plunges into the real business of his letter by expressing his indignation at the defection of his converts, who appear to have transferred their allegiance to another gospel, which was much concerned with the importance of the Jewish rite of circumcision. This matter soon leads him, significantly, to embark upon a personal apologia, in which he vehemently seeks to demonstrate his independence, in matters of faith, of the Church of Jerusalem. His apologia falls into three distinct parts, which feature seems to indicate, and correspond to, three lines of attack on his own position.

In the first he is concerned to show how he was originally converted to faith in Christ by the direct interposition of God, and that at this most crucial moment of his career he was absolutely independent of the Christian community of Jerusalem.[1]

The second part is constituted by what is clearly a very embarrassed account of a later visit which he paid to Jerusalem.[2] In this almost incoherent narrative Paul endeavours to show that he was led to undertake the journey "by revelation", but he next has to admit that he had to make a report of his work to the leaders of the Jerusalem Church, "lest by any means I should be running, or had run, in vain". Then he has to relate, significantly in this context, some incident concerning the circumcising of his follower Titus, and so obviously uncomfortable is he about the matter that his grammar becomes involved to such a degree as to defy all analysis of its meaning.[3] He continues to describe the transactions of this visit, and he does so with a degree of circumlocution and qualification in his references to the leaders of the Jerusalem Church which must truly reflect his sense of embarrassment towards these authorities when his own position *vis-à-vis* them was in question. For all his professed indifference, the profundity of his concern is evident in the most revealing fashion when he writes: "But from those who were (are) reputed

[1] Gal. 1. 17 ff. Cf. pp. 58 *seq.* above.   [2] Gal. 2. 1–10.
[3] The elaborate explanatory notes of Lightfoot, *Galatians*, pp. 105–7, on "the broken grammar" are significant. Cf. Lietzmann, *An die Galater*, pp. 10–11; Goguel, *La Naissance du Christianisme*, pp. 324–7.

to be somewhat (whatsoever they were, it maketh no matter to me: God accepteth not man's person)—they, I say, who were of repute imparted nothing to me . . ." However, despite this avowal of unconcern for the standing of the Jerusalem leaders, Paul proceeds to tell his readers, obviously making the most of the fact, that he had obtained some measure of recognition for his work among the Gentiles from James, Cephas, and John, "who were (are) reputed to be pillars". Unfortunately for our understanding, the exact nature of this recognition is tantalizingly vague.[1] As we noted in an earlier chapter, Paul in this passage draws a strange distinction in the teaching of Christianity between a gospel of the circumcision and a gospel of the uncircumcision, ascribing the commission of the former to Peter and claiming that the latter was entrusted to himself. The fact of these two particular vocations, Paul states, was recognized by the Jerusalem leaders, but in the subsequent act of amity Barnabas is included with Paul as a recipient of the "right hand of fellowship" from the three "pillars", although no special recognition had been made of his special role in the assignment of the evangelical commissions. The episode ends with a note that Paul and Barnabas were specially asked to provide economic support for (presumably) the poor of the Jerusalem Church.

When we complete our reading of this passage the first question that naturally arises is that of what exactly took place on this occasion at Jerusalem. Since our only evidence is this obviously *ex parte* statement of Paul's, we have to content ourselves with certain inferences which on consideration seem to be reasonable. The first is that quite clearly Paul felt obliged in his apologia to the Galatian Christians to give an explanation of this particular visit to Jerusalem, which fact must surely mean that his adversaries had been using the events of the visit in some way which was decidedly detrimental to his position. The signs of Paul's embarrassment, which we have noticed above, indicate that there was substance in the case which his detractors made from the transactions on this occasion at Jerusalem, and three points certainly seem to emerge, namely that Paul's work had been called into question and he had to submit to an examination by the leaders of the Jerusalem Church (which fact constituted evidence of his subordination to their authority), that Paul's position about the circumcision of Greek converts had in some way been compromised, and that the most he can claim is that the leaders recognized some truly amazing dichotomy of spheres of evangelization for himself and Peter (which, according to the evidence of 1 Cor. 1. 12; 3. 22, the latter does not appear to have respected) and had given a token of

---

1 "*Un tale accordo, di cui gli Atti non hanno il minimo sentore, è del tutto inverosimile. O Paolo si è esaltato oltre misura nella considerazione della sua missione provvidenziale o il testo non è autentico. Gli anziani di Gerusalemme non potevano pensare né a rivendicare per sé soli l'evangelizzione di tutti i Giudei del mondo né e rimettersi al solo Paolo per l'evangelizzione di tutti i Gentili. Una simile spartizione non può esser stata concepita in una prospettiva di realità*" (Loisy, op. cit., p. 145). "*Assurément, Paul simplifie en imaginant une sorte de partage de l'œuvre de conversion entre lui et Pierre*" (Guignebert, *Le Christ*, p. 306).

fellowship and communion to him and Barnabas.   It is possible that, in thus claiming a different sphere of activity from that of Peter, Paul sought expressly to define his position relative to this eminent Apostle.   The fact of the request for alms must be noted, for it will be found to have a considerable significance in our examination of other Pauline material.

The third episode of this apologetical narrative comprises certain events which took place at Antioch, apparently rather subsequent to the Jerusalem visit.[1]   Here again it seems that Paul is particularly concerned to justify his position relative to Peter, although incidentally he also reveals how he stood with regard to James.   The subject of the dispute on this occasion was the possibility of table-fellowship, a matter of great concern in the ancient world,[2] between Jewish and Gentile Christians.   Peter by his example had decided in favour of such a notable measure of social intercourse, but retracted on the protest of certain emissaries of James. Peter's obvious subservience here to the authority of James is significant, as we have already noted; its consequences for Paul appear to have been decisive.   From his vigorous repudiation of Peter's conduct it is evident that he then ceased to have any further amicable relations with that distinguished leader, for it is scarcely likely that, if Peter had consequently accepted Paul's side in the dispute, the fact would have gone unrecorded in the Galatian Epistle.[3]   Moreover, it must be noted that, despite the boasted right hand of fellowship from James, it was his emissaries, clearly representing his views as is evident from the reaction of Peter, who first and effectively pronounced the prohibition on an act which Paul regarded as of fundamental significance for his interpretation of Christianity.   Thus it is obvious that we must understand this Antiochene episode as constituting for Paul and his readers an occasion of essential decision; that as such its transactions are invested with definitive importance; that consequently it means that whatever degree of acceptance Paul may have thought that he succeeded in gaining at Jerusalem was completely negatived by the subsequent events at Antioch, and that henceforth in fundamental policy and basic sympathy he stood professedly apart from James and Peter, and in the issue was even deserted by his erstwhile companion, Barnabas.

The remainder of the Galatian Epistle shows how gravely Paul viewed the point at issue.   The immediate question is that of the necessity of circumcision, but it was clearly for Paul but one of the most obvious aspects of the deeper underlying problem.   The adversaries remain unnamed, but there can be no doubt about their identity, namely that they are representatives of the Jerusalem Church, for the remark in 4. 17 that "They zealously seek you in no good way; nay, they desire to shut

---

[1] Gal. 2. 11 ff.

[2] "*Tischgemeinschaft ist mehr als nur Nebeneinandersitzen; sie ist für den antiken Menschen in einem besonderen Sinn Koncretisierung der Gemeinschaft*": G. Kittel, *Z.N.T.W.* (1931), p. 150.

[3] "*immer wieder fällt der Schatten des Petrus auf den Weg des Paulus*" (Lietzmann, *Gesch. der alten Kirche*, I, p. 108).   Cf. Nock, *St. Paul*, p. 110, n. 1; Loisy, *Le Origini del Cristianesimo*, p. 149; Knox, *Jerusalem*, p. 197, n. 6; Guignebert, op. cit., p. 308; Goguel, op. cit., pp. 321, 330, 333 *seq.*

you out, that ye may seek them" clearly alludes to the policy which produced the schism at Antioch.[1] Consequently the vehemence of Paul's condemnation of his antagonists' attempt to undermine the loyalty of the Galatians must be seen as ultimately reaching back to the leaders at Jerusalem, and that vehemence is very great—"If any man preacheth unto you any gospel other than that which ye received, let him be anathema. For am I now persuading men, or God? or am I seeking to please men? if I were still pleasing men, I should not be a servant of Christ",[2] and "but he that troubleth you shall bear his judgement, whosoever he be. But I, brethren, if I still preach circumcision, why am I still persecuted? then hath the stumbling-block of the cross been done away. I would that they which unsettle you would even cut themselves off." [3] The doctrinal significance of the condemnation of those who force circumcision on the Galatians, "only that they may not be persecuted for the cross of Christ", has been discussed at length above.[4]

The outcome of the attack on Paul's authority which is implicit in the Galatian Epistle is unknown, but that the attack was not limited to this particular part of his chosen mission field is evident from the Epistles to the Corinthians. The first of these writings begins by showing that at Corinth something had happened which caused Paul's converts to divide themselves into parties under the names of Cephas, Apollos, and Christ, as distinct from Paul.[5] There can be little reasonable doubt that this situation must have been caused by the dissemination of teaching among the Corinthian Christians which led them to identify themselves severally, in all but one instance, with certain well-known contemporary leaders. The significance of this fact is immense, and its full import must be drawn out. When we consider the names, with the exception of the Christ sect, it is seen that the parties claimed allegiance severally to three persons, who from what we otherwise know of them divide into two groups, namely of Paul and opponents of Paul. To be more explicit: the Galatian Epistle sufficiently proves that a breach existed between Paul and Peter, while we have already given reasons for regarding Apollos as a representative of a Church which was out of communion with that of Paul, or at least not favourably regarded by it; [6] here in Corinth the names of Peter and Apollos signalized parties in apparent conflict with that of Paul. This situation must accordingly mean that in Corinth, which was peculiarly Paul's field of work, either Peter and Apollos or their repre-

---

[1] Knox, op. cit., p. 229, n. 18, suggests that εἰ μή τινές εἰσιν κ.τ.λ. of Gal. 1. 6, 7 means: "'only they who trouble you and would pervert the Gospel of Christ are somewhat' (i.e. are persons of some importance), τινές being used in the same contemptuous sense of persons regarded as τι in 2. 6 and τινα in Acts 5. 36". Cf. Sieffert, *Der Brief an die Galater*, p. 18; Goguel, *La Naissance du Christianisme*, pp. 144, 174, n. 1, 340–1.

[2] Gal. 1. 9, 10.

[3] Gal 5. 11, 12. "*Dieser Satz* (i.e. 6. 12) *erläutert den dunkleren Spruch* 5. 11: *die Judaisten fürchten Verfolgungen, wenn sie das Kreuz Christi als einzigen Heilsgrund bekennen, weil dies nach* 1 Cor. 1. 23 *ein* σκάνδαλον *für die Juden ist*" (Lietzmann, *An die Galater*, p. 41). See above, p. 71.

[4] Gal. 6. 12; see above, pp. 71, 78.

[5] 1 Cor. 1. 11–13; cf. 3. 21, 22.   [6] See pp. 17–18, 24–6 above.

sentatives had operated, and perhaps still did operate, in propounding to the Christians there interpretations of Christianity which were recognized as seriously different from that taught by Paul. That these rivals of Paul had met with an effective measure of success is evident, and, when it is remembered that they had achieved it in a Church of which Paul was the founder, the fact must surely indicate that the prestige of their authority must have more than offset the sentiment which the Corinthian Christians should naturally have felt for Paul. A further clue to understanding the situation is perhaps to be found in the identity of the mysterious Christ party. We have seen in an earlier chapter [1] that Palestinian Christology was especially concerned with the status of Jesus as the Jewish Messiah. Of this theology Peter certainly was a leading exponent, and we may recall too that, according to Acts, the Christology of Apollos had been regarded as seriously defective by the friends of Paul—a tendentious presentation which is tantamount to a condemnation of the Christianity taught at Alexandria. Now if Peter had visited the Christian community at Corinth and had propounded to them the theology of the Jerusalem Church as the original and authoritative interpretation of the faith, it would be likely that considerable, and to the Corinthians a new, emphasis would have been laid upon the Messianic vocation of Jesus. Consequently, it would be a reasonable inference that the Gentile Christians of Corinth, unable to appreciate the significance of the Jewish context of this new doctrine, regarded the special presentation of Jesus as the Messiah as some distinct doctrine and that those to whom it especially appealed enthusiastically espoused the cause of its propagation and styled themselves "Christ's" ('Εγὼ δὲ Χριστοῦ).

In the immediate sequel Paul surely reveals his preoccupation with the personal issue involved for him in the presence of these rivals or their continuing influence among his converts. He writes, after his fine impassioned conclusion to his passage about the conflicting parties, in a quick and significant transition: "Let a man so account of us, as of ministers of Christ, and stewards of the mysteries of God. Here, moreover, it is required in stewards, that a man be found faithful. But with me it is a very small thing that I should be judged of you, or of man's judgement . . ." [2] Then after a bitter passage about the sufferings of the Apostles, in which it is not certain whether he is associating himself with Apollos, Paul changes to a sudden tenderness and writes: "I write not these things to shame you, but to admonish you as my beloved children. For though ye should have ten thousand tutors in Christ, yet have ye not many fathers: for in Christ Jesus I begat you through the gospel. I beseech you therefore, be ye imitators of me." [3]

In chapter 9 Paul returns again suddenly to the personal issue and enters at once into an impassioned defence of his apostleship. The terms

[1] Chapter Five. Goguel, op. cit., p. 336, n. 2, finds the reference to the Christ party so difficult to explain that he dismisses it as "*une glose maladroite*".
[2] 1 Cor. 4. 1–3.   [3] 1 Cor. 4. 14–16.

of his apologetic indicate that his opponents charged him with not having
seen the Lord and therefore with not having the status or authority of
an Apostle. He consciously formulates his defence "to them that examine
me (ἀνακρίνουσιν)".[1] It is to explain why he had not claimed or
enjoyed the same economic support as did the distinguished leaders of
the Church, and in describing these latter it is a significant revelation of
Paul's mind that he particularizes "the brethren of the Lord, and Cephas".
This defence also throws some interesting light on Paul's personal conduct
in evangelizing and shows how that conduct laid itself open so easily to
misinterpretation as unprincipled: "And to the Jews I became as a Jew,
that I might gain Jews; to them that are under the law, as under the law,
not being myself under the law, that I might gain them that are under
the law; to them that are without law, as without law, not being without
law to God, but under law to Christ, that I might gain them that are
without law"; there is incidentally no recognition here of a demarcation
between a gospel of the circumcision and one of the uncircumcision,
which in his Galatian Epistle Paul had so earnestly claimed had been
drawn to determine the spheres of Peter and himself. Again in the
celebrated passage about the Resurrection tradition Paul seems to be
brought to the question of his personal authority by the mention of the
original witnesses, including Cephas and James, and from equating his
own spiritual experience with theirs he is significantly led on to assert
his superiority to them in evangelistic achievement, although he is "the
least of the apostles".[2] The chief topic of the final chapter of this
Epistle has a crucial meaning in Paul's career, which we have yet to
consider; here it will suffice to note that Paul is particularly concerned
about a collection of alms for "the saints" and that he plans to go himself
to Jerusalem with the delegates who bear it, "if it be meet for me to go"
(ἐὰν δὲ ἄξιον ᾖ τοῦ κἀμὲ πορεύεσθαι).[3]

The same spirit of personal apologetic, combined with a kind of veiled
polemic against certain unnamed opponents, soon shows itself in the so-
called Second Epistle to the Corinthians. We find Paul writing, "For
we are not as the many, corrupting (or, making merchandise of) the
word of God: but as of sincerity, but as of God, in the sight of God, speak
we in Christ."[4] Of the identity of those to whom this bitter description
is applied there is a clearer indication in the following verse. "Are we
beginning again to commend ourselves? or need we, as do some, epistles
of commendation to you or from you? Ye are our epistle . . ."[5]
Clearly then those whom he designates as corrupters of the word of God
are no mere freelance charlatans, but Christians who were in some way
emissaries of certain accepted authorities, whose letters of commendation
were effective in the Corinthian Church. Moreover, these verses reveal

---

[1] 1 Cor. 9. 3. "*Sensu forensi de iudice questionem habente*" (C. H. Bruder, *Concordantiae Novi
Test. Graeci*). "Here is my reply to my inquisitors" (Moffatt, *First Corinthians*, p. 115).
[2] 15. 5, 7, 8, 9.   [4] 2 Cor. 2. 17.
[3] 16. 4.   [5] 2 Cor. 3. 1, 2.

11

that to Paul's own special Gentile converts there came emissaries with high credentials and that they operated in such a way among them as thus to incur his bitter denunciation. In the verses which immediately follow those which have just been considered we find that Paul continues to develop the theme of the superiority in ministry of himself and his friends to their rivals, and the terms of reference in his comparison are very significant. He states that this claim of sufficiency is not egotistical, since God is the source of their sufficiency, "who also made us sufficient as ministers of a new covenant; not of the letter, but of the spirit: for the letter killeth, but the spirit giveth life".[1] Here not only the well-known Pauline antithesis between the letter and the spirit, but also the sequel about the significance of the inability of the children of Israel to look upon the face of Moses, proves that Paul contrasts himself and his followers with rivals who are attached to the Jewish Law.[2]

Following the present sequence of this Epistle, we come to a section which comprises Paul's instructions and exhortations about the collection of alms for "the saints". Especially significant in the passage are the verses in which are explained the reasons for this offering. Not only are the alms calculated to relieve the economic wants of the Christians of Jerusalem, but they will dispose them favourably towards the Corinthians who have sent them.[3]

Chapter 10 is wholly concerned with matters of Paul's status and reputation with his converts and in contrast with some anonymous rivals. After what seems to be another reference to the Christ sect, Paul alludes to his ability to exult in the authority which the Lord has given him for the building up of the Corinthians, and he asserts his readiness to use his power in warning those who, apparently during his absence, have despised him. Then comes a pregnant comparison: "For we are not bold to number or compare ourselves with certain of them that commend themselves: but they themselves, measuring themselves by themselves, and comparing themselves with themselves, are without understanding. But we will not glory beyond our measure, but according to the measure of the province ($\tau o \hat{v}$ $\kappa \alpha \nu \acute{o} \nu o s$) which God apportioned to us as a measure, to reach even unto you." Then, after declaring what appears to be his observance of the limits of his commission in evangelizing the·Corinthians, Paul adds "not glorying beyond our measure, that is, in other men's labours ($\grave{\epsilon} \nu$ $\grave{\alpha} \lambda \lambda o \tau \rho \acute{\iota} o \iota s$ $\kappa \acute{o} \pi o \iota s$)". He continues with some involved and obscure remarks about the effect of the growth of the Corinthians' faith upon his future evangelistic work: "so as to preach the gospel even unto the parts beyond you, and not to glory in another's province in regard of things ready to our hand ($\grave{\epsilon} \nu$ $\grave{\alpha} \lambda \lambda o \tau \rho \acute{\iota} \omega$ $\kappa \alpha \nu \acute{o} \nu \iota$ $\epsilon \grave{\iota} s$ $\tau \grave{\alpha}$ $\grave{\epsilon} \tau o \iota \mu \alpha$). But he that glorieth, let him glory in the Lord. For not he that commendeth himself is approved, but whom the Lord commendeth." This language is admittedly obscure, but it would appear that it is not because

---

[1] 2 Cor. 3. 4–6.   [2] Ibid. 7–18. Cf. Knox, *Gentiles*, pp. 130–1.   [3] 2 Cor. 9. 12–14.

Paul is writing vaguely, but rather allusively, and there can be little doubt that, as he writes, he has in mind definite persons who had been doing the things from which he here insistently claims that he has abstained.[1]

The climax of this apologetic is reached in chapter 11 and completes in a most vivid manner the evidence which has been accruing of a most grave challenge to Paul's authority in what might fairly be regarded as the strongest centre of his influence. The situation clearly arises out of the fact that the Corinthian Christians had been subjected to some propaganda which Paul regards as entirely pernicious: "But I fear, lest by any means, as the serpent beguiled Eve in his craftiness, your minds should be corrupted from the simplicity and the purity that is toward Christ." Then in the next verse comes the amazing charge, which, however, can be paralleled in the Galatian Epistle and thus has high significance: "For if he that cometh preacheth another Jesus, whom we did not preach, or if ye receive a different spirit, which ye did not receive, or a different gospel, which ye did not accept, ye do well to bear with him ($\kappa\alpha\lambda\hat{\omega}s$ $\dot{\alpha}\nu\acute{\epsilon}\chi\epsilon\sigma\theta\epsilon$)."[2] From this exposure of doctrinal disloyalty Paul at once passes to the thought of the disloyalty to himself which it implied, and this consideration was significantly associated in his mind with a questioning of his apostolic authority: "For I reckon that I am not a whit behind the very chiefest apostles ($\tau\hat{\omega}\nu$ $\dot{\nu}\pi\epsilon\rho\lambda\acute{\iota}\alpha\nu$ $\dot{\alpha}\pi\sigma\sigma\tau\acute{o}\lambda\omega\nu$). But though I be rude in speech, yet am I not in knowledge; nay, in everything we have made it manifest among all men to you-ward." Again, as in the Galatian Letter, we find that Paul in defending his authority does so in terms of asserting the soundness and effectiveness of his knowledge, which fact must surely mean that the particular point on which he was attacked by his opponents was that of his understanding of what were the essentials of the faith. Moreover, the fact of Paul's assertion of his equality with the Apostles *par excellence* is revealing of the source from which the challenge to his position came. There follows a second explanation of why he, Paul, had not claimed financial support from his converts, obviously in refutation of a charge that his failure to put forward this claim was evidence of his inferiority to the Jerusalem leaders. In the sequel to this Paul exceeds all his former vehemence in his denunciation of his adversaries, and whether it is legitimate to assume from the context that he inveighs here against the actual leaders of the Jerusalem Church or against their representatives, it is just to interpret his invective as proof of the serious proportions of the breach which existed between him and the authorities of the Mother Church. So emphatic is his denunciation that a paraphrase cannot do justice to it and it must be given *in extenso*:

---

[1] Cf. Knox, op. cit., p. 129, n. 4.
[2] A truer rendering is undoubtedly given by Moffatt (*A New Translation of the Bible*): "You put up with it all right". "*So verträget ihr's billig*": Luther. See M. Aurelius, viii. 19: οὐ οὖν πρὸς τί; τὸ ἤδεσθαι; ἴδε, εἰ ἀνέχεται ἡ ἔννοια. Epictetus, I, vi. 27: ἀλλ' οἶμαι ὅτι ταῦτα πάντα ἀντιτιθέντες πρὸς τὸ ἀξιόλογον τῆς θέας φέρετε καὶ ἀνέχεσθε.

"For such men are false apostles, deceitful workers, fashioning themselves into apostles of Christ. And no marvel; for even Satan fashioneth himself into an angel of light. It is no great thing therefore if his ministers also fashion themselves as ministers of righteousness; whose end shall be according to their works."

Any further question there may be about the identity of these opponents of Paul is surely removed by his subsequent remarks. They are men whose activity among the Corinthians can be described corporately as that of a man who "bringeth you into bondage", who "devoureth you", who "taketh you captive", who "exalteth himself", a series of charges which are strikingly reminiscent of those brought against the adversaries in the Church of Galatia. The Corinthian enemies are, moreover, Hebrews, Israelites; they boasted that they were the seed of Abraham; they are recognized as "ministers of Christ".

After an eloquent recitation of his own personal experiences of sufferings and of spiritual exaltation, Paul once more returns to the significant subject of the comparison between himself and the Jerusalem leaders: "for in nothing was I behind the very chiefest apostles", and he cites as evidence of his possession of "the signs of an apostle" the achievements of his work at Corinth.[1]

Of the true nature of the situation which these Corinthian documents imply there can be little real doubt. Quite clearly into this essentially Pauline community envoys of the Jerusalem Church, probably including Peter himself and perhaps some of "the brethren of the Lord", had come and had given Paul's converts teaching which differed so seriously from that of Paul that it could reasonably be described as "a different gospel", concerning "another Jesus". This teaching, moreover, was imparted on the authority of the leaders of the Jerusalem Church, the Apostles *par excellence*, and it was accompanied by a repudiation of Paul's doctrine on the ground of his lack of apostolic authority and knowledge. This anti-Pauline propaganda had not been completely successful, but it had significantly won a notable following in this Pauline citadel, and Paul himself was very seriously concerned to combat it. It is, however, further evident that, despite his obvious animus against them, Paul found himself in an embarrassing position, since the paramount authority of the Jerusalem leaders in the Church was unchallenged and unchallengeable, while his own in comparison could only be maintained by special

---

[1] 2 Cor. 12. 11, 12. Remarking on Paul's silence about James and Peter, compared with his fierce inveighing against their emissaries, Lietzmann, *An die Galater*, I, p. 109, observes: "*aber wer genauer zusieht, lernt es, zwischen den Zielen seiner Briefe zu lesen, und erkennt hinter den Satansdienern und Lügenaposteln und falschen Brüdern die Schatten der Grossen von Jerusalem.*" Cf. Schweitzer, *Mysticism of Paul*, pp. 155–8; Loisy, *Le Origini del Cristianesimo*, p. 168; Knox, *Jerusalem*, p. 365; Nock, *St. Paul*, p. 169. The arguments put forward by Lake, *Earlier Epistles*, pp. 219–32, in favour of identifying Paul's opponents at Corinth as πνευματικοί, and not as Judaizers, would now appear to be largely irrelevant, since he fails to appreciate that the controversy about circumcision was but a practical issue (perhaps only of local currency) and was symptomatic of a far graver difference on the fundamental interpretation of the person and mission of Jesus. See also Simon, *Verus Israel*, pp. 310–11.

pleading; so in his apologia he could not retort by an open attack upon his opponents, and he was obliged to weaken his case by the use of circumlocution, veiled innuendoes, and anonymous denunciations. Furthermore, as evidence of the inherent weakness of his own position, Paul obviously had to preserve some semblance of communion with the Jerusalem Church, and he clearly regarded the collection of alms for its members as an important factor to this end.

If the Galatian and the Corinthian writings show that the leaders of the Jerusalem Church did not respect any arrangement which might have been made with Paul to confine their activities to the Jews, the Epistle to the Romans in its turn provides evidence that Paul was equally ready to win a position for himself in a Church which had undoubtedly been founded by representatives of Jewish Christianity. We must now accordingly turn to examine this latter document, for from it much valuable information may be gleaned on the critical situation obtaining in the Church in the course of the fifth decade of the first century.

One of the most fundamental of the many problems connected with the Epistle to the Romans is constituted by the fact that Paul is clearly writing to Gentile Christians and yet so large a part of his letter is taken up with the question of Israel's failure to accept the Christian Gospel. However, as we have already seen,[1] Paul shows signs of embarrassment in his approach to the Roman Christians and he is clearly at pains to vindicate his teaching, thereby implying that those to whom he wrote had cause already to regard him with suspicion. It is necessary, therefore, to find some situation which will correspond to these facts. This means that an occasion must be sought when Paul would have felt that he could write to the Gentile members of the Roman Church with some hope of winning them to his views, and when, accordingly, the original Jewish influence in the community had been very seriously diminished or removed.

A situation which well conforms to the pattern of these facts can be discerned to have existed in the years immediately following the expulsion of the Jews from Rome by the Emperor Claudius.[2] According to the record of the Acts, Paul met at Corinth Aquila and Priscilla, Jews who had recently come from Rome as a result of the imperial order.[3] Now it is likely that Paul made many inquiries of his new friends about the position of the Gentile members of the Roman Church who were thus left to their own resources by the expulsion of their Jewish brethren.[4]

---

[1] See above, pp. 54–5.

[2] Acts 18. 1, 2; Suetonius, *Claudius* 25; Dio Cassius, lx. 6; Orosius, vii. cap. vi (*Patr. Lat.* ed. Migne, t. 31, 469). Cf. Tacitus, *Ann.* xii. 52. On the question of date see *B.C.*, vol. v, pp. 459–60, which notes that Orosius' reckoning for 49–50 well fits the date given by Acts for Paul's arrival at Corinth, but stresses the weakness of the unsupported statement of Orosius. Momigliano, *L'Opera dell'Imperatore Claudio*, p. 76, seems inclined to date the expulsion for 49, with the qualification, "*se dobbiamo prestar fede al dato di fonte ignota di Orosio*". A. D. Nock, *Camb. Anc. Hist.*, vol. x, p. 500, dates the event for 49 without comment.

[3] Acts ibid.

[4] Adequate reason is given in *B.C.*, vol. iv, p. 222, for presuming that Aquila and Priscilla were already Christians before their coming to Corinth.

The opportunity of winning a foothold in such a community, to be followed up later when it was possible by a personal visit, must have been very attractive to Paul, and to this end he addressed the letter which has come down to us.

His approach is very diplomatic, for he is fully conscious that he is entering upon "another man's foundation",[1] and that those to whom he is addressing himself had been taught another interpretation of the faith [2] and would probably be still attached to the memory of their Jewish teachers and sharing their dislike of his doctrine. Consciousness of what was his chief obstacle, therefore, undoubtedly determined Paul's choice of the destiny of Israel as his main theme, but, despite this and his circumspect treatment of some spiritual and ethical matters, he clearly reveals his purpose to have "some fruit in you also, even as in the rest of the Gentiles" [3] in his frank claim: "I write the more boldly unto you in some measure, as putting you again in remembrance, because of the grace that was given me of God, that I should be a minister of Christ Jesus unto the Gentiles, ministering the gospel of God, that the offering up of the Gentiles might be made acceptable, being sanctified by the Holy Ghost." [4]

In making suggestions about his future visit to Rome Paul gives some invaluable hints concerning the time of his writing and his own immediate plans. He tells his readers that before he can come to Rome he has to undertake a journey to Jerusalem for the purpose of presenting the Church there with the offerings of the Christian communities of Macedonia and Achaia.[5] As is so often the case in his writings when he touches upon a matter of deep concern, his preoccupation with the significance of the collection to himself leads Paul on to say more than is strictly necessary in the present context. Thus, obviously conscious that his sponsoring of the contribution of money made by the Gentiles to the Church at Jerusalem might be construed as incompatible with his claims to be the Apostle to the Gentiles, Paul is induced to give a careful explanation of the matter. But his preoccupation carries him further and he unwittingly reveals his anxiety by appealing to the Roman Christians: "Now I beseech you, brethren, by our Lord Jesus Christ, and by the love of the Spirit, that ye strive together with me in your prayers to God for me; that I may be delivered from them that are disobedient in Judæa, and that my ministration which I have for Jerusalem may be acceptable to the saints; that I may come unto you in joy through the will of God, and together with you find rest." [6]

When the Roman Epistle is interpreted in this light, the problematical 16th chapter is seen to be patient of an explanation which is consistent

---

[1] Rom. 15. 20. [2] See above, pp. 54–5. [3] Rom. 1. 13.
[4] Rom. 15. 15, 16. [5] Rom. 15. 22–26.
[6] Rom. 15. 30–32. Cf. Dodd, *Romans*, pp. 232–3. Goguel, *La Naissance du Christianisme*, pp. 187–9, 343–4, thinks that Paul tried to anticipate the Judaizing of the Roman Church, in which considerable Jewish influence already prevailed.

both with the fact of the apparent weight of external and internal
evidence for its independence of the preceding chapters of the Epistle
and with that of its original connection with them.[1] Apart from the
manuscript evidence that this chapter was not originally an integral part
of the Epistle, a serious objection has been seen in the fact that, if, as
the Epistle makes absolutely clear, he had never visited Rome, it is very
strange that Paul should know so many members of the Church there
by name.[2] If, however, Paul met at Corinth with Aquila and Priscilla,
who were obviously distinguished members of the Roman Church, it
is likely that he would also have met there other refugees of that community. Moreover, if, as the evidence of Acts shows, Paul had succeeded
in establishing a close friendship, undoubtedly implying acceptance of
his teaching, with Aquila and his wife,[3] there is much reason for believing
that he similarly won other Roman Christians to his way of thinking.
Now our thesis above has been that, having learned from the Roman
Christian refugees at Corinth that a situation existed among the remaining
Gentile members of the Roman Church which might be successfully
exploited in his interests, Paul wrote the letter which comprises chapters 1–15 of the present Epistle, and its preservation is evidence that it
achieved an effective measure of success. Obviously Paul would have
been intent on following up and maintaining his contact with the Roman
Christians. Now we know from the fact that Aquila and Priscilla set
up house elsewhere, probably in Ephesus,[4] that some of the Roman
refugees did not intend to settle permanently at Corinth, and it is reasonable to suppose that in process of time, as the political situation cleared,
many of the refugees returned to the imperial city.[5] This would mean,
of course, that many of Paul's erstwhile acquaintances at Corinth migrated
back to Rome, so that he came thus to know personally many members
of the Church there before his own arrival in the city. Consequently
chapter 16 can reasonably be regarded as a subsequent note sent under
the form of a commendation of Phœbe to maintain Paul's contacts with
the Roman community, especially through the instrumentality of his
former Corinthian friends. Moreover, there is also evidence that
divisions had now appeared in the Roman Church, which must be
regarded as a likely consequence of the influx of Pauline ideas and the
opposition of those who remained faithful to the older teaching, or of
those Jewish refugees who, still hostile to Paul, had also returned to their
former homes. And so we find Paul writing to encourage his supporters:
"Now I beseech you, brethren, mark them which are causing the divisions
and occasions of stumbling, contrary to the doctrine which ye learned:
and turn away from them. For they that are such serve not our Lord

---

[1] Cf. Moffatt, *Intro. to N.T.*, pp. 134–9.
[2] Cf. Moffatt, op. cit., pp. 137–8; Sanday and Headlam, *Romans*, pp. xcii–xciii; Lake,
Earlier Epistles, p. 326; Dodd, op. cit., pp. xvii *seq.*
[3] Acts 18. 2, 3, 18, 26.   [4] Acts 18. 18, 19. Cf. 1 Cor. 16. 19.
[5] Acts 28. 17 ff. clearly presupposes the return of the Jewish community to Rome.

Christ, but their own belly; and by their smooth and fair speech they beguile the hearts of the innocent." [1]　And then the significant words which begin the final doxology, so striking in their bold contrast to the earlier apologetic approach to the Roman Christians in 1. 15, 16: "Now to him that is able to stablish you according to my gospel and the preaching of Jesus Christ (κατὰ τὸ εὐαγγέλιόν μου καὶ τὸ κήρυγμα Ἰησοῦ Χριστοῦ), according to the revelation of the mystery which hath been kept in silence through times eternal . . ." [2]

It is now time to draw up the conclusions of this extended survey of the evidence of the Acts and Paul's Epistles.　Despite the frequent disagreements and inconsistences of the two sources, these conclusions can be of positive value, since the discrepancies generally are due either to the *ex parte* statement of Paul or to the apologetic purpose of the author of the Acts—factors, in other words, which are certainly known and can be reckoned with accordingly.

From both the Galatian and the Corinthian Epistles it is clear that Paul's authority in his own churches was being seriously challenged by powerful adversaries.　From the Galatian Letter we learn that Paul was conscious of great embarrassment about his position relative to the leaders of the Jerusalem Church.　He endeavours to show in a passage which abounds with inconsistencies that on a second visit which he had paid to the Holy City some form of recognition or *modus vivendi* had been accorded to him by the three chief leaders.　However, he is himself forced to admit that bad relations soon arose and at Antioch Peter, who appears to have been for a time conciliatory, and even Barnabas, broke with him, owing to the intervention of emissaries of James; the very *raison d'être* of the Galatian Epistle is proof that that breach, instead of being healed, had grown more serious in that among Paul's own converts agents of Jewish Christianity were teaching an interpretation of the faith which was effectively different from that given by Paul.

In Corinth a similar situation to that in the Galatian Church appears to have existed, although the immediate point at issue was not that of the essentiality of circumcision.　Most significant is the fact that factions had been created there which identified themselves with various facets of Jewish Christianity in opposition to Paul.　This fact and the vehemence of Paul's defence of his apostleship and his denunciations of his adversaries' pretensions and teaching all point to the operation of representatives of the Jerusalem Church, including perhaps Peter, among Paul's converts at Corinth to undermine his authority and doctrine and to substitute their own.

The hostile disregard of Paul's position in his own Gentile mission fields which this Galatian and Corinthian material indicates is, however,

[1] Rom. 16. 17, 18.　Cf. Sanday and Headlam, op. cit., pp. 439–40.
[2] Rom. 16. 25.

on Paul's side to be paralleled by his attempt to ingratiate himself with the Gentile Christians of Rome during the eclipse of the original Jewish influence there. Thus it would appear that each side in this struggle was opposed to the teaching of the other and did not hesitate, when occasion allowed, to propagate among its adversary's converts its own peculiar interpretation of the faith.

However, in this conflict Paul's position was inherently weak. The Jerusalem Church was the original and accepted source of the tradition of the faith, and that position Paul could not openly challenge. To the Jerusalem Christians, on the other hand, Paul clearly appeared as an upstart who had made himself the champion of a policy towards the Gentiles which they would not accept, or would only accept with serious reservations. But probably even more shocking to them was his theological temerity, which seemed to be transforming the traditional faith in ways which were almost blasphemous to their orthodox scruples, and, moreover, by its speculative daring and implied antinomianism constituted a very serious obstacle to their own aim of establishing a better position for themselves with their countrymen, especially the Pharisees. To meet the danger of Paul and his teaching their line of action was obvious and capable of great effectiveness, namely to repudiate Paul's authority as a qualified exponent of the faith. To this end their emissaries went to Paul's churches and presented the teaching of the Jerusalem Church as the authentic and original faith, consequently repudiating Paul as a late-comer to Christianity, who had not shared the original experiences or understood their proper significance. To this line of attack Paul was peculiarly vulnerable, because he could not deny the primal authority of the Jerusalem leaders or gainsay the fact that he had not been one of the original disciples of Jesus. Thus we find him developing the only line of apologetic which lay open to him, namely to minimize the importance of the knowledge of the historical Jesus, and to assert that his own conversion was due to the direct interposition of God and that in acquiring his knowledge of the faith "he communed not with flesh and blood". However, he could not escape the inherent weakness of his position, since even his highly spiritualized interpretation of the faith had ultimately to base itself upon certain essential facts of the historical tradition, and even in his most vehement invective he realized that he could not openly repudiate the superlative authority of the Jerusalem leaders and had to content himself with veiled references to the identity of his opponents in his denunciations.

Since the three Epistles concerned necessarily show us severally a local situation in this connection, we cannot trace any course of development in this struggle between Paul and the Jerusalem leaders. We do, however, possess some evidence which permits us to believe that a definitive crisis did develop in Paul's relations with the Church of Jerusalem. We have noted Paul's concern in his Corinthian writings for the success of the collection of alms among his churches for the Jerusalem community, and especially his statements about the offerings helping to make the members of the Mother Church favourably disposed; and he plans to take the alms personally to Jerusalem, "if it be meet for me to go". In the Roman Epistle we find the measure of Paul's concern in this matter so great that he is even led to ask the Roman Christians for their prayers, so that his visit to Jerusalem for the purpose (he now seems to have lost any hesitancy about going) may be well received by the Jerusalem community and he may safely escape from those who are unbelieving (τῶν ἀπειθούντων) in Judæa. On turning to the Acts we find Paul undertaking a journey to Jerusalem with great foreboding of coming ill and against clear spiritual warnings; Luke, however, gives no adequate reason for this undertaking and says nothing at all about the alms.[1] Now, on comparing the testimony of these two different sources we see Paul himself first hesitating and then deciding to take the alms personally to Jerusalem, fully conscious of the dangers involved and doubtful of his reception by the Jerusalem Christians. Luke in his later narrative depicts Paul making what was clearly to be his last and fateful visit to the Jewish metropolis; he gives no reason for the visit, but clearly indicates that the Apostle must have had some very pressing cause which led him gratuitously to run into such grave peril. We have, therefore, to predicate some crisis in Paul's affairs which corresponds to the evidence of our data. Such a situation we may reasonably conceive as follows: the hostile activity of the emissaries of the Jerusalem Church continued to grow in effectiveness, so that Paul's position in his own churches at last became untenable and he was obliged to decide on a desperate solution. This was to make a final personal appeal to the Jewish leaders to accept some *modus vivendi*, and to this end, to reinforce his case, he made a special effort to raise an impressive sum of alms, in order to take it, together with a delegation of supporters from the various churches, to the Mother Church as an eloquent token of the worth of his co-operation.[2]

We are dependent on the tendentious narrative of the Acts for the sequel. As we have seen, despite all his manifest desire to put the best possible interpretation on the events at Jerusalem, Luke has to admit that Paul was charged with disloyalty to Judaism and required to submit to a public test of his orthodoxy. If, therefore, our reconstruction of the crisis has been justified so far, we may reasonably extend it to cover the transactions at Jerusalem. Accordingly it would appear that Paul's move embarrassed the Jerusalem leaders, but their head, James, was more than a match for Paul in astuteness, and he proposed the test which was designed to put Paul in a fatal dilemma. If he refused to give this proof of his orthodoxy, then he was in effect declaring himself an apostate from

---

[1] But see above, p. 133, n. 3.
[2] Cf. Klausner, *From Jesus to Paul*, p. 396; Dodd, *Romans*, pp. 232–3; Goguel, *La Naissance du Christianisme*, p. 248.

Judaism and thus would merit excommunication. On the other hand, he had come to Jerusalem, with a delegation of his converts, as the champion of Gentile right to full participation in the new faith; if, therefore, he submitted to the order of James and provided evidence of his orthodoxy, his position in the eyes of his Gentile followers would be gravely compromised, for they would know that he, their champion, recognized his subordination to the Jerusalem authorities and proclaimed his adherence to the doctrine of the essentiality of Judaism by the performance of an obscure Jewish ritual act. For Paul the dilemma was inescapable. For all his gospel of the sufficiency of faith in Christ, he had illogically continued to recognize the claims of Judaism upon a Jew, and now that he was faced with the consequences of this fatal weakness in his logic, he obviously felt that he could not formally repudiate his national faith and accordingly submitted to his opponent's astute demand.

Paul's arrest while performing the purificatory rites of the Nazarite vow must have been as disastrous to his cause as it was convenient to the authorities of the Jerusalem Church.[1] For it meant that, having suffered a serious loss of prestige and gravely compromised himself in the eyes of his converts by his submission to the demand of James, and before he had the chance of re-establishing his reputation with them, if this were then possible, he was arrested, not as a Christian but as a violator of a Temple taboo,[2] and removed from effective communication with his followers. The record of the Acts, as is well known, ends without telling what was the outcome of Paul's appeal to Cæsar. However, there are weighty reasons for believing that it was not favourable,[3] for it is difficult to accept that Luke would have failed to commemorate such a triumph for the faith, if Paul, having been condemned by the Jewish national authorities, had been acquitted before the imperial tribunal; moreover, full consideration must be given to the fact that he patently represents Paul's last journey to Jerusalem as surrounded by forebodings of ill, amounting in Paul's own statement to an expectation of death. If, therefore, Paul had been ultimately acquitted in Rome, which fact would undoubtedly have been well known to Luke's readers, the culminating drama of the last chapters in Acts would have been insipid and meaningless, for it would have meant that all the solemn divine warnings and Paul's own forebodings had issued in nothing more than his arrest in Jerusalem and easy imprisonment until he was acquitted in Rome. On the other hand, if it were already known that Paul had finally suffered the extreme penalty, then the full poignancy of such a prophecy as that of Agabus, "So shall the Jews at Jerusalem bind the man that owneth this girdle, and shall deliver him into the hands of the Gentiles", would

---

[1] Cf. Weiss, *Urchristentum*, p. 550.

[2] Cf. Klausner, op. cit., pp. 399–400. Goguel, op. cit., p. 533, thinks that the true cause of the riot over Paul in the Temple was that the Jews regarded him as an apostate.

[3] Cf. *B.C.*, vol. i, pp. 349–50; Loisy, *Le Origini del Cristianesimo*, p. 183; Guignebert, *Le Christ*, pp. 319–23; Goguel, op. cit., pp. 346–7.

have been felt by Paul's readers, and this last journey to Jerusalem seen as the beginning of the awful drama of his martyrdom.

However that may be, it is significant that, after his arrest in Jerusalem, there is no further record of Paul's effective contact with his churches. The consequences of this fact must have been immense. The Gentile delegates would have returned to their home churches with their disturbing tale of Paul's subservience to the authorites of the Jerusalem Church and his subsequent uninspiring fate. We may well imagine the distress and perplexity of those who had believed Paul that his interpretation of Christianity was God-given, and the triumph of those who had been persuaded by his adversaries that he was an impostor. Moreover, the field was now left open to those adversaries, and we cannot doubt that James and his friends would quickly have followed up their success against Paul himself by intensifying their propaganda among his churches, in order to win over his converts to a full acceptance of their authority and doctrine. The consequences of this it will be our task to investigate later; here we must endeavour to appreciate the proportions of the crisis which was thus created for nascent Christianity.

Paul's arrest in Jerusalem seems to have taken place somewhere about the year 55.[1] In the year 62 James, the brother of the Lord, met his death [2] in what appears to have been an act of violence engineered by the High Priest, as we have already seen. The martyrdom of James, although undoubtedly causing a profound shock and a very serious loss to the Jerusalem Church, seems if anything to have redounded to its reputation, and, according to the testimony of Hegesippus, he was immediately succeeded, without any recorded opposition, by his cousin Symeon, the dynastic principle being clearly effective already.[3] Thus it appears that, whereas Paul was removed from the active leadership of his communities about 55, the Jerusalem Church continued strong and united and able to exploit to the fullest the opportunities of propaganda in those churches which were now deprived of their founder. That the campaign of the Jewish Christians must have won a large measure of success is patent, when it is remembered how even when he was able to exercise a personal influence over them, Paul had to fight a hard, and by no means a successful, battle to keep the allegiance of his converts. And now that his personal intervention was no longer possible (and tradition has preserved the name of no successor), it would appear inevitable that in process of time the Pauline achievement in theological interpretation and missionary enterprise would have ceased to survive in any effective degree, being replaced by the Jerusalem teaching and administration, which was conceived to keep the new faith strictly within the confines of Judaism. Such a situation it would appear that Luke recalls, when he causes Paul

---

[1] Cf. *B.C.*, vol. v, pp. 470–3.
[2] Cf. Lewin, *Fasti Sacri*, sects. 1929, 1931; Klausner, *Jesus of Nazareth*, p. 42; Schürer, *G.J.V.*, I, p. 583, n. 47.
[3] *Apud* Euseb., *Eccl. Hist.*, III. xi. Cf. Streeter, *Primitive Church*, p. 40.

gloomily to foretell to the Ephesian elders: "I know that after my departing grievous wolves shall enter in among you, not sparing the flock; and from among your own selves shall men arise, speaking perverse things, to draw away the disciples after them." [1]

Thus from the year 55 a crisis of the most fundamental import for the future of Christianity emerged. Each year from then saw the realization of Paul's conception of Christianity as a universal religion grow steadily more remote before the increasing control of Jerusalem. What would have been the final result of this process, if left unchecked, is necessarily a matter for speculation, but it would seem that there can be little reasonable doubt that Christianity would have been something very different from that which it did actually become, and that its connection with its Jewish origins would have remained more intimate and essential. However, it was destined that the process should not develop unchecked, and the critical decade after the arrest of Paul was suddenly and catastrophically terminated in the year 66 by the raising of the standard of revolt by the Jewish nationalists of Palestine against the government of Rome, and for Christianity the crisis of the ten years was merged into another of even greater consequence.

To appreciate the profundity of this situation and its revolutionary effects will now be our task, and we shall approach it best by undertaking a study of the course and results of the terrible war against Rome which convulsed and finally destroyed the Jewish nation between A.D. 66 and 70.

[1] Acts 20. 29, 30. Cf. Goguel, *La Naissance du Christianisme*, p. 222.

8

The Jewish War against Rome, A.D. 66 to 70

JOSEPHUS found the immediate cause of the Jewish rebellion against
Roman suzerainty in a dispute which occurred at Cæsarea between
the Jewish and the Gentile inhabitants of the city. The blame for
this outbreak and the series of provocative acts which followed Josephus
imputes to Gessius Florus, the procurator, whose conduct he explains was
prompted by the desire to goad the Jews into insurrection, so that in the
general confusion which would ensue his own misdeeds might be forgotten. The extreme nature of the guilt of Florus in this matter becomes
rather suspect owing to the persistent emphasis which the Jewish historian
places upon it, and also the fact that he goes on to show how, even after
the procurator had obtained his end and the revolt assumed serious
proportions, he nevertheless strangely continued to aggravate the affair,
even to the extent of laying himself open to the charge of neglecting his
obvious military duties, the prompt fulfilment of which might well have
redounded to the increase of his own reputation with the Emperor.[1]
Moreover, Josephus has to admit that the Jews were in arrears with their
tribute,[2] and there is a strange, and in the circumstances a significant,
silence about the reaction of the Zealots to all the unreasonable provocation
of Florus. However, although allowance must be made for his obvious
apologetic tendencies here, it would seem that Josephus had much ground
for seeing in Florus the man whose criminal conduct at length stirred
Jewish discontent beyond the point of endurance, and this view is borne
out by a brief statement of Tacitus [3]—"*duravit tamen patientia Judaeis
usque ad Gessium Florum procuratorem; sub eo bellum ortum*".

The provocative conduct of Florus did thus undoubtedly provide the
immediate cause of the war, but there were deeper and more serious
causes which had been steadily producing a situation of discontent and
recklessness which must sooner or later inevitably have expressed itself
in armed rebellion. We have already seen, in another context, that

---

[1] Jos., *Ant.*, xx. 11. 1; *Wars*, ii. 14. 2–15. 6 (277–332). According to Josephus (ibid.,
ii. 17. 4: 417), Florus refused to send troops to succour the Roman garrison and the peace party
at Jerusalem. He also blames Florus for the disastrous retreat of C. Gallus from the insurgent
capital (ibid., ii. 19. 4). One detail may here be given to illustrate the inconsistency of Josephus'
account at this point. He says (ibid., ii. 16. 5–6) that Florus tried to gain possession of the
Antonia, but according to other evidence which he gives and the testimony of Acts (ibid.,
v. 5. 8; Acts 21. 31–34) this fortress was regularly in the hands of a Roman garrison.
[2] *Wars*, ii. 16. 5; 17. 1 (404, 405).
[3] *Hist.*, v. 10. Cf. Jerome, trans. *Euseb. Chron.*, col. 455a (*Patr. Lat.*, ed. Migne, t. xxvii);
Sulp. Severus, *Chron.*, ii. 29.

Josephus blamed the politico-religious fanaticism of the Zealots for leading the Jewish people ultimately into the disastrous war with Rome,[1] and the vital part which the Zealots took in the actual fighting certainly goes far to substantiate his charge.   But the very fact of the Roman suzerainty was a standing insult to the most deeply cherished ideal of all faithful Jews, which was that of Israel as a theocracy, with Yahweh as its supreme king.   And Rome on its side signally failed to understand the religious susceptibilities of the Jews and by a policy of discreet conciliation to recommend its government to this difficult people, whose country formed a vital strategic link in the communications and defence of the Empire, and whose influence through their Diaspora was felt in almost every city of the Græco-Roman world, and extended even to the domain of Parthia, ever the potential enemy of Rome in the East.[2]   The Romans, however, not only failed to conciliate the Jewish mind on this delicate and most essential matter, but they appear deliberately to have sought to inflame Jewish feeling by senseless insults, such as those for which Pontius Pilate was responsible,[3] and finally, through the insane attempt of Caligula to erect his statue in the Temple,[4] they succeeded in creating in the Jews an ever-present fear that such a threat of desecration might at any time again be made by their heathen governors.[5]   This constant apprehension, which must have touched every pious Jew, together with the sufferings caused by the maladministration of the procurators, steadily increased the volume of Jewish discontent, so that a survey of the history of this period truly appears as the tracing of the course of some tragic drama which moves relentlessly towards its awful climax.

Eduard Meyer,[6] in commenting on the fact that Josephus blames the misgovernment of the Romans for provoking the Jews to revolt, observes that, despite the essential part played by the religious factor, the rising assumed rather the character of a social revolution and a civil war. The religious factor is undoubtedly underestimated in such a judgement, but it does serve nevertheless to draw deserved attention to an aspect of the matter which has frequently been overlooked.   The basic economic fact is that the larger part of the population of ancient Palestine was concerned with agriculture [7] and that the stability of its means of living

---

[1] See p. 105 and n. 1.

[2] Josephus found it expedient to address his book on the Jewish war to the Jews of Parthia. Cf. Goodenough, *Politics of Philo Judaeus*, pp. 19–20.

[3] Philo, *Leg. ad Caium*, sect. 38; Jos., *Ant.*, xviii. 3. 1–2, *Wars*, ii. 9. 2–4.   Cf. also the trouble over the custody of the High Priest's vestments in the time of Claudius (Jos., *Ant.*, xx. 1. 1), and Florus' taking of the seventeen talents from the Temple treasury (Jos., *Wars*, ii. 14. 6–9).

[4] See p. 108 and references there given.

[5] This fear possibly lies behind the antichrist idea as expressed in 2 Thess. 2.

[6] *Ursprung und Anfänge des Christentums*, I, p. 74, n. 2; cf. Momigliano, *Camb. Anc. Hist.*, vol. x, p. 850; F. C. Grant, *Economic Background of the Gospels*, p. 55.

[7] Cf. F. Delitzsch, *Jewish Artisan Life in the Time of Christ*, p. 17; M. Rostovtzeff, *Social and Economic Hist. of Roman Empire*, pp. 248–9.   K. Kautsky, *Foundations of Christianity*, pp. 255–6, gives no evidence in support of his statement that by this time the Jews had generally ceased to be an agricultural people and were now mainly traders and capitalists.   However, the statement might be considered true if it is meant to include the Diaspora.   Cf. Grant, op. cit., p. 71; J. Juster, *Les Juifs dans l'Empire romain*, p. 305.

depended vitally upon the maintenance of peace and good order. And it was just this which the Roman government of the country failed to provide. Taxation was heavy, officials were unjust and rapacious, and little public security was given. In the country districts large bands of malcontents, some genuine patriots but many undoubtedly little more than mere brigands, maintained themselves, very probably by levying a toll on the local population, as their modern representatives have done in the same land. Therefore the economic situation must steadily have deteriorated in the country, producing in turn a large and desperate proletariat, filled with both social and religious grievances. It was composed of men with little to lose in the overthrow of the prevailing social structure; famished and reckless as they were, they eagerly grasped at any promise of the quick coming of the Messiah and the attraction of the Messianic banquet;[1] they were men with a natural hatred of the heathen Roman overlord and that hatred easily and quickly extended to the sacerdotal aristocracy at Jerusalem, whose pro-Roman policy was dictated by its desire to preserve its position of wealth and social prestige. This dangerous condition of things in the country began to be paralleled in Jerusalem itself. About this time the completion of the Temple buildings threw a large body of men (eighteen thousand according to Josephus) out of work, and although the Jewish prince Agrippa employed them temporarily in paving the city with white stone,[2] they went to form a discontented proletariat in the city. Their ranks too must have received many recruits from the inferior orders of the priesthood, who were reduced to abject poverty by the violence and rapacity of the chief sacerdotal families of Jerusalem.[3] This social antipathy expressed itself in time in the plundering and massacring of the rich during the civil violence which preceded the siege of the city by Titus.[4]

From the point of view of our purpose of assessing the effects of the Jewish War on the Christian Church it is especially necessary for us to pay careful attention to the geographical extent and the intensity of the warfare and the consequent Jewish losses. There is much difficulty to be faced in attempting to estimate these facts, for Josephus, who is practically our only authority for these events, is clearly more concerned to recount his own rather doubtful exploits, especially in Galilee, than to give a balanced account of the war as a whole. For instance, as we shall see, his treatment of the Samaritans' part in this Jewish rebellion is most

---

[1] Cf. Luke 14. 15; 13. 29, 30; Mark 10. 37. Cf. Papias, in Lightfoot's *Apostolic Fathers*, pp. 521–2, sect. xlv.

[2] Jos., *Ant.*, xx. 9. 7; cf. Holtzmann, *Das Ende des jüdischen Staatswesens*, p. 636.

[3] Jos., op. cit., xx. 8. 8; 9. 2. It is probably the violence of the high-priestly families at this time which is celebrated in a street ballad preserved in the *Talmud* (*Pesahim*, 57a; *T. Menahoth*, xiii. 21), given in Klausner, *Jesus of Nazareth*, p. 305, n. 10; cf. Derenbourg, *Essai sur l'Histoire et la Géographie de la Palestine*, pp. 232–4; Graetz, *Hist. of the Jews*, vol. ii, p. 238.

[4] Jos., *Wars*, iv. 3. 1–5 (121–46). Note also the burning of the city archives, ibid., ii. 17. 6 (427). Cf. Stapfer, *La Palestine au Temps de Jésus-Christ*, p. 85; Schlatter, *Geschichte Israels*, p. 322.

unsatisfactory, particularly when it is remembered that this heterogeneous people constituted a barrier between the two Jewish centres of activity in Judæa and Galilee.

When by the cessation of the daily sacrifice in the Temple for the Emperor and by the massacre of the various Roman garrisons in Palestine [1] the Jews irrevocably committed themselves to a death struggle with the might of Rome, the general course of Roman action appeared clear.   For any large-scale military operation the procurator of Palestine relied upon the support of the governor of the Syrian province, who had four legions at his disposal.[2]   The governor of Syria at this time was Cestius Gallus, who had already had cause to interfere in the affairs of Palestine,[3] and so it would seem that he must have been well informed about the situation and able to form a shrewd estimate of what action was needed.   To the modern investigator it appears that the best course at this juncture must have been for the legate to enter Palestine with a strong force before the Jewish rebels could consolidate their position and fortify their cities and strongholds.   Moreover, although the Jewish province was relatively small, the importance of its people far exceeded its territorial expanse, so that the spectacle of rebellion there was likely to have a disturbing effect upon the position of Rome in the eastern provinces, and there was the possibility of repercussions in Parthia.[4]   Therefore, prompt action appears to have been essential.   However, Gallus, either from incompetence or through some unknown necessity, delayed his expedition for three months.[5]

It is rather difficult to estimate the Jewish policy and outlook at this point, because confusion reigned in Jerusalem and as yet there was no generally acknowledged leader.   The Zealots, of course, were the driving force of the revolt, but for a time their energies were absorbed in combating the efforts of the aristocracy, who were supported by the Roman garrison

---

[1] Jos., *Wars*, ii. 17. 1–2 (405–10).   According to Josephus, *Contra Apionem*, ii. 6, the Jews themselves paid for these sacrifices.   Philo, *Leg. ad Caium*, sects. 157, 317, states that the Emperor paid.

[2] Cf. Jos., *Ant.*, xviii. 4. 2, *Wars*, ii. 12. 6 (239, 241–4); Tac., *Ann.*, xii. 54; Arnold, *Roman Provincial Administration*, pp. 127–8.   On the subject of the legions see Mommsen, *Roman Provinces*, vol. ii, p. 210, n. 1.   Cf. Ginsburg, *Rome et la Judée*, pp. 124–5.

[3] Jos., *Wars*, ii. 14. 3; 16. 1–2 (280–3, 333–5).

[4] The victories of Corbulo had only recently rendered the eastern frontier tolerably safe. Some of the kinsmen of Monobazus, king of Adiabene, did fight on the Jewish side; Jos., *Wars*, ii. 19. 2 (520).   Rev. 6. 1–3 illustrates the fear of a Parthian invasion which always beset the inhabitants of Syria.   Cf. B. Pin, *Jérusalem contre Rome*, p. 13.

[5] The *terminus a quo* of the beginning of the revolt is Berenice's petition, which is dated for the 16th of Artemisios (Jos., *Wars*, ii. 15. 2: 315–17), and the *terminus ad quem* is the 15th of Loos, the date of the assault on the Antonia (ibid., ii. 17. 7: 430).   This involves a difference of three months.   From internal evidence the cessation of the imperial sacrifices must have occurred in Panemos, probably early in the month.   C. Gallus finally attacked Jerusalem on the 30th of Hyperberetaios (ibid. 19. 4: 528); computation will show that he was at Beth-Horon on the 23rd of that month (ibid. 19. 2–4); so, since his march was rapid, it is probable that he set out in the same month.   In *The Wars* Josephus unfortunately employs the Macedonian months for chronological purposes, and it is impossible to tell whether he equates them with the months of the Julian or the Jewish calendars; cf. Schürer, *G.J.V.*, I, pp. 755–60.

of Jerusalem and a detachment of troops sent by Agrippa—the Jewish prince being intent on limiting the effects of the rising.[1]   Thus until this opposition could be overthrown in the capital the Zealots were unable to organize the country to resist the expected punitive expedition of the Syrian legate and his legions.   The raising of the standard of revolt against Rome, however, had its repercussions throughout the whole of Palestine and a large part of the Diaspora.[2]   The movement appears quickly to have become widespread in Palestine, involving it would seem such places as Tiberias, Tarichæa, and the Peræan Julias, which were special possessions of Agrippa II.[3]   Of the attitude of Samaria to this Jewish revolt Josephus gives us very little information, which is unfortunate, since the intense antipathy which existed between the Jews and the Samaritans is well known.   From the meagre references of the Jewish historian it would seem that the majority of the Samaritans were coerced into an outward allegiance to the Jews; possibly the city of Sebaste resisted, since it was garrisoned by a Roman contingent and had to be reduced by force.[4] The news of the revolt, and especially of the slaughter of the Roman garrison at Jerusalem, had a disastrous consequence for the Jewish population of Cæsarea.   This city, which had long been the headquarters of the procurator, had undoubtedly many attachments with the Roman military and so its reaction to the news was most violent and a complete massacre of the Jews ensued.[5]   This bloody act naturally provoked Jewish reprisals.   The Gentile cities of Philadelphia, Sebonitis, Gerasa, Pella, Scythopolis, Gadara, Hippos, Kedesa, Ptolemais, Gaba, and of the district of Gaulonitis were attacked, the neighbouring Syrian villages were laid waste, and without doubt Gentiles throughout Palestine generally perished as victims of Jewish fanaticism.[6]   The hour of Jewish vengeance had come, and it would seem that, though as yet national feeling was unorganized, such was its strength and intensity that it infected the whole people, with a few exceptions, and swept them irresistibly into a frenzy of religious exultation and violent hatred for the heathen Gentile. Such passions alone could sustain them in their act of rebellion, for humanly speaking their cause was hopeless, since sooner or later it was certain that Rome would put forth her mighty strength and crush their puny resistance, taking for their crime a most bloody revenge.   Hence there is a certain nobility in the Zealot action as they led their country into this awful war, for the Zealots had not taken up arms because they

---

[1] *Wars*, ii. 17. 3–10 (411–55); see *Life*, 5. Cf. Schlatter, op. cit., p. 325.

[2] Pogroms broke out in Tyre, Alexandria, Damascus, and in many other Syrian cities; Jos., *Wars*, ii. 18. 2–5, 7–8; 20. 2 (461–8, 487–98, 559–61). The massacre at Damascus occurred after the defeat of Gallus; Jos., *Life*, 6; Euseb., *Eccl. Hist.*, II. xxvi.

[3] Jos., *Wars*, iii. 9. 7 (445 *seq.*); *Life*, 9, states that Tiberias was divided on the question of war.

[4] Cf. Jos., *Wars*, ii. 18. 1 (460). Cf. Thomson, *The Samaritans*, p. 39.

[5] Jos., op. cit., ii. 18. 1 (457).

[6] Jos., op. cit., ii. 18. 1 (458–60). Josephus also mentions Cæsarea and Askalon, but it is known from ibid., iii. 2. 1 (9–25), that Askalon was not taken, and it is also very improbable that Cæsarea suffered such a fate, since there is evidence of cohorts there during these times. Cf. ibid, iii. 4. 2 (66); Ricciotti, *Flavio Giuseppe*, vol. ii, p. 328, n. on 458–60.

thought that they were stronger than the Romans, but because they hoped for a saving miracle from God.[1] When we remember too the inspiration which must have come to these men from their nation's great past—the wonderful deliverances which Yahweh had wrought for their fathers from the bondage of Egypt, from the threat of Sennacherib, and from the cruel impiety of Antiochus Epiphanes—we can understand the burning faith which lies enshrined in the words which they engraved on their new coins : שנת אהת לגאלת ישראל (the first year of the redemption of Israel).[2] For the moment the insurgents' policy probably consisted of no more than a determination to put down all opposition to the sacred cause of Israel's liberty and to await behind the walls of their Holy City the inevitable attack of the impious Roman, with full confidence in Yahweh's succour.

The attack, though delayed, was powerfully delivered. Cestius Gallus at length entered Palestine with a strong force of legionary and auxiliary troops. He encountered little opposition in Galilee or Samaria, owing undoubtedly to the Jewish lack of organized effort, and he advanced with confidence straight on to the insurgent capital.[3] Here, despite some minor reverses, the legate succeeded in pushing his attack to the very point of breaching the Temple walls, when suddenly for some inexplicable reason he ordered his troops to withdraw from the final assault, and then, after a short stop on Mount Scopus, to retreat northward from the city.[4] The

---

[1] Cf. Schlatter, *Geschichte Israels*, pp. 325–6.

[2] Madden, *Coins of the Jews*, p. 198; cf. pp. 203, 206. These coins also bear the names שמעון נשיא ישראל : אלעזר הכהן; Madden, *Hist. Jew. Coinage*, pp. 174–5, would assign the coins stamped with the legend "Simon, prince of Israel" to the Head of the Sanhedrin, Simon, son of Gamaliel; cf. Schürer, *G.J.V.*, I, pp. 765–72. The importance of these two men, Eleazer and Simon, which these coins attest, does not appear in Josephus' records, which fact indicates that he cannot be entirely relied upon to give an accurate account of what happened within the walls of Jerusalem. Cf. Eisler, *ΙΗΣΟΥΣ ΒΑΣΙΛΕΥΣ*, II, p. 560, n. 4.

[3] Jos., op. cit., ii. 18. 9–19. 4 (499–527). Smith, *Historical Geography*, p. 299, condemns Gallus for his swift rush across the frontiers of Judæa. But on Josephus' evidence (*Wars*, ii. 18. 10–11; 19. 1 : 507–12, 513–14) all opposition had been subdued in Galilee, while it was unlikely that Samaria would give trouble.

[4] Jos., op. cit., ii. 19. 1–7 (513–45). Josephus blames Florus for this retreat, explaining that he plotted to achieve this in order to increase the seriousness of the war. It is scarcely credible that the legate should thus have allowed himself to be turned away when at the point of victory; possibly Josephus inferred this from the report of Gallus to Nero (ibid., ii. 20. 1 : 588). Schürer, op. cit., p. 605, briefly intimates that the legate found his forces insufficient for a successful assault; but this cannot be the case, considering the degree of success which he had already attained. Schürer's suggestion seems to be based on the size of the forces later employed by Vespasian and Titus, but it is clear that the revolt at the time of the expedition of Gallus had by no means developed to the extent to which it attained after his defeat. Graetz, *Hist. of the Jews*, vol. ii, p. 263, thinks that Gallus deemed it inadvisable to embark on a lengthy campaign at so late a season of the year. This explanation cannot be accepted in view of the fact that the Roman advance had been rapid and Gallus had already committed himself to the siege of Jerusalem. Schlatter, op. cit., does not attempt to explain the mystery. Momigliano, *Camb. Anc. Hist.*, vol. x, p. 856, states that the retreat was due to Gallus' fear of an attack upon his flanks, but he does not specify from whom this was likely to come, and Josephus gives no indication of the possibility of such a movement. Ricciotti, op. cit., vol. ii, p. 348, rightly emphasizes the discrepancies of Josephus' account of the matter; his own opinion is that Gallus underestimated his task when preparing the expedition—a conclusion which is scarcely borne out by his rapid success. Cf. Jones, *Herods of Judaea*, p. 247; Ferrero e Barbagallo, *Roma Antica*, vol. ii, p. 308; Eisler, op. cit., I, p. 320. In the author's opinion Josephus has omitted, intentionally or unintentionally, to record certain essential facts in his account; with this view Dr. Eisler in a letter has kindly signified his concurrence.

Jews, who had been in a desperate plight and fully expecting the Romans to break into their sanctuary, were astonished to see their enemies so strangely turn their backs upon almost certain victory, and, when once their fears of some stratagem were dispelled, their joy was unbounded. The miracle of Sennacherib's army had been repeated; Yahweh in some mysterious way had saved his shrine and turned the triumph of the heathen into the ignominy of retreat. Filled then with the burning conviction of divine assistance, the Jews eagerly pursued after the retreating Romans, harassing their march and inflicting many losses. In the rocky defiles of the Beth-Horons the Roman position became most serious, and only nightfall and the subsequent sacrifice of their rearguard enabled the remnants of the legate's force to struggle to safety beyond the frontiers of Palestine.[1]   And thus the first great contest between the Jews and the Romans ended.   For the Romans it was undoubtedly the greatest military disaster since the loss of the legions of Varus in the German forests.   It meant that a Roman army under the leadership of an important provincial governor had been defeated by the unorganized insurgents of a small country, which, however, held the key position between the rich province of Syria and the granary of Egypt.   For the time Roman prestige was seriously lowered in the East and an important line of communication endangered.[2]   Such a situation, of course, could not be accepted, and for once Nero showed something of his latent ability in selecting Vespasian, whose military experience had been hardly won in Britain, for the difficult task of subduing the rebellious Jews and restoring the Roman position in their rugged land.[3]   To the Jews the defeat of Gallus was the hoped-for demonstration of Yahweh's power and saving care.   It seemed indeed as if his Temple was inviolable, for so soon as the heathen had laid their impious hands upon that sacred structure confusion had fallen upon them, and in their fatal retreat nearly six thousand of their number had perished by the victorious arms of his chosen people.   Before such a manifestation of divine succour all opposition to the revolt inevitably faded away,[4] and this victory over the army of Cestius Gallus had for the

---

[1] Jos., op. cit., ii. 19. 7–9 (540–55). On the difficult nature of the road through the Beth-Horons see Smith, *Historical Geography*, p. 210, n. 2; Lightfoot, *Horae Hebraicae*, vol. i, pp. 43–4. The pass was the scene of the victory of Joshua over the Amorites (Josh. 10. 10, 11) and of Judas Maccabæus over the Seleucid army under Seron (1 Macc. 3. 13–24), which facts must now have appeared very significant to the Jews. Cf. Ricciotti, op. cit., vol. ii, pp. 349–50, nn. on 542, 546.

[2] The Romans suffered two other heavy defeats at this time in Britain and Armenia; see Suet., *Nero*, 39; Tac., *Ann.*, xiv. 29, xv. 8; Dio Cassius, lxiii, Epit. Zonaras, 11, 13.   Rostovtzeff, *Social and Economic Hist. of Roman Empire*, p. 306, clearly underestimates the potential significance of this defeat in the eyes of the Romans when he describes the Jewish War as "a local colonial war which did not affect the Empire as a whole".   The appointment of Vespasian to undertake the subjugation of Palestine indicates the degree of concern felt by the imperial government. Cf. Ferrero e Barbagallo, op. cit., vol. ii, pp. 308–9; Peretti, *La Sibilla babilonese*, pp. 18–20.

[3] Cf. Henderson, *Life and Principate of the Emperor Nero*, p. 372; Bersanetti, *Vespasiano*, pp. 17–18.

[4] Cf. Schlatter, op. cit., p. 327; Holtzmann, *Das Ende des jüdischen Staatswesens*, p. 644. Josephus does state that many eminent Jews fled from the city after the defeat of Gallus (*Wars*, ii. 20. 1 : 556), but he gives the names of three only, all of whom were closely connected with King Agrippa II (cf. ibid., ii. 17. 4 : 418).

Jews the fatal consequence of pledging them henceforth, with all the fervour of religious conviction, to their disastrous struggle with Rome.

The actual course of Jewish affairs immediately after the Roman defeat is not clear, owing to the partial accounts of Josephus. From what he chooses to tell it appears that a party of moderates now assumed control in Jerusalem, led, and this is very surprising, by the High Priest; Eleazer, the Zealot commander in the recent fighting, was excluded from the government.[1] This moderate party now began to organize the defence of the whole country, and generals were appointed and dispatched to various places. Among these was, according to his own testimony, the future historian Josephus, who received the charge of Galilee.[2] The appointment of such an inexperienced young man to a district which must bear the brunt of the Roman attack is certainly strange, and there is much ground for doubt about the exact nature of his commission, as there is also about his conduct in its execution.[3] However, this problem does not concern us here; what is more relevant to our subject is the state of Galilee at this time. Of this unfortunately we can only be certain of one thing, namely that much disorder and violence were rife there. Josephus in his *Wars of the Jews* and in his *Life* gives us two conflicting accounts.[4] In the former work he tells how he succeeded in fortifying all the chief cities and strong places of Galilee and that he raised and trained an army of one hundred thousand Galilæans. Such a tale of energetic straightforward preparation does not appear in his auto-biography, which was written later. On the contrary, in this we have a long account of unsavoury intrigues and exploits in which it appears that there were many pro-Roman elements in Galilee, while there was no unity of command among the insurgents. One fact, however, must be carefully given its full weight, namely, that one of the chief opponents of Josephus in Galilee was John of Gischala, who later was one of the two Jewish leaders in the terrible siege of Jerusalem, where he defended the Temple with the Zealot forces. That such a man should have been active then in Galilee and that he should fiercely have opposed the treacherous activities of Josephus indicates surely, amid all the welter of Josephus' apologetic, the fact that Zealot policy was strong and ably enforced in Galilee, and the subsequent campaign of Vespasian amply confirms this view.

In the spring of the year 67 Vespasian entered Palestine with three legions and a strong body of auxiliary troops.[5] But now a different

---

[1] Jos., *Wars*, ii. 20. 3 (562–5); *Life*, 7. Cf. Graetz, op. cit., vol. ii, p. 270; Stapfer, *La Palestine au Temps de Jésus-Christ*, p. 86.
[2] Jos., *Wars*, ii. 20. 3–4 (563–8). Cf. Graetz, op. cit., vol. ii, p. 280.
[3] Josephus gives two different accounts of his appointment, namely in *Wars*, ii. 20. 4 (568), and *Life*, 7. Cf. Krauss, *Jew. Encycl.*, vol. 7, p. 274; Thackeray, *Josephus: the Man and the Historian*, pp. 10–12, 20–1; Eisler, *Messiah Jesus*, pp. 183 *seq.*, ΙΗΣΟΥΣ ΒΑΣΙΛΕΥΣ, I, pp. 261 *seq.*
[4] *Wars*, ii. 20. 6–21. 10 (569–640); *Life*, 7–73. Cf. Milman, *History of the Jews*, vol. i, p. 533.
[5] Jos., *Wars*, iii. 4. 2 (64–9).

situation existed from that of the previous year, for a series of fortified cities barred the way, in Galilee especially, to Jerusalem. Since the Jews would not give him the opportunity of deciding the issue in one great pitched battle, Vespasian saw the necessity of reducing provincial Palestine first before attacking the centre of the revolt at the metropolis; [1] moreover, it would be impossible to maintain a large army on the barren hills of Judæa, unless communications northward were free and supplies could be drawn from Galilee and the Plain of Esdraelon.[2] Consequently the operations of the Romans during the campaigning season of this year were confined to the reduction of the insurgents of Galilee and other neighbouring districts. It was an arduous task, for it meant a succession of sieges of well-fortified places, and the Jews, while unable to oppose the Roman legionaries in the open field, excelled in this type of fighting, where fanatical courage and individual resource equally matched the discipline and military science of the Romans. But it was a mode of warfare which finally involved the defenders in even more terrible losses than the attackers, for the taking of a city generally meant an almost total massacre of its inhabitants. The towns of Gabara, Jotapata, Japha, Tarichæa, Gischala, Gamala, and Joppa suffered in this way.[3] The Samaritans also became involved in the slaughter and Josephus tells us that in an obscure action over eleven thousand of them were slain by the Romans.[4] The fall of Tarichæa apparently led to the capitulation of the rest of insurgent Galilee, and the end of the first year's campaign saw the Romans in possession of Galilee, Samaria, and the seaboard west of Judæa.[5]

During the course of this fighting in the north, and to a certain extent as a result of it, a situation of terrible confusion rapidly developed in Jerusalem. Possibly owing to the defection of Josephus, the moderate party began to lose its power; and the arrival of John of Gischala in the city gave the Zealots a capable leader, so that, with the aid of a force of

---

[1] Josephus, *Wars*, iii. 6. 3 (129), does say that he attempted to oppose the Romans in the open field at Garis, but the result was a fiasco, the Jews fleeing on the mere report of the approach of the enemy.

[2] Cf. Smith, *Historical Geography*, pp. 298–9. Abrahams, *Campaigns in Palestine*, p. 34, considers that the Jews made a strategic blunder in allowing themselves to be shut up in Jerusalem. It is, however, more in keeping with the facts to think that the military superiority of their opponents gave the Jews no choice of strategy; moreover, their obvious belief in the inviolability of the Temple must also be remembered; cf. Jos., op. cit., vi. 2. 1 (99); Schlatter, *Geschichte Israels*, p. 329.

[3] Jos., op. cit., iii. 7. 1, 3–31, 33–36; 9. 2–4; 10. 1–6, 9–10; iv. 1–2 (132–306, 316–39, 414–31, 462–505, 522–42, 1–120); *Life*, 74. Cf. Madden, *Coins of the Jews*, pp. 222–3.

[4] *Wars*, iii. 7. 32 (307–15). Possibly the Samaritans had been infected with something of the fanaticism of the Jews and had assembled on their holy mountain to await the advent of their *Taheb*. Lightley, *Jewish Sects*, pp. 233–4, thinks that they made common cause with the Jews, but there is no evidence for this view, nor is it consistent with what we otherwise know of them. The suggestion of Thomson, *The Samaritans*, pp. 39–40, that the Samaritans could not make Cerealis, the Roman commander, understand the object of their assembly, appears very plausible. Cf. Gaster, *Samaritans*, pp. 89–90.

[5] Op. cit., iv. 2. 5 (120). There is certainly no evidence for the statement of Graetz, op. cit., vol. ii, p. 293, that the Romans were so exhausted by the fighting in Galilee that, after its reduction, Vespasian had to declare a truce.

patriotic but ferocious Idumæans, they eventually succeeded in destroying the moderates and seizing the control of the war against Rome.¹

The next year Vespasian continued his careful policy of reducing the
insurgent centres outside the capital.   He subdued Peræa and Idumæa,
and occupied the towns of Antipatris, Lydda, Emmaus, Jericho, and
Adida, thus isolating Jerusalem, the headquarters of the revolt.²   The
results of this year's campaign certainly appear rather meagre, but it is
difficult to decide whether this was due to Vespasian's caution in the face
of a stubborn Jewish resistance, or to his unwillingness to involve himself
too deeply in operations while the affairs of the Empire were in so pre-
carious a position after the death of Nero.   That this latter fact must have
weighed heavily with Vespasian is clear from his subsequent election to
the purple.³   For the rest of his stay in Palestine his activity was confined
to destroying the remaining rebel strongholds outside Jerusalem, with the
exceptions of Herodium, Masada, and Machærus.⁴   When at last the
legate of Syria and the governor of Egypt concurred in proclaiming
Vespasian as Emperor, the Judæan campaign came to a standstill and
Vespasian left Palestine with a large part of his army.⁵

Dr. Schlatter has wisely observed ⁶ that this cautious campaign of
Vespasian, in which so little spectacular progress was made, had the effect
of stimulating and strengthening the hopes of the insurgent Jews that
Yahweh was concerning himself with the safety of Zion.   Although
Jerusalem was still considerably disturbed by the warring factions of the
various groups of patriots which had concentrated there for its defence,
it seems that the chaos could not have reached the destructive dimensions
described by Josephus, for we know from his own testimony that the great
festivals were still being celebrated in the Temple and attended by the
people generally.⁷   That such men should continue to remain as the
defenders of a city upon which a relentless enemy was steadily closing in
is not consistent with the character of mere brigands and desperadoes, as
Josephus would have us see them, but it clearly points to men animated,
fanatically perhaps, but genuinely, with a dynamic belief that they were

---

¹ Jos., *Wars*, iii. 9. 6, iv. 3. 6 seq. (438–42, 121 seq.); Tac., *Hist.*, v. 12. Cf. Derenbourg,
Essai sur l'Histoire et la Géographie de la Palestine, pp. 269–70; Stapfer, *La Palestine au Temps de
Jésus-Christ*, p. 88; Graetz, *Hist. of the Jews*, vol. ii, p. 296; Momigliano, *Camb. Anc. Hist.*, vol. x,
p. 860 (who thinks that the Idumæans joined the fight, not so much on account of their
hatred of Rome, as for their loathing of the Jewish upper classes, whom they regarded as
oppressors).

² Jos., op. cit., iv. 7. 3–8. 2; 9. 1 (410–50, 486–90). For the position of Adida see Smith,
Historical Geography, Plate iv; Schürer, *G.J.V.*, I, p. 238, n. 36.

³ Cf. Bersanetti, *Vespasiano*, p. 22.

⁴ Jos., ibid.; Tac., op. cit., v. 10. This was during the winter of 68–9.

⁵ Tac., op. cit., ii. 79; Suet., *Vespasian* 6, *Vitellius* 15; Jos., op. cit., iv. 10. 3–6; Dio Cassius,
lxiv. 9. 2 (Epit. Xiph. 196 f.). Cf. G. H. Stephenson, *Camb. Anc. Hist.*, vol. x, pp. 827–9.
On the question of what proportion of the Roman army remained in Palestine see Mommsen,
Provinces, vol. ii, p. 213, with which compare J. Rendel Harris, *Some Interesting Syrian and Palestinian Inscriptions*, p. 10.

⁶ Op. cit., p. 332.

⁷ Op. cit., v. 3. 1, vi. 9. 3 (99–102, 421). The offering of the daily sacrifice continued until
there was not a priest left to make it; Jos., op. cit., vi. 2. 1 (94). Thackeray, Loeb ed., loc. cit.,
suggests that ἀρνῶν should be substituted for ἀνδρῶν.

waging a holy war, in which they could be certain of divine help. And thus from their exultation over the defeat of Cestius Gallus and from the slackening of Roman efforts in 68–9 there grew the unshakable confidence in the ultimate success of their cause and they could regard with calm equanimity the gradual encirclement of the Holy City by the forces of the heathen.[1]

The suspension of the war which had been occasioned by the election of Vespasian was brought to an end when in the spring of the year 70, some few days before the Passover, Titus, the eldest son of the Emperor, gathered his forces before the walls of Jerusalem for the final overthrow of the Jewish rebels.[2]　The Roman army was far stronger than it had been for the previous campaign, and it now consisted of four legions and a great force of auxiliary troops;[3] the issue could now no longer be left subject to any chance, since the Jews had already succeeded in defying the power of Rome for nearly four years, and, moreover, the new dynasty of the Flavii badly needed some striking military success to enhance the prestige of its government.

The siege which followed was one of the most terrible in history.　The approach of the Romans immediately united the Jews, and under their two commanders, John of Gischala and Simon ben-Gorias, they fought as loyally as did their opponents under the son of the Emperor.[4]　Since Jerusalem was subdivided by walls and possessed three separate places of great strength, namely the fortress of Antonia, the Temple, and the Herodian palace with its massive towers, it could not be taken by the breaching of its outer defences, but it had to be won by sections, which meant fighting in constricted spaces, in which, as we have seen, the Jews excelled.[5]　The Jewish cause was naturally hopeless from the start.　The city was "kept in on every side" by a great Roman feat of circumvallation, and hunger and disease proved to be enemies as potent as the Roman legionaries.[6]　Nevertheless the Jewish patriots refused every offer of terms and fought with indescribable fury in contesting every foot of the Roman advance.　The Temple, of course, was the great storm centre of the siege, for it stood as the concrete embodiment of all that the Jews hoped, and fought, and suffered for; in its defence they had risen in revolt

---

[1] When Josephus took the opportunity of the cessation of the daily sacrifice to urge the Jews to surrender, John of Gischala replied with scorn that he never feared the taking of the city, because it was God's own city (θεοῦ γὰρ ὑπάρχειν τὴν πόλιν); Jos., *Wars*, vi. 2. 1 (98).

[2] Jos., op. cit., v. 1. 6–3. 1 (40–99).　Cf. Lewin, *Fasti Sacri*, 2116.

[3] Jos., op. cit., v. 1. 6 (40–6).

[4] Jos., op. cit., v. 6. 4 (277–8); Tac., op. cit., v. 12.

[5] For descriptions of Jerusalem at this period see Jos., op. cit., v. 4–5 (136–247); Tac., op. cit., v. 11–12.　For modern accounts see Smith, *Jerusalem*, vol. i, pp. 32–9, Map 3 (for comparative profile of the hills), chap. viii (for a discussion of the walls); *Palestine Exploration Fund Quarterly*, 1905, art. by C. Wilson, cf. ibid. (1886), pp. 92–113; arts. by J. Garstang and R. Levy, in *Wonders of the Past*, vol. iii; Olmstead, *Jesus in the Light of History*, pp. 71–91; Albright, *Archaeology of Palestine*, pp. 154–6, 158.

[6] Jos., op. cit., v. 9. 2; 11. 4–12 (356–9, 466–518), for the circumvallation of Jerusalem.　Cf. Luke 19. 43 and Creed's note, *St. Luke*, pp. 353–4.　On the sufferings of the Jewish population see Jos., op. cit., v. 10. 2–5; 12. 3–4; 13. 7; vi. 3. 3–4 (424–45, 512–26, 567–72, 193–213).　Cf. Euseb., *Eccl. Hist.*, III. vi; Derenbourg, *Essai sur l'Histoire et la Géographie de la Palestine*, p. 285.

and in its inviolability they had put their trust.   If Dr. Charles' surmise [1] is correct and we have in the first three verses of the eleventh chapter of the Apocalypse a fragment of a Zealot prophecy, we can well see the nature of this hope—the outer court of the Temple may indeed be trodden under foot of the Gentiles, but the sanctuary and they who worship there would go untouched; Yahweh would suffer the heathen thus far but no farther.   But the miracle for which they hoped did not come.   The heathen stormed the Temple; the heathen polluted its courts with Israel's blood and set fire to Yahweh's noble house, but still Yahweh did not answer, nor did his Messiah descend to blast the impious invader with his breath; instead thousands of his people were butchered in those holy courts or found in that sacred edifice their funeral pyre, while the victorious Romans did sacrifice to their heathen standards and hailed their commander as Imperator.[2]

The destruction of the Temple was the virtual end of Jewish resistance; a stupor seems to have settled upon the Jews at the sight of such inexplicable desecration: they lost all heart for further fight, and were just slaughtered by the ferocious legionaries, and when at length the carnage was stayed the Holy City of Jerusalem was a desolation of dead bodies and smoking ruins.[3]

The fall of Jerusalem marked, with a few small exceptions, the collapse of the Jewish revolt against Rome.[4]   It had been a long and desperate struggle stretching over some four years, and the Jewish losses had necessarily been enormous.   Josephus gives in different places in his work the figures of the Jewish losses, which amount for the whole war to the prodigious number of 1,356,460.[5]   Such a total, because it is given by Josephus, is naturally to be suspected of exaggeration, but the words of the Lukan Apocalypse,[6] whether a genuine prophecy or a *vaticinium post eventum*, were surely terribly fulfilled—"And they shall fall by the edge of the sword, and shall be led captive into all the nations: and Jerusalem shall be trodden down of the Gentiles, until the times of the Gentiles be fulfilled."   The numbers of those who perished, or were deported [7] as

---

[1] *I.C.C.*, vol. i, pp. 270 *seq.*, 274 *seq.*; cf. Streeter, *Four Gospels*, pp. 517–8.   An echo of this belief is found in the *Sibylline Oracles*, v. 401–2 (ed. Charles, *Apoc. and Pseudepig.*, vol. i, p. 404): (the Temple) "made with holy hands and such that men from their soul and body itself trusted would be ever immortal".   Jos., *Wars*, vi. 5. 2 (285), tells of a "false prophet" who on the very day of the destruction of the Temple urged the people to await their divine deliverance there. He also records that the "tyrants" thus employed such "false prophets" to encourage the people.

[2] Jos., op. cit., v. 4. 4–8; 5. 1–2; 6. 1 (224–7, 271–87, 316).   For such a picture of the Messiah see 2 Esdras 13. 3, 4, 9–11.   Oesterley, *New Com.*, Apoc., p. 32, and Charles, op. cit., vol. ii, pp. 551–2, date this part of 2 Esdras for just before A.D. 70.   Cf. Williams, *Hebrew-Christian Messiah*, pp. 254–5.

[3] Jos., op. cit., vi. 6. 2–3; 7. 1–3; 8. 1–5 (323–55, 358–73, 374–408).

[4] The strongholds of Herodium, Machærus, and Masada were captured a little later; Jos., op. cit., vii. 6. 1, 4; 8. 1–2, 4–7; 9. 1–2 (163–4, 190–209, 252–79, 295–388, 389–406).

[5] The compilation is made by Milman, *History of the Jews*, vol. ii, pp. 100–1.

[6] Luke 21. 24.   Cf. Taylor, *Behind the Third Gospel*, pp. 118–24.   It may, however, be one of what Creed describes (*St. Luke*, pp. 135 *seq.*) as "the Lukan modifications due to history".

[7] On the number and fate of the Jewish captives see Jos., op. cit., vi. 9. 3; vii. 2. 1; 3. 1 (420, 23–5, 37–40).   In the *Talmud* (*Gittin*, f. 57a) the immolation of Israel in the arenas of the Empire is remembered: "For seven years did the nations of the world cultivate their vineyards with no other manure than the blood of Israel."   Milman, ibid., gives the number of prisoners as 101,700.

captives or maimed, or otherwise suffered in this national calamity must certainly have been proportionate to the length and extension of the war and the extreme ferocity with which it was waged on both sides. And, further, these losses must have been sustained by all ranks of society, for the rich had suffered in the class war which preceded the real conflict with Rome, the non-combatants had been subject to the hunger and disease occasioned by the many sieges, and generally they had been involved in the subsequent massacres which marked the taking of their towns, and those who had actively participated in the fighting, of course, met their inevitable fate either in battle or in defeat. To all this physical suffering which overwhelmed the Jewish people must be added the destruction of their homes and goods and of their economic resources, involving, as Dr. Büchler has well shown,[1] terrible hardships in the years immediately following the war. The Jews did, then, indeed receive a blow from which, as a nation, they never recovered. Although later, in the time of Hadrian, they rose once more in armed revolt against Rome, their national existence had really terminated in A.D. 70, for on the razed site of their Holy City a heathen soldiery now had its camp,[2] and, as Holtzmann has well said,[3] "*Die nationale Selbständigkeit des Volkes war für immer vernichtet. Ein Neues Zeitalter musste für den jüdischen Glauben beginnen. Der Mittelpunkt des bisherigen Judentums, der Tempel zu Jerusalems, war nicht mehr.*" Judaism was left to find for itself a new bond of union in the study of the Law and the worship of the synagogue; the *Talmud*, not the Temple, would from henceforth symbolize the spirit of Israel's race.[4]

[1] *Economic Conditions of Judaea after the Destruction of the Second Temple*, pp. 29–55. Cf. Albright, *Archaeology of Palestine*, pp. 240–1.

[2] Jos., *Wars*, 7. 1. 1 (1–4); cf. vi. 9. 1 (413). For a rabbinical account of the razing of Jerusalem see *Taanith*, iv–v (Maimond), quoted by Stapfer, *La Palestine au Temps de Jésus-Christ*, p. 90; but see also Milman, op. cit., vol. ii, pp. 132, n. 2, 136, 139, n. 3. Cf. Schürer, *G.J.V.*, I, p. 634; Albright, op. cit., pp. 166, 168.

[3] *Das Ende des jüdischen Staatswesens*, p. 673. Cf. Windisch, *Der Untergang Jerusalems* (*Anno* 70) *im Urteil der Christen und Juden*, p. 548; H. J. Schoeps, *Die Tempelzerstörung des Jahres 70, in der jüdischen Religionsgeschichte*, pp. 2–3, 27–8; Cohen, *Il Talmud*, pp. 10 seq.

[4] Cf. Oesterley and Box, *Literature of Rabbinic and Mediaeval Judaism*, pp. 20 seq.; Schürer, *G.J.V.*, I, pp. 652–60; Milman, op. cit., vol. ii, pp. 115 seq.; Oesterley, *Hist. of Israel*, vol. ii, p. 251; R. T. Herford, *Effect of Fall of Jerusalem upon Character of Pharisees*; O. Spengler, *Decline of the West*, vol. ii, pp. 210–12; Toynbee, *A Study of History*, vol. ii, pp. 285–6, vol. v, pp. 74–6. Pin, *Jérusalem contre Rome*, pp. 129 seq., suggests that the fall of Jerusalem in A.D. 70 was not fatal, since the Diaspora survived, whereas the overthrow in A.D. 135, consequent on the Bar Cochba revolt, was definitive. As a further index to the complexity of the politico-religious factor in Palestine during this period see the interpretation of the so-called *Damascus Script* put forward by Dr. R. Eisler in the *Gaster Anniversary Volume* (London, 1936), pp. 110–143. See also the interpretation recently set forth by Professor André Dupont Sommer, in a paper read before the Académic des Inscriptions et Belles Lettres, of the commentary on Habakkuk which was among the so-called Dead Sea Scrolls discovered in 1947 (a summary of the paper appeared in *The Times* of May 30, 1950, and in *The Spectator* of July 7, 1950, pp. 8–9). This interpretation should also be compared with that advanced by Dr. R. Eisler in a letter to *The Modern Churchman*, vol. xxxix (1949), pp. 284–7.

9

The Fate of the Palestinian Church

THE destruction of their Holy City and the consequent cessation of the Temple worship had a paralysing effect on the life of the Jewish people, and from it they only slowly recovered and settled to an essentially maimed existence, with their cherished religion bereft of much of its *raison d'être*. The profundity of the disaster finds a curiously paradoxical expression in that the record of Israel's sufferings is only preserved by a renegade member of the race, Josephus, for the gratification of the heathen conqueror; but of the agony of mind which this terrible test of faith in Yahweh's providence caused among those who survived there remains a poignant proof in the so-called Salathiel Apocalypse.[1] Herein the author asks, with the passionate urgency of one whose deepest convictions had been shaken by the rude contradiction of fact, bitter questions of the God whom he had been taught to trust: "Are their deeds any better that inhabit Babylon? and hath she therefore dominion over Sion? . . . For I have seen how thou sufferest them sinning, and hast spared the ungodly doers, and hast preserved thine enemies; and thou hast not signified unto any how thy way may be comprehended. Are the deeds of Babylon better than those of Sion? Or is there any other nation that knoweth thee beside Israel? Or what tribes have so believed thy covenants as these tribes of Jacob?"[2]

To those Jewish Christians who survived the carnage of A.D. 70 the same heart-rending questions must have presented themselves, but of their reactions thereto no certain record remains. Among all the documents which comprise the New Testament canon, and indeed among the other extant writings of the sub-apostolic age, there is no description of the terrible events which attended the defeat of Israel's cause against Rome, or of the fortunes of the Palestinian Christians amid the convulsion and overthrow of their nation's life, neither is there any conscious reference

[1] Preserved in 2 Esdras 3. According to 3. 1, 29 the Apocalypse is to be dated for thirty years after the destruction of Jerusalem. Cf. Oesterley, *New Com.*, Apoc., p. 33. On different aspects of the Jewish reaction to the destruction of Jerusalem see *Sibylline Oracles*, v. 11, 408–11 (ed. Charles, *Apoc. and Pseudepig.*, vol. ii, p. 405; cf. p. 373); Baruch 3. 9–end. Cf. Peretti, *La Sibilla babilonese*, pp. 467 seq.,; Thackeray, *New Com.*, Apoc., pp. 104–5; Schürer, *G.J.V.*, III, pp. 223 seq., 239, 443; Edersheim, *Hist. of Jew. Nation*, pp. 20–30; Farrar, *Early Days of Christianity*, vol. ii, p. 327, n. 1; Herford, op. cit., pp. 12 seq.; Derenbourg, *Essai sur l'Histoire et la Géographie de la Palestine*, p. 303, p. 1; Schoeps, *Die Tempelzerstörung*, pp. 2, 9, 14–17, 28–9, 31 seq., 44–5; Simon, *Verus Israel*, pp. 19–24, *R.H.P.R.*, t. xxvi (1946), p. 134.

[2] 2 Esdras 3. 28, 30–32. Cf. *Tractate Sabbath*, Fol. 119b (*Der babylonische Talmud*, ed. L. Goldschmidt, I, pp. 804–6); H. Loewe, *Judaism and Christianity*, I, p. 170, nn. 1 and 2.

to the significance of the catastrophe for Christianity. Indeed so complete a silence is maintained in these primitive documents that on their testimony alone nothing would be known of the disaster which overwhelmed Israel in A.D. 70.

The fact of this remarkable silence raises a twofold problem, namely why the Jerusalem Christians themselves left no record of their fortunes or indications of their mental and emotional reaction to such a tremendous experience, and what was the reason which led the Gentile Christians apparently to allow so epoch-making an event as the destruction of the citadel of Judaism and the disappearance of the Mother Church to pass uncommemorated. We clearly have here a problem which demands a thorough and extensive investigation, for the *a priori* presumption must be, in the light of our foregoing studies, that here we have to do with a matter which is inextricably bound up with the issues at stake in the crisis of A.D. 55–66.

In the absence of any explicit statement in the New Testament or sub-apostolic documents we are left to find our earliest and our only information about the fate of the Jerusalem Church in the fourth-century *Ecclesiastical History* of Eusebius, which is substantially reproduced in the next century by Epiphanius.

Eusebius, after relating how the Apostles were finally driven from Judæa by the hostility of the Jews (μυρία εἰς θάνατον ἐπιβεβουλευμένων), goes on to describe the fortunes of the Christian community in Jerusalem: [1] "However, when the people of the church in Jerusalem, having been commanded by an oracle (κατά τινα χρησμὸν), given by revelation to men there approved before the war, to depart from the city and to dwell in a certain city of Peræa, namely, Pella, (and) when those who believed on Christ had migrated thither from Jerusalem . . ." Eusebius then proceeds to show that, when all faithful Christians (ἁγίων ἀνδρῶν) had left Jerusalem and the whole land of Judæa (σύμπασαν τὴν Ἰουδαίαν γῆν), the judgement of God then fell upon the unbelieving Jews in the form of the Roman armies. The accounts of Epiphanius, while agreeing on the main fact, contain variations of statement about the warning oracle. According to the passage in the *Adversus Haereses*,[2] it was Christ himself who gave the warning (Χριστοῦ φήσαντος), and the flight was made just before the commencement of the siege of Jerusalem (ἐπειδὴ ἤμελλε πάσχειν πολιορκίαν). But in the relevant passage of the *De Mensuris et Ponderibus* [3] the advice to leave the city was given by an angel (προεχρηματίσθησαν ὑπὸ ἀγγέλου); the time here is noted with reference to the delivery of the warning and is apparently in effect the same as that given for the flight in the other passage ('Ηνίκα γὰρ ἔμελλεν ἡ πόλις ἁλίσκεσθαι ὑπὸ τῶν Ῥωμαίων). Epiphanius concludes this

[1] *Eccl. Hist.*, III. v. 2–3.
[2] Epiphanius, *Adv. Haer.*, xxix. 7 (*Patr. Gr.*, ed. Migne, t. xli). Cf. ibid., xxx. 2. 2.
[3] Epiphanius, *De Mens. et Pond.*, xv (*Patr. Gr.*, ed. Migne, t. xliii).

brief account with the note that the disciples subsequently returned to Jerusalem, thereby contradicting the explicit statement of Eusebius in another part of his *History* [1] that the Church of Aelia, the Roman city which Hadrian caused to be constructed on the site of Jerusalem, was composed of Gentiles (ἐξ ἐθνῶν συγκροτηθείσης).

Several questions at once suggest themselves on the first reading of these passages and others soon appear on further consideration. The primary one, of course, is that of the source or sources from which these two late Christian writers derived their information. In view of their previous accounts of James the Just the presumption naturally is that Hegesippus was their authority for statements about the original Church of Jerusalem. [2] However, such an inference cannot be regarded as certain, for Eusebius seems to have made a special point of mentioning the fact, if Hegesippus was his authority for any particular statement. [3] The most that can be said in this connection, therefore, is that Eusebius and Epiphanius both knew of a tradition, the authority of which they did not regard as specially notable, that the Jerusalem Christians had fled to Pella, on the advice of an oracle, some time prior to the investment of the city; and it should be noted that Epiphanius does not seem herein to have been merely dependent on the record of the Bishop of Cæsarea.

The reason for the flight and the choice of Pella are represented as being due to an oracle. Epiphanius' contradiction of himself in assigning the warning to both Christ and an angel is not serious, and more important is the fact that all accounts agree that the flight was regarded as being made in response to a divine monition. That such an oracle is conceivable is adequately attested by the Little Apocalypse in Mark and the references made in Acts to the activity of prophets in the Jerusalem community. [4] But the choice of Pella as an asylum presents a serious difficulty to our understanding and demands a detailed discussion.

The city of Pella in Peræa was Greek in origin and tradition, being one of the cities of the Decapolis; indeed there is reason to think that it may have been a foundation of Alexander the Great himself and that its name was intended to commemorate his Macedonian birthplace. [5] Consequently it would appear on *a priori* grounds very improbable that pious Jews, such as we have every reason for believing the Jerusalem Christians to have been, should have chosen so thoroughly Gentile a centre for refuge. [6] But there are other more serious objections.

---

[1] *Eccl. Hist.*, IV. vi. 4.

[2] Lawlor, *Eusebiana*, pp. 28–34; Lawlor and Oulton, *Eusebius: Eccl. Hist.*, vol. ii, p. 82 : these writers think that the two accounts come from a common source, which is probably Hegesippus; they think that Epiphanius did not derive his version from Eusebius. Hort, *Judaistic Christianity*, p. 175, thought that Hegesippus was the source of Eusebius' account, and so did Harnack, *Die Mission und Ausbreitung des Christentums*, II, p. 78, although he suggests as an alternative source Julius Africanus.

[3] E.g. *Eccl. Hist.*, II. xxiii; III. xx, xxxii; IV. viii, xxii.   [4] Acts 11. 27, 28; 21. 11.

[5] Cf. Schürer, op. cit., II, pp. 137–140; Smith, *Hist. Geography*, pp. 593, 597–8, 602.

[6] Renan, *Antichrist*, p. 151, suggests that the choice was made because Pella was one of the two nearest neutral cities to Jerusalem; the other being Scythopolis, where Roman sympathies

Pella was some sixty miles north-eastward from Jerusalem, and the route thither would have necessitated crossing the river Jordan at some point. Accordingly the possibilities of a journey there by a number of persons in a body would have been decisively conditioned by the military situation prevailing at any specific time. Now the time of the flight according to our authorities is not clear.[1] Eusebius states that the warning oracle was given "before the war" (πρὸ τοῦ πολέμου), while Epiphanius specifies, as we have seen, that it was made either just before the commencement of the siege of the city or before its fall. But, whichever of these times is to be preferred, there are serious difficulties to be faced.

The time indicated by Eusebius may be interpreted to mean that the Jerusalem Christians fled from the metropolis either before the expedition of Cestius Gallus in 66, or before the campaign of Vespasian in 67. If the former time be preferred, it means either that the Jerusalem community was in Pella when the city was attacked by the Jewish insurgents or that it arrived there shortly afterwards. Since, according to Josephus,[2] Pella and other neighbouring cities were sacked (ἐπόρθουν πόλεις . . . καὶ Πέλλαν) in revenge by the Jews when they learned of the massacre of their countrymen by the Gentile inhabitants of Cæsarea, either alternative appears impossible. For if the Jerusalem Christians had taken refuge in Pella before the Jewish attack, it would seem unlikely that they, a party of renegades, would have survived the vengeance of their ferocious countrymen. Equally impossible does it appear that, after the sack of Pella, they would have chosen the place for a refuge, for not only would a devastated city have offered no shelter, but a party of Jews, whatever their particular religious tenets, would scarcely have been welcomed by any Gentile survivors of the Jewish reprisal. This last objection also applies to the supposition that the flight took place about a year later, just before the campaign of Vespasian, and to it must be added other difficulties.[3] As we have seen, the defeat of the expedition of Cestius Gallus inspired the Jews with fresh zeal and courage and confirmed them in their belief that they were fighting a holy war and that their God was with them to give the final victory. If then the flight on Eusebius'

were strong. A city which had been attacked by Jewish rebels, such as was Pella (see below), is scarcely likely to have been a neutral city. Moreover, on Renan's argument, Philadelphia should have been a more obvious choice. It is interesting to note that Lietzmann, *Gesch. der alten Kirche*, I, p. 185, gives exactly the opposite reason to that of Renan for the choice of Pella, namely, "*das war eine heidnische und den Juden bitter verhasste Stadt im Ostjordanlande*".

[1] The difficulties involved in dating the presumed flight to Pella do not generally seem to be appreciated by scholars. E.g. Lietzmann, op. cit., I, p. 185, thinks that the death of James the Just was the immediate cause of the flight, but he does not consider what would have been the subsequent fortunes of the Christians, if they had fled at that time. Streeter, *Four Gospels*, p. 512, seems to have held a similar opinion about the time of the flight. Harnack, op. cit., p. 78, n. 4, appears to perceive some of the difficulties, but he does not attempt a solution. Schürer, *G.J.V.*, I, p. 619, dates the flight for the winter 67–8 (*wenn nicht schon früher*), but he gives no reason for his preference, and seems to relate the flight to the civil war which was waged in Jerusalem at this time.

[2] *Wars*, ii. 18. 1 (458). Cf. Ricciotti, *Flavio Giuseppe*, vol. ii, p. 328, n. on 458–60.

[3] Renan, op. cit., p. 150, dates the flight for 68, but gives no precise reasons for his choice of this year.

reckoning is to be dated for the period between the defeat of Gallus and the opening of Vespasian's operations in the spring of 67, we are asked to believe that a body of renegade Jews, apparently non-combatant, could have passed unmolested through a considerable tract of insurgent country, patrolled as it was undoubtedly at such a time by bands of nationalist troops,[1] that they crossed the Jordan safely at some ford, and that they finally settled in peace in a city recently destroyed by Jewish rebels. Further, if they had succeeded in surmounting these apparently fatal difficulties, they would have been subject to the perils which must have beset every Jew when the troops of Vespasian subjugated Peræa in 68,[2] for the legionaries or their auxiliaries are not likely to have discriminated between orthodox and Christian Jews.

If either of the times given by Epiphanius for the flight is regarded as preferable, each of these is found on closer scrutiny to be subject to serious objection. To take the earlier alternative first, namely that the Christians escaped from Jerusalem on the eve of the final siege by Titus, when they saw the city about to be encompassed by armies:[3] we are asked to believe that a considerable body of Jewish pacifists succeeded in eluding the attention of their zealous countrymen and travelled safely, with some proportion of their goods, through territory now held by the Romans and probably still carefully patrolled[4] owing to the fact that it had only recently been subdued, and finally that they settled in safety among Gentiles who had so cruelly suffered from Jewish fanaticism and who were now undoubtedly watching with satisfaction the last agonies of Jewish national life, regarding them as the just penalty for all of which they held the Jews to be guilty. These objections remain if the other reference of Epiphanius ('Ηνίκα γὰρ ἔμελλεν ἡ πόλις ἁλίσκεσθαι) be interpreted to mean that the Christian community finally escaped from the doomed city when they saw that its fall was imminent. And this timing would in addition involve special difficulties of its own, in that it would mean that the Christians until then had been prepared to share the fate of all patriotic Jews, but in the eleventh hour had changed their minds and succeeded in escaping both the vigilance of their own fanatical countrymen and that of the investing Romans and conveyed themselves in safety some sixty miles away to a Gentile city which had suffered severely from the hands of the Jews.

In addition to these problems involved in the question of the time of the flight there are others of general relevancy. It is true that both

---

[1] Jos., *Wars*, v. 10. 1 (420–3), tells of the attitude of the patriots to Jewish deserters.

[2] Jos., op. cit., iv. 7. 3–6 (413–39).

[3] Cf. Luke 21. 20. Hort, op. cit., p. 175, thought that the flight probably took place late in the course of the war and was due to the supremacy of the Zealots in Jerusalem. In this view he has been followed by Kidd, *Hist. of the Church*, vol. i, p. 48. Holtzmann, *Das Ende des jüdischen Staatswesens*, p. 669, was inclined to think that the Christians fled when Titus offered terms after the cessation of the daily sacrifice. Goguel, *La Naissance du Christianisme*, p. 154, prefers a date early in 70, but is clearly not aware of the difficulties.

[4] Jos., op. cit., v. 13. 4–5, tells a horrible story of the fate of certain Jewish deserters in the Roman camp.

Eusebius and Epiphanius state that the movement was the outcome of
a divine warning; nevertheless the demands of inspired utterance often
embody a shrewd appraisal of the relevant situation, and consequently
the choice of Pella is very difficult to understand, for there were several
other cities, both Jewish and Gentile, nearer at hand than this Trans-
Jordanian city.   Then there are the obvious economic factors to be considered.   With what proportion of their goods and by what means could
a mixed body, such as the Jerusalem Christians must have been, travel
such a distance, involving the crossing of a river, through country in a
state of war?   And finally, unless they had succeeded in forming a substantial caravan for the conveyance of their goods, on what did they rely for
their economic support in devastated Pella among embittered Gentiles? [1]
And then in general comment it should be noted, against the view that
the statements of Eusebius and Epiphanius are likely to be records of
fact, that the Christian community of Pella appears to have played no
important part in the life of the Church during the first and second
centuries; this insignificance would surely be strange and surprising, if
the Church of Jerusalem, with all its unchallenged authority and prestige,
had migrated *en bloc* to the Peræan city.

These difficulties are truly serious and we are thus justified in not
accepting the accounts of Eusebius and Epiphanius as accurate records
of fact; [2] whatever may have been the fate of the Jerusalem Church, it
is not credible that it migrated as a body to the Greek city of Pella in
Peræa.   But this conclusion does not necessarily imply that the accounts
of the two Christian writers are complete fabrications, for the fact of the
unlikely nature of Pella as a place of refuge for the Jerusalem Christians
must surely indicate that the assertion that it was such was not a natural
inference made by subsequent Christians on the basis of its obvious
suitability as an asylum for Jewish refugees, but must rest upon some
genuine tradition of Pella having once given shelter to a body of
Jewish Christians.   What was the origin of such a community and when
did it settle in Pella are clearly questions beyond the possibility of solution
for us, but it is useful to remember that there were other Christian communities in Palestine besides that in Jerusalem and we have noticed
evidence for the existence of a strong centre of independent tradition in
Galilee—and Galilee was much closer to Pella than was Jerusalem.
Consequently it is reasonable to believe that some time during the course
of the suppression of the revolt, or shortly after, Christians from one or
more churches in the vicinity of Pella may have sought refuge there and
gradually constituted themselves into a vigorous community, which grew

---

[1] Renan, *Antichrist*, p. 152, made the rather naive suggestion that they lived on their savings.
[2] According to Meyer, *Ursprung und Anfänge des Christentums*, III, p. 585, n. 1, Schwartz
(*Göth. Nachr.*, 1907, 284. 1) had doubted the truth of this celebrated flight.   Meyer, however,
accepts it as true.   Hoennicke, *Das Judenchristentum*, p. 104, declares categorically of Eusebius'
account that, "*An dieser Nachricht zu zweifeln, liegt kein Grund vor*"; but he is obviously not aware
of its difficulties; nor are Schmidtke, *Neue Fragmente*, p. 233; Goguel, op. cit., pp. 154 *seq.*; Simon,
Verus Israel, pp. 88, n. 3, 89, 288, 304–5.

in self-confidence and in process of time naturally came to claim that it represented the descendants of the famous Mother Church at Jerusalem. If Epiphanius is to be trusted in his statement that the community at Pella later moved to Jerusalem, we may possibly see a little more of the way in which the tradition evolved. Eusebius tells us that, when Hadrian rebuilt and repopulated the devastated Jerusalem, the Church which established itself there was composed of Gentiles.[1] He does not tell us whence these Christians came, but it is permissible to think that many may have come from Pella and, bringing with them the tradition that their Church had originated from some Jewish Christian refugees, may naturally have supposed that they, their founders, were members of the original Church of Jerusalem, and so in turn may have regarded themselves as their representatives when they settled on the revered site of the Holy City.

We have now to face the question of the possibility that there may be discerned in the New Testament documents some trace of a memory of the experiences of the Palestinian Christians during the last days of Jerusalem. We have seen that the Markan Gospel contains fragments of an older apocalypse, which apparently expressed the hopes and fears of the Palestinian Christians during the threat of Caligula to violate the sanctity of the Temple.[2] Now, since the Gospel of Matthew is distinguished for its Hebrew outlook and feeling, there is a reasonable *a priori* case for supposing that the Matthean editing of the Markan Apocalypse may contain indications of the knowledge which that author had of the fate of the Palestinian Christians, a knowledge which would conceivably be revealed as he deals with a subject which had essential reference to current affairs.

The first significant difference in Matthew's version of the Markan Apocalypse is that, in the place of the passage about persecution in Mark 13. 9, he substitutes a passage (24. 10–12) in which are described the internal strife which will torment the Church during the days of tribulation and the falling away of many because of false prophets and an increase of antinomianism. This change may fairly be regarded as significant and may perhaps reflect a period of bitter internal strife in the Palestinian Church and the consequent apostasy of many under the strain of some general calamity.

If Matthew in his rendering of the Markan Apocalypse is consciously developing a time sequence to correspond with the succession of the events of the war, which is by no means certain, his treatment of the famous Abomination passage is problematical. His addition to the

---

[1] *Eccl. Hist.*, IV. vi. 3–4. On Aelia Capitolina see Albright, *Archaeology of Palestine*, pp. 166, 168. The tradition that a Church continued to exist in Jerusalem until the time of Hadrian (Euseb., *Dem. Evang.*, III. v. 10) must be understood according to Goguel, op. cit., p. 160, rather in "*un sens moral et non matériel*".

[2] See pp. 107–8 above.

13

Markan text of the words "in a holy place" (ἐν τόπῳ ἀγίῳ), made with
reference to the location of the Abomination, may well be interpreted
as a detail consciously added in the light of the happenings at Jerusalem
in A.D. 70.[1]   Josephus tells us that the victorious legionaries erected their
standards in the Temple and did sacrifice to them.[2]   That the Jews well
understood that the standards of the Roman army were the sacred
emblems of a heathen religion is certain from the fact of their violent
reaction to the introduction by Pilate of military standards into the Holy
City.[3]   Consequently to a pious Jew the erection of the standards and
the performance of sacred rites by the triumphant Romans in the Temple
would obviously have constituted a veritable manifestation of the
Abomination of Desolation, foretold by Daniel.   The probability, therefore, that Matthew here consciously emended the Markan account in the
light of historical fact makes his subsequent reproduction, with only one
slight addition, of Mark's text about the flight into the mountains
significant.   Its significance is of a negative nature, but it is nevertheless
valuable to note that Matthew, who seems in his rendering of the Markan
Apocalypse to be conscious of its applicability to the catastrophe of
A.D. 70, did not find it necessary to emend Mark's words about the
flight, despite the highly impracticable character of the advice they
contain; thus, although it is an *argumentum a silentio*, it may be noted as
remarkable that Matthew apparently saw no need to change the Markan
picture of a sudden unorganized flight of individuals after the actual
violation of the Temple to an orderly communal exodus, at some time
prior to the virtual collapse of Jewish resistance, such as Eusebius and
Epiphanius suggest.

There is another passage in Matthew which has the appearance of
reflecting a time of persecution and flight.   Jesus is represented as saying
to the Twelve,[4] whom he had just commissioned, "when they persecute
you in this city, flee into the next: for verily I say unto you, Ye shall
not have gone through (τελέσητε) the cities of Israel, till the Son of
man be come."   This passage constitutes a well-known exegetical
difficulty, and it has been invoked as basic evidence for at least one
ingenious interpretation of Christian Origins.[5]   Its primary importance
to us here depends on the question of whether it does or does not reflect
the experience of a subsequent generation of Palestinian Christians.   To
find an answer we must first note that the passage is made by Matthew
to follow on immediately after that section on persecution which, as we

[1] Matt. 24. 15, 16.   Streeter's rejection of the words ἐν τόπῳ ἀγίῳ (*Four Gospels*, pp. 517
seq.) in support of his theory of the Antiochene origin of Matt. is discussed below, pp. 245–6.

[2] *Wars*, vi. 6. 1 (316).

[3] Jos., *Ant.*, xviii. 3. 1; *Wars*, ii. 9. 2–3 (169–74).   Eisler, *Messiah Jesus*, p. 315, points out, in
another connection, that Jerome (*Com. Matt.*, xxiv. 15) had reason to think that contemporary
Jews had actually seen in Pilate's act a fulfilment of Daniel's prophecy: "τὸ βδέλυγμα τῆς
ἐρημώσεως *potest . . . accipi . . . de imagine Caesaris, quam Pilatus posuit in templo.*"   Cf. Eisler,
ΙΗΣΟΥΣ ΒΑΣΙΛΕΥΣ, II, pp. 166–170; I, Tafel xxxiv.

[4] Matt. 10. 23.

[5] Cf. A. J. Grieve, *Peake's Commentary*, p. 710a.

have just seen,[1] he omitted in his rendering of the Markan Apocalypse, replacing it there by verses which he felt to be more pertinent to the situation which he then had in mind; the Markan section which he thus decided to omit from his own version of the traditional Apocalypse he evidently had reason for transferring to a place earlier in his narrative. Now this originally Markan passage deals with the sufferings of Jewish Christians, apparently outside Palestine, and it has been reasonably suggested that Mark probably had in mind therein the example of Paul.[2] What Matthew does, therefore, in effect is to transfer the application of a passage which he is likely to have known had reference to Paul and his followers, to the essentially Judaistic Twelve. We shall have cause later to deal at length with the fact of the existence of an anti-Pauline motive in Matthew, which this observation tends to presuppose. Here it is necessary to note that Matthew, who thus at this point in his work is clearly concerned to fabricate an interested presentation of the status and mission of the Twelve, has already represented Jesus as definitively limiting the scope of their mission to Israelites.[3] Hence in verse 23 it would follow that the Dominical instruction means that the mission of the Twelve to Israel will not have been completed before the *Parousia*, thus implying that no time would be left for evangelizing the Gentiles.[4] That Matthew should have set forth in his Gospel such a statement when the majority of the original disciples must already have died, thus seemingly creating gratuitously an awkward problem of the manifest failure of the Lord's words to find fulfilment, appears to have only one satisfactory explanation. It is that he was instinctively identifying himself and the community to which he belonged with the ideal band of the chosen disciples of Jesus, and thus he passes, unconsciously, to assigning to the Twelve experiences which were really those of his own community. Accordingly, it is possible that the references to a succession of flights, which apparently take place in Palestine, reflect the experiences of some community of Palestinian Christians, of which Matthew was a member. The time of such experiences appears to be indicated by the fact, noted in an earlier chapter, that both the Pauline and the Lukan documents show that the Church of Jerusalem, and so by inference other Palestinian Christians, enjoyed a stable life until at least the year 55 and in no way could be depicted as a community of persecuted itinerants.[5] It would seem to follow, therefore, that we must look to some time after this year for a situation which would conceivably correspond to that implied in the Matthean saying, and no other is known that is more suitable than that in which the Palestinian Christians may well have found themselves during the revolt against Rome and its suppression. Why persecution should then have broken out against the Jewish Christians cannot be known certainly, but it would be reasonable to believe that either during

---

[1] See above, p. 173.
[2] See Streeter, op. cit., p. 494.
[3] Matt. 10. 5, 6.
[4] Cf. Streeter, op. cit., p. 255.
[5] See above, pp. 93–4.

the early stages of the revolt or in the years immediately following the destruction of Jerusalem, both occasions when loyalty to Judaism became so crucial an issue,[1] the former tolerance shown to the Christians may have been abandoned and the movement regarded as disloyal to the cause of Israel's existence, especially in the light of the memory of Paul's anti-nomian activity.

There is another piece of possible evidence bearing on the question of a concerted flight of the Palestinian Christians which has also to be considered. In the twelfth chapter of the Apocalypse of John there is the strange vision of the woman arrayed with the sun, who is in travail with a man child, who is to rule all nations with a rod of iron. A great red dragon awaits to devour her son, but he is saved by God and the woman flees for refuge into the wilderness, "where she hath a place prepared of God, that they may nourish her a thousand two hundred and three-score days".[2] Then, after an interlude in which the defeat of the dragon by Michael and the heavenly host is described, the account of the fortunes of the woman is resumed, but at a point previous to that described in verse 6. It is then told how the dragon persecuted the woman and how she miraculously flew to her place in the desert, being saved from the flood of water which the dragon sent forth from his mouth.[3] Ernest Renan[4] saw in this bizarre imagery an account of the flight of the Christian Church from the Jewish insurgents, and in the mention of the flood he believed that there was an allusion to some incident of the flight, possibly an attempt to drown the fleeing Christians in the Jordan. The great English authority on apocalyptic matters, the late Dr. R. H. Charles, has written[5] in comment on verses 14–16 that "if the source is Christian (these verses) refer to the flight of the primitive Christian community to Pella before the fall of Jerusalem (cf. Eusebius, H. E. iii, 5); but, if the source is Jewish, to that of the élite of the Jews to Jabneh, which became the seat of Jewish scholarship after the fall of Jerusalem". Against the second of these alternatives the objection must be made that Jabneh could not possibly have been considered desert,[6] and therefore a purely Jewish connotation is unlikely. We are thus left with the pos-sibility, on the authority of Dr. Charles, that the passage contains a refer-ence to a Christian flight. It is naturally tempting then in this case to look for indications of locality, as Renan did. The "water as a river" of verse 15 at once presents the attractive suggestion of its being a refer-ence to the only great river of Palestine, namely, the Jordan; and this suggestion, if accepted, would therefore fix the direction of "into the

---

[1] Cf. Herford, *Effect of Fall of Jerusalem upon Character of Pharisees*, pp. 19 *seq.*
[2] Rev. 12. 1–6. The subject of τρέφωσιν is obscure.
[3] Rev. 12. 13–16.
[4] *Antichrist*, pp. 150 *seq.*
[5] *I.C.C.*, vol. i, pp. 299–314; cf. p. lxiii.
[6] "Yebna, as the town is now called, lies in a fertility of field and grove that helps us to understand the repute of the district for populousness": Smith, *Historical Geography*, p. 194; cf. Schürer, *G.J.V.*, II, pp. 98–9.

wilderness" of verse 6 as across the river into the desert country of Trans-Jordania. However, plausible as such identifications may be, we must carefully remember that we are dealing here with apocalyptic imagery, and it is dangerous to press it too closely for precise information. Moreover, it must be recognized that it is very unlikely that the passage would ever have been regarded as containing an allusion to a concerted flight of Jewish Christians across the Jordan to Pella, if the comparatively late accounts of Eusebius and Epiphanius of such an incident had not provided the stimulus to seek for this interpretation.

Our examination of what might be considered to be evidence of the flight of an important body of Palestinian Christians, presumably the Church of Jerusalem, from involvement in the national uprising against Rome has shown that this evidence is not satisfactory, and at the most it may only safely be accepted as witnessing to some small-scale and unorganized exodus of Christians from one or more centres, not necessarily including Jerusalem. Moreover, it has to be noted that tradition has associated no important personage or group of the Church of Jerusalem with any of these flights, which fact is significant when it is recalled that rabbinic tradition preserved the memory of the escape of Rabbi Johanan ben Zakkai from beleaguered Jerusalem.[1]

The destinations of these various groups of refugees are unknown, although, as we have seen, there survived a tradition that Pella had provided shelter, perhaps to some Galilæan Christians. However, the general direction of flight appears to be obvious, when the geographical development of the Roman campaign of suppression is considered. As we have seen, Vespasian entered Palestine from the north and worked southwards to Jerusalem, Galilee thus naturally receiving the first impact of his attack.[2] It would accordingly be expected that any movement of Jewish refugees would have been away from the avenging Roman armies in a southerly direction. Some may have turned eastward to cross the Jordan into Trans-Jordania, as indeed the statements of Eusebius and Epiphanius show, but considering the desolate nature of this territory and the fact that the only cities there, with the exception of Heshbon, were Greek and that they had suffered from Jewish attacks, it is unlikely that there was a general movement thither. The natural goal for such refugees was Jerusalem, and Josephus tells us that the city was abnormally crowded when the siege commenced.[3] But it is also possible that many

---

[1] Cf. Derenbourg, *Essai sur l'Histoire et la Géographie de la Palestine*, pp. 282–3; Moore, *Judaism*, vol. i, pp. 83–4.

[2] See above, pp. 161–2.

[3] *Wars*, vi. 9. 3 (420–1). Josephus says that this overcrowding was due to the Passover pilgrims, who were suddenly prevented from returning home by the investment of Jerusalem. This scarcely seems an adequate reason in view of the fact that it would be most improbable that pilgrims would have come from the Roman-occupied zones to insurgent Jerusalem for the festivals; it is surely more likely that the large numbers were due to the refugees who had gradually gathered in the metropolis as the Romans advanced.

of the more far-seeing of the refugees, and undoubtedly many of the more
prudent inhabitants of Jerusalem itself, realized that no final safety was
to be obtained in the city and so sought shelter where Hebrews for many
long centuries had found asylum in times of national danger and distress,
namely in Egypt.   Thus it is reasonable to suppose that to the ancient
land of the Nile, whither the patriarchs had gone in times of want, to
which Israel had turned for succour from the Assyrian terror, where the
broken remnants of Judah, dragging with them the protesting Jeremiah,
had found shelter from Babylonian vengeance, where multitudes of Jews
under the patronage of the Ptolemies had settled and prospered, and
whither after the destruction of Jerusalem, as Josephus tells us,[1] even
many of the fierce Sicarii fled for refuge—that there also many Jewish
Christians fled at various times and from various places during the course
of the war.   We have already noticed the evidence of a flourishing centre
of Christian life existing in Alexandria and that it undoubtedly owed its
origin to the Palestinian Church;[2] it would be easy to understand, therefore, that such refugees were likely to have found a ready welcome with
their brethren in the Egyptian metropolis, and they would have gone
to reinforce the original Palestinian tradition of the Church there, thus
constituting a situation of great significance for our apprehension of the
factors effective in the evolution of Christianity in the first century, as
we shall later have cause to see.

We have been occupied so far with the problem constituted by the
apparent evidence that the Jewish Christians, or at least some of them,
saved themselves from the fate of thousands of their countrymen by
timely flight.   We must now turn to consider whether any notable community of the Palestinian Christians was likely to have escaped comparatively untouched by the disasters of the war.   By inference from the
Lukan writings there seems to have been one such community, namely
that of Cæsarea.   According to Josephus[3] the Gentile population of
Cæsarea, which was the headquarters of the Roman government in
Palestine, at the instigation of the procurator Florus, wreaked vengeance
on the Jewish inhabitants of the city, for Jewish outrages elsewhere, by
massacring them.   These Cæsarean Gentiles do not appear to have
suffered any Jewish reprisal in turn, and the city continued to remain in
Roman hands.[4]   Now the narrative of the Acts shows several signs of a
special acquaintance with a Christian community at Cæsarea.   The story
of the conversion of Cornelius may well be regarded as an ecclesiastical
foundation tradition whereby the origin of the Church in Cæsarea was
traced to the leading Apostle of the Lord.[5]   But Philip, a distinguished
representative of the anti-Judaic movement associated with Stephen,

---

[1] Op. cit., vii. 10. 1 *seq.* (409–10).   Cf. M. Simon, *R.H.P.R.*, t. xxvi (1946), p. 123.
[2] See pp. 17–18, 23–6, 140.   [4] See above, p. 158, n. 6.
[3] Op. cit., ii. 18. 1 (457).   [5] Acts 10.   Cf. Knox, *The Acts of the Apostles*, p. 33.

appears to have had an earlier connection with the city [1] and is later depicted as settled there with his family and obviously enjoying a considerable reputation.[2]   Moreover, Paul seems, significantly, to have been welcomed by the Church there.[3]   Consequently these facts, together with that of the location of one of the "we" passages there, constitute a reasonable case for believing that the author of Acts had some special contact with the Christian community of Cæsarea.[4]   And to these considerations can be added the possibility, already noticed, that the cycle of stories about the Jerusalem Resurrection Appearances and the death of Judas Iscariot, and the sympathy shown for the Samaritans, especially in the Gospel,[5] point to an environment separated in time and sympathy from the primitive source of tradition and yet essentially Palestinian from its topographical knowledge, which requirements Cæsarea admirably fits. If these points are valid in the present context, it would follow that a vigorous community of Christians, undoubtedly of Gentile origin, existed in Cæsarea in the first few decades after A.D. 70.   Whatever may have been the origin of this Church, and, as we have noted, the story of Cornelius and the position of Philip are significant, its survival of the Jewish catastrophe must have meant the confirmation and development of those tendencies to universalism of which the Cornelius tradition is so complete an expression.   It is further feasible that such a Church, having thus preserved its identity through the turmoil and loss of the years 66–70, emerged therefrom the strongest Christian body in Palestine and in consequence became a depository of Palestinian tradition, howbeit coloured and conditioned by its own peculiar experience and outlook.

We have so far dealt primarily with whatever positive evidence there seems to be of the fate of the Palestinian Christians.   We have now to turn our attention to what might be termed the negative evidence, namely to the significance of the failure of tradition to preserve any adequate account of the fortunes of the Jewish Christians during the fatal years of the war against Rome and especially of the passing of the Mother Church.

From our earlier studies we found reason to conclude that the political factor played a far larger part in Palestinian Christianity than the New Testament documents consciously allow to appear and that many Jewish Christians were deeply concerned in the cause of Israel's liberation from the yoke of heathen Rome.   What was the reaction of those Christians when the standard of revolt was raised in 66 and when Yahweh seemed so patently to manifest his providence for his people in the amazing defeat of Cestius Gallus we may well surmise.   The situation held for them every feature that could excite their eschatological hopes; the issue must

---

[1] Acts 8. 40.   [2] Acts 21. 8, 9.   [3] Acts 9. 30; 18. 22; 21. 8–14.
[4] Acts 21. 8–14.   Cf. Streeter, *Four Gospels*, p. 219; Creed, *St. Luke*, p. lxx.
[5] E.g. Luke 9. 51–56; 10. 33–37; 17. 11–19; Acts 8. 5–25.

have lain clear before them of the fulfilment of Israel's destiny and the utter overthrow of the impious heathen, and in that glorious climax of history surely their Master must appear mightily, with the hosts of heaven, as God's Messiah.   Indeed in this supreme crisis that Jew must have been cold and apathetic beyond belief who could remain untouched by the dynamic of a popular passion so charged with religious feeling and who could stand aside as his people prepared themselves for this tremendous proof of their faith.   Consequently it would seem to be certain that many of the Jewish Christians of Palestine must have made common cause with their countrymen, taking up arms against the Romans, and thus sharing the common fate of either death in battle or subsequently, as captives, death in the arenas of the Empire.   The memory of those who fell fighting for their nation's liberty was certainly not likely to be preserved by Gentile Christians, for to them rather they would have appeared as Jewish rebels against their lawful overlord, and their fate would be seen as divine punishment for their blindness in failing to separate themselves from their obdurate countrymen.

There were also doubtless Jewish Christians, more pacifically disposed, who did not resort to arms, and who did not seek safety in flight. Such probably just waited where they lived, hoping that in their humble obscurity they would eventually be spared, for the records of warfare in all ages and places show that many, for want of the necessary energy, or plans, or means, have always taken this line of action.   The fates of such would have been various.   Where their town or village surrendered without resistance the majority probably escaped death and slavery and suffered only the evils of military occupation, though in the ancient world, as in the modern, these could be terrible enough.   In those places where resistance was offered very few are likely to have escaped death or slavery, for, as Josephus tells us, a massacre, at least of the males, generally followed the taking of such a rebel city.

The fact then that Christian tradition has preserved no other account of the fortunes of the Mother Church of Jerusalem than that, obviously inaccurate, given by Eusebius and Epiphanius must surely mean that in whatever was known of the passing of that famous Church there was found nothing which could be conveniently utilized in the growing taste for hagiography.   Such silence, in view of the former unique authority and prestige of the Jerusalem Church, is significant, and, when it is seen in its context with that knowledge which we have reached of the nature and outlook of Jewish Christianity, the conclusion appears in every way reasonable and necessary that the Jerusalem Church fell together with the Jewish nation in the catastrophe of A.D. 70, because that Church in its principles and the loyalties of its members was essentially one with the nation.

It is probable, as we have seen, that the Church in Palestine was not completely obliterated, but those Jewish Christians who had remained in their country and had survived the perils and sufferings of the war must have faced conditions of terrible privation and distress after A.D. 70. We are informed by Josephus [1] that, after assigning a tract of land at Emmaus to eight hundred of his veterans, Vespasian ordered the whole of Judæa to be sold. Very probably a large portion of this land was bought by some of those wealthy Jews who had managed to escape to the Romans, for there is in rabbinic literature the record of a special law permitting Jews to buy land in Palestine, if the consent of its former owners was first obtained.[2] But, since the Jewish Christians were not in general of the wealthy classes, they must have shared in the terrible economic hardships which, as Dr. Büchler in his monograph on this subject has well shown, were certainly endured by the Jews after their crushing defeat.[3]

Therefore the havoc of these four disastrous years must cruelly have thinned the numbers of the Jewish Christians in Palestine by death, slavery, and flight, while the wretched remnant which survived in their homes were reduced to extreme want. Thus in so short a space of time this flourishing Jewish Christian Church, with its revered company of original disciples and witnesses at Jerusalem and its sturdy peasant members in the country districts, was so fatally shattered by the blast of war that it fades almost completely out of the life of the Catholic Church, and its miserable descendants appear later as strange, struggling sects of *Ebionîm* (poor men) in the eyes of the supercilious Gentiles, who had gained so large a part in the heritage of their faith.[4]

Such were some of the material effects of the four years of war upon the Jewish Christians, and it is certain that through them the position of unique prestige and unchallenged authority which the Palestinian Church enjoyed up to A.D. 66 was irrevocably destroyed. The spiritual effects of the disaster, though not so easily to be estimated, must have been equally profound. Their Holy City had been laid in ruins by the heathen, their splendid Temple desecrated and its sacred rites abolished, and yet the Messiah of their nation had not come. How could so terrible a problem be explained? Could Paul have been right after all, that with God there is no real difference between Jew and Greek? Or was there some other solution, more congenial to their innate pride of race and faith, a solution which God had revealed in the very disaster which had overwhelmed them? In this moment of deep perplexity many a Jewish Christian must have turned back for guidance and consolation

---

[1] *Wars*, vii. 6. 6 (216–17).

[2] *Mishnah, Gittin*, v. 6, given in Derenbourg, *Essai sur l'Histoire et la Géographie de la Palestine* p. 294; cf. Edersheim, *Hist. of Jew. Nation*, p. 81.

[3] *Economic Conditions of Judaea after the Destruction of the Second Temple*, pp. 29–55. For archaeological evidence see Albright, *Archaeology of Palestine*, pp. 240–1.

[4] Cf. Lietzmann, *Gesch. der alt. Kirche*, I, pp. 189 *seq.*; Meyer, *Ursprung und Anfänge des Christentums*, I, pp. 597 *seq.*; Burkitt, *Christian Beginnings*, pp. 71–5; Schmidtke, *Neue Fragmente*, pp. 175 *seq.*; Goguel, *La Naissance du Christianisme*, pp. 154–67; Schoeps, *Symmachusstudien*, pp. 66–79; Simon, *Verus Israel*, pp. 277–307.

to the records of his people's wondrous past, and in such a quest his attention must have dwelt with earnest care on the accounts of the two previous acts of desecration which the Temple had suffered. The Temple had twice been destroyed, but Israel continued, because the real bond of its faith lay not in the cultus but in the divine Law, which was its guide and sanction. Once more the Temple lay in ruins; once more then let Israel find its unity and pride in the Law. This strengthening of the Pharisaic position [1] must surely have increased the difficulties and perplexity of those Jewish Christians who had survived. For the very survival of Israel itself seemed then to depend upon an utter loyalty to the Law and all that it signified, and the temptation must have been sore to cleave to the remnant of the nation in its hour of adversity, renouncing all that made for separation from Israel and for kinship with the hated Gentile. Doubtless many Jewish Christians gradually reverted to complete orthodoxy, and those who did not were condemned to live more completely as sectaries, out of communion with their nation's faith and life and separated by their own scruples from Gentile Christianity.

Of the thoughts of those Jewish Christians who remained faithful to their acceptance of Jesus there survives no certain evidence, but there are some verses in the twenty-first chapter of the Apocalypse of John which seem to fit no situation so well as that in which the Jewish Christians of Palestine conceivably found themselves in the first decades following A.D. 70.[2]

In verse 10 of this chapter the prophet tells how he saw "the holy city Jerusalem, coming down out of heaven from God, having the glory of God". Now, while it is indeed true that developing Christianity deepened its Jewish content, it is hard to believe that a Gentile Christian, even by the end of the first century, would have instinctively formulated his eschatological hopes in terms of the descent from God of a Holy City and that the name of that City should be Jerusalem. But to a Jewish Christian such a concept and such nomenclature would be natural and easy. To him Jerusalem, although it lay in ruins at the hand of a heathen conqueror, was still the Holy City, and for him a Holy City was an essential of his faith. The next particularly significant verse in the passage is 22, in which the prophet declares of the city: "I saw no temple therein: for the Lord God the Almighty, and the Lamb, are the temple thereof." The consciousness herein revealed of a problem about a temple must surely indicate a time when such a problem was pertinent, and no time would seem more suitable than in the first decades following the overthrow of Jerusalem and the destruction of its Temple. Clearly it would

---

[1] Cf. Herford, *Effect of Fall of Jerusalem upon Character of Pharisees*, pp. 16 *seq.*; Kilpatrick, *The Origins of the Gospel according to St. Matthew*, pp. 109–11; Simon, *Verus Israel*, pp. 29 *seq.*, 302–7.

[2] Cf. Charles, *Studies in the Apocalypse*, pp. 185–9; cf. Goudge, *New Com. N.T.*, p. 706; Windisch, *Der Untergang Jerusalems*, p. 526; Goguel, op. cit., pp. 171–2; A. Causse, *R.H.P.R.*, t. xxvii (1947), pp. 12–36.

seem that the writer was conscious of the inadequacy of the old Temple, an inadequacy now demonstrated by its desecration and destruction, but a temple occupying the central position in his new Holy City was an instinctive necessity. Thus, as this Jewish Christian prophet looked out on to the future from the darkness and depression of his own present circumstances, his hopes clothed themselves in familiar, though idealized, guise, and with the eye of faith he saw a new Holy City, a new Jerusalem, complete with its Temple, not of stones and wood but constituted by God Almighty himself and by the Lamb, who was the Christian's Lord. It is a noble vision, but also a melancholy one, for it surely reveals how deep-seated was the conviction of the peculiar election of Israel, since even the tragedy of A.D. 70 could not finally eradicate the feeling that the economy of God demanded a Holy City, which, though idealized, conformed to the pattern of the earthly Jerusalem in both its name and its possession of a unique temple. And so after A.D. 70 the Jewish Christian who survived his nation's fall could not finally shake himself free from the particularism of Judaism and commit himself to the universalism of Christianity, as proclaimed by Paul and others, but instead an insistent nostalgia turned back his gaze to the past and limited his hopes to the re-establishment by God of an idealized Jerusalem.

The documentary evidence for the fate of Palestinian Christianity during these crucial years is admittedly meagre in quantity and poor in its quality. But probably the most eloquent evidence is to be seen in the indisputable fact that after A.D. 70 the Church of Jerusalem disappears completely from the life and concern of the Catholic Church. As was noted in the first chapter of this work, there is a kind of tunnel in the course of the life of the Church in the second half of the first century. In the period before we see the Church strongly centralized around the mother community of Jerusalem, whose authority and prestige are unchallenged, even by the daring Paul. From this period, which is so well illumined by the writings of Paul and the narrative of Acts, we pass on in our survey to find the life of the Church disappearing into obscurity with the passing of Paul. It emerges again for us in the other New Testament writings and the documents of the sub-Apostolic age, but we see it then changed completely in its organization and outlook, for of Jerusalem and its unique authority nothing is heard, either in reference to the present or in reminiscence of the past; it is as though a curtain of complete oblivion had descended to obliterate the former order and, whatever may be the source of the twenty-first chapter of the Apocalypse of John, it would seem that the prophet divined that an epoch had ended and another had dawned when he depicted the Almighty, enthroned in heaven, declaring, "Behold, I make all things new".

Thus the Mother Church of Christianity passed away from any further effective part in the life of the movement to which it had given birth.

The cause of this sudden and complete demise, so far as we have been able to establish it, was that that Church had identified itself too closely with the nation from which it had originally emerged and in Israel's virtual annihilation it consequently shared. The survivors of Israel were able gradually to re-integrate their life after the disaster of A.D. 70, because the logic of their faith, though terribly shaken, remained single and harboured no contradictory element. But with the logic of Jewish Christianity it was fatally otherwise. As Paul's interpretation had shown, the movement which took its origin from Jesus of Nazareth contained some essential elements the *raison d'être* of which demanded a universalist explication. This factor the Jewish Christians had striven to ignore, and even when events extorted from them certain concessions, they sought to avoid the intrinsic issue by an illogical compromise, designed to conserve the essentiality of Judaism while admitting a qualified possibility of Gentile participation in the new faith. But the contradiction involved was fatal, and, even if the surviving remnants of Jewish Christianity in Palestine after A.D. 70 had indeed possessed the necessary personalities and disposed of adequate economic resources to maintain their supreme authority, it is difficult to believe that they could have given to Christianity a *Weltanschauung* of sufficient consistency and dynamic to ensure the future of the movement as a world faith.

That the crisis of A.D. 55–66 was thus resolved radically by the elimination of one of the parties involved, and that party too which on the eve of the Jewish revolt looked more likely to conquer, is obvious. It remains, however, our task to trace in detail the repercussions which the destruction of Jerusalem had for Christians other than those living in Palestine.

The Markan Reaction to A.D. *70*

ACCORDING to the general consensus of learned opinion the four Gospels of the New Testament canon, with one possible exception, were produced after the year A.D. 70. The exception is the Gospel of Mark, for estimates of its date vary between A.D. 65 and 75; [1] it will be our thesis here that the internal evidence of the document points indubitably to a date shortly after A.D. 70.

The Gospels, and pre-eminently the three known as Synoptic, constitute what appear to be the most important writings of the New Testament corpus, since they purport to be historical narratives of the life of Jesus of Nazareth. In them Jesus is set forth in his contemporary environment, and knowledge and interest are evidently displayed in depicting the relevant historical and topographical setting. Now this concern appears to be new in Greek-speaking Christian circles when comparison is made with the writings of Paul, in which, as we have seen, historical interest is not only almost non-existent, but also consciously repudiated. It is true that these Gospels incorporate earlier material which may, at least in that which relates to the Passion, have attained some semblance of a narrative form, and this material is certainly traceable to a Palestinian source. However, there is no evidence that any connected narrative of the life of Jesus was composed and attained an effective circulation in the Gentile Church prior to the production of the Gospel of Mark; indeed, to the contrary, the fact that both Luke and Matthew adopt the Markan narrative framework in their own Gospels points irresistibly to the conclusion that the Gospel of Mark was their only prototype and that the non-Markan material of which they disposed merely lent itself to incorporation into the Markan scheme, with the exception of their diverse Birth legends. It follows, therefore, that we are justified in regarding the Gospel of Mark as an innovation in Christian faith and practice, and so the question accordingly arises of the cause or causes of this unprecedented and highly pregnant departure.

When we consider the matter, various possibilities suggest themselves in explanation of the novelty which the Gospel of Mark constitutes. The genius of its author may be advanced as the cause of so momentous a departure from previous Christian practice. There is undoubtedly

---

[1] Cf. Moffatt, *Intro. to N.T.*, p. 213; Guignebert, *Jesus*, p. 41; Goguel, *La Naissance du Christianisme*, p. 141.

considerable truth in this proposition, but alone it does not adequately answer the question, for genius rarely expresses itself without some essential reference to its environment. We have then to consider what contemporary factor could have provoked the original genius of Mark to find so notable an expression. It is at once natural to seek for an answer in the needs of the Church at the time, and we are guided in our inquiry by the necessary inference that whatever the need or needs may have been consciousness thereof first made itself felt at some particular time. We have accordingly to look for some specific situation in the life of the Church which might be recognized as being likely to have produced the consciousness of a need for the composition of a biography of Jesus such as the Markan Gospel.

In view of the fact that the decade A.D. 65–75 is generally thought to be that in which the Gospel of Mark was probably composed, it is natural to see in the destruction of Jerusalem an event which might conceivably have produced a situation in the Gentile Church such as could have called forth a new type of writing. This supposition would appear to be reasonable on *a priori* grounds, but it might naturally be expected that the document itself should show some signs of a recognizable concern in those issues which were likely to have faced the Gentile Christians after A.D. 70. For to describe the career of Jesus of Nazareth inevitably involved the adoption of an attitude of censure of, or agreement with, those individuals and groups, Jewish and Roman, with whom he had decisive contact, and this attitude in turn is likely to have been strongly conditioned by the feelings which were entertained towards the contemporary representatives of such persons. In other words, if the Gospel of Mark was a product of the reaction of some body of Gentile Christians to the overthrow of the Jewish national state, it may fairly be regarded as a mirror in which may be found reflections of the mind of such Christians when they considered what that event had meant for them.

Among the various groups of Palestinian Jews with whom Mark has to do we may conveniently select first the religious leaders and investigate his handling of them as he describes their relations with Jesus. The general impression which is conveyed by Mark's many references to these leaders is that of the bitter and determined enemies of Jesus, who constantly thwart and oppose him in his work, and finally plan and accomplish his death, being blind all the while to his divine character and mission and wilfully obdurate to the witness of his miracles. From the beginning of the Gospel onwards, with an ever-increasing clarity of intention, the Jewish leaders are set forth in this light.

The first note of this tendentious representation is given in 1. 22, where Jesus is described as teaching at Capernaum at the beginning of his Ministry "as having authority, and not as the scribes". This incident is soon followed by the account of the first clash with the scribes over the healing of the paralytic man.[1]   Here the theme of the superiority of Jesus' authority over the official Jewish teachers' is boldly stated in the words addressed to the scribes: "But that ye may know that the Son of man hath power on earth to forgive sins . . ." Next "the scribes of the Pharisees" [2] are censured for their self-righteousness, an incident which is followed by the Dominical decision on the problem posed by the ritual fastings observed by the disciples of the Baptist and of the Pharisees, which leads the author in turn to find appropriate comment in the apophthegm of the Patch and the Wine-skins in 2. 21, 22.   Herein clearly the author has sought to indicate the presence of a fundamental change in that "one cannot preserve the old garment of Judaism by new patches, nor conserve the new wine of Christianity in old wine-skins".[3] This passage is immediately succeeded by an account of a controversy between Jesus and the Pharisees on the subject of Sabbath observance, which concludes with the rebuff of the latter and the consequent assertion that "the Son of man is lord even of the sabbath",[4] a claim surely denoting a contemporary Christian feeling of independence from a former obligation.   Having introduced what must have been the very pertinent question of Sabbath observance, the Markan writer is then moved to add another story of the Dominical dispensation from the same taboo,[5] and he utilizes this to introduce his fundamental thesis that the Jewish authorities were responsible for the death of Jesus: he shows the Pharisees as turning in their chagrin to plot with the Herodians "how they might destroy him".

Mark next proceeds in the development of this theme to accuse the "scribes which came down from Jerusalem" of imputing demoniac possession to Jesus as the cause of his miraculous power, a charge which constitutes, significantly, the Unforgivable Sin.[6]   The next reference to the Jewish authorities (Pharisees and scribes) is 7. 1–15, where the question of ritual cleanliness is made the occasion for quoting the significant words of Isaiah 19. 13 as a prophetic explanation of the failure of the Jews to serve God aright.[7]   The account of the Transfiguration then allows the writer to answer another objection from the Jewish scribes to the divine mission of Jesus: [8] "The scribes say that Elijah must first come." The answer in verse 13 is indicative of the line adopted in the apologetic which was current in Markan circles, namely that a suffering precursor must be followed by a suffering Messiah.[9]   In the next encounter with the

---

[1] 2. 6–12.

[2] The alternative reading here (καὶ οἱ Φαρισαῖοι) makes no material difference to the argument.

[3] Klostermann, *Das Markusevangelium*, p. 33; cf. Turner, *New Com. N.T.*, p. 56 loc. cit.; Guignebert, op. cit., pp. 303–4; Rawlinson, *St. Mark*, p. 32.

[4] 2. 23–28.   [5] 3. 1–6.   [6] 3. 22–29.

[7] Cf. Klostermann, op. cit., p. 78.

[8] 9. 11–13.   On the true sequence of this passage see Klostermann, op. cit., p. 100.

[9] Cf. Klostermann, op. cit., p. 101.   See the interesting suggestion of Bacon, *Jesus and Paul*, pp. 158–9, that Mark used the story of the Transfiguration to show how the "pillar" Apostles were taught the Pauline gospel of the mystery of the Cross.

Pharisees they are depicted as asking Jesus a question about divorce, "tempting him". [1]

The narrative moves on to its climax in the events of the last days at Jerusalem, and the author quickly picks up his theme again in describing the reaction of the Jewish authorities to the action of Jesus in the Cleansing of the Temple. In reply to their question about the nature and source of his authority Jesus counters with another question which is regarded as placing Jewish opposition in a dilemma: according to the Markan statement here the position of the Jewish leaders in their rejection of the claims of the Baptist was incapable of a logical defence even to their own countrymen.[2] The relation of this incident then prompts the author to anticipate the development of his theme in its historical sequence by the interposition of his philosophy of Jewish history in the form of the Parable of the Wicked Husbandmen, which has as its conclusion the significant statement: "What therefore will the lord of the vineyard do? he will come and destroy the husbandmen, and will give the vineyard unto others." [3] Mark then records the anger of the Jewish authorities, as they realize "that he spake the parable against them", and their desire "to lay hold on him".[4]

The story of the Tribute Money, which follows, constitutes a kind of anticlimax to the Parable and its conclusion, but it has a supreme significance for our purpose, since it shows that Mark was desirous of representing to his readers two of the leading Jewish parties as attempting to compromise Jesus (ἵνα αὐτὸν ἀγρεύσωσι λόγῳ) on the subject of the Jewish payment of tribute to Rome. The significance of the question which Mark describes them as putting to Jesus is crucial, for it amounts to nothing less than a request to the Christians' Lord to define his views about the right of the Jews to rebel against their Roman masters. However, before entering into a detailed discussion of the evidence of the passage, it will be convenient to complete this stage of our survey by noticing another important account of a Dominical correction of official Jewish teaching. In 12. 35–37 Jesus is represented as commenting, during his public teaching in the Temple, on the scribal doctrine of the Davidic descent of the Messiah and exposing it to condemnation on the score of illogicality by a quotation from Psalm 110. This passage is then followed by another containing a bitter condemnation of the scribes and ending with the significant words: "these shall receive greater condemnation"—the use of the comparative here perhaps suggesting the punishment of another group of people, whose identity would have been known to the readers of the Gospel.[5]

---

[1] 10. 2. Cf. Bultmann, *Die Gesch. der Synopt. Trad.*, pp. 25–6.   [2] 11. 27–33.

[3] 12. 1–9. "*Die Drohrede ist hiermit (v. 9) völlig abgeschlossen*" is the opinion of Klostermann, op. cit., p. 137, in answer to Loisy's suggestion that the brevity of the threat indicates that Jerusalem was not yet destroyed.

[4] 12. 12.

[5] 12. 38–40. "*Ein schlimmeres Urteil (Jac. 3. 1) als die gewöhnlichen Sünder werden diese γραμματεῖς deshalb empfangen, weil sie in ihrer Stellung es empfangen*" (Klostermann, op. cit., p. 145). The

We have now reached a point in our survey of this part of the relevant material when we must pause and try to decide what is the significance of its testimony concerning the intention that informed the author in this obviously tendentious representation of the Jewish leaders. We may best undertake this task by a careful consideration of the two important passages which we have just noticed.

The passage dealing with the Davidic descent of the Messiah constitutes a well-known difficulty of New Testament exegesis, for the clear denial of such a descent which is made herein by Mark appears to be strange in the light of other New Testament evidence of a regular ascription of the Davidic descent to Jesus current in various Christian circles.[1] Several solutions have been proposed,[2] but the crucial point seems generally to have been missed or its full significance not properly appreciated, namely that Mark definitely says that the Davidic descent of the Messiah was a doctrine of the Jewish scribes (Πῶς λέγουσιν οἱ γραμματεῖς). Clearly Mark's purpose here is to refute a piece of teaching which he represents as coming from official Jewish sources and not just to discuss a question of precedence, for the final question, "whence is he his son?", surely implies the expectation of a negative answer.

This Markan denial of the Davidic descent of the Messiah opens up a very complicated problem, for, although with one exception all our evidence of the primitive Christian ascription of the title "Son of David" to Jesus is post-Markan, that exception is of crucial significance. In the opening salutation of his Epistle to the Romans (1. 3) Paul describes Jesus as "born of the seed of David according to the flesh", a description which the Apostle seems to assume would be readily accepted by his readers at Rome. This means that the concept of the Davidic descent must have been current in the Christian community at Rome, and this community, as we have already seen, was a pre-Pauline foundation and originally closely associated in thought, sympathy, and organization with the Church of Jerusalem. Therefore it follows that the belief in the Messiahship of Jesus connoted for both the Jerusalem and the Roman Christians acceptance of his Davidic descent, which is, of course, consistent with all that we otherwise know of the Christology of the Jerusalem Christians.

Now the concept of the Messiah as the Son of David was, as we have already seen, essentially political in its inspiration and outlook. We reach, therefore, a position of great interest. The idea of the Davidic

identification of the other party of the comparison as "*die gewöhnlichen Sünder*" has no obvious support from the context; the identity must have been apparent to Mark's readers and, considering Mark's apologetic theme, those who in comparison will receive the lesser condemnation must be the Jewish people.

[1] Matt. (genealogy) 1. 1, 6–16; 9. 27; 12. 23; 15. 22; 20. 30, 31; 21. 9, 15; Luke (genealogy) 3. 23–31; 18. 38, 39; Rom. 1. 3.

[2] Bousset, *Kyrios Christos*, p. 5; Guignebert, *Jesus*, pp. 109–14; Goguel, *Jesus*, pp. 255–8; Klostermann, op. cit., p. 145; Eisler, *ΙΗΣΟΥΣ ΒΑΣΙΛΕΥΣ*, II, p. 178, and see also the important note on p. 177. Cf. Goguel, *La Naissance du Christianisme*, pp. 136–7; T. W. Manson, *Teaching of Jesus*, p. 266, n. 2.

14

descent of the Messiah, which was essentially connected in contemporary apocalyptic thought with nationalist aspirations, had very early been employed both in Palestine and in Rome by Christians in their interpretations of the role of Jesus; then somewhere between the years A.D. 65 and 75 we find Mark, writing probably for the Christian community in Rome, repudiating such an idea and ascribing it to the scribes of the Jews.

To appreciate the full significance of this action we must pause to notice Mark's use of the words "the scribes" (οἱ γραμματεῖς), in order to understand their true import in this passage. Mark uses the term twenty-two times in the course of his Gospel, and, as we have been noting, he uses it in passages in which the class as such is condemned on some point of its life or teaching. Moreover, from the first mention in 1. 22 he uses the term, without any explanation, to describe the official teachers of Judaism, thus evidently assuming that it was well known in this connection to his readers. The question naturally arises, therefore, of what knowledge Mark's readers could have had of such Jewish teachers, if they were resident outside Palestine. To supply an answer we have but meagre evidence upon which to draw, but, such as it is, it does seem to provide a clue to our understanding of Mark's action here. First we may notice that Mark reserves the Hebrew and Aramaic titles of ῥαββὶ and ῥαββουνὶ for Jesus only,[1] the reason possibly being that tradition had handed on the memory of this primitive title for Jesus and that Mark, out of reverence for a sacred word, would consequently not use it as a designation for the rabbis with whom so often he and his Christian brethren were in bitter conflict. Then, secondly, there is evidence from Jewish grave-stones at Rome of a somewhat later period (2nd to 5th century) that the Greek word γραμματεύς was in current employment among the Diaspora there.[2] If these facts are relevant, then we may reasonably infer that the term γραμματεῖς was well known to the Roman Christians as a designation for the local rabbis, who represented to them the official teachers of the Jews. Hence when Mark uses the term it is likely that for his readers it included two meanings, namely both a nearer one, which was embodied in the persons of the Jewish rabbis of the Roman Diaspora, and a more remote one, signifying a similar class of official exponents of Judaism in far-off Palestine. In either case, however, the term meant for them in an accepted sense the official representatives of Jewish life and thought. When Mark, therefore, wrote "how say the scribes", he undoubtedly had primarily in mind, as did also his readers, the official representatives of Judaism of his own day and experience. Thus his attributing to the scribes of the doctrine of the Davidic descent of the Messiah and his disavowal of the association of the Davidic sonship with the title κύριος are tantamount to an attempt

---

[1] 9. 5; 11. 21; 14. 45; 10. 51. Cf. Dalman, *Jesus-Jeshua*, p. 13; Black, *An Aramaic Approach to the Gospels and Acts*, p. 21.

[2] Schürer, *G.J.V.*, II, pp. 314, n. 7, 320. For LXX use see 1 Esdras 8. 3; 2 Macc. 6. 18. Paul employs it, without explanation, in 1 Cor. 1. 20. Cf. Moore, *Judaism*, vol. i, pp. 40–4.

to dissociate the Christian interpretation of Jesus from any connection with what was regarded as the distinctive current Jewish interpretation of the Messiah. The cause of such an action on the part of Mark is clearly of fundamental importance as a factor indicative of his mind and purpose in composing his Gospel, but here it will now suffice to emphasize the significance of the fact that in the Markan Gospel we find a definitive attempt to repudiate an interpretation of the status of Jesus which would connect him with the nationalist aspirations of the Jews, and this is done despite the consequent rejection of an important piece of primitive Christian teaching.

The importance of determining its current value, as we have done in the case of the passage just discussed, in order to evaluate its significance, is even greater in the case of the Markan account of the Tribute Money incident. Considering the almost total lack in this account of any apparent spiritual worth to a non-Palestinian Christian community, living under very different political conditions from those which presumably obtained in Judæa about A.D. 30, it is difficult to understand its inclusion by Mark into his short Gospel, unless it had some very pertinent contemporary significance, some vital *Sitz im Leben* for the community for which he wrote, but one which is not immediately apparent to us.

As we have seen, the passage (12. 13–17) is equivalent to a discussion of the Christian attitude towards the question of the right of the Jews to rebel against their Roman overlords. Now, while Bultmann [1] is probably right in regarding verses 14–17 as a well-established piece of Christian tradition of pre-Markan origin, the question remains of what purpose Mark intended it to serve when he incorporated it into his narrative, an act implying selection from much other material which lay ready to hand; or, to put the question in a more illuminating form from our point of view, why did Mark deem it necessary to present his readers with a discussion of the right of the Jews to adopt a course of action which was tantamount to rebellion against the Imperial Government? Again we have a question which must be related to the time of the composition of the Markan Gospel, and now the answer here and to the question implicit in the preceding passage appears to be irresistibly obvious, namely that the author was endeavouring to meet the situation which must have arisen in many Christian churches outside Palestine as a result of the Jewish war against Rome. The two passages which we have been considering give us the essential lines along which Mark formulated his apologetic to meet this situation. The Messianic hope was known to be a potent factor in the development of extreme Jewish nationalism, and so the Markan repudiation of an interpretation of the Lord in terms of a decidedly Jewish nationalist concept is easily understandable. And so also is the discussion of the matter of the Jewish tribute to Rome. The Jewish authorities are represented as putting the question to Jesus in

[1] *Die Gesch. der synopt. Trad.*, p. 25.

order "that they might catch him in talk", and Jesus, before answering, perceives "their hypocrisy" and prefaces his answer with the condemnatory remark, "Why tempt ye me?" Such remarks are significant, and perhaps it is not over-subtle to see in them a reaction to some situation in which the Christians were in danger of being associated in popular thought with the rebellious Jews, an association which Mark would here attribute to Jewish malice.[1] Whether the answer of Jesus came from pre-Markan tradition or not, it was singularly appropriate to the Markan apologetic here, for it sounded just the right note of prudent compromise [2] for a community which, while desirous of separating itself from any appearance of complicity with the cause of the Jewish rebels, was, nevertheless, still painfully mindful of the persecution which it had but recently suffered at the instigation of Cæsar. Therefore, "render unto Cæsar the things that are Cæsar's" would have constituted an adequate answer to what was deemed the purely political affair of the Jewish rebellion, while the balancing clause "and unto God the things that are God's" satisfied the nearer interests of the Roman community with regard to their consciousness that resistance had been, and might have again to be, made to the Imperial Government.

In the light of the evidence which these two passages provide, the part played in the plan of Mark's apologetic by the other condemnatory references to the Jewish leaders is obvious. The Jewish leaders, the official representatives of Jewish life and thought, are plainly set forth as the constant opponents of Jesus, who repeatedly incur his condemnation and whose authority is eclipsed by his divine calling. But this pillorying of these men reaches its climax in the part of the Markan narrative which we have not yet surveyed, so that it is necessary now to proceed to an examination of that, in order to appreciate the full proportions of the tendentious presentation of the official exponents of Judaism which is therein involved.

As we have already seen, Mark early in his narrative had stated that the Jewish authorities had determined to destroy Jesus; [3] in 14. 1, 2 the hint is again taken up and elaborated into an account of a definite plot to accomplish his death. This part of the Markan theme must surely

---

[1] Merrill, *Essays in Early Christian History*, p. 47, has suggested that official Roman differentiation of the Christians from the Jews was first made during the reign of Nero, which would thus account for the persecution at Rome. This differentiation, he thinks, was due to the prior protests of both Jews and Christians to the early official confusion of their respective faiths. However, no potent cause is known for such a Christian protest before the events of A.D. 66–70. Tacitus' famous reference to Christianity (*Ann.*, xv. 44) clearly shows how an educated Roman instinctively traced the new faith back to its Jewish origin. On the complexity of the problem here see A. D. Nock, *Camb. Anc. Hist.*, vol. x, pp. 502–3, A. Momigliano, ibid., pp. 725–6, 887–8; Goguel, *La Naissance du Christianisme*, pp. 520–4, 598–603; Parkes, *Conflict of Church and Synagogue*, pp. 85–92; Carcopino, *La Vie quotidienne à Rome*, p. 163; Simon, *Verus Israel*, p. 90, n. 2; Piganiol, *Histoire de Rome*, p. 281.

[2] "*Jesus entzieht sich trotz seines Mutes und seiner vermutlich antirömischen Gesinnung dem Dilemma mit einer Antwort, die sich gleich weit von der relativen Staatsfreundlichkeit des römischen Bürgers Paulus . . . wie von revolutionären Zelotentum hält*" (Klostermann, *Das Markusevangelium*, p. 139). See Chapter Six, p. 104. Cf. Loisy, *Les Origines du N.T.*, p. 101.

[3] 3. 6. Cf. 12. 12.

be pure invention, for an analysis shows that there are many obvious inconsistencies in his statements, some of which also presuppose a knowledge of what was transacted in exclusively official conclaves, which were apparently of a secret nature.[1] For example, Mark professes to know what was said at the meeting at which the plans for the death of Jesus were laid, and, while he states that the Jewish leaders were then desirous of taking Jesus "with subtilty (ἐν δόλῳ)", because they feared that "a tumult of the people" might ensue, he later depicts them as deliberately stirring up the people to force the hand of Pilate (15. 11), a statement which is also at variance with the story that the Jewish authorites only succeeded in arresting Jesus through the treachery of Judas Iscariot.[2] The tendentious nature of the consequent account of the Trial of Jesus before the Sanhedrin is manifest in the opening verse: [3] "Now the chief priests and the whole council sought witness against Jesus to put him to death; and found it not" (15. 55).

The account of the Trial before Pilate, which follows, quickly reveals an intention to create the impression that the Roman recognized the innocence of Jesus, but that his hand was forced by the Jewish leaders who were set on Jesus' destruction.[4] The crudity of Mark's handling of this theme, which is supremely demonstrated in the Barabbas incident, is perhaps indicative of its originality and novelty to contemporary Christian thought. The basic assumption herein that a kind of amnesty was a regular feature of the Passover Festival under Roman procuratorial rule is quite without non-Christian historical corroboration,[5] a fact which cannot be passed over on a plea of the logical unsoundness of the *argumentum a silentio*, for in such a matter we may reasonably expect to have been informed by Josephus, who was especially concerned to emphasize any privileges which his countrymen enjoyed at the hands of the Romans; moreover, there is the obvious practical objection to the existence of a custom of such a nature in a state so noted for its restlessness as was Judæa, particularly when in the case in point the prisoner was connected with some insurrection (στάσις). It follows, therefore, that the assertion of the existence of such a custom could only have been made, with any chance of acceptance, to a public that, owing to its situation with regard

---

[1] 14. 1, 2, 53 ff. Cf. Guignebert, *Jesus*, p. 451.

[2] Cf. Guignebert, op. cit., pp. 451–7; Klostermann, op. cit., p. 161.

[3] Cf. Klostermann, op. cit., p. 173; Guignebert, op. cit., pp. 462–5.

[4] Cf. Meyer, *Ursprung und Anfänge des Christentums*, I, p. 202; Guignebert, op. cit., p. 465; Goguel, op. cit., pp. 475–7.

[5] Cf. Klostermann, op. cit., pp. 177–8; Schürer, *G.J.V.*, I, pp. 468–9; Guignebert, op. cit., pp. 469–70; Goguel, *Jesus*, pp. 516–21; Loisy, op. cit., p. 112, *Le Origini del Cristianesimo*, p. 77. "*Einen als schuldig erkannten und verurteilten* στασιαστής *zu begnadigen, hatte dagegen ein römischer Statthalter bekanntlich gar nicht das Recht, und er würde sich damit eines von dem argwöhnischen Tiberius sicher nie geduldeten Eingriffs in das Vorrecht des Kaisers schuldig gemacht haben*" (Eisler, ΙΗΣΟΥΣ ΒΑΣΙΛΕΥΣ, II, pp. 464–5). The papyrus report of the legal ruling of the prefect G. Septimius Vegetus in A.D. 88 has been cited as a parallel to Mark 15. 15 (e.g. H. G. Wood, *Did Christ Really Live?*, p. 117), but on comparison the Egyptian case concerned so trifling a matter that it cannot reasonably be considered relevant. Cf. C. H. Roberts, *Legacy of Egypt*, p. 265; Deissmann, *Licht vom Osten*, pp. 229–30.

to both place and time, could not possibly be in a position to question its veracity. However that may be, the Barabbas episode enabled Mark, howbeit with a certain illogicality in view of his statement in 14. 1, 2, to represent the responsibility for the death of Jesus as falling solely upon the Jewish people and their leaders: "And Pilate said unto them, Why, what evil hath he done? But they cried out exceedingly, Crucify him" (15. 14).[1] This Markan thesis of the criminal responsibility of the Jews and the virtual innocence of the Romans reaches its significant conclusion in 15. 39, where the Roman centurion on Calvary, undoubtedly in contradistinction to the blasphemy of the Jewish leaders, is depicted as testifying to the divine nature of Jesus: "Truly this man was (the) Son of God."

We have then a studied presentation of the Jewish authorities as the enemies of Jesus, who from the beginning reject him and who in the end foully accomplish his death. Consequently to any reader of Mark's narrative it would appear not only that Jesus was independent of Judaism in his teaching and deeds, but that he was definitively repudiated as such by the official representatives of Judaism, and thus must be regarded as being essentially in isolation from the religion and national interests of the Jews. This presentation we have now to see was further supported by a similar picture of the Jewish people.

The Parable of the Sower is provided with an interpretation [2] in which a contrast is drawn between the disciples of Jesus and those who, having heard, had remained unconverted. To the former "the mystery of the kingdom of God" is revealed, while the indifference of the others is explained as part of the divine plan by a quotation from Isaiah 6. 9, 10. Then the account of the visit of Jesus to "his own country" ($\tau\dot{\eta}\nu$ $\pi\alpha\tau\rho\dot{\iota}\delta\alpha$ $\alpha\dot{\upsilon}\tau o\hat{\upsilon}$) [3] enables a striking picture to be drawn of the obduracy of his own countrymen, and an explanation is put forth in the form of a Dominical logion about the prophet's lack of honour in his own country. The inclusion of such an episode, which is apparently devoid of any purely spiritual value for a Christian community in Rome, can surely only be explained, as others of a similar nature, on the assumption that it was designed by the author to meet some current situation, and what that situation was is eloquently suggested by the words of Jesus: "A prophet is not without honour, save in his own country, and among his own kin, and in his own house." And once more we must also notice that such a saying is scarcely calculated to have been treasured by the Palestinian Christians, among whom the kin of Jesus enjoyed a position of great authority and prestige and who were also intent on fostering a *rapprochement* between themselves and the leading religious party of their nation.

---

[1] The account following (15. 16–20) of the Mocking is probably to be explained as a well-established part of the Passion Narrative which Mark felt that he could not safely or rightly exclude.

[2] 4. 11, 12. Cf. Black, *An Aramaic Approach to the Gospels and Acts*, pp. 153–8.

[3] 6. 1–5. Cf. Bacon, *Jesus and Paul*, pp. 151–2.

But in the Gentile Gospel of Mark its purpose is clearly intelligible as its readers found occasion to detach their Lord ever more completely from his racial background.

This process of separating Jesus from his historical *milieu* is further illustrated in an interesting way by Mark's treatment of both the actual kindred of Jesus and his Twelve Apostles. In 3. 21 we have the remarkable statement that his relatives (οἱ παρ' αὐτοῦ),[1] having heard of his evangelizing activity, came "to lay hold on him: for they said, He is beside himself". Then, after the ensuing Beelzebub episode, the family of Jesus (ἡ μήτηρ αὐτοῦ καὶ οἱ ἀδελφοὶ αὐτοῦ) is depicted as visiting him, while he is occupied in the work of his ministry, apparently in order to restrain him.[2] The occasion is accordingly represented as the cause of the significant Dominical question: "Who is my mother and my brethren?", and then the equally authoritative answer, with reference to those "which sat round about him": "Behold, my mother and my brethren! For whosoever shall do the will of God, the same is my brother, and sister, and mother." Later in the narrative (6. 2, 3) acquaintance with his family is made the basis of the taunting question of the incredulous Jews about the authority of Jesus in spiritual matters.

Now such obvious disparagement of the Lord's kinsfolk is certainly strange when it is recalled that in the primitive Christian community of Jerusalem James, the Lord's brother, came to acquire such prestige and authority that, as we have seen, there was once every likelihood that Christianity would develop a kind of caliphate based on blood relationship with Jesus. Accordingly it must be concluded that the author of the Markan Gospel was writing at a time when he found it expedient to belittle the status and reputation of those who had recently been the leaders of the Jerusalem Church: at a time, in other words, when such disparagement would not be deemed a dangerous disloyalty to a strong and accepted authority, and before the memories of the persons concerned had become invested with an unassailable halo of sanctity. As we have seen, James met his death in A.D. 62 and up to that time there is reason to believe that he and the Church over which he immediately presided had maintained their position of prestige and authority unchallenged; indeed, according to the later witness of Eusebius, James had been immediately followed in office by another relative of the Lord.[3] Therefore, it is improbable that Mark should have chosen before that time to present the kinsmen of the Lord in such unflattering terms, while it is also difficult to believe that such a representation would have been current

---

[1] Cf. Klostermann, *Das Markusevangelium*, p. 42; Turner, *New Com. N.T.*, p. 62 loc. cit.; Rawlinson, *St. Mark*, pp. 41–2.

[2] 3. 31–35. "*Mutter und Brüder Jesu sind die angekommenen* οἱ παρ' αὐτοῦ": Klostermann, op. cit., p. 44. Goguel, *La Naissance du Christianisme*, pp. 130–3, would see therein traces of an earlier antidynastic polemic.

[3] *Eccl. Hist.*, III. xi. 1. Eusebius dates this for μετὰ . . . τὴν αὐτίκα γενομένην ἅλωσιν τῆς Ἱερουσαλήμ. The rest of the account, however, shows signs of the working of a pious imagination.

in the Church when its centre was still the original community of Jerusalem. Hence some event after A.D. 62 must be sought which can supply an intelligible cause for such a change, and so here we find another line of evidence converging to emphasize the crucial nature of the events in Palestine which ended with the overthrow of Jerusalem and the disappearance of the Mother Church in A.D. 70.

The suggestion was made just above that the Markan treatment of the Twelve Apostles also witnesses to the trend of the Gospel's apologetic purpose of detaching Jesus from his national background by describing some piece of Jewish hostility towards him or some incident illustrating his independence of his original environment. Thus in this Gospel the Apostles are represented as a weak, vacillating band, who generally fail to understand their Master's true nature and mission [1] and completely lack his power.[2] They quarrel among themselves on the matter of precedence,[3] one of their number actually betrays Jesus to his enemies,[4] and they all finally desert him in his hour of need and flee.[5] The sketch of Peter, the leader of the apostolic band, is instructive. While he is depicted as the first of the disciples to recognize Jesus as the Christ, he is also shown immediately afterwards as so signally failing to perceive the necessity of the Passion as to merit the fierce denunciation of Jesus: "Get thee behind me, Satan: for thou mindest not the things of God, but the things of men." Indeed it is possible that in the Cæsarea Philippi story we have a definite piece of anti-Petrine polemic. It was known that Peter had been the first to recognize the Messiahship of Jesus, but to Mark this had little significance compared with his failure, as a celebrated champion of Jewish Christianity, to perceive the soteriological meaning of the death of Jesus and that Jesus' true role was that of *Salvator mundi*.[6] The same Apostle is later described in a celebrated scene as denying all knowledge of his Master through fear.[7]

Now such an unflattering portrayal of the original Christian leaders as this may appear to us as a clear proof of the veracity of the Gospel record, but such a mode of presentation at the time of its composition was surely unusual. To the Christians of the third and fourth decades such men as Peter were the revered leaders of their faith; [8] even if the personal desire of such men to humiliate themselves by commemorating their failures is allowed for, it is improbable that their followers would have been desirous of perpetuating the memory of such bygone lapses. Thus we are brought to look for a reason to explain such disparagement

---

[1] Mark 9. 6, 10; 10. 13–16, 28–31, 32. Cf. Bacon, op. cit., pp. 149–50.
[2] 9. 18.   [3] 9. 34; 10. 35–45.   [4] 14. 10, 11, 20, 21, 43–45.
[5] 14. 50. Cf. Loisy, *Les Origines du N.T.*, p. 109.
[6] Mark 8. 29–33. Werner, *Der Einfluss paulinischer Theologie im Markusevangelium*, pp. 180–1, in attempting to rebut the suggestion of J. Weiss that Mark definitely sets out to show that the Twelve did not understand the soteriological significance of the Passion can only cite in his own support 1 Cor. 15. 3, which, as we have seen, indicates Jewish Christian apologetic, not soteriology. Cf. Bacon, op. cit, pp. 158–9.
[7] 14. 66–72. Cf. M. Goguel, *Harvard Theological Review*, vol. xxv, pp. 1–27.
[8] E.g. 1 Cor. 1. 12; 9. 5; Gal. 1. 18; 2. 9, and the Peter saga in the early chapters of Acts.

of the original Christian leaders, and again the catastrophic events of
A.D. 66–70 alone appear to supply a convincing answer. In his treatment
of both the kinsfolk of Jesus and his Apostles we find revealed the same
motive which informs Mark's presentation of the Jewish leaders and their
people, namely, the desire to detach Jesus from any vital connection
with Jewish national life in its manifold aspects, and thereby to demonstrate
Christianity in its origins as a faith misunderstood and persecuted from
the beginning by the Jews, who thus avowed it as something essentially
different from their own national faith and incompatible with it.

To this diverse material, with its converging testimony, there may also
be added that which is constituted by Mark's treatment of Galilee and
Jerusalem in the course of his narrative. In a notable monograph,[1]
Professor Lohmeyer has shown that the difference which is to be discerned
in the treatment accorded to the two places forms a vital factor in the
understanding of the Gospel. For Mark "Galilee is the holy land of the
Gospel, the place of its eschatological fulfilment",[2] while, on the other
hand, all the events of the Passion are located at Jerusalem: "Jerusalem
is the city of deadly enmity to Jesus, of sin, and of death." [3] Now,
although there is certainly good reason, as we have seen, for believing
that Galilee had played a far greater part in Palestinian Christianity
than is apparent on a cursory reading of our sources, from the point of
view of our present study the question may well be asked why Mark,
writing for a Gentile public who lived far from Palestine, concerned
himself in his narrative of the life of Jesus with enhancing the reputation
of Galilee at the expense of Jerusalem. We have, of course, no means
of knowing the extent of the geographical knowledge of Mark's readers,
but it would seem nevertheless a reasonable assumption that to the
majority of them Jerusalem would have been known as the metropolis
of the Jews, while a provincial district such as Galilee would scarcely
have been known at all. If then Mark shows clear signs of attributing
to the obscure Galilee the happier events of the Ministry of Jesus (and
possibly his Resurrection manifestation), while he depicts Jerusalem as
the city which rejected and destroyed him, thus ignoring any other earlier
contacts which Jesus doubtless had with the Holy City of his people,
surely we may reasonably infer that once more we witness the working
of the Markan apologetic, seeking to show that what it held to be official
Judaism misunderstood and persecuted the Lord. And once more the
question inevitably follows of the purpose of this Markan attempt—
when would the need have arisen to discredit Jerusalem, the metropolis
of the Jews, in the eyes of the Christians? No more probable answer
appears to be forthcoming than that which gives A.D. 70, the time when
Jerusalem, the centre of Jewish national life and the heart of the Jewish

[1] *Galiläa und Jerusalem.* Cf. Lightfoot, *Locality and Doctrine in the Gospels.*
[2] Lohmeyer, op. cit., p. 29; cf. Lightfoot, op. cit., pp. 62–5, 111.
[3] Lohmeyer, op. cit., p. 34; cf. Lightfoot, op. cit., pp. 111, 123, 124.

rebellion, was overwhelmed with terrible, and to the Gentiles merited, destruction.

. . .   .

The diverse material which we have now surveyed accordingly points, with a wealth of cumulative evidence, to the presence of an apologetic theme running through the Markan Gospel.   The aim of this apologetic is to disentangle Christianity from its Jewish origins by showing that Jesus lived in conscious independence of those natural ties of blood and tradition which must ordinarily have been regarded as an indissoluble bond uniting him to his race, and by demonstrating the rejection of and the hostility towards the mission and person of Jesus on the part of the Jewish leaders and people.   We have also seen evidence of a significant desire to prove that Jesus in no wise associated himself with what are depicted as the political aims of Jewish nationalism.   The logic of this apologetic consequently demands a definite situation which it was designed to meet, and the known historical situation which alone will satisfactorily answer to such a demand is that which was created for nascent Gentile Christianity by the overthrow of Jerusalem in A.D. 70. But other evidence still remains to be considered before we can fully appreciate the significance of the Markan Gospel as the first witness of a new and pregnant reorientation of Christianity.

.   .   .

In an earlier chapter we saw that there is evidence for believing that the Jewish Christians in Palestine were probably more deeply involved in the cause of their nation's freedom from the Roman yoke than is generally thought on a cursory reading of the relevant New Testament documents.   We have now to notice a fact, to which reference has already been made, which would seem to indicate some consciousness on the part of Mark of such embarrassing knowledge.   In giving the list of the Twelve he designates one of the two Simons as "the Cananæan" (τὸν Καναναῖον), whereas Luke twice describes him by the compromising title of "the Zealot" (τὸν καλούμενον Ζηλωτήν: ὁ Ζηλωτής).[1]   We have already discussed the political significance of the title; we must here note the significance of the treatment of it.   The Gospel of Mark is notable for its preservation of Aramaic expressions which had undoubtedly firmly fixed themselves in the tradition either by virtue of their supposed curative potency or by the poignancy of the memories with which they were associated.   In five instances [2] in which they are given in Greek transliteration Mark attaches thereto an explanation of their meaning, thus clearly indicating that he was writing for a public to whom Aramaic was unknown.   However, to the description of Simon as "the Cananæan" no such explanatory note is appended.   When it is recalled, therefore,

---

[1] Mark 3. 18; Luke 6. 15; Acts 1. 13.   See above, p. 105 and n. 2.
[2] 3. 17; 5. 41; 7. 34; 15. 22, 34.

that the necessary explanation would have read "which is, the Zealot", it must surely mean that Mark's failure here to keep to his customary practice attests his consciousness of the fact that to point attention to the existence among the Lord's Apostles of a Zealot was at least inconvenient. And this in turn necessarily presupposes that Mark's readers would have known that the Zealots were the leading Jewish revolutionary party against the government of Rome, a fact which also points to a time shortly after A.D. 70, probably when the memory of the Flavian triumph at Rome was still fresh in the mind.[1]

Having seen reason to believe that the Markan Gospel was inspired by an apologetic motive to present Jesus as definitely independent of his national origins and background, we now have the task of inquiring whether the form in which this motive finds expression, namely an historical or biographical narrative, was adopted merely because of its appropriateness or whether its use may also be regarded as due to factors inherent in the situation of Gentile Christianity during this period.

Since, as we have already noted from the evidence at our disposal, it would appear that the Gospel of Mark was an innovation in what had until then been normal Christian thought and practice, it follows that the adoption of the historical narrative form is more likely to be explained by a consideration of the position of Christian affairs in the fifth and sixth decades of the first century.

In our earlier studies we have seen that the Church of Jerusalem was distinguished for its emphasis upon the ways in which the historical career of Jesus of Nazareth fulfilled ancient prophecies, thus attesting the truth of his Messianic status and mission. This emphasis upon what would now be termed "the Jesus of History" was found by Paul to be inconvenient both for his own interpretation of Jesus and for his own personal authority, and he accordingly sought to minimize its value and even once proceeded as far as to repudiate it completely. Now we have also seen that, after Paul's arrest and effective removal from active contact with his converts in 55, the Jerusalem Christians were able to intensify their efforts to controvert his teaching and establish their own authority in his churches. This situation continued until the beginning of the Jewish revolt in 66. During this period, then, the Gentile Christians of Paul's foundation or following were subjected to the propaganda of Jewish Christianity, and this undoubtedly took the form, in matters of teaching, of presenting "the Jesus of History" in narrative accounts of his career in Palestine.

However successful the doctrinal teaching of the Jerusalem emissaries may have been, there can be little doubt that the attraction of their vivid stories about Jesus must have been very great to the imagination of most

---

[1] According to Jos., *Wars*, vii. 5. 3 (118), John of Gischala, the commander of the Zealots, figured in the triumphal procession in Rome, as did, undoubtedly, many of his followers.

Gentile Christians. In comparison the esoteric teaching of Paul demanded of his hearers no mean faculty for abstract thinking, and it was scarcely calculated to compete successfully with heroic narrative in popular appeal. Hence it would appear that the decade of uncontested predominance which the Jerusalem Church enjoyed among the Gentile Christians left behind it at its passing at least one indelible effect, namely an appreciation on the part of the Gentile Christians of the tradition of the historical Jesus.

The obliteration of the Mother Church of Jerusalem, the source of the traditions which they had come to value so highly, must consequently have faced the Gentile Christians, *inter alia*, with the need of preserving such records of their sacred history as they possessed. It is understandable, therefore, that a member of some Church, very possibly that of Rome, was led by convergent causes to undertake a composition which should give a durable literary form to traditions which, existing as treasured memories in that Church, were now threatened with progressive oblivion by the fact of their being severed definitively from their original source, while at the same time he was desirous of providing such an apologia as he felt the situation of his faith required after the terribly disturbing events in Palestine between A.D. 66 and 70.

However, the influence of Jewish Christianity, despite its decade of unchallenged supremacy, was not absolute, and the author of this innovating document, which we now know as the Gospel of Mark, was clearly inspired by the theology of Paul.[1] Whether this inspiration was the outcome of a loyalty preserved during the period of Paul's eclipse we do not know, but it is most likely that the catastrophic overthrow of Judaism and the sudden disappearance of the Jerusalem Church caused many of Paul's former adherents to recall the great principle of Christian freedom from Judaistic control for which the Apostle of the Gentiles had so passionately contended, and that they saw in the disaster which had so signally overwhelmed Israel divine confirmation of Paul's message. Of course, it is not to be expected that the theology of Paul, unsystematic and sometimes inherently inconsistent as we know it in his Epistles, was thoroughly comprehended by his followers, but the Markan Gospel does reveal that some of his most important concepts had been grasped and retained even under the impact of the Jerusalem propaganda; indeed the historical tradition of the Mother Church was utilized to express them. Thus in its theological exposition Mark may fairly be regarded as definitively representing the recognition of the Messiahship of Jesus by Peter as an early and imperfect stage in the understanding of his true

---

[1] Cf. Bacon, *Jesus and Paul*, pp. 16, 143–54; Moffatt, *Intro. to N.T.*, pp. 235–6. The thesis of Werner, *Der Einfluss*, that Mark is in no wise under the influence of Paul, is based essentially on the presupposition that the contrary thesis must be able to demonstrate a literal dependence of Mark on Paul in order to prove its truth. Werner ignores the obvious conditioning influence of Mark's circumstances and the changes in expression and concept which must inevitably arise in the course of some twenty or thirty years.

nature, which was, namely, that of the Son of God [1]—this truth being significantly perceived first by the demoniac forces and finally by the Gentile centurion on Calvary.[2] The death of Jesus, moreover, is set forth not as an accident, to be explained apologetically by means of Old Testament quotations, but as an event of universal soteriological significance,[3] which could not be understood by the celebrated representative of the Jewish Apostles.

There are indeed in this Gospel clearer signs of an antipathy towards the leaders of the Jerusalem Church than those already cited in evidence of the author's desire to dissociate Jesus from essential connection with his Jewish environment. We are shown John being rebuked by Jesus for his intolerant exclusivism:[4] "John said unto him, Master, we saw one casting out devils in thy name: and we forbade him, because he followed not us. But Jesus said, Forbid him not: for there is no man which shall do a mighty work in my name, and be able quickly to speak evil of me." When Mark wrote these words it must surely have been with a lively recollection of him who had laboured so devotedly in the service of the Master and yet had not followed the "very chiefest apostles" and had consequently been ostracized by them. Then there is the significance of Jesus' answer to Peter's boast of the sacrifices made by himself and his companions in accepting their apostleship:[5] none who has made personal sacrifice for the gospel's sake shall go unrewarded, but rather, and surely in rebuke, "many that are first shall be last; and the last first". Thus came the first signs of a rehabilitation of the reputation of Paul, as his followers, struggling free from the influence of the Jerusalem Church, perceived afresh the truth of his witness, against the lurid background of the awful overthrow of Jewish spiritual arrogance.

The apocalyptic portion of Mark's Gospel is illuminating when viewed in the light of the foregoing interpretation. We have already in another context [6] discussed the significance of Mark's contradictory statements about Christ's prophecy of the destruction of the Temple, seeing that, whereas in the introduction to the Little Apocalypse he clearly represents Jesus as making such a prophecy, in his account of the Trial before the Sanhedrin he describes the ascription of such a prophecy to Jesus as a malicious calumny of false witnesses. We saw then that in his account of the Trial he was undoubtedly setting forth the tradition of the Jerusalem Church, which had cause definitely to repudiate any suggestion that Jesus had foretold the destruction of the Temple which they revered and in which they worshipped. A cause must consequently be sought for Mark's contradiction of his record by putting this prophecy into the mouth of Jesus, and none can surely be found which is more convincing

---

[1] Cf. Hoskyns and Davey, *Riddle of New Testament*, pp. 147 *seq.*
[2] 1. 24; 3. 11; 5. 7; 15. 39.
[3] 10. 45.
[4] 9. 38–40. Cf. Bacon, op. cit., p. 150.
[5] 10. 28–31. Cf. Bacon, op. cit., pp. 149–50.
[6] Pp. 37–40.

than that of the historic fact itself. It was not the general practice of Roman commanders to destroy temples, and both Josephus and Sulpicius Severus have described how the fate of the Jewish sanctuary was previously debated by Titus and his officers.[1] Therefore, a prophecy of destruction so precise as that which Mark ascribes to Jesus, that "there shall not be left here one stone upon another, which shall not be thrown down", would be a temerarious one to make before the event. But when the catastrophe had happened (accidentally according to Josephus) and when the fact had been so vividly recorded in the subsequent Flavian triumph in Rome in 71, it is easily understandable that a Christian writer was so impressed by this evidence of the divine condemnation of Judaism [2] that he felt obliged to show that his Lord had anticipated its coming, despite the fact that thereby he contradicted his own subsequent statement in the record of the Sanhedrin Trial.

If Mark's preface to the Little Apocalypse thus so clearly indicates the time of his writing, his subsequent version of the Apocalypse well reveals his *Weltanschauung* as he wrote in the aftermath of hope and doubt which followed the destruction of Jerusalem. The clue to our understanding of this would seem to lie in the fact that the warning against deception by false Christs appears in two different contexts, thereby suggesting that the passages in which they severally occur are of separate origin.[3] Now since one of these is the section which, as we have seen,[4] so well corresponds to what might reasonably be presumed to have been the expression of the reaction of the Palestinian Christians immediately after the failure of Caligula's attempt to desecrate the Temple, it would seem to be probable that this gives the original version and context of the admonition. If this inference be sound, then the other version may well be understood as a piece of plagiarism on the part of Mark, designed to make an effective addition to a section which he had composed in the light of the contemporary situation. Recent wars, civil and foreign, with

---

1 See pp. 120–1.

2 See Josephus' graphic account of the triumphal procession, *Wars*, vii. 5. 6 (132–57). Both the tableaux ($\pi\acute{\eta}\gamma\mu\alpha\tau\alpha$) and the spoils of the Temple must have created a tremendous impression upon any thoughtful Christian onlooker that day in the streets of Rome. The existing Arch of Titus in the Forum, with its precious reliefs of two scenes from the triumphal procession, was not erected until after the death of Titus. The inscription on the present Arch does not refer to the Jewish War, but another arch in the Circus Maximus, which was destroyed in the fourteenth or fifteenth century, bore the mendacious inscription: *Senatus populusque Romanus imp. Tito Caesari divi Vespasiani f. Vespasiano Augusto . . . quod praeceptis patri(is) consiliisque et auspiciis gentem Judaeorum domuit et urbem Hierusolymam omnibus ante se ducibus regibus gentibus aut frustra petitam aut omnino intemptatam delevit* (given in Schürer, *G.J.V.*, I, p. 635, n. 128). Cf. Mommsen, *Provinces of Roman Empire*, vol. ii, p. 216, n. 1; Ricciotti, *Flavio Giuseppe*, vol. iv, pp. 246–8; E. Hutton, art. "Rome" in *Wonders of the Past*, vol. ii, pp. 481, 494; L. Curtius-A. Nawrath, *Das Antike Rom* (Wien, 1944), pp. 39–40, Bilder 40–4. The Jewish victory was also well celebrated in contemporary Roman coinage. Coins of Vespasian, Titus, and Domitian exist which bear the legends: *ΙΟΥΔΙΑΣ ΕΑΛΩΚΥΙΑ*, IVDÆA CAPTA, IVDÆA DEVICTA, and some representation of Judæa as a captive; see Madden, *Coins of the Jews*, pp. 208–29; cf. F. Gnecchi, *Monete Romane* (Milan, 1935), p. 200; Bersanetti, *Vespasiano*, p. 42; Hunkin, *Palestine in General History*, Plate xii and pp. 83–4.

3 Mark 13. 5, 6, 21–23.

4 Pp. 107–8.

other calamities,[1] had deeply stirred the eschatological expectations of his fellow Christians, and the excitement had reached a climax with the destruction of the Jerusalem Temple and the overthrow of all for which it stood. Wild rumours had undoubtedly circulated and many had abandoned themselves to an unhealthy frenzy of speculation, becoming thereby the easy prey of any impostor. Mark urges caution, for these events are only the beginning of the final cataclysm, and he admonishes his readers to give heed to their own staunchness in the faith, reminding them of the recent sufferings, probably under Nero.[2] But to Mark himself the destruction of Jerusalem and the desecration of the Jewish sanctuary were true portents, and he sees in them the fulfilment of the short apocalypse which had been called forth some thirty years earlier by the impiety of Caligula. And so he inserts this earlier document into his own writing, thus producing a chronological sequence of portents, running from the wars which marked the end of Nero's reign and the establishment of the Flavian dynasty, with a backward glance to the persecution of 65, and then on to the Jewish overthrow, with a covert reference to the profanation of the Temple by the legionaries "(let him that readeth understand)". "But take heed: behold, I have told you all things beforehand"; with this warning Mark concludes the series of signs which he and his contemporaries had recently witnessed and prepares to deal with the coming of the final catastrophe. "But in those days", i.e. after the period which had reached its culmination in the desecration of the Jewish Temple, a series of cataclysms will overthrow the present cosmic order, and then will follow the *Parousia* of the Son of Man and the gathering together of his elect.[3]

When Mark wrote it would seem that there was then some need to sound a note of caution against the expectation that the *Parousia* was absolutely imminent. Although he is firm in his belief that the supreme event would come in the lifetime of his own generation,[4] he finds it necessary to assert the lapse of some indefinite period before its realization. The gospel must first be preached unto all the nations;[5] what was the exact connotation of "all the nations" it is impossible to tell, but quite clearly the term had not been reached when Mark wrote. But an even stronger caveat was needed and it was given in the significant words: "of that day or that hour knoweth no one, not even the angels in heaven, neither the Son, but the Father".[6]

The situation which lies behind this Markan Apocalypse thus indicates itself clearly. The eschatological expectations of the Christians for whom Mark wrote had been progressively stimulated by stirring events which

---

1 Mark 13. 7, 8. For an account of the anxiety and fear engendered in Rome by the disasters of the civil wars and the rebellions which marked the end of the reign of Nero, see Bersanetti, *Vespasiano*, pp. 40–1; M. P. Charlesworth, *Journal of Theological Studies*, xliii (1942), p. 106; *Camb. Anc. Hist.*, vol. xi, pp. 44–5. The earthquake at Laodicea in A.D. 60, which Tacitus mentions (*Ann.*, xiv. 27), may have been in the mind of Mark as it was in that of the writer of the *Sibylline Oracles*, iv. 107; cf. Peretti, *La Sibilla babilonese*, p. 470. See also de Labriolle, *La Réaction Païenne*, p. 53.

2 13. 8, 9.   3 13. 24–27.   4 13. 30.   5 13. 10.   6 13. 32.

seemed to be veritable portents of the *Parousia*. Persecutions, wars, natural disasters had appeared to lead up to the overthrow of Jerusalem, the city to which Christians had been taught, as also the Jews, to look as the supreme centre on earth of spiritual authority. Now surely at last their Lord must appear in glory to vindicate his own; excitement was high, rumour and speculation were rife. And yet the Coming tarried; the tension was extreme, but a sense of anticlimax and consequent puzzlement was beginning to be felt. And so Mark wrote that the signs of the times did truly point to the presence of the last days and he affirmed his conviction that within the lifetime of himself and his readers the supreme climax would come. But nothing more definitive could be said; the present interval was necessary, for the gospel had still to be spread abroad; the duty of the faithful Christian was to be ready and watch, for only God knew the time of the final visitation.

In the Gospel of Mark we thus have embodied the first reactions of a Gentile Church, probably that of Rome, to the destruction of Jerusalem. So profound were the consequences of the event for that community that the author was completely unable to view it with detachment; indeed, to the contrary, he was so deeply immersed in the problem it created that his whole interest was absorbed by the immediate issues which it had produced for himself and his fellow Christians. Accordingly we find that the very *raison d'être* of the Gospel is the situation which faced the Gentile Christians in consequence of the annihilation of the Mother Church in the course of Israel's disastrous attempt to challenge the supremacy of Rome. In this situation many different factors were involved, and it is undoubtedly to the genius of Mark that we owe the conception of the attempt to solve the many ensuing problems in the form of a biography of Jesus of Nazareth, although in choosing this medium he was essentially influenced by the Jewish Christian predilection for an historical presentation of Jesus, which had firmly established itself throughout the Gentile churches after the removal of Paul. This biography was made to serve several needs. It provided a defence of Christianity by showing that its Lord, though born a Jew, had no essential connection with his race, which now had by its fanatical excesses increased the general odium in which it was held by Gentiles. Jesus was shown to be one far greater than the Jewish Messiah, and thus the old traditional interpretation of the Church of Jerusalem was transcended by that of Paul, namely the interpretation of Jesus as the Son of God. And so the rehabilitation of Paul's teaching begins: it is not the original Jewish disciples who first perceive the true nature of Jesus; they go so far as to recognize his Messianic character but fail to understand the need and significance of his death, and it is left to a Gentile soldier on Calvary to pierce through the mystery of the Crucifixion and apprehend that the Crucified was truly the Son of God. Then finally the obsolescence of

Judaism, already pronounced by Paul, is proclaimed definitively in significant juxtaposition to the Centurion's Confession: "And the veil of the temple was rent in twain from the top to the bottom." [1]   A vision of the charred desolation which was once Yahweh's famous shrine must have risen vividly in his mind as Mark wrote those solemn words, explaining thereby to his readers that the Old Dispensation, prolonged for them wrongly by the Jerusalem Christians, had thus at last in A.D. 70 been so signally brought to its end.

[1] Mark 15. 38.   Cf. Loisy, *Les Origines du N.T.*, pp. 114–15; Goguel, *Jesus*, p. 544, *La Naissance du Christianisme*, pp. 282–3; Eisler, *ΙΗΣΟΥΣ ΒΑΣΙΛΕΥΣ*, I, pp. 161–2 and notes.

The Lukan Literature and the Rehabilitation of Paul

IN date of composition the Gospel of Mark constitutes our earliest evidence of the reaction of Christians to the fall of the Jewish state and the destruction of its capital city. Indeed so close is the document to the event that it finds therein its veritable *raison d'être*. For evidence of the next stage of that reaction we have to look to the Gospel of Matthew and the Lukan writings as being our next likely sources of such information. To choose between these two groups of documents on grounds of priority of composition is difficult; so, in view of the fact that the Acts is manifestly concerned with an heroic presentation of Paul, we may accordingly make a convenient start by examining the Lukan writings, since they promise to show some phase of that rehabilitation of Paul, consequent on the events of A.D. 70, of which the Markan Gospel affords initial proof.

Turning first to the Gospel of Luke we may note that, whatever the form in which Luke's special material may have originally existed,[1] the extant Gospel incorporates the narrative framework of Mark, which means, of course, an effective respect on the part of Luke for that document. But there are signs that Luke did not appreciate the urgency of the Markan apologetic which was called forth by the situation consequent for Gentile Christianity on the Jewish rebellion and its calamitous suppression. We may notice, for example, that in reproducing the apophthegm of the Wineskins Luke fails to understand Mark's intention of contrasting the new dynamic of Christianity with the obsolescence of Judaism and adds a verse which tends to reverse the original meaning.[2] Similarly the Markan account of the rejection of Jesus by his own countrymen loses its former apologetical force and is made to bear a universalist interpretation by the addition of the rather academic references to Elijah and Naaman.[3] This lack of appreciation of the Markan concern to extricate Jesus from any essential connection with Judaism indicates a time when the issue with Judaism was no longer urgent, and it reasonably corresponds to the sense of detachment with which the destruction of Jerusalem is contemplated. The catastrophic overthrow of the Jewish state is for Luke essentially a *fait accompli* and it is seen in its historical perspective

---

[1] Cf. Streeter, *Four Gospels*, chap. viii; Taylor, *Behind the Third Gospel*; Goguel, *Jesus*, p. 139, n. 2; Clarke, *New Test. Problems*, pp. 66–70.

[2] Luke 5. 37–39. Cf. p. 187 and n. 3 above.

[3] Luke 4. 24–27. Cf. pp. 194–5 above. The expansion of the Markan passage certainly appears to be better explained in terms of Luke's well-known universalism and not, as Streeter, op. cit., p. 209, suggested, by the hypothesis of a special non-Markan source.

as an act of divine vengeance for the slaying of Christ: "these are days of vengeance (ἐκδικήσεως), that all things which are written may be fulfilled . . . for there shall be great distress upon the earth and wrath unto this people (τῷ λαῷ τούτῳ). And they shall fall by the edge of the sword, and shall be led captive into all the nations: and Jerusalem shall be trodden down of the Gentiles, until the times of the Gentiles be fulfilled." [1] Although detailed knowledge is shown of the siege in the reference to the Roman circumvallation of the city,[2] nothing explicit is said of the fortunes of the Christian community there; the issue concerns only the majestic Christ and the Jewish people; Jerusalem must perish because it knew not the time of its visitation,[3] and the daughters of Jerusalem are admonished to weep not for Christ as he goes to Calvary, but for themselves and for their children in view of the awful fate which is to be theirs.[4]

The same attitude of relative detachment from concern about the effects of the overthrow of the Jewish state is to be seen also in Luke's incautious recording of facts indicative of a serious degree of involvement on the part of the Palestinian Christians in their nation's cause against Rome. In contrast to Mark he has no hesitation in noting that one of the Lord's company of Apostles was a Zealot,[5] while he gratuitously underlines the significant fact that Jesus' disciples were armed in Gethsemane by his account of the disciples' anticipation of their Master's instructions in this respect.[6] He also records the curiously suspicious episode of the report about the Galilæans slaughtered by Pilate.[7] Mark's obvious embarrassment about facts which revealed the presence of a political factor in the original Christian movement in Palestine is thus clearly not shared by Luke, and the fact is doubtless to be explained by the date of Luke's writing, namely at a time when the likelihood that Christians would incur some of the odium felt for the Jewish rebels was a danger which had effectively passed away.

---

[1] Luke 21. 20–24. Cf. Bultmann, *Die Gesch. der synopt. Trad.*, pp. 129, 134; Klostermann, *Das Lukasevang.*, pp. 202–3; Creed, *St. Luke*, pp. 253–4; Streeter, op. cit., pp. 494, 540; Meyer, *Ursprung und Anfänge des Christentums*, I, p. 127. The words ἄχρι πληρωθῶσι καιροὶ ἐθνῶν may give some apparent sanction to the suggestion of Taylor, op. cit., pp. 118 *seq.*, that this section of Luke may represent a Jewish Christian apocalypse written about A.D. 67–9; but the idea implicit therein is as likely to have had a Gentile as a Jewish currency at this period. Cf. Peretti, *La Sibilla babilonese*, pp. 473 *seq.*; Knox, *Gentiles*, chap. i.

[2] 19. 43. Cf. Jos., *Wars*, v. 12. 1–2 (491–510). According to Josephus this work was only undertaken as a special measure after some successful Jewish sallies, in which the Romans' usual siege-works were destroyed. Cf. Ricciotti, *Flavio Giuseppe*, vol. iv, pp. 117–19.

[3] Luke 19. 41–44. Cf. Bultmann, op. cit., p. 130; Klostermann, op. cit., p. 190; Creed, op. cit., pp. 353–4; Weiss, *Urchristentum*, p. 557. The attempt of Streeter, op. cit., pp. 215, 222, and Taylor, op. cit., p. 123, to assign the passage to their hypothetical first draft of Luke, thus dating it before A.D. 70, shows a failure to appreciate the significance of the circumvallation of the city, referred to in verse 43, in the light of the above-cited passage of Josephus.

[4] 23. 28–31. Cf. Montefiore, *Synoptic Gospels*, vol. ii, p. 623; Lietzmann, *Gesch. der alt. Kirche*, I, pp. 227–8; Luce, *St. Luke*, p. 243; Taylor, *Formation of Gospel Tradition*, p. 75; Knox, *Hellenistic Elements*, p. 12. The passage may well be derived from some Palestinian original, but it is certainly presented by Luke with reference to A.D. 70.

[5] 6. 15. See above, pp. 198–9.

[6] 22. 36–38. See above, pp. 102–3.   [7] 13. 1, 2. See above, p. 106.

This absence of any urgency of concern in the significance of the events of A.D. 66–70 for Christianity is carried over from the Gospel into the Acts of the Apostles. As we have already had abundant cause to note, the Acts, although purporting to be a record of the fortunes of the infant Church during the first three decades of its life, exhibits an almost complete indifference towards the relations of Christianity with contemporary events, both social and political. Hence it is clear that the purpose of Luke in composing this work was essentially specialized, and what he intended it to be appears to find concise expression in the first chapter. Herein we are shown the original Jewish disciples being implicitly rebuked by the Risen Lord for their narrow nationalist view of the mission of their Master and their part in it. And then their view is reorientated by him and given a universalist focus: "ye shall be my witnesses both in Jerusalem, and in all Judæa and Samaria, and unto the uttermost part of the earth."[1] The theme which is thus adumbrated is then gradually unfolded in a narrative which clearly divides into three consequent stages. The first is that of the initial establishment of the Church in Jerusalem. This is followed by the transitionary stage of the realization by the original Jewish disciples that the new faith had a universal validity and that Gentiles were to be admitted to its benefits. The third and longest stage is constituted by the record of Paul's world-wide evangelizing work, which appropriately concludes with a picture of the Apostle in Rome, after his declaration that the Jews had rejected the salvation of God which the Gentiles will gladly receive, "preaching the kingdom of God, and teaching the things concerning the Lord Jesus Christ with all boldness, none forbidding him".[2] Thus the description of the Acts as the record of the God-directed course of Christianity from its origins in provincial Jerusalem to its establishment in the metropolis of the Roman Empire is justified and apt.[3]

Since there is every reason for believing that the Acts is an original and unique production of primitive Christian literary activity, the question naturally arises of the cause or causes which led to its conception. To seek an answer we can but interrogate the document itself.

The clearly tendentious nature of the narrative of the Acts strongly suggests a clue to understanding the motive which actuated its author in composing it. As we have seen, he was concerned to depict the evolution of primitive Christianity under a very special guise, which meant that many probable formative factors were deliberately ignored. What in effect Luke succeeds in producing is an idealized picture of the progress of the Church, in which the movement goes forward unhampered by any serious obstacle. Jewish and pagan opposition is gloriously sur-

[1] Acts 1. 6–8. See Bacon, *Jesus and Paul*, pp. 155–7, on the "Paulinization" of Peter in Acts; also Guignebert, *Le Christ*, p. 55.
[2] 28. 31.
[3] Cf. Streeter, op. cit., p. 531; Weiss, op. cit., p. 525; *B.C.*, vol. ii, pp. 175 *seq.*; Lake, *Landmarks*, pp. 59 *seq.*; McNeile, *Intro. N.T.*, pp. 79 *seq.*; Guignebert, op. cit., pp. 58–9.

mounted by divine aid, while internal dissension is only described in the course of an edifying account of its quick and decisive solution.[1] Such a representation, as we have already observed on many occasions, in no wise finds support from the writings of Paul; indeed, to the contrary, it reveals a manifest failure to appreciate the true nature and seriousness of the points at issue between Paul and the leaders of the Jerusalem Church. From this discrepancy many scholars have been led reasonably to infer that Luke did not have at his disposal in composing the Acts those letters of Paul which are preserved in the present *Corpus Paulinum*.[2]

The idyllic picture of the internal life of the Church which Luke constructs does, however, on closer examination reveal signs of its author's consciousness of factors, in the historical situation which he purports to describe, which have for him a serious contemporary concern. We have already had cause to comment upon the significance of his handling of James the Just.[3] We saw that James is suddenly introduced into the narrative, with no explanation of his antecedents, as a personage of primary standing in the Jerusalem community. We noted also that a complete silence is preserved about his kinship to the Lord. Thus clearly it would seem that, unless Luke is to be charged with an amazing lack of elementary literary ability, his *gaucherie* in this respect is to be explained as due to some need which he felt of not commemorating the cause of James' position of unique authority in the primitive Church. Some similar motive must also be presumed to account for the abrupt dismissal of Peter from the narrative in which he had hitherto held the foremost place; we know from Paul's First Corinthian Epistle that Peter had probably operated at Corinth, but Luke certainly did not find it convenient to describe any of his further exploits when once Paul had been introduced as the supreme champion of Christianity. Then there is the matter of his curious handling of Apollos, which we have discussed at length in an earlier chapter.[4] The motive operative here is undoubtedly to be traced to his attitude towards the form of Christianity which was professed at Alexandria, and that attitude was distinctly hostile.

Consideration of these features suggests that Luke composed his narrative with reference to a specific situation then existing in those parts of the Church with which he was concerned. Primarily he believed that that situation demanded of him the presentation of an idealized picture of the origins of the Christian Church, and this fact must surely mean that he was writing at a time when the original issue between Jewish and Gentile Christianity had but an academic interest and when also

---

[1] Cf. Loisy, *Le Origini del Cristianesimo*, p. 31; *B.C.*, vol. ii, pp. 181–4.

[2] E.g. H. Windisch, in *B.C.*, vol. ii, p. 306; K. and S. Lake, *Intro. N.T.*, pp. 68–9, 71; Moffatt, *Intro. to N.T.*, p. 300; Nock, *St. Paul*, p. 84; Klausner, *From Jesus to Paul*, p. 224. Cf. Guignebert, op. cit., pp. 53–4.

[3] See above, pp. 27–8, 45–8.

[4] See above, pp. 24–6.

such a picture was not likely to be challenged as false by those who still retained a lively memory of those early days. Moreover, the bias in this representation was strongly in favour of Paul, and even the Jerusalem leaders, whom the Apostle's own writings show to be implacably hostile towards him,[1] are depicted as strong and whole-hearted in their support of principles which were essentially Pauline, and edifyingly fraternal in their relationships with the exponent of them.[2] We may consequently justly infer that Luke was writing when it was possible thus boldly to espouse the cause of Paul and to set him forth as the supreme Apostle, whose unique position was recognized, and whose example was praised, by the leaders of the Jerusalem Church. The Lukan narrative, therefore, certainly represents a stage far more advanced in the process of the rehabilitation of Paul than that indicated in the Gospel of Mark.

When Luke wrote, obviously Jewish Christianity no longer constituted a danger or even an effective cause of concern. However, as we have seen, Luke was not entirely without embarrassment in his portrayal of the two leading members of the Jerusalem Church, James and Peter. Though he claims that they are supporters of Paul and champions of the freedom of Gentile Christians from the yoke of Judaism, he refrains from any explanations which will in the case of the former point attention to his unique prestige and with regard to the latter record his activity outside Palestine. That these two leaders had long been dead when Luke wrote is certain, so that his attitude towards them is more likely to have been conditioned by factors operative in his own environment. It seems that a clue to these is to be found in the feeling of hostility which he shows towards Alexandrian Christianity. When he wrote some decades after A.D. 70, the Church of Jerusalem was then but a memory and unjustified statements could be made about it with little fear of serious contradiction. But if the Jerusalem Church had ceased to be the opponent of Paul and his teaching, it clearly had a successor, according to Acts, in Alexandria. The doctrine of that Church was an offence to Luke, and he makes it clear that an Alexandrian Christian could not be permitted to operate in the churches he himself was associated with until his Christology had been brought to the required Pauline standard.[3] Hence we may conclude that, when Luke wrote, the Church of Alexandria held a position relative to Paul, or rather to the teaching which had come to be associated with him, which was similar to that formerly occupied by the Mother Church of Jerusalem. Consequently the silence preserved by Luke about the origins of Christianity at Alexandria suggests that the Church in the Egyptian metropolis was probably founded by and had been closely connected with the Church of Jerusalem.

In the light of this suggestion Luke's curious dismissal of Peter from his narrative assumes a special significance. After his miraculous escape from the prison of Agrippa I, Peter is described as going to the house of

---

[1] See above, pp. 136–145.   [2] Acts 15. 6–29; 21. 17, 20, 25.   [3] See above, pp. 24–6.

the mother of John Mark, evidently a recognized rendezvous of the Christians of Jerusalem, to inform the household of his deliverance and to request them to pass on the news to James, who thus makes his first appearance in the narrative, and then "he departed, and went to another place (εἰς ἕτερον τόπον)".[1]   There has naturally been considerable discussion among scholars about Peter's destination and various suggestions have been made.[2]   But in any discussion it seems that there is a crucial point about which a decision has first to be made, namely whether Luke's vagueness here is merely due to his unconcern about literary completeness in his narrative or is the result of an intention to suppress some fact which he regarded as inconvenient to his purpose.   Obviously nothing like demonstration can be expected either way in a matter such as this, considering the nature of the material at our disposal, but there are two facts which seem to be relevant and which would suggest that the latter alternative is the more probable.   We may note that in the case of Philip, when Luke wishes to dismiss him from his narrative after recounting a series of his exploits, he does so by giving a brief note of his career until he reaches Cæsarea, in which precise locality he is left.[3]   Now Luke shows this degree of literary care, despite the fact that he is about to commence that part of his narrative which he clearly regards as the more important, namely his account of the work of Paul.   But in the account of Peter's fortunes he has no crucial matter to the description of which he might be eager quickly to pass; indeed, to the contrary, the sequel to the story of Peter comprises an account of the deeds and fate of King Agrippa, which is really irrelevant to the theme of the Acts.   There is accordingly reason for regarding Luke's vagueness about Peter's destination as intentional and as due to his dislike of commemorating the fact of this distinguished Apostle's sojourn in some specific place.   From our studies so far there would seem to be three possible places in which Peter may have sojourned for some time and which Luke might conceivably not desire to mention in such a connection in his narrative.   They are Rome, Corinth, and Alexandria.[4]   If we are to select among these the most likely city which Peter would have chosen as a place of refuge, granting the substantial truth of his escape from an imprisonment ordered by Agrippa I,[5] the claims of Alexandria are the strongest on grounds of distance and general suitability.   Now if Peter, the rival of Paul, had settled for a time in the Egyptian capital, undoubtedly becoming intimately associated with

---

[1] Acts 12. 17.

[2] Cf. *B.C.*, vol. iv, p. 138 loc. cit.; Streeter, *Primitive Church*, p. 12; Rackham, *Acts*, pp. 179–80; Lake, *Earlier Epistles*, pp. 284–5; A. Menzies, in *Peake's Commentary*, p. 790b; Goguel, *La Naissance du Christianisme*, p. 184.

[3] Acts 8. 40.

[4] Antioch has frequently been suggested as Peter's place of refuge, on the strength, it would seem, of the later tradition which claimed him as the first bishop of the city, and Gal. 2. 11. The suggestion is obviously made without any consciousness of the need of explaining Luke's vagueness here.   See below, pp. 232–3.

[5] Cf. *B.C.*, vol. iv, p. 135, n. on verse 7; J. W. Swain, *Harvard Theological Review*, vol. xxxvii (1944), pp. 346–7.

the Church there, as is consistent with what we have already inferred about the relations of the Jerusalem and Alexandrian Christian communities, it is easily understandable that Luke, when he came to dismiss Peter from his story, found it inconvenient to record that the great Apostle had found refuge in that Church which he was concerned to represent as defective in its Christology.

We thus emerge from our examination of the Lukan writings with a number of reasonable inferences which will help us to appreciate the significance of those writings in terms of the consequences of the destruction of Jerusalem for the Christian Church.   To Luke the actual event itself appears as a *fait accompli*, which can be regarded academically as a demonstration of divine justice on the Jewish nation for its guilt in rejecting and slaying Jesus Christ.   Clearly Luke wrote at a time when the immediate repercussions of the Jewish overthrow, with which Mark was so deeply concerned, had ceased to be effective.   But that event had consequences of a more enduring nature and which indeed went to form powerful factors in the situation of Christianity in the latter decades of the first century.   It was in reaction to a certain phase of this situation that the writings of Luke were produced.   He clearly belonged to that part of the Church in which the rehabilitation of Paul had effect.   When he wrote, the process had doubtless developed well beyond the tentative stage which finds expression in the Markan Gospel and the atmosphere was favourable to the bold presentation of Paul as the Apostle of Christianity *par excellence*.   The perils and passions of Paul's original conflict with the Jerusalem Christians had long passed away, and either the significance of the principles at issue therein was not understood or it was deemed to be a matter of which it was not helpful to revive the memory.[1]   On the contrary it was felt to be more convenient to present the story of the beginnings of the Christian Church in an idealized form, under which the first Christians appear a godly and zealous brotherhood, who under the guidance of the Holy Spirit edifyingly overcome every occasion of dispute, thus preserving a wonderful harmony of co-operation in furthering the interests of the gospel of Christ.   However, although the original antagonists of Paul were no more, there was in Alexandria a community of Christians who still held their views, and who probably invoked the memory of the great reputation of the Jerusalem leaders, especially of James and Peter, in their maintenance.   Hence when Luke wrote, although his work was destined for members of his own part of the Church, he was keenly conscious that there existed in Egypt powerful opponents of his teaching, and so we find him betraying embarrassment in his handling of James and Peter, despite the fact that he actually claims that these leaders warmly supported Paul, and he only breaks his silence about Alexandrian Christianity once, and then it is to insinuate that its doctrine of Christ was seriously defective.

[1] Cf. Creed, *St. Luke*, p. lxxi.

If the Acts of the Apostles may thus be fairly regarded as a most notable monument to that restoration of the prestige of Paul which was an outcome of the destruction of Jerusalem in A.D. 70, we may rightly seek for other evidence of the process as indicative of the further effects of that crucial event.   The most obvious instance to demand our attention is that of the *Corpus Paulinum* itself, for the number of Paul's Letters preserved in the New Testament canon and their diversity of address and content surely point to a definite effort to collect the Apostle's writings together as documents having a special value for the collector and his public.

We have seen that there is a consensus of authoritative opinion to the effect that Luke in composing the Acts did so without reference to the writings of Paul which we possess, and the presumption is naturally that he did not know them.   It accordingly seems to follow that the extant *Corpus Paulinum* was made some time subsequent to the publication of Acts, and the reasonable suggestion has been advanced that the interest in Paul which the Acts either created or stimulated was the cause of its formation.[1]   However that may be, the suggestion can only legitimately be regarded as one which, on *a priori* grounds, is reasonable, and for our purpose it remains necessary to investigate the relevant data in order to appreciate the significance of the *Corpus Paulinum* relative to the overthrow of the Jewish national state.

The first document which appears to be relevant to our inquiry is the so-called *First Epistle of Clement*, which is generally dated for about A.D. 96. The locations of the writer and his addressees are peculiarly significant, since both Rome and Corinth had close associations with Paul.   Clement, who clearly had a great respect for Paul and expected that such a sentiment would be shared by the Corinthian Christians, is intent on provoking in his readers a sense of their duties by any argument which he believed to be cogent.[2]   Consequently it is significant that in invoking the example of Paul he limits his references to the Apostle's witness at Corinth to one passage from his First Epistle to the Corinthians.[3]   The meaning of the passage is indeed very pertinent to the situation then existing in the Corinthian Church, but it certainly seems strange that, if he knew the Acts, Clement did not use the fact that Paul had founded the Church there, being encouraged by the words of the Lord, "I have much people in this city".[4]   But, be that as it may, the *Epistle of Clement* witnesses to the fact that by the year 96 the First Corinthian Epistle was known in both Rome and Corinth, whereas it was possible that in a hortatory communication between these two Christian centres no explicit reference

---

[1] See Goodspeed, *New Solutions to New Test. Problems*, pp. 1 seq., *An Intro. to the New Test.*, p. 215.   Cf. Streeter, op. cit., pp. 159–60; K. and S. Lake, *Intro. N.T.*, pp. 96–101.
[2] E.g. his account of the phœnix, ch. xxv.
[3] Ch. xlvi.   Reminiscences of 1 Cor. appear in ch. ii. 8, v. 5, xlvi. 7.
[4] Acts 18. 9–11.   Although he records that Aquila and Priscilla were already in Corinth, it would seem that Luke intends to make Paul responsible for the establishment of the Church there.

was felt to be necessary to the Lukan record of Paul's unique association with them.

The thorough linguistic investigation of the Pastoral Epistles made by Dr. P. N. Harrison enabled him to show that the author of these documents, living about the end of the reign of Trajan or the beginning of that of Hadrian, knew well the ten Epistles of the present *Corpus Paulinum*, holding them in great respect as the writings of one whose example and teaching had already come to be accepted as authoritative.[1]   Therefore the formation of the *Corpus* may be regarded as having been effected at a date sufficiently prior to this time to enable it to become established as authoritative.   Support for this view is also forthcoming from the fact that Polycarp seems to have been inspired by some well-known example when he immediately set to work to collect the letters of Ignatius after that martyr's death;[2] while the author of 2 Peter significantly seeks to increase his prestige by referring to the Epistles of "our beloved brother Paul".[3]

From an examination of the Pastoral Epistles another interesting fact emerges, namely that the author, despite his manifest desire to give his compilation the appearance of an authentic Pauline composition, never, except in one ambiguous instance, seems to avail himself of the vivid narrative of the Acts;[4] indeed, to the contrary, he seems to draw upon another source of tradition about the activities of Paul.

The *Epistle of Clement* and the Pastoral Epistles may accordingly be regarded as providing evidence of a peculiar significance to our inquiry. The former witnesses to the currency of the First Corinthian Epistle in the two important churches of Rome and Corinth at the end of the first century, but it shows no knowledge of the Acts of the Apostles, or at least no appreciation of the value of its testimony to the matter in hand. A similar ignorance or neglect of the Acts is exhibited by the author of the Pastoral Epistles, while he bears witness to the existence of an authoritative *Corpus Paulinum*, which included the extant ten Epistles, in the early decades of the second century.   The conclusion indicated, therefore, is that appreciation of Paul's writings existed in circles which show no knowledge of the Acts of the Apostles, so that the further inference naturally suggests itself that the work of Luke does not appear on examination to have been a likely cause of the formation of the *Corpus Paulinum*.

We must now pass from this external evidence to consider what testimony the *Corpus* provides concerning its own origins and purpose.

---

[1] *Problem of the Pastoral Epistles*, pp. 84–6, 88. Cf. Moffatt, *Intro. to N.T.*, pp. 398–9, 416; Burkitt and Creed, *Camb. Anc. Hist.*, vol. xii, pp. 453–4; Guignebert, *Le Christ*, pp. 132–3.

[2] See Streeter, *Four Gospels*, p. 161; Moffatt, op. cit., p. 60.

[3] 2 Pet. 3. 15. The date of the witness of this document is taken to be about A.D. 150. Cf. K. and S. Lake, op. cit., p. 168. See Bacon, *Jesus and Paul*, p. 155, on the Pauline interest in 1 Peter.

[4] 2 Tim. 3. 11 : see Harrison, *Problem of Pastoral Epistles*, pp. 124, 126, App. iv, text loc. cit. Harrison, ibid., p. 9, says cautiously that the author of the Pastorals was acquainted "perhaps with Acts", but he gives no indication of this knowledge. Cf. Moffatt, op. cit., p. 416.

The feature which first arrests the attention is that of the unsatisfactory state in which some of the Letters have been preserved. The most notorious instance of this is the present Second Epistle to the Corinthians, which is commonly recognized to be a veritable mosaic of fragments of several of Paul's Letters, which the editor has endeavoured to fit together to the best of his ability. There is also the puzzle about the sixteenth chapter of Romans, while it would appear that the Epistle to the Laodiceans had been completely lost, although a little personal note such as Philemon survived.[1] As we have already noticed, the state of the preservation of Paul's writings constitutes the most eloquent evidence of a temporary eclipse of the Apostle's reputation, during which the survival of his Letters depended wholly on local circumstances. That process of rehabilitation, consequent on the downfall of Israel, of which Mark affords our earliest testimony did not gather sufficient momentum in time to secure the complete preservation of even those Epistles the designation of which we know, and when finally the effort was made to collect them together irreparable losses had occurred.[2]

The contents of the *Corpus* provide cogent proof of the honesty of purpose which actuated its composer. Considering the nature and variety of the Epistles, we can be confident that no writing of Paul's is likely to have been excluded because of its incompatibility with the ideas which a later generation of Christians might have held of the origins of their faith. The background of strife, the contempt shown for Paul, the unedifying conflict at Antioch, the fierce invective, are features calculated to scandalize any who held the Lukan view of an idyllic past. The man who faithfully gathered together these documents must have been one who had a deeper appreciation of Paul and a keener insight into the issues involved in his controversies than Luke; indeed we may justly regard his work of honest compilation as the surest proof that Paul had a later disciple who did not find in his writings "some things hard to be understood, which the ignorant and unsteadfast wrest . . . unto their own destruction".[3] Whoever this unknown Pauline was, not only did he perceive the principles for which his master contended, but he was himself able to see the past conflict in its context in a nobler vision, of which he has left us an eloquent expression.

The true nature of the Epistle to the Ephesians has long been the subject of diverse interpretation, but, when the writing is viewed in terms of its place in the *Corpus Paulinum*, the most apt description of it seems to be that it was originally intended to serve as an introduction to the collected writings of Paul.[4] "The writer combines a real measure of

---

[1] See above, pp. 8–9. Cf. K. and S. Lake, op. cit., pp. 98, 146; Lake, *Earlier Epistles*, p. 334.

[2] Lake's suggestion, op. cit., p. 366, explaining the growth of the *Corpus Paulinum*, appears to overlook the significance of the two facts that the existence and use of the Epistles of Paul is not attested before 96 (Clement) and that the extant documents are obviously incomplete.

[3] 2 Pet. 3. 16.

[4] Cf. Knox, *Gentiles*, p. 184; K. and S. Lake, op. cit., p. 142; A. J. Grieve, Supplement to *Peake's Commentary*, p. 35a.

originality with a deep understanding of Paulinism and a thorough loyalty
to it; he has no ulterior motive of the kind usually found in pseudepi-
graphic writings." [1]   In the person of Paul he expounds a theology
which is really an epitome of the great Apostle's teaching as contained in
his Epistles: that the Gentiles, who were "alienated from the common-
wealth of Israel, and strangers from the covenants of the promise, having
no hope and without God in the world", now "are made nigh in the
blood of Christ.   For he is our peace, who hath made both one, and
brake down the middle wall of partition." [2]   But what was an urgent
living issue for Paul, to his Ephesian disciple has become a position well
achieved and secure in the divine economy.   Judaism and its cultus of
the Temple are no longer a powerful entity to which Gentile Christians
had apologetically to adjust themselves; after the ancient strife the new
synthesis had been effected: "So then ye are no more strangers and sojourners, but ye are fellow-citizens with the saints, and of the household
of God, being built upon the foundation of the apostles and prophets,
Christ Jesus himself being the chief corner stone; in whom each several
building, fitly framed together, groweth into a holy temple in the Lord." [3]

And so we may well leave at this decisive point of development the
process of the rehabilitation of Paul, which was one of the most pregnant
of the consequences of the destruction of Jerusalem for the Christian
Church.   As we have seen, already by about the beginning of the second
century it was productive of two distinct lines of interpretation.   In the
Lukan Acts a high reverence for the great Apostle of the Gentiles is
revealed and he is set forth as the Apostle *par excellence*; but it is an idealized
portrait and is weakened by the author's ignorance of, or design to exclude,
the real nature and proportions of the conflict in which Paul was involved
with the Jerusalem Christians.   A truer and a fearless appreciation of
the principles at stake is adumbrated in the Gospel of Mark and finds
its effective expression later in the deliberate formation of the *Corpus
Paulinum*, with its noble preface, in which the editor shows himself to have
perceived the significance of Paul's contendings and yet is able, for all
his obvious devotion to Paul, to refrain from any exultation over the fall
of Israel and to construct from the testimony of the past a superb synthesis
of Jewish concept and Christian faith.

[1] Knox, op. cit., p. 184.   [2] Eph. 2. 11–14.   [3] Eph. 2. 19–21.

12

The Gospel of Matthew and the Origins of Alexandrian Christianity

THE Markan Gospel and the writings of Luke represent two phases of the repercussions of the overthrow of the Jewish nation in A.D. 70 which may fairly be regarded as successive and consequential, although, as we have seen, Luke does not develop all the ideas of Mark. The repercussions which we trace in them were clearly conditioned by specific situations in the Gentile churches, and thus they may truly be interpreted as the most significant expressions of the mind of Gentile Christianity as it recovered from the first shock of its definitive severance from the Mother Church of Jerusalem, the original source of authority in faith and practice. There now presents itself for our consideration another document, namely the Gospel of Matthew, which seems to be contemporaneous with the Lukan writings, but which obviously is not in the same sequence of reaction, since it represents a more thoroughly Jewish outlook.

On a general view the Gospel of Matthew exhibits some strange and apparently contradictory features. Whereas its Greek is good compared with that of some other of the New Testament writings,[1] its cultural interests appear to be essentially Jewish; it contains some of the fiercest invective against the Pharisees, yet the authority of this Jewish sect is strangely exalted; a narrow intolerance characterizes so much of its attitude towards the Gentiles, but its last verse apparently expresses a universalism as wide and as noble as any to be found elsewhere in the New Testament corpus. It may indeed be granted, in explanation, that the document in its extant form probably contains material of diverse origin and date, but this does not alone adequately account for the seeming contradictions, and the problem remains of finding some ethos of which it may fairly be considered an intelligible literary expression.

Various places have been suggested for the provenance of Matthew. Among them English-speaking scholars have generally preferred Antioch, and the late Dr. Streeter in particular elaborated a strong case in favour of this location.[2] Since the theory of the Antiochene origin of the

[1] Cf. Allen, *I.C.C.*, pp. lxxxv–lxxxvi; Bacon, *Studies in Matthew*, p. 134; Knox, *Hellenistic Elements*, p. 64 and n. 4; B. Weiss, *Das Matthäus-Evangelium*, p. 8.

[2] *Four Gospels*, pp. 12, 500–26, *Camb. Anc. Hist.*, vol. xi, pp. 260–1, *Primitive Church*, pp. 58–60; F. Jackson and K. Lake, *B.C.*, vol. i, p. 330; Goodspeed, *Intro. N.T.*, pp. 175–6. A Palestinian origin for Matthew has been championed by Meyer, *Ursprung und Anfänge des Christentums*, I, p. 241; cf. III, p. 226. There are, however, several serious objections to this view: (1) The Greek of Matt. shows little of the awkwardness which might naturally be expected of a Palestinian

Matthean Gospel has thus been so powerfully supported, but since it would appear that another city has stronger claims to the distinction, it is necessary briefly to examine the arguments advanced by Dr. Streeter in favour of the Syrian city.

It will be convenient to begin with the explanation given for the presence in the Greek city of Antioch, which had been the original headquarters of the Gentile Mission, of such Judaistic material as that which Matthew contains. The suggestion is made that some time after the death of James, the Lord's brother, in the year A.D. 62, a party of Jerusalem Christians may have fled for refuge to Antioch. However, Dr. Streeter unfortunately is not clear about whether the immediate cause of this flight was the death of James or the beginning of the Jewish War; his reference to Eusebius' account of the flight to Pella tends to show that he connected this movement with the approaching siege of Jerusalem, and he appears to think also that the imminence of this disaster led the Jerusalem Christians for the first time to commit their traditions to writing.[1] But that such a flight northward to Antioch should have been undertaken at any time during the course of the war by a party of Jews is most improbable. Both Cestius Gallus and Vespasian, who conducted the two Roman campaigns against the insurgents, entered Palestine from the north, so that the natural direction of those Jews who preferred flight to resistance was southwards or to the east across the Jordan.[2] To have fled towards Antioch would have taken them directly into the theatre of war and towards the advancing armies of the heathen, and such a course would have been obviously suicidal. Moreover, it is difficult to

Jew; e.g. Josephus, an educated man with literary pretensions, was obliged to employ Greek literary assistants (cf. Thackeray, Loeb *Josephus*, vol. ii, pp. xiv–xv; Ricciotti, *Flavio Giuseppe*, vol. i, p. 150); cf. note 1 above. (2) In the light of Streeter's thesis that each of the four Gospels represents the tradition of some great Church, it seems very improbable that a Gospel current among the depressed fragments of the Palestinian Church after A.D. 70, especially one which speaks so slightingly of the Gentiles, should have commended itself to Gentile churches. (3) It is difficult to understand how a Gospel which is "clearly a Greek composition" (McNeile, *St. Matthew*, p. xxviii) was produced for an Aramaic-speaking community; cf. V. Taylor, Suppl. to *Peake's Commentary*, pp. 27–8. The later Jewish Christian sects of Syria, mentioned by Jerome and Epiphanius, apparently had for their Gospel a Hebrew translation of the Greek Matthew. Bacon, op. cit. pp. 19–23, has argued that Matt. originated in the Greek-speaking Jewish Christian communities of northern and north-eastern Syria, and was brought thence to Antioch; cf. Green, *St. Matthew*, pp. 19–22. There seems to be one particularly serious objection to this view, namely that Josephus, when composing an account of the Jewish War against Rome for the large Jewish population in these same parts, wrote in Aramaic (τῇ πατρίῳ : *Wars of the Jews*, Preface, 1–2), this clearly being the common language there. B. Weiss, *Das Matthäus-Evangelium*, p. 17, gives no convincing reason why the polemic in Matt. against libertinism should mean that the Gospel originated in Asia Minor. Kilpatrick argues for a Phœnician location (*The Origins of the Gospel according to St. Matt.*, pp. 132–3) on the ground of Matt.'s alteration of the Syro-Phœnician Woman of Mark to a Canaanite (15. 22). But surely, if it has significance, this alteration points in quite the opposite direction? For it would seem more reasonable to expect a writer in Phœnicia to have preserved such an interesting reference to his own locality as this in Mark. If Matthew were written in Alexandria, such an alteration would have point, since the term "Canaanite" would afford a good traditional contrast with the Chosen of Israel. Incidentally Kilpatrick's other points that Matt. indicates a wealthy city community (pp. 124–5) and a seaport (p. 132) all agree with an Alexandrian origin.

[1] Op. cit., p. 512.
[2] See above, pp. 177–8.

see why, of all possible places of refuge, the most Judaistic of the Jewish Christians should have chosen to seek shelter in the very city which had been the fount and centre of that liberalizing movement which they had so bitterly opposed.[1]

Secondly, we must consider the suggestion of Dr. Streeter that the Gospel of Matthew represents a compromise between James' ideas and Paul's under the ægis of the mediating Peter.[2] Of the Judaistic side of this Gospel there is no doubt, but its apparent liberalism may be easily exaggerated and misinterpreted. The strongest piece of evidence in favour of this liberalism is found in the last two verses of the Gospel, where the Risen Lord commissions the Apostles to make disciples of all nations. But, as we shall attempt to show presently, the whole meaning of this passage is qualified by the words: "teaching them to observe all things whatsoever I commanded you"; and both it and other similar evidence which may be cited in support of a liberalist outlook are patient of a very different interpretation, and one which is consistent with the Judaistic interest displayed throughout the Gospel. Moreover, the uncompromising nature of this interest does not seem to have been sufficiently appreciated by Dr. Streeter. A Gospel which records Christ as saying: "I was not sent but unto the lost sheep of the house of Israel",[3] and "Go not into any way of the Gentiles",[4] and which gives the warning: "in praying use not vain repetitions, as the Gentiles do: for they think that they shall be heard for their much speaking",[5] and probably with reference to the Gentiles says: "Give not that which is holy unto the dogs, neither cast your pearls before the swine" [6]—such a Gospel can scarcely be regarded as designed to conciliate Gentile Christians. Furthermore, a writing which holds up as a worthy ideal a well-instructed scribe after the Jewish pattern [7] and which counsels its readers to give respect and obedience to the scribes and Pharisees [8] does not look like a compromise between James' ideals and Paul's effected in a Gentile city.

The great interest in Peter which is shown in Matthew, which Streeter has interpreted as evidence in support of his theory of a compromise, can be adequately explained, and also more convincingly as we hope to show below, in quite another way.

---

[1] Gal. 2. 11 ff.; Acts 11. 19–26; 13. 1–3; 14. 26–15. 2.

[2] Op. cit., pp. 512–16.

[3] 15. 24. Cf. J. Weiss, *Urchristentum*, pp. 284–5.

[4] 10.5.   [5] 6. 7. Cf. 18. 17.

[6] 7. 6. Cf. Allen, *I.C.C.*, p. 67. According to Strack and Billerbeck, *Kommentar*, I, pp. 449–50, rabbinic writers refer to Rome, i.e. the non-Israelitish world, under the name of swine.

[7] 13. 52. Cf. Strack und Billerbeck, op. cit., I, p. 676; Moffatt, *Intro. to N.T.*, p. 255.

[8] Matt. 23. 1–3. Cf. J. Weiss, *Urchristentum*, p. 586. Bacon, *Jesus and Paul*, pp. 162–3, makes the interesting suggestion that Matt. 17. 24–27 reflects the Jewish Christian policy of paying the customary Temple-tax and that the reference of the words "lest we cause them to stumble" is to the orthodox Jews, whose sympathy they sought to win or retain. However, it is to be noted that Eisler, *Orpheus the Fisher*, pp. 94 *seq.*, has presented a good case for identifying the reference as made to the Roman tribute imposed on the Jews after A.D. 70 (Jos., *Wars*, vii. 6. 6: 218). Cf. Kilpatrick, *The Origins of the Gospel according to St. Matthew*, pp. 41–2.

Dr. Streeter further supports his theory by citing a number of textual variants in Matthew which he interprets as proof that what he regards as the Antiochene group of manuscripts gives the best tradition of the text of the Gospel, thus indicating their proximity to the original. However, on a detailed examination of the variant readings of Matthew it would appear that in most cases quite an opposite interpretation can reasonably be made out, and in contradiction to Dr. Streeter's conclusion the evidence seems to show that the Alexandrian manuscripts provide the best authority for the text of this Gospel. Since this question necessarily involves a detailed discussion of the variants the subject is treated in an appendix to this chapter, in order to avoid obscuring the main theme here.

Another objection to Dr. Streeter's thesis is to be found in the fact that the author of the Acts of the Apostles clearly had very close connections with Antioch and that he has incorporated Antiochene traditions into his work.[1] Indeed Eusebius actually says that Luke was of Antioch (Λουκᾶς δὲ τὸ μὲν γένος ὤν τῶν ἀπ' 'Αντιοχείας),[2] and, if the reading of Codex Bezae for Acts 11. 28 be accepted, the "we" passages start significantly at Antioch;[3] it may also be added that Streeter himself admitted that Luke was probably "a member of the congregation of Antioch".[4]

Now in the Acts there appears an account of the death of Judas Iscariot which is quite different from that given by Matthew.[5] It is accordingly difficult to believe that one who was probably a member of the Antiochene Church, and who was well acquainted with its traditions, should have put on record an account of the death of Judas which contradicted that already in circulation there. Secondly, the post-Resurrection accounts of Luke, in both the Gospel and the Acts, make Jerusalem definitely the stage upon which the whole drama was enacted, while Matthew, perhaps following Mark, preserves the tradition that Christ appeared only in Galilee after the Resurrection and from there ascended into the heavens.[6] Now there is much reason for believing that this difference over the locality of the appearances was rooted in a difference of theological outlook,[7] and so again it is not likely that documents embodying such important differences emanated from the same Church or from members

---

[1] E.g. Acts 11. 19–30; 13. 1 ff.; 15. 1 ff. Cf. Jackson and Lake, *B.C.*, vol. ii, pp. 127–9, 153, 200–4. These scholars recognize the strength of the tradition that Acts was originally written in Antioch.

[2] *Eccl. Hist.*, III. iv. 6.

[3] See the edition of the text by J. H. Ropes, *B.C.*, vol. iii, p. 109 and note; cf. *B.C.*, vol. ii, pp. 158 *seq.*, vol. iv, p. 130.

[4] *Four Gospels*, p. 554.

[5] Acts 1. 18–20; Matt. 27. 3–10. Bacon, *Studies in Matthew*, p. 252, says, "Cæsarea, Antioch, and the Pauline mission-field are not the regions in which to look for legendary accounts of the fate of Judas conflicting as Matt. 27. 3–10 does with Acts 1. 18–20 and with Papias' account derived from 'the Elders'." Cf. Streeter, *Primitive Church*, pp. 50–1; *B.C.*, vol. v, pp. 22–30.

[6] Luke 24.; Acts 1. 1–4; Matt. 28. 10, 16–20. Cf. Mark 14. 28; 16. 7.

[7] Cf. Lohmeyer, *Galiläa und Jerusalem*; Lightfoot, *Locality and Doctrine in the Gospels*: see above, pp. 197–8.

of the same Church. And this same consideration applies with equal force to the Infancy Narratives, for the divergences between the Lukan and Matthean versions imply two distinct and dissimilar traditions, which can scarcely have been current in the same Church.[1] Indeed, when full weight is given to the fundamental differences which exist between the Lukan and Matthean records, the fact of Luke's connection with Antioch irresistibly demands that the sphere of Matthew be located far from the Syrian city.

The rejection of the claim of Antioch to be the place of origin of Matthew's Gospel leaves but one other city as a likely candidate for the position, namely Alexandria, and to that conclusion we have already noticed that the evidence of the MS. tradition for Matthew clearly points. It now accordingly becomes our task to seek for further positive evidence of the Alexandrian origin of Matthew and to investigate the beginnings of Christianity in the Egyptian metropolis. We shall best approach our task by considering generally the situation of Alexandria relative to the beginnings of the Christian movement.

Alexandria was the second greatest city of the Græco-Roman world [2] and was the capital of that land with which the Jews had had age-long cultural and political relations and to which they instinctively turned for refuge in times of national distress. The city of Alexandria itself had long been the home of a large Jewish population; indeed about one-third of the city was in Jewish hands, and as a community the Jews were wealthy and flourishing, possessing many synagogues and enjoying many peculiar privileges.[3] Philo estimated the number of Jews living in Alexandria and other parts of Egypt as not less than one million,[4] which, according to M. Juster, was over an eighth of the entire population of the country.[5] According to Jewish writers anti-Semitism was strong in Alexandria, but it would appear that such antipathy was partly provoked by Jewish fanaticism and by their interested support of the Roman government against the political pride and aspirations of the Greek inhabitants of the city.[6]

Consideration of these facts certainly leads to the conclusion that

1 Cf. Streeter, *Four Gospels*, pp. 266 *seq.*; *Primitive Church*, pp. 50–1.
2 Cf. H. I. Bell, *Camb. Anc. Hist.*, vol. x, pp. 296–7, F. Oertel, ibid., pp. 398–400, 412.
3 Cf. Bell, *Juden und Griechen im römischen Alexandreia*, pp. 10–14, *Jews and Christians in Egypt*, pp. 11 *seq.*, *Camb. Anc. Hist.*, vol. x, p. 296; H. Box, *Philonis Alexandrini In Flaccum*, pp. xx *seq.*; Schürer, *G.J.V.*, III, pp. 21 *seq.*; Jouget, *L'Impérialisme Macédonien et l'Hellénisation de l'Orient*, p. 399; Oesterley, *Hist. of Israel*, vol. ii, p. 404, *Legacy of Egypt*, pp. 237–8.
4 *In Flaccum*, 43.
5 *Les Juifs dans l'Empire Romain*, p. 209.
6 See Bell, *Jews and Christians in Egypt*, p. 11, *Camb. Anc. Hist.*, vol. x, p. 308. Cf. Oesterley, op. cit., vol. ii, p. 404. The bulk of the evidence for Alexandrian anti-Semitism comes from Philo and Josephus. The careful wording of the Letter of Claudius (*Select Papyri*, II, Loeb ed., pp. 85–7) indicates a view that either side was equally guilty. Perhaps one of the most significant pieces of evidence (because of its simplicity of statement) of the destructive power of Jewish fanaticism in Egypt is the letter of Apollonius, *strategus* of the Apollonopolite-Heptacomia *nome*, written about A.D. 120, during the Jewish revolt (op. cit., II, pp. 306–9). Cf. Goodenough, *Politics of Philo Judaeus*, *passim*; Bell, *Egypt*, pp. 89–90.

16

Christianity should early have felt the attraction of Alexandria as both a natural and a promising mission-field. But, except for the late and patently fabricated accounts of Eusebius,[1] Christian tradition has nothing to tell of the genesis of the faith there, and when light is finally thrown on the Christian situation in the second century we find that Alexandria has already developed a flourishing Church, in which Pantænus and Clement attest the vigour of its intellectual life, as do also the great heresiarchs Valentinus and Basilides,[2] while evidence has recently been forthcoming of the fact that the Gospel of John was being read even in Upper Egypt during the first half of the same century.[3] The natural inference to be drawn from these facts is, of course, that Christianity must have arrived early in Egypt, and that the silence preserved in Christian tradition about its origins must be considered strange. Consequently it is understandable that scholars have closely questioned the reference of the words of the Emperor Claudius in his letter to the Alexandrians when he warns the Jews of the city: "not to bring in or admit Jews who come down the river from Syria or Egypt ($\dot{a}\pi\dot{o}$ $\Sigma\nu\rho\dot{\iota}as$ $\ddot{\eta}$ $Ai\gamma\dot{\nu}\pi(\tau)o\nu$ $\kappa a\tau a$-$\pi\lambda\dot{\epsilon}o\nu\tau as$), a proceeding which will compel me to conceive serious suspicions; otherwise I will by all means take vengeance on them as fomenters of what is a general plague infecting the whole world ($\kappa a\theta\dot{a}\pi\epsilon\rho$ $\kappa o\iota\nu\dot{\eta}\nu$ $\tau\epsilon\iota\nu a$ $\tau\hat{\eta}s$ $oi\kappa o\nu\mu\dot{\epsilon}\nu\eta s$ $\nu\dot{o}\sigma o\nu$ $\dot{\epsilon}\xi\epsilon\gamma\epsilon\dot{\iota}\rho o\nu\tau as$)."[4] The vigour of this warning certainly presupposes the existence both in Alexandria and elsewhere of some serious form of Jewish unrest, and it has been tempting to connect it with the expulsion of the Jews from Rome by Claudius, which Suetonius and the Acts have recorded;[5] moreover, the last sentence is curiously reminiscent of the charge which Tertullus brought against Paul on behalf of the Jewish leaders: "we have found this man a pestilent fellow, and a mover of insurrections among all the Jews throughout the world (κai $\kappa\iota\nu o\hat{\nu}\nu\tau a$ $\sigma\tau\dot{a}\sigma\epsilon\iota s$ $\pi\hat{a}\sigma\iota$ $\tauo\hat{\iota}s$ $'Io\nu\delta ai o\iota s$ $\tauo\hat{\iota}s$ $\kappa a\tau\dot{a}$ $\tau\dot{\eta}\nu$ $oi\kappa o\nu\mu\dot{\epsilon}\nu\eta\nu$)".[6] Some scholars have definitely interpreted the reference as made to the agitation produced in the com-

---

[1] *Eccl. Hist.*, II. xvi (note his errors about Philo in this connection, xvii–xxiv). Mark's connection with Alexandria is not mentioned by Clement or Origen, and in the second half of the 3rd century Dionysius, Bishop of Alexandria, could write of Mark without recording so notable a tradition about his own see.

[2] Cf. Lietzmann, *Gesch. der alten Kirche*, I, pp. 134, 279 *seq.*, 301 *seq.* It has been suggested that the legend of Mark's evangelization of Alexandria is a reminiscence of the help originally given by Rome to the Alexandrian Church to free it from gnostic influence; see Burkitt, *Camb. Anc. Hist.*, vol. xii, p. 478; Creed, in *Legacy of Egypt*, p. 310; Bell, *Harvard Theological Review*, vol. xxxvii (1944), pp. 185 *seq.*, *Egypt* (1948), pp. 86–8; de Labriolle, *La Réaction Païenne*, pp. 50–2.

[3] See C. H. Roberts, in *Legacy of Egypt*, p. 262. Partly on the strength of this fact K. and S. Lake, *Intro. N.T.*, p. 53, have actually suggested assigning the Gospel of John to Alexandria as its place of origin. Cf. Bell, *Harvard Theological Review*, vol. xxxvii, pp. 199–200.

[4] Translation and text, A. S. Hunt and C. C. Edgar, *Select Papyri*, II, p. 86, ll. 96–100, p. 87; cf. Bell, *Jews and Christians in Egypt*, p. 25, also p. 29.

[5] *Claudius*, 25: "*Iudaeos impulsore Chresto adsidue tumultuantes Roma expulit*"; Acts 18. 2; cf. Dio Cassius, ix. 6. Cf. V. M. Scramuzza, *B.C.*, vol. v, pp. 295–6; A. D. Nock, *Camb. Anc. Hist.*, vol. x, pp. 500–1; Guignebert, *Le Christ*, p. 16; Eisler, *ΙΗΣΟΥΣ ΒΑΣΙΛΕΥΣ*, Bd. I, p. 132, n. 4.

[6] Acts 24. 5.

munities of the Diaspora by Christian evangelization.[1] Such a certain identification, however, is not justified by the relevant evidence, which at the most will only allow the earlier verdict of Dr. Idris Bell,[2] the original editor of the Letter, namely that the passage does not contain a direct allusion to Christianity, but perhaps the earliest historical indication of the unrest which the propagation of Christianity must have caused. This verdict has great significance for us here when it is set together with other fragments of evidence which we are considering, relative to the beginnings of Christianity at Alexandria.

Another such fragment seems to be provided by a contemporary incident at Alexandria. Philo records that when Agrippa passed through the Egyptian metropolis on his way home to Palestine as the newly appointed King of the Jews, the Gentile inhabitants of the city staged a mocking mime (ὡς ἐν θεατρικᾶς μίμοις), in which an idiot was decked out in the trappings of royalty and derisively saluted by the Syrian word Μάριν.[3] Now while the incident can well be explained, as indeed it is by Philo, in terms of the well-known caustic wit of the Alexandrians, and while the word Μάριν could easily have been familiar to the cosmopolitan population of the great commercial port, it is, nevertheless, significant that this particular form of parodying Jewish kingship was adopted to insult the local Jewish community. It must be remembered that for over forty years, since the death of Herod the Great, there had been no official King of the Jews, so that, when Agrippa arrived as the Jewish King in Alexandria in A.D. 38, the title must have been a novelty for the Alexandrians, except possibly (and the exception would be a significant one) as a current expression of Jewish Messianic hopes. Now, if Christianity had already become an effective force in the Egyptian city and it was known that certain Jews were claiming that the crucified Jesus of Nazareth was the true King of the Jews and were accustomed to refer to him by the Syrian word Μάριν, which was certainly in current use in Christian circles elsewhere,[4] the derisive parody which the Alexandrians

---

[1] E.g. S. Reinach, *Orpheus*, p. 244. Oesterley, *Hist. of Israel*, vol. ii, p. 409, n. 3, has suggested that a Jewish Baptist sect, of which Apollos was a member, may have caused some such disturbance in Alexandria; it might fairly be asked how far Christianity might then have been described as "a Jewish Baptist sect". Eisler, *Enigma of Fourth Gospel*, pp. 96–7, believes that the Letter refers to the agitation caused by some Nasoræan Messianists.

[2] *Juden und Griechen im römischen Alexandreia*, p. 27. Cf. Loisy, *La Naissance du Christianisme*, p. 163; Momigliano, *L'Opera dell'Imperatore Claudio*, pp. 66–70. Guignebert in his last work, *Le Christ* (1943), p. 17, professed himself unconvinced that the Letter provided one of our earliest pagan references to Christianity. See also the useful review of opinion in Goguel, *La Naissance du Christianisme*, p. 18, n. 6, and de Labriolle, op. cit., pp. 20–4. It must be noted that Dr. H. I. Bell now holds that no possible reference to Christianity may be legitimately inferred from the Letter (*Harvard Theological Review*, vol. xxxvii, pp. 189–90).

[3] *In Flaccum*, 5–6 (25–42, ed. H. Box) ; cf. Schürer, *G.J.V.*, I, p. 497.

[4] 1 Cor. 16. 22. Cf. Clarke, *New Test. Problems*, p. 148; *B.C.*, vol. i, pp. 409–10; Deissmann, *Licht vom Osten*, p. 127; Burkitt, *Christian Beginnings*, pp. 49–52; Nock, *Early Gentile Christianity*, p. 85; Guignebert, *Le Christ*, pp. 84–5. Philo's curious explanation in the passage under discussion should be noted: ᾔδεσαν γὰρ 'Αγρίππαν καὶ γένει Σύρον καὶ Συρίας μεγάλην ἀποτομὴν ἔχοντα, ἧς ἐβασίλευε. Was the use of Μάριν due to the mob's striving after ethnological exactitude in its farce, or to a spontaneous seizing upon a current term which they knew had already for many Jews an opprobrious meaning? See the note of S. H. Hooke

staged to insult Agrippa's newly acquired office assumes a greater significance both in itself and in relation to the notable passage in the Letter of Claudius. At this point we must for a time leave the matter and turn our attention to some other aspects of the problem of Christian Origins at Alexandria.

Accepting then the general probability which is indicated by the fragmentary evidence which we have just discussed, and by *a priori* inference from the contemporary cultural and geographical situation, namely that Christianity in some form arrived early in Alexandria, we must now turn to consider the significance of the silence which we have noted in the New Testament about the beginnings of the faith in the Egyptian capital. To appreciate the true proportions of the problem involved here, we must carefully bear in mind the fact that our knowledge of the geographical progress of first-century Christianity is derived exclusively from the Epistles of Paul and the Acts of the Apostles. These documents agree in representing the movement as starting from Palestine and developing in a north-westerly direction to reach its goal in Rome, the metropolis of the then-known world, with a suggestion of future progress westwards to Spain. However, we have already had abundant occasion to note the essentially controversial and tendentious character of both the Pauline and the Lukan writings; in them we have in fact the *ex parte* statement of one side in a conflict of fundamental import. Why there should survive in the New Testament corpus no document providing a conscious description of the origins of Christianity elsewhere in the Roman Empire, particularly in Egypt, is a question which we have still to answer, and the key to that answer paradoxically lies in the elucidation of the nature of Alexandrian Christianity in the first crucial decades after A.D. 30.

There is fortunately a clue to guide us out of this impasse. Despite the unsatisfactory nature of the Acts as a reliable historical record, the document does contain two valuable indications of Luke's attitude to Alexandrian Christianity, which we have already discussed in another context. The more significant is that constituted by the account of Apollos, and from our examination of the passages concerned we found reason for believing that the author of Acts definitely sought therein to depict the Christianity of Alexandria as defective in its Christology from the Pauline standpoint;[1] it appeared, moreover, from Luke's remarks, that this Alexandrian Christology took the form of a kind of rabbinical

thereon, cited by H. Box, op. cit., p. 92; see also the note on p. 91. The interpretation of the incident by Frazer, *Golden Bough*, "The Scapegoat", pp. 418–19, has a certain relevancy to the view put forth above. Cf. Eisler, *ΙΗΣΟΥΣ ΒΑΣΙΛΕΥΣ*, II, p. 278, n. 2.

[1] See above, pp. 24–6, 209. It is also interesting to note that W. Bauer (*Rechtgläubigkeit und Ketzerei im ältesten Christentum*, Tübingen, 1934, pp. 49 *seq.*, cited by Goguel, op. cit., pp. 19–20) suggested that the silence in ecclesiastical tradition about the origin of Egyptian Christianity is due to the fact that it was known to have been heretical in the beginning from the later orthodox point of view. Cf. C. H. Roberts, *J.T.S.*, vol. 1 (1949), pp. 161–2.

exposition of the Messiahship of Jesus.   The second, and admittedly less certain, indication of Luke's attitude towards Alexandria is contained in his curious dismissal of Peter from his narrative "to another place".   If this mysterious destination was Alexandria, and we have seen that this identification is reasonable,[1] then the pattern of Christian beginnings in Egypt becomes more distinct and intelligible.

It would accordingly appear that Christianity reached Alexandria early, being brought thither by persons who had learned their faith in Jerusalem and who continued loyal in their allegiance to the Mother Church there.   This firm establishment of Jewish Christianity in the Egyptian metropolis satisfactorily accounts for Paul's remarkable omission of Egypt from the wide field of his missionary endeavour and supplies the reason why he turned northwards and then westwards in his evangelizing journeys.   Clearly he could have expected little success in Alexandria, and the opportunity never offered itself there, as it did at Rome,[2] of evading the vigilance of the Jewish members of the Church and addressing a prospecting letter to its Gentile members, if such there were then.

From what we have seen of the nature of the Christology of the Jerusalem Church and from what we have inferred from Luke's account of the teaching of Apollos, it would follow that the new faith as presented in Alexandria was calculated to excite Messianic hopes and controversies among the Jewish population of the city, thus producing a situation in terms of which the Alexandrian Greeks' insult to Agrippa I and the severe language used by Claudius in his letter can be easily understood.   It is interesting also to note that, if our suggestion that Peter spent some time in effective work in the Egyptian city be justified, then his presence there would approximately coincide with the disturbances to which Claudius refers.[3]

Prior to A.D. 70 we accordingly find that there existed a kind of Jewish Christian axis, constituted by the churches of Jerusalem and Alexandria, which was hostile in its attitude towards Paul and his policy and which was in turn, so far as possible, shunned by him.   This position was decisively changed by the catastrophic overthrow of the Jewish nation, and after A.D. 70 the Church of Alexandria remained the only effective representative of the primitive Christianity of Jerusalem.   The immediate aftermath of the Jewish downfall produced a peculiar situation in the Alexandrian Church.   As we have already seen,[4] it is probable that during the course of the war against Rome many of the Palestinian Christians sought refuge with their brethren in the Egyptian capital.

---

[1] See above, pp. 210–2.   [2] See above, pp. 145–8.
[3] The Preface to the Letter of Claudius, added by the prefect Lucius Aemilius Rectus, gives the date (ἔτους) β′ Τιβερίου Κλαυδίου Καίσαρος Σεβαστοῦ κ.τ.λ. Momigliano, op. cit., p. 70, would date the Edict for after A.D. 41: "*è certo posteriore a quei primi editti e può quindi anche congetturarsi posteriore ai fatti di Roma* (the disturbances referred to by Suetonius)".
[4] See above, pp. 177–8.

Consequently the passing of the Mother Church of Jerusalem resulted in the strengthening of the Jewish Christians of the Church of Alexandria.

About the Alexandrian Christians' state of mind at this time of crisis and distress we may reasonably make certain *a priori* inferences. First, it is obvious that the overthrow of their nation and the destruction of their sacred city, with its Temple, must have been a most grievous blow to their national faith and pride. For those who still, under the impact of the calamity, retained their faith in Jesus as the Christ, it is clear that much readjusting of their ideas and their outlook was imperative. If they remained convinced of the essentiality of Judaism and continued to regard Jesus primarily as the Messiah, the inescapable logic of fact demanded that they should find some explanation for the overthrow of their nation by the heathen which would square with their faith. Then in turn the failure of their own people to accept the person and mission of Jesus raised more acutely than ever the question of the admittance into the Church of those Gentiles who were willing to accept Jesus as their Lord. A third problem which had in time also to be faced by them, although it did not immediately arise, was that constituted by the rehabilitation of Paul in the Gentile churches and the challenge which that fact implied to the essentially nationalistic factor in Jewish Christianity. It is in this mental atmosphere and in response to such needs that we believe that the Gospel of Matthew was produced.

The Gospel in its extant form clearly dates from some decades after A.D. 70; indeed a sufficient time must be allowed after that year to enable the Gospel of Mark to become known in Alexandria and its challenge recognized, and for the general readjustment of the Church to the obliteration of the mother community of Jerusalem to reach that degree of crystallization to which, as we shall see, Matthew responds. However that may be, there can be little doubt that some elements of the extant work come from the period immediately subsequent to the upheaval of A.D. 70.

The most vivid expression of the consciousness of locality as felt by a Jewish Christian refugee in Alexandria is surely to be found at the beginning of the Gospel in the Story of the Flight into Egypt. The significance of the Story is at once obvious when it is recalled that elsewhere in his book Matthew shows a manifest reluctance to admit that Jesus passed beyond the frontiers of the Holy Land by emending Mark's account of the Syro-Phœnician Woman, so that Jesus is represented as remaining within the sacred confines of Palestine.[1] And yet despite this evident dislike of allowing that the Messiah had entered into Gentile territory, his is the only Gospel to make the remarkable assertion that the Anointed

---

[1] Mark 7. 24, 31; Matt. 15. 21, 22. "*Jesus hat selbst das heidnische Gebiet nicht betreten; das war aber nicht die Meinung des Mc*" (Klostermann, *Das Matthäusevangelium*, p. 134); cf. B. Weiss, *Das Matthäus-Evangelium*, p. 283. The fact that Matt. also omits Mark's statement that Jesus entered into a house (Gentile?) may also be significant. Werner, *Der Einfluss paulinischer Theologie im Markusevangelium*, pp. 198–9, is probably right, however, in thinking that in Mark there is no reference here to the question of social intercourse with the Gentiles.

of God, while indeed born in the holy land of Yahweh's ancient promise, had found refuge in his infancy in Egypt from the menace of the hated Herod, thus fulfilling Hosea's prophecy: "Out of Egypt did I call my son."[1] It requires but little imagination to understand how this tradition of Christ's sojourn in Egypt would have been eagerly accepted and treasured by those Christians there who also had found sanctuary in the land of the Nile from the terror of the heathen. No other Church could claim that the Lord had once actually lived in its land; that was the proud boast of the Church of Alexandria alone, which recorded the tradition vividly in its own Gospel.

The effect which the overthrow of the Jewish nation had upon the Gentile churches has been described; momentous as that effect was, the event could be viewed by Gentiles, and by those Jews who had ceased to regard Judaism as still valid within the Christian dispensation, with a degree of detachment which was quite impossible for those who still believed in the essentiality of the Law. Hence to the members of the Alexandrian Church the calamity which had befallen their nation in A.D. 70 presented an urgent and intimate problem, the challenge of which to their faith took several forms.

The first was naturally that of the significance of the disaster as a judgement of God upon the nation. The fact could not be denied; it could only be interpreted in such a way, if possible, as would make intelligible God's delivery of his people to the will of the heathen and would vindicate the belief of the Jewish Christians that Jesus was the Messiah of their nation. To meet this aspect of the challenge of A.D. 70 Matthew develops a veritable philosophy of history, which finds expression mainly by way of a consistent emendation of Markan or *Q* material. Its general theme is that the failure of the Jews to recognize the true nature of Jesus was the cause of their downfall; the theme itself is not particularly original and it appears in various forms in both Mark and Luke, but in its treatment by Matthew there is a poignancy of feeling which surely reveals the intimacy of the problem.

A good example of this process of emendation with which to start is afforded by Matthew's version of a *Q* logion which he significantly attaches to the story of the Healing of the Centurion's Servant, but which appears in a different context in Luke, who probably gives it in its original

---

[1] Matt. 2. 13–15. There is other evidence of the tradition of the sojourn in Egypt in *Tractate Sanhedrin* 107b, and Origen, *Contra Celsum*, i. 66; cf. Strack und Billerbeck, *Kommentar*, I, pp. 84–5; Levertoff and Goudge, *New Com. N.T.*, p. 132b; Allen, *I.C.C.*, p. 16. The idea of a *Wunderkind*, born of a virgin, was well known in Alexandria; cf. Clarke, *New Test. Problems*, pp. 2–3. The Osiris legend also would have familiarized the Egyptian Jews with the *motiv* of the rescue of the *Wunderkind* from the enemy who sought to destroy him; cf. Erman, *Die Religion der Aegypter*, p. 74. Klostermann, op. cit., p. 17, however, would see the influence of the legend of the infancy of Moses here. The parallel to Matt. 21. 15 (καὶ τοὺς παῖδας τοὺς κράζοντας ἐν τῷ ἱερῷ καὶ λέγοντας, Ὡσαννὰ τῷ υἱῷ Δαβίδ)which Almqvist (*Plutarch und das Neue Test.*, p. 42) cites from Plutarch's *De Is. et Os.* 14, concerning the Egyptians' belief in the mantic power of children, especially while in temples, has also a possible significance here.

form.[1]   According to Jesus many shall come from all parts of the world
and feast with the Jewish patriarchs in the kingdom of heaven, but (to give
the Lukan version) "ye (i.e. the Jews) shall see . . . yourselves cast
forth without".   Matthew's version reads: "but the sons of the kingdom
(οἱ δὲ υἱοὶ τῆς βασιλείας) shall be cast forth into the outer darkness".
There can be little doubt about who "the sons of the kingdom" are, and
here we begin to see Matthew's interpretation of the catastrophe of A.D. 70
emerge.   His countrymen, who had not accepted Jesus, were nevertheless
by race the rightful "sons of the kingdom", but they had been cast out of
their heritage for their lack of faith, and, as he wrote, he saw the Gentiles
entering in to take their place.

Two other short but important passages, expressive of this apologetical
theme, come in Matthew 10. 34 and 12. 6.   The first is probably based on
a Q saying, which appears in Luke 12. 51 in a different context.   In the
Matthean version Jesus says: "Think not that I came to send (βαλεῖν)
peace on the earth: I came not to send peace, but a sword."   In the
Lukan parallel "division" (διαμερισμόν) appears in the place of "sword"
(μάχαιραν).   Reason has been shown[2] for thinking that the Matthean
passage here may be a conflation of Q with Micah 7. 6, in which case it
would follow that Luke gives the more primitive form of the saying, and so
the change which Matthew makes of "sword" for "division" accordingly
acquires a special significance.   In a strikingly similar passage in the
Apocalypse[3] the symbolism of the sword to the Jewish mind appears very
clear.   The prophet John sees a rider on a red horse going forth to take
peace from the earth, "and there was given unto him a great sword".
The sword means war, and it is wielded by Jesus.   We see herein a further
phase of Matthew's philosophy of recent history.   The cause of the disastrous war which had ruined his people was to be found in the advent of
Jesus; from the way in which the Jews reacted to his personality and
teaching ensued the civil strife, in which converted and unconverted Jews
alike suffered.

The second of these brief passages is actually an addition which Matthew
makes to the Markan story of the controversy with the Pharisees about the
sanctity of the sabbath.   Matthew expands Mark's reference to David
and Abiathar by citing the case of the priests working in the Temple on the
sabbath and yet being free from offence against the Law.   The mention of
the Temple seems then to have led him to a further comment as from the
mouth of Jesus: "But I say unto you, that one greater (μεῖζον) than the
temple is here."   The exact interpretation of the neuter comparative
μεῖζον is somewhat uncertain, but the use of the neuter comparative πλεῖον
in Matt. 12. 41, 42 and Luke 11. 31, 32 seems to indicate a more personal
meaning, referring directly to Jesus.   Therefore we have here an actual

---

[1] Matt. 8. 11, 12; Luke 13. 28, 29.   Cf. Streeter, *Four Gospels*, p. 514.
[2] Streeter, op. cit., p. 494, n. 1.
[3] Rev. 6. 4.   Cf. Strack und Billerbeck, op. cit., I, p. 585.

comparison made by Matthew between Jesus (or his principle for the interpretation of the Law) and the Temple. The purpose of the comparison is clear; the Temple had indeed perished, but it could now be seen that its loss was not fatal, for Jesus and the Law (which witnessed to him and which he fulfilled) were greater and still endured.

An addition which is made to the Markan parable of the Wicked Husbandmen finally expresses this Matthean interpretation of the Jewish overthrow in unequivocal words.[1] The Jewish leaders have been the Wicked Husbandmen of God's Vineyard, and their crowning sin was the slaying of his Son.[2] The Markan version already contained the threat of divine vengeance, but Matthew felt obliged to emend it slightly but significantly by the addition in his own account of the words κακοὺς κακῶς.[3] The Jewish authorities were to Matthew not merely husbandmen; they were wicked. The destruction, as he viewed it in the light of the terrible experiences of A.D. 70, was not sufficiently described by the impersonal ἀπολέσει of Mark, and he felt moved to qualify it with κακῶς. Then, after he had finished transcribing the Markan parable, he again felt that he must still further reinforce its lesson, and so in v. 43 he places his interpretation beyond all doubt. The Kingdom of God, by Dominical pronouncement, is taken away from the unbelieving of the Jews and given to a nation "bringing forth the fruits thereof". The overthrow of the nation and the destruction of the national sanctuary were after all no inexplicable tragedy which seemed to contradict the providence of God.[4] They were the inevitable consequence of the nation's failure to recognize in Jesus the long-promised Messiah. Of the identity of the nation to whom the Kingdom of God is to be given there can be little doubt. A remarkable parallel to this Matthean passage is to be found in 1 Peter 2. 7–10. There the symbolic Corner-Stone again appears as a cause of division, and those who believe are called an "elect race . . . a holy nation"; the Epistle itself is significantly addressed to the "elect who are sojourners of the Dispersion". It appears certain, therefore, that the Jewish Christians, and probably those who, having fulfilled the necessary conditions, joined them, are to Matthew this other nation to whom the Kingdom of God is given. That Matthew also employed the same concept of the Corner-Stone is shown to be probable in the appendix to this chapter.

We may note in conclusion here that, in one of his additions[5] to the Passion Narrative of Mark, Matthew succeeded in concentrating his philosophy of recent history into ten short words of such power and meaning that they have echoed down the ages, giving a seeming justification to the anti-Semitism of each Christian generation. He depicts Pilate as

[1] Matt. 21. 43. Cf. J. Weiss, *Urchristentum*, p. 522.
[2] Matt. 21. 45. Von Gall, *ΒΑΣΙΛΕΙΑ ΤΟΥ ΘΕΟΥ*, p. 353, makes the interesting suggestion that the βιασταί of Matt. 11. 12 signified the Zealots; see above, p. 106, n. 1.
[3] Matt. 21. 41; cf. Mark 12. 9. Cf. B. Weiss, *Das Matthäus-Evangelium*, pp. 369–70.
[4] Cf. Windisch, *Der Untergang Jerusalems (Anno 70) im Urtheil der Christen und Juden*, p. 520.
[5] Matt. 27. 24, 25. Cf. Bultmann, *Die Gesch. der synopt. Trad.*, p. 305.

convinced of the innocence of Jesus and desirous to release him. But the fierce importunity of the Jewish mob forces him to sanction a judicial murder. The uneasy Roman publicly disavows his guilt by a symbolic washing of his hands. But no such compunction is felt by the Jews, and they are accordingly depicted as eagerly accepting full responsibility for the crime in the ominous words which they shout back to the conscience-stricken governor: "His blood be on us, and on our children." As Matthew penned those words a vision of awful carnage, lit by the fatal flames of the burning Temple, must surely have arisen before his eyes.

Although by birth the Jews were the original "sons of the kingdom", the logic of fact was inescapable and Matthew was sufficiently a realist to see that the admittance of the Gentiles into the Church had to be accepted. But if their admittance could not be prevented, at least it should be rigorously controlled, and Matthew was prepared to preserve in his Gospel the record of an old Dominical prohibition of evangelizing any but Jews,[1] so that it might clearly be known that the conversion of Gentiles was not at first sought for by the Master. In his treatment of the problem of their admission elsewhere in his Gospel, although he appreciated as keenly as did the Pharisees the value of docile Gentile converts,[2] Matthew was severe and ungracious. We have already seen that in his version of the Q saying which he appends to the story of the Healing of the Centurion's Servant the Gentiles enter the Kingdom of God as substitutes for the real heirs, because of the latters' failure of faith. In contradistinction to Paul's advocacy of the free and unconditioned admission of Gentiles into the Church, the essentiality of the Law is upheld, and this policy receives its final expression in the last two verses of the Gospel, when the Risen Lord is depicted as sending the Apostles to make disciples of all nations, "teaching them to observe all things whatsoever I commanded you": [3] among these commands, according to Matthew, are not only the precepts of the Sermon on the Mount, but also those undisguisedly Judaistic ones of 5. 17–19 and 23. 2, 3.

A particularly interesting insight into Matthew's mind on this issue is afforded by his version of the Parable of the Wedding Feast.[4] There seems to be adequate reason for believing that Luke gives the Parable in its more original form,[5] since Matthew's version shows characteristic touches to heighten the effect in the interests of his philosophy of the ruin of the Jewish state. For instance, the Guests do not merely make excuses

---

[1] Matt. 10. 5, 6. [2] Cf. Matt. 23. 15.

[3] How far the instruction to baptize in the names of Father, Son, and Holy Spirit represents the original text of Matt. it is now impossible to know. However, it must be noted that the text, as it stands, can only be considered Trinitarian if interpreted anachronistically; cf. B. Weiss, op. cit., p. 508 loc. cit.

[4] Matt. 22. 1–14.

[5] Cf. Streeter, op. cit., p. 516. The somewhat different account for the origin of the Matthean version suggested by T. W. Manson, *The Teaching of Jesus*, pp. 84–5, does not invalidate the interpretation given below in the text.

for refusing the invitation, as in Luke, but they assault and kill the servants who had been sent to call them; the king (οἰκοδεσπότης, according to Luke) not only is angry at their refusal and declares that they will not taste of his supper, but sends forth his army to slay the murderers and to burn their city—obviously from the use of the singular a reference to Jerusalem. Matthew's version, after describing the subsequent furnishing of Guests from divers places, adds the strange story of the Guest who comes without a Wedding Garment. As it stands in Matthew's text, the meaning of the story is quite inexplicable, since it would be grossly unjust to blame one who had thus been urgently requested to come to the Feast for not being suitably attired. Clearly we have here a fusion of two distinct parables, each with a different purpose,[1] and the fact of their strange fusion illustrates the working of the author's mind. The allusion to the destruction of Jerusalem naturally led Matthew on to think of its consequences, and in particular of one of its great problems: that of the personal preparedness of the Gentiles for the privilege of Church membership. The logic of events, as we have seen, had forced him to recognize that the invitation of the Gospel had to be extended to the Gentiles, but he was not altogether happy about it. The example of Paul's work was ever before his eyes, and probably, as in Alexandria more and more Gentiles desired to enter the Church, he felt obliged to utter a grave warning against any kind of promiscuous admission. To him the Jews, despite their final rejection, were the rightful Guests and had enjoyed the proper preparation of the Law; but this was not so with the Gentiles. They had unexpectedly been called from the highways of heathenism; therefore, they must be carefully scrutinized and instructed (i.e., in the terminology of the Parable, they must be provided with the necessary Wedding Garment) before they could be safely admitted into the fold of the Church.[2]

That the admission of the Gentiles into the privileges of the faith was not uncontested in the Alexandrian Church possibly finds illustration in the Parable of the Labourers in the Vineyard.[3] The Jews, who had borne the heat and the burden of the day in serving God, naturally resent the admittance of the late-coming Gentiles into their full rights and privileges. Their complaint is rejected, but it is to be noted that a not very flattering picture is given of the capabilities of the late-comers; they had obviously stood idle in the market-place because they showed little promise of good service, and they are finally given the full wage not on their merits but through the compassion of the Lord of the Vineyard. If the entry of the Gentiles into the Church had to be accepted, the Jewish Christians would have it made clear that it was because of an inexplicable piece of divine grace and not for any deserving Gentile quality.

[1] Cf. Streeter, *Four Gospels*, p. 243, n. 2; A. J. Grieve, *Peake's Commentary*, p. 718b.
[2] "*R. Jochanan b. Zakkai hat gesagt: Wenn die Schrift von weissen Kleidern spräche, wieviel weisse Kleider haben die Völker der Welt! . . . Siehe, sie spricht aber nun von Gebotserfüllungen u. guten Werken u. Torastudium*": *Midr. Qoh.* 9. 8 (42a), in Strack und Billerbeck, *Kommentar*, I, p. 878.
[3] Matt. 20. 1–16.

We saw that in the Gospel of Mark the first adumbration of the rehabilitation of Paul is to be found. Whether this fact was recognized at Alexandria when the Markan Gospel reached there we have no certain means of knowing, but the continuance of the process of rehabilitation, which is evident in the Acts of the Apostles and the formation of the *Corpus Paulinum* and other documents, must soon have been felt as a challenge to their position by the Alexandrian Christians, and it was consciously met in their version of the tradition which was put forth in the form of the Gospel of Matthew.

To combat the rising reputation of Paul Matthew adroitly used the unrivalled claims of Peter, who had been so closely connected with Alexandrian Christianity. Thus in his Gospel Peter appears more prominent than in the other Synoptic writings.[1] In the list of the Apostles Peter is definitely πρῶτος,[2] and this theme of the magnification of Peter's position and authority reaches its climax when to the Markan account of Peter's Confession at Cæsarea Philippi there is added the extraordinary statement:[3] "And I also say unto thee, that thou art Peter, and upon this rock I will build my church; and the gates of Hades shall not prevail against it." The statement is followed by the promise to Peter of the gift of the keys of the kingdom of heaven, together with the special power of binding and loosing, as distinct from the general gift to all the Apostles recorded in 18. 18. The authority and prestige which this Matthean addition to Mark's narrative confers on Peter are tremendous, and the comment of J. Weiss[4] is certainly justified, that "this extraordinary exaltation of Peter at the expense of the other Apostles must have some special ground. It is only conceivable in a community in which Peter was 'the Apostle', and for which, in opposition to others, he represented the right tradition."

Before we may proceed from this point we must answer the arguments put forward particularly by Weiss[5] and Streeter[6] to the effect that this prominence was given to Peter at Antioch, where he held a position of unique authority. The chief ground of these arguments appears to be in the claims which were advanced by the see of Antioch, in the course of the ecclesiastical controversy of the fourth and fifth centuries, that certain precedence belonged to it because Peter had been its first bishop. But such evidence is extremely flimsy, and it is more likely to be expressive of ecclesiastical desire than of historical fact.[7] Further, it is certainly remarkable

[1] Cf. Streeter, op. cit., pp. 258, 504, 514 *seq.*; J. Weiss, *Urchristentum*, p. 585; Bacon, *Jesus and Paul*, pp. 160–3; Kilpatrick, *The Origin of the Gospel according to St. Matthew*, pp. 43–4.

[2] Matt. 10. 2.

[3] 16. 18, 19. Cf. Dibelius, *Die Formgeschichte des Evangeliums*, p. 112; Loisy, *Le Origini del Cristianesimo*, p. 99.

[4] Op. cit., p. 585; cf. Guignebert, *Jesus*, pp. 319–24; Loisy, op. cit., p. 100, *Les Origines du N.T.*, p. 142. Loisy suggests that the rebuke to Peter is a fiction inspired by Pauline interests.

[5] Ibid.

[6] Op. cit., pp. 504, 515. Cf. *B.C.*, vol. i, p. 330: Jackson and Lake here admit that the hypothesis cannot be demonstrated as correct.

[7] Cf. Merrill, *Essays in Early Christian History*, p. 277.

that Ignatius, one of the earliest bishops of Antioch and one who had a special interest in episcopacy, in all his letters makes no reference to Peter as the illustrious founder of his own see,[1] while that diligent collector of early Church tradition, Eusebius, names Evodius as the first bishop of the Syrian metropolis.[2]   When these facts are considered, there appears to be great force in the suggestion of Professor C. Schmidt, in his work on the Clementine literature,[3] that the author of the initial draft of the writings (*Verfasser der Grundschrift der Pseudo-Clementinen*) was originally responsible for inventing, on the strength of Gal. 2. 11, an important administrative sojourn of Peter at Antioch.   The evidence of Paul's Galatian Epistle is in fact clearly indicative of quite the opposite conclusion.   As we have seen, Antioch was the headquarters of Paul and the original centre of Gentile Christianity.   There Paul clearly felt himself to be in such a strong position that he was able to rebuke the vacillating Peter to his face on a matter of vital importance to Gentile Christianity.   The memory of Peter's capitulation to the Judaizing emissaries of James and its humiliating consequence could scarcely have been quickly effaced from the minds of the Antiochene Christians, especially if a copy of Paul's Epistle to the Galatians was preserved by them among their venerated archives.

Thus from the evidence of the Galatian Epistle it would seem that Peter's behaviour at Antioch certainly did not recommend him for any position of unique authority there, such as that envisaged in Matthew, or even for that of a mediator, as Dr. Streeter supposes; and to this Pauline evidence we may also add that which truly comes from the silence of Acts about any such position of Peter in the Syrian city.   There is furthermore considerable significance in the fact that the passage which gives such superlative authority to Peter is absent from the parallel account of Luke. This means that the emphasis on the Petrine authority is made by the most Judaistic of the Gospels, while a definitely Gentile document like Luke preferred to reproduce the original Markan account, and Luke also, as we have seen, had very close connections with Antioch.

With this exaltation of Peter as the Apostle *par excellence* of Christ and the Rock upon which the Church was built, there goes in the Gospel of Matthew a thinly veiled polemic against Paul and his teaching.   It appears as a personal attack in two passages.   The first is 5. 17–19, which is probably a Matthean elaboration of a *Q* saying.[4]   This passage begins with the significant words from Christ: "Think not that I came to destroy the law or the prophets: I came not to destroy, but to fulfil."   Then

---

[1] Indeed Ignatius shows remarkably little interest in Peter; he mentions him twice only (Romans iv. 3; Smyrnæans, iii. 2), as he does Paul.

[2] *Eccl. Hist.*, III. xxii. Cf. Lawlor and Oulton, vol. ii, p. 92, who think that the insignificance of Evodius in Christian tradition proves that Eusebius was right in this statement.   Schmidt, *Studien zu den Pseudo-Clementinen*, p. 369, thinks that Evodius probably stood at the head of the list of Antiochene bishops in the *Chronicle* of Julius Africanus.

[3] Op. cit., p. 368.

[4] See Streeter, op. cit., pp. 256–7, 286–7; cf. Bultmann, *Die Gesch der synopt. Trad.*, pp. 146–7. Goguel, *La Naissance du Christianisme*, p. 360, admits the anti-Pauline reference here, but believes that it was in Matthew's source and unrecognized as such by him.

follows the *Q* logion about the immutability of the Law, after which Matthew adds: "Whosoever therefore shall break (λύσῃ) one of these least commandments, and shall teach (διδάξῃ) men so, shall be called least (ἐλάχιστος) in the kingdom of heaven: but whosoever shall do and teach them, he shall be called great in the kingdom of heaven." As Weiss has remarked, this passage becomes most intelligible when it is regarded as a tacit attack against the work and teaching of Paul.[1]

The second attack is made in metaphorical language in the Parable of the Tares (13. 24–30). This statement, however, requires careful qualification, since it has been ridiculed by at least one New Testament scholar of standing as being due to a presumed "Tübingen tendency".[2]

We must begin by noticing carefully the subject of the Parable. It is quite clearly the problem presented by the existence of the evil together with the good in the Church, and of the policy which should consequently be adopted to deal with the situation. The wheat, which springs from the good seed sown by the owner of the field, has, of course, the right to grow therein. But the tares are sown by one whom the owner describes as a "hostile man" (ἐχθρὸς ἄνθρωπος), and, therefore, they have no rightful place in the field, but, since they are so intermingled with the wheat, their separation cannot be effected until the harvest. Now, as Dibelius has noted,[3] the author introduces the enemy as though he were a known personality. The question accordingly arises to whom the expression ἐχθρὸς ἄνθρωπος could have referred, so that it could have been recognized by Matthew's readers without further explanation. The answer can readily be made that it was the Devil, especially since this identification is expressly given in the explanation of the Parable in vv. 37–43. But this answer would not have been so obvious if the explanation had not been added, for ἐχθρὸς ἄνθρωπος is a rather strange and a surprisingly mild description for the Devil, even if we allow for the need of a measure of consistency with the rest of the Parable; and the action of sowing tares, annoying but not essentially fatal to the purpose of the owner of the field, appears a rather weak thing to attribute to the Devil, especially after the description of his soul-destroying activity which had just been given in the Parable of the Sower (e.g. in vv. 4 and 19). This view receives confirmation from the suspicion which justly attaches to the explanation by reason of its patent artificiality and its clear disruption of the order of the text. In the first place it may be noted that the style of the explanation of the Parable of the Tares is stilted when compared with that of the Parable of the Sower (vv. 18–23),[4] and the interpretation of the successive details is mechanical. Further, it is very remarkable that this elaborate allegorical explanation should be given to the Parable of the Tares, for actually its

---

[1] Op. cit., p. 585. Cf. Streeter, *Primitive Church*, p. 56; B. Weiss, *Das Matthäus-Evangelium*, p. 106, footnote.
[2] McNeile, *St. Matthew*, p. 197; cf. Moffatt, *Intro. to N.T.*, p. 256. J. Weiss, op. cit., pp. 522–3, thinks that an attack on either Paul or his disciples is to be seen here.
[3] *Die Formgeschichte des Evangeliums*, p. 254.   [4] See McNeile, op. cit., pp. 202–3.

meaning is much clearer than that of the Parable of the Sower, and yet it is explained in far greater detail; moreover, while this interpretation is given to this straightforward parable, a series of obscure parables is allowed to follow without any comment on their respective meanings.[1]   It surely seems, therefore, considering these facts, that a careful explanation was regarded as necessary for the Parable of the Tares.   Then, secondly, there is the very obvious dislocation of the narrative sequence and the literary pattern due to the insertion of the explanation of the Parable.[2]   For instance, after telling the Parable of the Sower to the people, Jesus, according to the Markan parallel (Mark 4. 10), explained it in private to his disciples, and this clearly seems to be the meaning of Matthew from 13. 10 ff.   Therefore, according to the sequence of the narrative, the Parable of the Tares is also told in private (v. 24).   In v. 34, however, after the series of parables, which according to vv. 10–11 were addressed privately to the disciples, Jesus is, surprisingly, described as having all the while been speaking to the multitudes.   This inconsistency, however, can easily be removed if vv. 34–35 are regarded as a later editorial comment designed to introduce the explanation of the Parable of the Tares in v. 36.[3] It is further of very great significance that, if vv. 34–35 are omitted, then the string of parables (addressed to the disciples) continues uninterruptedly, and they form two groups of three parables, each either peculiar to Matthew or revised by him.   Moreover, an indication of the original literary pattern of this part of the Gospel is seen in the fact that the author had purposely arranged them in two groups, introducing the first group with the formula ἄλλην παραβολὴν παρέθηκεν (twice) or ἐλάλησεν αὐτοῖς, and the second with (πάλιν) ὁμοία ἐστίν.[4]   It must be recognized that there is no manuscript evidence for regarding the verses containing the explanation of the Parable as a later interpolation, but this seems to be the only adequate interpretation of the facts set out above.   The *raison d'être* of such an interpolation is, moreover, clear.   As we have seen, this very straightforward Parable was alone thought to need a careful detailed explanation.   Now if, as we hope to show presently, there was a decline of the Judaistic spirit in the Alexandrian Church in the first decades of the next century, the well-known reference to Paul under the guise of ἐχθρὸς ἄνθρωπος undoubtedly then caused much embarrassment.   Therefore, it is a reasonable supposition that, since reverence forbad the excision of this Parable from their Gospel, the Alexandrian Christians agreed to redirect its meaning by inserting an explanation, in which the compromising expression ἐχθρὸς ἄνθρωπος was definitely identified with the Devil; very possibly such an explanation had already gained currency through the medium of preaching and teaching in Alexandria.   If then these reasons be sound for regarding the explanation as an early official interpolation,

---

[1] Matt. 13. 31–34, 44–48.
[2] This is recognized by a conservative critic such as Allen, *I.C.C.*, pp. 149–52.
[3] Cf. Allen, ibid.; Levertoff and Goudge, *New Com. N.T.*, p. 162b.
[4] Matt. 13. 44, 45, 47.

we may justifiably see in the Parable of the Tares an attack on Paul's policy of allowing the morally lax Gentiles into the Church and the author's conclusion that nothing could be done about the situation for the present, but that the evil would be surely rooted out at the Last Day.

We have discussed the significance of Luke's caricature of the Christology of the Alexandrian Church, concluding that it indicates that the teaching of that Church in the first decades was representative of the doctrine of the Mother Church of Jerusalem, and we have noted other evidence confirming this view. By the time that the Gospel of Matthew reached its present form toward the end of the first century, it is obvious that some measure of development in Alexandrian Christology had already taken place, which fact is sufficiently understandable in terms of the stimulus which the Markan Gospel must have provided. However, on examination it would appear that Matthew reveals both vestiges of the older Christology and a conscious emending of the Markan interpretation in the interests of the prestige of the Alexandrian Church *vis-à-vis* the churches which were developing the Pauline tradition.

Of the older teaching relics appear in the introductory verses to the Gospel: the work is described as "The book of the generation ($\beta i\beta\lambda os$ $\gamma\epsilon\nu\epsilon\sigma\epsilon\omega s$) of Jesus Christ, the son of David, the son of Abraham".[1] This bold declaration of the essentially Hebraic origin of Jesus forms a striking contrast to the beginning of the Markan Gospel and to its apologetical theme, and the consequent genealogy is an eloquent testimony to the concern of the Jewish Christians to demonstrate the correctness of the lineage of Jesus in the interests of his Messiahship.

Matthew's treatment of the Markan account of the process whereby the Divine Sonship of Jesus was successively recognized is significant. Mark, it will be recalled, represented that Jesus was first hailed as the Son of God by the demoniac powers and finally by a human being in the person of the Gentile centurion on Calvary; the disciples advance no further than a recognition of their Master as the Jewish Messiah. Matthew retains the Markan instances, but he depicts the disciples as being the first of men to apprehend the Divine Sonship[2] and, more important still, that it was Peter who proclaimed the truth in its fullest form: "Thou art the Christ, the Son of the living God."[3] And then on to this superlative statement he causes to follow words which are surely by their juxtaposition of the most profound significance. Jesus speaks: "Blessed art thou, Simon Bar-Jonah: for flesh and blood hath not revealed it unto thee, but my Father which is in heaven." Surely no counter-claim to Pauline revelation could be more clear?[4] In these majestic words the quintessence of

---

[1] Matt. 1. 1. Cf. B. Weiss, op. cit., pp. 29 *seq.* The Lukan genealogy undoubtedly was derived from Palestinian sources, possibly via the Church of Cæsarea; cf. Guignebert, *Jesus*, pp. 109–11.

[2] Matt. 14. 33.

[3] Matt. 16. 16–19. See p. 232 above.   [4] Cf. Gal. 1. 15, 16.

Pauline Christology is claimed as the original percept of Peter, the supreme Apostle of Jewish Christianity.

The equilibrium constructed by Matthew was essentially artificial, for it was in reality an attempt to confine the new wine of Christianity in the old wine-skins of Judaism. And as such it was doomed either to perish or to be metamorphosed, for the position of the Jewish Christians in Alexandria could not by its very nature be successfully maintained into the future, unless it were assured of a continuous stream of Jewish converts who accepted its peculiar outlook, which envisaged a Church seeking to win "all the nations" to a faith which required their adherence to many obsolete and unmeaning Jewish laws and practices. The failure to secure such a stream of Jewish converts meant that, with the continued influx of Gentiles, the original Jewish character of Alexandrian Christianity must inevitably be lost, while Gentile influence steadily predominated. Of the actual course of this process we have no clear information, but there are certain facts which indicate some points in this course.

The first of these facts which we may notice is that the preservation of the works of Philo was undoubtedly due to early Christian appreciation of them. They were apparently written originally for a small eclectic circle of Hellenistic Jews in Alexandria; their appeal could only have been small, and after A.D. 70, when Judaism turned back upon itself and found congenial expression in Talmudic concepts, the liberalizing thought of Philo was doomed to extinction among those of his own race. It is a necessary inference, therefore, that sometime after the destruction of Jerusalem certain members of the Alexandrian Church, of either Jewish or Gentile extraction, must have begun to notice the works of the Alexandrian philosopher and to appreciate their worth in constituting an attractive bridge between the Jewish and the Gentile outlooks.[1]

A second factor which also worked to destroy the original Jewish character of Alexandrian Christianity must undoubtedly have been provided by political events. Dr. Idris Bell has shown[2] that the Jewish revolt and overthrow generally lost for the Jews the favour and protection they had enjoyed from the Roman Government, and their whole position must have been rendered very much worse by their risings in the reigns of Trajan and Hadrian. This increasing deterioration of the status of the Jewish Christians in the Church of Alexandria, with the corresponding increase of Gentile influence, suggests an intelligible background of controversy, despair, and exhortation against which to set three documents the origins of which have long been matters of considerable debate.

The first of these documents to be considered, since it appears to mark

[1] Cf. Lietzmann, *Gesch. der alt. Kirche*, I, p. 93; Klausner, *From Jesus to Paul*, pp. 198–205; Guignebert, *Le Monde Juif vers le Temps de Jésus*, pp. 294–5; Schürer, *G.J.V.*, III, p. 490; J. M. Creed, in *Legacy of Egypt*, p. 316; Goodenough, *Politics of Philo Judaeus*, pp. 298–307.
[2] *Juden und Griechen in römischen Alexandreia*, p. 32; cf. Simon, *Verus Israel*, pp. 53–64.

17

the first stage in the evolution of Alexandrian Christianity from its Judaistic beginnings, is the Epistle of James. The question of the origin of this writing is still a matter of dispute. The traditional view that the Epistle is an authentic work of the Lord's Brother still finds its supporters,[1] but the general trend of critical opinion seems to be towards regarding it as a fairly late composition, i.e. after A.D. 70, perhaps incorporating earlier material from a Jewish source.[2] Its place of origin is naturally equally disputed, but we may well notice the general deductions relative to this matter which have been drawn by Professor Windisch:[3] "The author of our writing lives in a circle in which ritualism had long since disappeared, but where Pauline soteriology was not effective, and where the Law, purged in the way in which Jesus advocated, was the foundation of piety. . . . Generally, James attests a Christianity, as is so often the case in the apostolic period, which is outside Jerusalem and outside the Pauline sphere of influence." Such a situation would well correspond to that which we have already seen as probably obtaining at Alexandria after A.D. 70. This general compatibility of situation is, however, strengthened in favour of Alexandria by a number of small but significant points. For example, there are in the Epistle so many reminiscences of the Gospel of Matthew that they can scarcely be accidental; on the contrary, they point strongly to a dependence on a well-known work.[4] Then the use of the simile of the tossing of waves as an illustration in 1. 6 would indicate a familiarity with the sea, which might be expected of a writer in a seaport city, and, further, the great interest in ships, and especially the note about their size, would well fit in with an Alexandrian authorship, for Alexandria was famous for its great corn ships;[5] again the reference to trading in 4. 13 would be natural to an inhabitant of a great commercial centre such as Alexandria. There are also a number of ideas scattered throughout the Letter which are strongly reminiscent of Philo, thus perhaps indicating the growing interest of the Alexandrian Church in the works of the philosopher.[6]

If then there is reason to believe that the Epistle of James was an Alexandrian composition, we have a document of great value for the history of Christianity in the Egyptian capital. Accordingly the undoubted

---

[1] E.g. G. H. Rendall, *Epistle of St. James and Judaic Christianity.* Cf. C. T. Dimont, *New Com. N.T.*, pp. 627–8; J. H. Moulton, *Peake's Commentary*, p. 902.

[2] Cf. Moffatt, *Intro. to N.T.*, pp. 468–75; Lietzmann, op. cit., I, pp. 212–13; Guignebert, *Le Christ*, pp. 42–3; W. L. Knox, "Epistle of St. James", *J.T.S.*, vol. xlvi.

[3] *Die katholischen Briefe*, pp. 21, 36.

[4] See list given by Dimont, *New Com. N.T.*, p. 627a. Goodspeed, *Intro. N.T.*, pp. 291 *seq.*, recognized the affinities of James with Matthew to the extent of ascribing the Epistle to Antioch, which he believed was the place of origin of Matt. Cf. Moffatt, op. cit., p. 466.

[5] Knox, op. cit., p. 15, points out that "the ship and the rudder are regular hellenistic commonplaces". This may be, but τὰ πλοῖα, τηλικαῦτα ὄντα are not likely to have been familiar objects in Palestine, whereas they correspond well with the πλοῖον Ἀλεξανδρῖνον of Acts 27. 6. Knox, op. cit., p. 13, cites Philo, *De Post. Cain* 100, as a parallel to the simile in Jas. 1. 6.

[6] Cf. Knox, op. cit., pp. 13, 14, 15, 16. For the Orphic connotation of τὸν τροχὸν τῆς γενέσεως and φύσις θηρίων (3. 6, 7) and the influence of Orphism on the Alexandrian Jews see Eisler, *Orphische-dionysische Mysteriengedanken*, pp. 86, 393–4.

polemic which the Epistle contains against the teaching of Paul constitutes a fact of peculiar significance, as does also the author's assumption
of the mask of James, the great antagonist of Paul.[1]   It would, therefore,
appear that what we have in this writing is a Jewish attempt, made in
Alexandria, probably at the end of the first century, to stem the rising tide
of Paulinism.   The document is ostensibly addressed to the Diaspora, but
we may well doubt whether it had, or was designed to have, much currency beyond Egypt.   It would seem that we may reasonably regard it as
a monument of the beginning of the decline of Jewish predominance in the
Church of Alexandria, for the danger of Pauline doctrine is clearly urgent
and local.

A further stage in this process of transition in Alexandrian Christianity
can fairly be discerned in the Epistle to the Hebrews.   The first pertinent
question here to be considered is that of its date.   There are certain passages in the document which seem to indicate a date before the destruction
of the Temple, but these can be adequately explained,[2] while the fact of
its patent artificiality of composition points to a late period, for, as Lietzmann has noted, "it is certainly . . . a writing which begins as a theological tractate and continues as such, with homiletical interjections, but
ends as a pseudo-Pauline Letter".[3]   That the writing is influenced by
Alexandrian thought of the Philonic type has been the opinion of many
scholars, even though they have not all agreed that the work therefore
originated from the Egyptian city.[4]   However, while it must be frankly
admitted that the Alexandrian origin of Hebrews cannot be demonstrated, the fact that the document was received into the canon of the New
Testament largely on the advocacy of the Church of Alexandria seems to
indicate that the Christians there must have had a special interest in it,
and this would be likely if they knew that the writing was a product of
their own Church.[5]   Then, as we have already suggested, the state of the
Alexandrian Church towards the end of the first century and the beginning
of the next well provides a setting consistent with that presupposed in the
Epistle.   In the words of Dr. Nairne,[6] "the broad clear view we get is of

[1] Meyer, *Ursprung und Anfänge des Christentums*, III, p. 227, n. 2.   Cf. Lietzmann, op. cit., I,
p. 212; J. Weiss, *Urchristentum*, p. 585; Knox, op. cit., p. 10; Moffatt, op. cit., pp. 465–6.   It
is a significant fact that the Epistle was regarded with great suspicion in Syria as late as the
fifth century.   Streeter's attempt (*Primitive Church*, p. 191) to explain its tardy acceptance into
the canon by supposing that the writing was originally anonymous and that the ascription in
the first verse was added by some Alexandrian scholar in the second century points in favour
of its Alexandrian origin, although Streeter himself preferred to associate it with Rome.

[2] Cf. McNeile, *Intro. to Study of N.T.*, pp. 220, 224–5; Moffatt, op. cit., pp. 445–6.

[3] Op. cit., I, p. 217.

[4] Cf. Moffatt, op. cit., pp. 27–8, 427–8; McNeile, op. cit., p. 194; S. C. Gayford, *New Com.
N.T.*, p. 596; Goodspeed, op. cit., p. 262.

[5] It would appear that the curious explanation which Clement of Alexandria gave of the
origin of the Epistle to the Hebrews, *apud* Euseb., *Eccl. Hist.*, VI. xiv. 2–4, may well indicate the
scholar's concern to recommend a revered writing of his Church, the true origin of which had
become forgotten with the passing of the situation with which it dealt.   Cf. Westcott, *On the
Canon of the N.T.*, pp. 323 seq.; H. Windisch, *Der Hebräerbrief*, pp. 4–5.

[6] *The Epistle of Priesthood*, p. 20.   Cf. A. S. Peake, *Critical Intro. to N.T.*, pp. 75–6; Moffatt,
op. cit., pp. 443 *seq.*   It is difficult to understand what Moffatt means by a "theoretical
Judaism" which became a source of temptation to Gentile Christians after A.D. 70.

Hellenistic Jews, now imperfect Christians, who are exposed to some particular temptation to give up their new faith and make common cause with their own nation". Such a temptation must have become increasingly strong for the original Jewish element in the Alexandrian Church as the growing numbers and power of the Gentile converts were steadily forcing them from their position of leadership and facing them with the distasteful prospect of being a weak minority in a thoroughly Hellenistic community. With their future thus so dismal, undoubtedly many Jewish Christians began to wonder whether after all Christianity was not essentially a Gentile faith, in which they were destined to lose their own treasured distinctions of race, and therefore they were led to look with increasing favour on their ancient national faith, now renewing its genius in rabbinic devotion to the study and practice of the Law. As signs of a secession grew alarmingly clear, some Jewish Christian of a stronger faith may well have been moved to proclaim to his despairing compatriots, as Matthew had done, "Stand fast, that no one take thy crown".[1] His thesis was that Jesus was superior in honour to Moses;[2] he develops the Pauline argument that the Law was given by angels,[3] and he emphasizes the superiority of the New Covenant by comparison with the Old: "that which is becoming old and waxeth aged is nigh unto vanishing away."[4] With what success the author of Hebrews was rewarded for his labour and zeal we do not know, but if his message was to any degree effective, that effectiveness was certainly only transitory.

A consequent stage in the evolution of Alexandrian Christianity, which reflects Gentile confidence in the superiority of their position over that of their erstwhile Jewish tutors, is found in the *Epistle of Barnabas*. Dr. Streeter has indeed used the testimony of this document against the possibility of the Gospel of Matthew being of Alexandrian origin. He writes:[5] "Alexandria is an impossible city in which to place the most Judaistic of the Gospels; *Barnabas*, the only certainly Alexandrian writing we possess of early date, is violently anti-Jewish in feeling." But Dr. Streeter appears to have overlooked the very significant fact that all the six Gospel quotations or reminiscences in *Barnabas* are to be found in Matthew;[6] four of them indeed can also be paralleled in Mark, but it is unlikely that it is to this Gospel that the source of these references is to be traced, since not only is the first quotation (22. 14) peculiar to Matthew and given verbally, but, as Westcott pointed out,[7] it is a conscious quotation by reason

---

[1] Cf. Levertoff and Goudge, *New Com. N.T.*, p. 125b; Kilpatrick, *The Origins of the Gospel according to St. Matt.*, pp. 109–115; Simon, *Verus Israel*, pp. 54 *seq.*
[2] Heb. 3. 1–6.
[3] Cf. Heb. 1. 4–14; 2. 2, 3, 9, 10, 16. Cf. Clarke, *New Test. Problems*, pp. 155–6; Gayford, *New Com. N.T.*, p. 603b.   [4] Heb. 8. 13.
[5] *Four Gospels*, p. 502; cf. *Primitive Church*, pp. 236–8. The Alexandrian origin of *Barnabas* seems to be a reasonable inference and is generally accepted; cf. Streeter, *Camb. Anc. Hist.*, vol. xi, p. 263; J. A. Robinson, *Barnabas, Hermas, and the Didache*, pp. 24 *seq.*
[6] Matt. 22. 14 (*Barn.* iv. 14), Matt. 9. 13 (*Barn.* v. 9), Matt. 26. 31 (*Barn.* v. 12), Matt. 20. 16 (*Barn.* vi. 13), Matt. 22. 44 (*Barn.* xii. 10), Matt. 22. 45 (*Barn.* xii. 11).
[7] *On the Canon of the N.T.*, p. 48.

of the introductory technical formula ὡς γέγραπται. Therefore, the *Epistle of Barnabas*, far from constituting a deep objection to the thesis of the Alexandrian origin of Matthew, as Streeter asserts, immensely strengthens the case in its favour, for quite obviously the author of the *Epistle* would have referred to that Gospel which was current in his Church and would naturally have assumed that his readers would understand the reference under the words ὡς γέγραπται.[1]

This use of, and consequently respect for, the Gospel of Matthew was not without its effect on the Gentile Christians, as represented by the author of *Barnabas*. As Harmer truly says in the Preface to his edition of the *Epistle*,[2] "The writer is an uncompromising antagonist of Judaism, but beyond this antagonism he had nothing in common with the Antijudaic heresies of the second century. Unlike Marcion, he postulates no opposition between the Old Testament and the New. On the contrary he sees Christianity everywhere in the Lawgiver and the prophets, and treats them with a degree of respect which would have satisfied the most devout rabbi. He quotes them profusely as authoritative. Only he accuses the Jews of misunderstanding them from the beginning to the end, and intimates that the ordinances of circumcision, of the sabbath, of the distinction of meats clean and unclean, were never intended to be literally observed, but had throughout a spiritual and mystical significance." His real attitude towards the Jewish minority in the Alexandrian Church, which still arrogated to themselves a position of special privilege and prestige, appears to be expressed when he writes of certain people (τισιν) who say, "that our covenant remains to them also. Ours it is; but they lost it in this way for ever, when Moses had just received it." And he continues: "their covenant was broken in pieces, that the covenant of the beloved Jesus might be sealed unto our hearts in the hope which springeth from faith in Him."[3] Thus reverence for the venerable traditions which were enshrined in the treasured Gospel of his Church indeed gave the writer of *Barnabas* a deep respect for the Jewish Law and the Prophets; yet he wrote conscious of the growing power of Gentile Christianity, not only in Alexandria, but throughout the Empire, and moved also by that increasing appreciation of the mission of Paul which, as we have already seen, had led to some amendment of the Gospel of Matthew itself; accordingly he felt obliged to combat with vigour the pretensions and objections of that dwindling, and probably despised, minority of

[1] This evidence from *Barnabas* negatives that which Streeter, *Four Gospels*, pp. 504–7, cites from Ignatius in favour of the Antiochene origin of Matthew. It might be noted here that the argument which Streeter advances (op. cit., pp. 507–11) for Antioch from the use of Matt. in the *Didache* depends for its force on the very early date (not later than A.D. 100) assumed for this document. However, several scholars, e.g. J. A. Robinson, J. Muilenburg, F. E. Vokes, have given good reason for a later dating and for the dependence of the *Didache* on *Barnabas*; cf. Streeter, *Camb. Anc. Hist.*, vol. xi, p. 289, n. 1.

[2] *The Apostolic Fathers* (J. B. Lightfoot), p. 239. Cf. Simon, op. cit., pp. 91, 112–14.

[3] *Barn.* iv. 6 (trans. Lightfoot-Harmer); λέγοντας ὅτι ἡ διαθήκη ἡμῶν μένει ἐκείνοις surely implies by the use of the possessive pronoun that the claim is not being made by Jews but by Jewish Christians.

Jewish Christians, who were prone to live too much in terms of the past.

A further possible link in this chain of development may be noted. Dr. Streeter has also presented a strong case for regarding the ancient Christian homily known as the *Second Epistle of Clement of Rome* as an Alexandrian composition, dating some time before A.D. 140.[1] If this attribution is correct, we have a further piece of evidence in favour of the Alexandrian origin of Matthew's Gospel, besides another insight into the mind of Alexandrian Christianity. In eleven passages which contain unmistakable reminiscences of the Gospels, while parallels can be found in each instance in both Matthew and Luke, those of the former generally appear to be nearer in words, order, or meaning.[2] As evidence of Alexandrian thought, this writing, like *Barnabas*, shows a consciousness of Jewish claims by emphasizing God's favour to the Gentiles.

The data which we have studied thus presents a picture of the first hundred years of Alexandrian Christianity, comprising four clearly defined and consequential stages. Founded within the first or second decade of the emergence of the Christian religion, undoubtedly by missionary effort from Palestine, and perhaps organized for some time by Peter, the Church at Alexandria was essentially Jewish in constitution, sympathy, and outlook, and it formed the southern pole of a kind of Jewish-Christian axis. The overthrow of the Jewish nation in A.D. 70 led to an effective increase of this Jewish element by the access of many refugees from Palestine. Out of the situation consequent on the destruction of Jerusalem the Gospel of Matthew was born as an apologia for Jewish Christianity and a polemic against the recrudescence of Pauline teaching. In a very real sense the Gospel of Matthew represents the apogee of Jewish influence in the Alexandrian Church. The steady decline of this Jewish predominance which ensued, perhaps after about A.D. 90, can be traced as it passed through its various phases of counter-attack on Paulinism, of compromising exhortation, and of Gentile attack,

---

[1] *Primitive Church*, pp. 238–47.

[2] *II Clem.* ii. 4—Matt. 9. 13; Mark 2. 17; Luke 5. 32. Mark is nearest here, though the difference in Matt. is only the addition of γάρ and the consequent altering of οὐκ to οὐ. Luke has ἐλήλυθα and εἰς μετάνοιαν. *II Clem.* iii. 2—Matt. 10. 32; Luke 12. 8. There are differences in regard to each of the Gospel references here. Matt. is nearer by the use of ὁμολογήσω. Luke has ὁ υἱὸς τοῦ ἀνθρώπου ὁμολογήσει. *II Clem.* iv. 2—Matt. 7. 21; Luke 6. 46. The first part of the sentence corresponds literally with Matt. The sense of the second part is that of the parallel portion in Matt.; Luke is very dissimilar. *II Clem.* v. 4a— Matt. 10. 16; Luke 10. 3. Matt. has πρόβατα for ἀρνία, but the meaning is the same. *II Clem.* v. 4b—Matt. 10. 28; Luke 12. 4, 5. Matt. gives the closer parallel in words. *II Clem.* vi. 1—Matt. 6. 24; Luke 16. 13. Luke only uses οἰκέτης. *II Clem.* vi. 2—Matt. 16. 26; Mark 8. 36; Luke 9. 25. Matt. has the closest parallel in words and order. *II Clem.* viii. 5— Matt. 25. 21; Luke 16. 10, 11. The second part is found identically in Luke; for the first part Matt. is somewhat nearer. The saying is quoted by Irenæus, *Adv. Haer.* II. 34. 3 (cf. Huck, *Synopse*, p. 140; Westcott, *On the Canon of the N.T.*, p. 164). *II Clem.* ix. 11—Matt. 12. 50; Luke 8. 21. Matt. is somewhat nearer in meaning, Luke in form. *II Clem.* xiii. 4— Matt. 5. 46; Luke 6. 32, 35. Luke gives the closer parallel. *II Clem.* xiv. 1—Matt. 21. 13; Luke 19. 46. The parallel is exact in both.

represented successively in the Epistle of James, the Epistle to the Hebrews, and the *Epistle of Barnabas*, and possibly also in the so-called *Second Epistle of Clement*. Thus the evolution of Alexandrian Christianity was completed from the simple Messianic creed, based upon a demonstration of Jesus as the Messiah of Jewish prophecy (which incidentally entailed a marked emphasis on the historical element implicit in the faith), to the highly complex speculations of the great Egyptian gnostics and to the philosophical expositions of Clement and Origen.

One final note of explanation must be added to meet a problem to which reference has already been made and which may be deemed to constitute a fatal objection to the thesis worked out in this chapter. This is the problem provided by the almost complete silence in early Christian tradition about the origins of the faith in Alexandria, if those origins and their subsequent evolution had indeed such a significance as we have suggested. The obvious answer is to be found in that very silence, as we have already partly seen in our study of the Pauline and Lukan material. Our picture of the evolution of Christianity in apostolic times is almost completely derived from the narrative of the Acts. But this is demonstrably an *ex parte* statement, and when we remember that the New Testament bears witness to many other interpretations of the Christ, or that the beginnings of the Church at Rome are almost equally obscure, we see that this silence is not really serious. The most crucial factor of all, however, is undoubtedly the destruction of Jerusalem in A.D. 70. This tremendous event, the effect of which has been so curiously ignored by New Testament scholars, produced a situation which really caused Christianity to be reborn. It was out of this rebirth that the Christianity represented by the Lukan writings emerged, and it was undoubtedly in response to some consciousness of a lack of clear tradition, *inter alia*, that the Acts of the Apostles was composed. The Church in Alexandria, however, had no such need to write up its traditions, for it was supremely conscious at that time of its unassailable pedigree. Thus, while Luke found it expedient to present in literary form a view of the past which was congenial to the churches for which he wrote, the story of the origins of Alexandrian Christianity went unrecorded. This failure of the Alexandrian Christians to provide a counterpart to the Acts was unfortunate, for owing to the decline in prestige of its Jewish element, and, even more perhaps, owing to the natural antipathy between Jew and Gentile, which was terribly aggravated by the Jewish rising in Egypt in the second century, in process of time the Alexandrian Church preferred rather to forget than to emphasize its origins, which were so essentially Jewish.

APPENDIX

The bearing of the evidence of textual variants on the problem of the origin of the Matthean Gospel *

The relevant variants differ considerably in the value of their respective testimony, but it will be more convenient to take them in the sequence in which they come in the Gospel.

The first variant thus to be noted, occurring in MS. Syr.S, which Streeter recognizes as providing the best evidence of the original text of Antioch, is in Matt. 1. 16; this need not detain us, since Dr. Streeter frankly admits that it has small claim to be regarded as the true text of Matthew.[1] The second variant reading given by MS. Syr.S is for Matt. 15. 24: "I have not been sent save after the flock, which hath strayed away from the House of Israel." This reading Streeter considered to be more Judaistic in tone than the usual Greek text here.[2] But such an opinion is purely subjective, for on comparison there seems to be no real difference in force between the two versions. Moreover, the words used in the Greek version here (τὰ πρόβατα τὰ ἀπολωλότα οἴκου Ἰσραήλ) appear again in Matt. 10. 6, which fact would seem to indicate that it was a well-known phrase to the writer of the Gospel, possibly coming from the missionary vocabulary of the community to which he belonged. Therefore, it appears that, contrary to Dr. Streeter's opinion, the Antiochene text represents an expansion of the original verse, thus indicating a weaker textual tradition for Matthew here. The next variant to be noticed is in Matt. 21. 44, the verse which tells of the crushing power of the symbolic Corner-Stone. This verse is omitted in MSS. D and Syr.S, etc., and is given by the MSS. of the Alexandrian group; the discrepancy has consequently led many scholars to regard the verse as a gloss from Luke 20. 18.[3] The assumption is reasonable, but there are some points in favour of the verse being an integral part of Matthew's original text which do not seem to have been sufficiently considered. Firstly, if v. 44 is a gloss from Luke, it has then to be explained why the scribe who was responsible for making it did not place it immediately after v. 42, so that it would preserve the sequence of Luke 20. 17, 18. As it is, v. 43 in Matthew really disrupts the natural connection between vv. 42 and 44, and this fact may well explain the absence of v. 44 from the MSS. cited, for a scribe unconsciously feeling the sequence of vv. 43 and 45, which is interrupted by v. 44, would have had a natural tendency to omit this verse. Secondly, it must be noticed that v. 44 is made up of a conflation of two Old Testament references, and thus it might well have appeared in *Q* in connection with some prophecy about the Corner-Stone, which was evidently a popular motif among the Jewish Christians;[4]

---

* The ensuing study is made in terms of Dr. Streeter's theory of textual origins. It must, however, be pointed out that subsequent research seems likely to present a somewhat different interpretation from that set out in *The Four Gospels*; see A. J. Grieve, Supplement to *Peake's Commentary*, pp. 21–3; C. C. Tarelli, *Journal of Theological Studies*, vol. xl, pp. 52 *seq.*, vol. xli, p. 258, vol. xliii, pp. 20 *seq.*

[1] *Four Gospels*, pp. 86–7, 267. Cf. Huck, *Synopse*, p. 1.
[2] Ibid., p. 261, n. 1. An interesting little variant, mentioned by Streeter, might be noted for 15. 6b. MSS. א and C give τὸν νόμον τοῦ θεοῦ, while the third correction of א and B, D, Θ, and the Syrian MSS. give τὸν λόγον τοῦ θεοῦ; cf. Huck, op. cit., p. 92.
[3] See Huck, op. cit., loc. cit., p. 166; cf. Streeter, op. cit., p. 319; Levertoff and Goudge, *New Com. N.T.*, p. 182; Klostermann, *Das Matthäusevangelium*, p. 173; Kilpatrick, *J.T.S.*, vol. l (1949), p. 150.
[4] E.g. Acts 4. 11; 1 Pet. 2. 6–8.

some confirmation of this is perhaps to be found in the fact that Luke does not give the complete Markan version in 20. 17, possibly since he preferred to give that of *Q*, which is longer. Moreover, since Matthew is here obviously preoccupied in interpreting the Parable of the Wicked Husbandmen in the light of the catastrophe of A.D. 70, he might well, after drawing out his conclusion in v. 43, have added v. 44 from *Q* as a kind of afterthought, which had then by force of association come naturally into his mind. As he pondered his nation's sufferings and recognized in them a divine visitation for the rejection of Jesus the Messiah, who, as the words of Mark reminded him, was the symbolic Corner-Stone, so in a kind of sequence of reverie he began to see here, as he had seen in 10. 34, the fatal consequences which the coming of Jesus had for his unbelieving people. There is one more small indication of Matthew's trend of mind here, when his choice of the demonstrative pronoun is compared with that of Luke. Matthew's ἐπὶ τὸν λίθον τοῦτον is more natural for a man to write who pondered the fulfilment of a prophecy in which he had perhaps himself suffered deeply than Luke's remote ἐπ' ἐκεῖνον τὸν λίθον.[1] In conclusion some further confirmation of the authenticity of this verse in Matthew may be found (if, as we have attempted to show, the Alexandrian origin of Matthew is a reasonable hypothesis) in *Barnabas* vi. 2, where the crushing power of Christ as the chief Corner-Stone is clearly set forth—ὡς λίθος ἰσχυρὸς ἐτέθη εἰς συντριβήν

Dr. Streeter has argued that in the Abomination of Desolation passage in Matt. 24. 15, Syr.S gives the original text against Bא, etc., by omitting ἑστὸς ἐν τόπῳ ἁγίῳ, the reason being that Matthew, writing in Antioch, had cause to detach the Anti-Christ expectation from its local connection with Jerusalem, possibly with a view to interpreting the Abomination prophecy in terms of the current *Nero-redivivus* myth.[2] Dr. Streeter's contention here, however, is sufficiently answered by the fact that the actual historical event so well corresponds to what Matthew says in 24. 15 that it is entirely unnecessary to seek for another interpretation, especially when it involves the altering of the extant text, supported as it is by the best Alexandrian MSS. The βδέλυγμα τῆς ἐρημώσεως . . . ἑστὸς ἐν τόπῳ ἁγίῳ is completely explained by the standards which the victorious legionaries erected in the Temple, for these standards were sacred emblems to the Romans, and Josephus expressly says that the soldiers sacrificed to them there.[3] It will be well to give this passage of Josephus in full, because of its great significance in this connection: Ῥωμαῖοι δὲ . . . κομίσαντες τὰς σημαίας εἰς τὸ ἱερὸν καὶ θέμενοι τῆς ἀνατολικῆς πύλης ἄντικρυς ἔθυσάν τε αὐταῖς αὐτόθι καὶ τὸν Τίτον μετὰ μεγίστων εὐφημιῶν ἀπέφηναν αὐτοκράτορα. When it is remembered how great a horror fell upon the Jews when Pilate introduced such standards into the city only,[4] it is easy to understand how a Jew would regard the solemn erection of heathen symbols within the sacred precincts of the Temple itself; and further that the son of the Emperor, whose deification must have been a well-known scandal to both Christian and Jew, had thus been triumphantly honoured in that holy place would clearly have fulfilled for such a writer as Matthew the prophecy of the βδέλυγμα τῆς ἐρημώσεως . . . ἑστὸς ἐν τόπῳ ἁγίῳ. There is one further point here which must be answered. Dr. Streeter argues that the omission of the article in the phrase τόπῳ ἁγίῳ indicates an interpolation. But it must be noted that Josephus in the above-cited passage does not say that the standards were erected in the sanctuary, but in the Temple, over against the eastern gate. The reason for this location was undoubtedly that the legionaries chose one of

---

[1] Luke 20. 18.   [2] Op. cit., pp. 512–20.
[3] *Wars of the Jews*, vi. 6. 1 (316). Cf. *Oxford Classical Dictionary*, p. 857b.
[4] Jos., *Ant.*, xviii. 31; *Wars*, ii. 9. 2–3 (169–174). Cf. p. 174, above.

the more extensive of the Temple courts, probably the Court of the Gentiles, for their parade service and the acclamation of their victorious commander. Thus, if Matthew had known this, as Josephus did, he might well have written τόπῳ ἁγίῳ designedly, instead of τῷ τόπῳ ἁγίῳ, which would have been too definite in this connection.

Then, in Matt. 24. 36, MS. Syr.S omits the important words οὐδὲ ὁ υἱός, which are given by the best Alexandrian MSS. Dr. Streeter has to admit that this omission cannot be defended.[1]

In Matt. 27. 4 there is an interesting difference about the adjective used to qualify αἷμα. The Alexandrian MSS., with the exception of L, give ἀθῷον, and Syr.S supports the use of δίκαιον.[2] Dr. Streeter imputes the corruption here to the Alexandrian MSS.[3] However, it is less likely that a rare word like ἀθῷον would have been substituted for a common one such as δίκαιον than vice versa; moreover, the use of the word ἀθῷος, in a different case, in 27. 24 shows that Matthew had a certain predilection for it. Thus again it would seem that the Alexandrian MSS. give the original text of the First Gospel against the Antiochene group of MSS.

Dr. Streeter lays considerable stress upon the fact that in Matt. 27. 17 the MSS. representing the Antiochene and Cæsarean texts, Syr.S and Θ, place the name of Jesus before that of Barabbas, thus implying a significant turn to Pilate's question, "Whom will ye that I release unto you? Jesus Barabbas or Jesus whom they call Christ?"[4] And by implication he explains that the omission of "Jesus" before "Barabbas" in the Alexandrian MSS. was due to an accident in copying: he suggests that since ὑμῖν Ἰησοῦν in such an uncial MS. as Θ would have been written YMININ, by an obvious haplographical error the second IN was omitted. However, Dr. Streeter fails to note here that MS. Θ places "Jesus" before "Barabbas" in verse 16 also, as does Syr.S as well.[5] Now this fact justly raises a suspicion that there is some measure of textual confusion here in this particular group of MSS., and the authenticity of this reading "Jesus Barabbas" is also clearly very improbable on consideration of other points. For instance, if λεγόμενον Ἰησοῦν Βαραββᾶν had originally appeared in v. 16, it would seem reasonable to expect from the contrast expressed in Pilate's question that the relevant part of v. 17 should have read Ἰησοῦν τὸν λεγόμενον Βαραββᾶν ἢ Ἰησοῦν τὸν λεγόμενον Χριστόν; especially since, as vv. 20 and 26 show, Matthew clearly thought that it was by the surname of Barabbas alone that the robber was known; the form Ἰησοῦν Βαραββᾶν, as used in Θ, badly spoils the tragic contrast which the double use of Ἰησοῦν in the question unmistakably implies. But there are more cogent reasons than this for doubting the authenticity of the reading. Matthew, except for one or two short anecdotes of his own, follows the narrative of Mark very closely during this part of the Passion Story. Now it is scarcely credible that a writer like Matthew, who did not scruple to alter the text of Mark in what he considered to be the interests of reverence to the person of Jesus,[6] should have added a word to the record of Mark which made a robber appear to have the same name as the Messiah, especially since he, Matthew, is distinguished among the Evangelists in stressing the divine significance of the name of "Jesus".[7] Therefore from a

[1] Op. cit., p. 135.   [2] Cf. Huck, op. cit., p. 204.
[3] Op. cit., pp. 566–7.   [4] Ibid., p. 136.
[5] Cf. Huck, op. cit., p. 206; Nestle, *Novum Test. Graece* (19th ed., 1949), p. 78.
[6] Cf. Matt. 19. 16, 17; Mark 10. 17, 18. Cf. Hoskyns and Davey, *Riddle of N.T.*, pp. 140 seq.
[7] Cf. Matt. 1. 21, 23, 25. Luke (1. 31; 2. 21) mentions the name without any comment on its meaning. Cf. B. Weiss, *Das Matthäus-Evangelium*, p. 41.

consideration of these points it appears that the interpretation of the fact of this variant reading justifies the holding of quite a different conclusion from that deduced by Dr. Streeter, and it goes to strengthen the reputation of the Alexandrian MSS. for preserving the original text of Matthew in a more trustworthy form than do the MSS. of the Antiochene tradition.

In all the Alexandrian MSS. there is appended to Matt. 27. 49 a short verse which tells of the piercing of the side of Jesus in almost the same words as are used by John 19. 34; it does not appear in Syr.S. That this verse in the Alexandrian MSS. is due to assimilation to the Johannine passage seems obvious, and most textual authorities regard it as such.[1] While the evidence against the authenticity of this reading appears overwhelming, there are, however, a few points in its favour which deserve consideration, and they may have the force of showing that there is no serious objection here to the view that the Alexandrian MSS. have preserved the best text for Matthew. In the first place it may be noted that the text of Matthew generally shows no clear signs of assimilation to the Gospel of John. Therefore, the question may be fairly asked why such assimilation should have taken place here. In John the recording of the incident had a distinct doctrinal value against Docetic teaching;[2] but here in Matthew it has no such value, since the incident is clearly described as happening before the death of Jesus. Moreover, here in Matthew it is not related to any prophecy, whereas in John it appears as a striking fulfilment of prophecy;[3] it seems truly strange that a scribe who considered the Johannine record deserving of interpolation into the text of Matthew did not also include the mention of its remarkable confirmation of prophecy. And to this last point there may be added a note on the general lack of motive in such an interpolation. As we have seen, the scribe who made it obviously could not have appreciated its Johannine significance as a testimony to the reality of the physical death of Jesus, for, if he had so done, he would never have inserted it after v. 49, but after v. 50, where it would have had its doctrinal value. It would seem that, if it were an interpolation, the scribe who made it must have been incredibly careless in that, after being sufficiently interested to copy the verse from John into his text of Matthew, he wrote it in the wrong place. The most feasible suggestion to meet this objection seems to be one which exonerates the Alexandrian MSS. in this connection, namely that the interpolation came through the copying of a marginal note into the text without due care about its juxtaposition to vv. 49 and 50. This interpolation is likely to have occurred early, for, as we have seen, the Gospel of John was already circulating in Upper Egypt in the first half of the second century. Thus perhaps interest in this striking incident in John caused the insertion of the relevant verse into Matthew, where it rapidly became the traditional reading.

From this survey it would accordingly appear that the evidence of the relevant textual variants on closer examination presents a formidable argument against Dr. Streeter's theory of the Antiochene origin of the Gospel of Matthew. In every case, with one possible exception, the MSS. which represent the text current in Antioch show a weaker tradition for Matthew than does the Alexandrian MS. group, and this fact, of course, militates against the view that

---

[1] E.g. it is double-bracketed by Westcott and Hort; the Revisers relegated it to the margin, as do Nestle, Souter, and Huck; it is, of course, rejected by Streeter, *Four Gospels*, p. 136.

[2] Cf. Streeter, op. cit., pp. 386–7; W. Lock, *New Com. N.T.*, p. 268b; A. E. Brooke, *Peake's Commentary*, p. 763b. Loisy, *Les Origines du N.T.*, p. 249, suggests a different interpretation, but it would not alter the force of the argument drawn from the doctrinal value of the passage here.

[3] John 19. 36, 37.

Matthew was the Gospel *par excellence* of the great Syrian metropolis, while it greatly strengthens the other evidence in favour of locating the origins of Matthew in Alexandria.[1]

---

[1] In this connection it is significant that more manuscripts of Matthew than of any other Gospel have so far been found in Egypt. C. H. Roberts, *J.T.S.*, vol. 1 (1949), p. 164, gives the following numbers: 9 texts of Matthew, 7 of John, 5 of Mark, and 4 of Luke. He comments thereon: "the preference for Matthew is surprising." There is no ground for surprise, if Matthew was in origin and purpose the Gospel of the Church of Alexandria.

EPILOGUE

IN our introductory survey of the problems of Christian Origins we saw that a kind of tunnel period existed in the course of the historical development of Christianity during the first century of its life.   Many aspects of the nascent faith which are revealed in its earliest documents, i.e. the Epistles of Paul, appear suddenly to have passed with the cessation of the production of the documents in which they find expression, and the next group of writings in chronological sequence bears witness to a contemporary situation in the Church which seems quite unrelated to that which had gone before.   This tunnel of obscurity into which the life of the Church seems to plunge and from which it later emerges metamorphosed, or, to change the illustration, this apparent hiatus in the consequential development of the Christian movement, concerns a period of some three decades, approximately from A.D. 55 to 85.   The middle year of this period is, significantly, A.D. 70, the year of the overthrow of the Jewish national state and the destruction of its holy city.   The apparent cruciality of this event for Christianity has been the subject of our investigation, and the conclusion has been reached that that cruciality is a fact of profound historical significance for the understanding of the nature of Christian Origins.   It would indeed not be an exaggeration to say that Christianity was in a certain sense reborn as a result of the Jewish catastrophe of A.D. 70.

The removal of Paul by his arrest was truly the defeat of that movement within the Church which was inspired to transcend the barriers of nationality and to proclaim the original historical Jesus of Nazareth as Lord and Saviour of all mankind.   Its defeat signified also the apparent assurance that the authority of the Church of Jerusalem had successfully surmounted a serious threat both to itself and to that interpretation of the faith which it held to represent the original and genuine tradition.   That interpretation envisaged the faith which had derived from Jesus of Nazareth as unquestionably an integral part of Judaism and having its relevance wholly within the bounds of Israel's national hopes.   Thus on the eve of the Jewish War against Rome in A.D. 66 the future of the nascent movement appeared to lie irretrievably in the hands of the Jewish Christians.

It would accordingly seem that any observer of the Christian situation before the standard of revolt was raised by the Jews in 66 must reasonably have forecast the future of Christianity as that of a Jewish Messianic sect, strongly centralized in Jerusalem, and too essentially nationalistic to permit of its effective extension among Gentile peoples. Hence its metamorphosis into the universalist Saviour-God cult to which the Gospel of Mark and the Lukan writings bear witness was so unexpected that it thus seems to constitute a veritable rebirth of the movement.

To the nature of the reborn faith many factors, implicit in the preceding situation, contributed. Perhaps the most momentous of these factors was the propagation of the Christology of the Jerusalem Church, with its essential emphasis on what would now be termed the Jesus of History, among the Pauline churches. The appeal of the historical tradition was great and it established itself so firmly among the Gentile Christians that the reaction to the events of A.D. 70 served rather to strengthen than to shake their appreciation of it. However, Paul's work had not been in vain and the rehabilitation of his reputation, consequent on the fall of the Jewish state, had the effect of reviving the influence of his teaching, though this was not perhaps always truly understood, which resulted in that fusion of the idea of the Saviour-God with the Jesus of History which finds expression in the Gospels.

To the same complex of causes, but also to the inspiration of a definitive apologetic conditioned by the situation in which some Gentile Christian community found itself placed shortly after A.D. 70, we further owe the initial concept of a theological interpretation of Jesus presented in the guise of an historical narrative, of which the Gospel of Mark is our exemplar. On the immensity of the import of this new departure in Christian thought and expression which Mark constitutes there is no need for comment.

Another consequence of A.D. 70, which dynamically changed the whole constitution of the Church and vitally affected the future development of its organization, was the complete obliteration of the Church of Jerusalem. We have not discussed this issue in our foregoing study, beyond noting the obvious contemporary importance of the fact of the disappearance of the original community, because estimate of its further repercussions for Christianity must necessarily be wholly speculative. However, there can be little reasonable doubt that the sudden removal of the original source of authority made possible the emergence of other local churches, especially that of Rome, to positions of decision and control in matters of faith and practice. It is, of course, a subject for conjecture how the organization of authority would have developed in the Church if the community of Jerusalem had continued to hold its original and unique position of authority and prestige, for in that case Christianity would necessarily have been a very different thing from that which it did actually become. Some guide to the possibilities of such a contingency may perhaps be found in the unique position maintained by Mecca in Islam, despite the establishment of that faith in such influential political and cultural centres as Baghdad, Cairo, and Constantinople. However, if Jerusalem had continued to remain the Christian centre of authority in faith and government, the movement must have continued in essential tutelage to Judaism. The quintessence of the drama of A.D. 70 is that the Church of Jerusalem did indeed strive to contain the new wine of Christianity within the old wine-skins of Israel's ethnic faith; until that year the attempt appeared to be successful, although the policy must inevitably have meant atrophy and death. But in the overthrow of the Jewish state the old wine-skins of Judaism were burst asunder and perished, liberating the new wine to flow freely abroad and to reach maturity in places more congenial to the original genius of its creator.

Thus we may conclude that, after the Resurrection experiences, the next most crucial event in the life of the Christian Church was the overthrow of the Jewish nation, which was dramatically epitomized in the destruction of its holy city of Jerusalem in A.D. 70.

BIBLIOGRAPHY I

Ancient Literary Sources

APOCRYPHAL LITERATURE (Jewish)—4 (2 Esdras) Ezra; 1 Baruch; Sibylline Oracles; Assumption of Moses; in *The Apocrypha and Pseudepigrapha*, ed. R. H. Charles, vol. ii, Oxford, 1913.

APOCRYPHAL LITERATURE (Christian)—*Apocrypha II, Gospels*, ed. E. Klostermann, Cambridge, 1904.
> *The Apocryphal New Testament*, ed. M. R. James, Oxford, 1926.

BARNABAS, *The Epistle*—ed. J. R. Harmer, in *The Apostolic Fathers*, ed. J. B. Lightfoot, London, 1891.

CLAUDIUS, Imperator—Letter to the Alexandrians, in *Select Papyri*, vol. ii, ed. A. S. Hunt and C. G. Edgar, *Loeb Classical Library*, London, 1934.

CLEMENT, *First Epistle*—ed. J. B. Lightfoot, in *The Apostolic Fathers*, London, 1891.
> *Second Epistle*—ed. J. B. Lightfoot, in *The Apostolic Fathers*, London, 1891.

Clementine Homilies—trans. T. Smith, *Ante-Nicene Christian Library*, vol. 17, London, 1870.

Clementine Recognitions—trans. T. Smith, *Ante-Nicene Christian Library*, vol. 3, London, 1867.

DIO CASSIUS—*Roman History*. Text and trans., E. Cary, *Loeb Classical Library*, vol. 7, London, 1924.

EPIPHANIUS—*Adversus (Octoginta) Haereses*, ed. J. Migne, *Patrologia Graeca*, tom. xli, xlii, Paris, 1858.
> *De Mensuris et Ponderibus*, ed. J. Migne, *Patrologia Graeca*, tom. xliii, Paris.

EUSEBIUS—*Ecclesiastical History*. Text and trans., K. Lake, *Loeb Classical Library*, 2 vols., London, 1926. Trans. H. J. Lawlor and J. E. L. Oulton, vol. i (trans.), 1927; vol. ii (notes), 1928, London.
> *Demonstratio Evangelica*, ed. Dindorf, vol. iii, Leipzig, 1867.
> *Chronica: S. Hieronymo Interprete et Ampliatore*, ed. Migne, *Patrologia Latina*, tom. xxvii, Paris, 1866.

Fontes Historiae Mysteriorum: Aevi Hellenistici—ed. N. Turchi, Rome, 1923.

HEGESIPPUS—in Eusebius, *Ecclesiastical History*.

JOSEPHUS—*The Wars of the Jews* (abbr. *Wars*); *Autobiography* (abbr. *Life*). Text and trans., H. St. John Thackeray, *Loeb Classical Library*, 3 vols., London, 1926–8. Italian trans. G. Ricciotti, *La Guerra giudaica*, vols. ii–iv, Turin, 1937.
> *The Antiquities of the Jews* (abbr. *Ant.*), text ed. S. A. Naber, Leipzig, 1892. English trans. W. Whiston.
> (For Slavonic version of Josephus' *Wars of the Jews*, see under Berendts and Eisler in Bibliography II.)

NEW TESTAMENT—*Nouum Testamentum Graece*, ed. A. Souter, Oxford, 1941 (1910).
> (Gospels), A. Huck, *Synopse der drei ersten Evangelien*, Tübingen, 1928.

ORIGEN—*Commentarium in Evangelium Mattheum; Contra Celsum*: ed. Lommatzsch, Berlin, 1834.

252

PHILO—*De Legatione ad Caium*, in *Bibliotheca Sacra Patrum Ecclesiae Graecorum*, pars ii, t. vi, Leipzig, 1829.
 In Flaccum, ed. H. Box, Oxford, 1939.
RABBINICAL LITERATURE—See Derenbourg, Lightfoot, J., Stapfer and Strack-Billerbeck in Bibliography II, and under (*Talmud*) below.
SUETONIUS—*Lives of the Caesars*, ed. C. L. Roth, Leipzig, 1898.
SULPICIUS SEVERUS—*Chronica*, or *Historia Sacra*, ed. Migne, *Patrologia Latina*, tom. xx, Paris, 1845.
TACITUS—*Annales; Historiae*: ed. C. Halm, 2 vols., Leipzig, 1891.
(*Talmud*) *Tractate Sabbath*, in *Der babylonische Talmud*, German translation by L. Goldschmidt, Band I, Berlin, 1930.

Secondary

AURELIUS VICTOR—*Historia Romana*, ed. T. C. Harley, vol. i, London, 1829.
CASSIODORUS—*Chronica*, ed. Migne, *Patrologia Latina*, tom. lxix.
Chronicon Paschale, ed. L. Dindorf, in *Corpus Scriptorum Historiae Byzantinae*, vol. i, Bonn, 1832.
EUTROPIUS—*Breviarium Historiae Romanae*, ed. H. Verheyk, London, 1821.
JEROME—*Commentarium in Isaiam*, ed. Migne, *Patrologia Latina*, tom. xxiv.
 Liber de Viris Illustribus, ed. Migne, *Patrologia Latina*, tom. xxiii.
OROSIUS—*Historia adversum Paganos*, ed. Migne, *Patrologia Latina*, tom. xxxi, Paris, 1846.
PHOTIUS—*Bibliotheca*, ed. Migne, *Patrologia Graeca*, tom. ciii, Paris, 1860.

BIBLIOGRAPHY II

Modern Works

ABRAHAMS, I. *Campaigns in Palestine from Alexander the Great* (Schweich Lectures, 1922), London, 1927.
ALBRIGHT, W. F. *The Archaeology of Palestine*, London, 1949.
ALLEN, W. C. *The Gospel according to St. Matthew* (*International Critical Commentary*), Edinburgh, 1907 (abbr. Allen, *I.C.C.*).
ALMQVIST, H. *Plutarch und das Neue Testament*, Uppsala, 1946.
ANGUS, S. *The Mystery-Religions and Christianity*, London, 1928.
 The Religious Quests of the Graeco-Roman World, London, 1929.
ARNOLD, W. T. *Roman Provincial Administration*, Oxford, 1906.
BACON, B. W. *Jesus and Paul*, London, 1921.
 Studies in Matthew, London, 1930.
BARNES, W. E. *The Testimony of Josephus to Jesus Christ*, London, 1920.
BARTLET, J. V. "Clementine Literature", article in *Encyclopædia Britannica*. vol. vi, 11th ed., 1910.
Beginnings of Christianity, edited by F. J. Foakes Jackson and Kirsopp Lake, 5 vols., London, 1920–33.
BELL, H. IDRIS. *Jews and Christians in Egypt*, London, 1924.
 Juden und Griechen im römischen Alexandreia (eine historische Skizze des alexandrinischen Antisemitismus), Leipzig, 1926.
 "Evidences of Christianity in Egypt during the Roman Period", article in *The Harvard Theological Review*, vol. xxxvii (1944).
 Egypt from Alexander the Great to the Arab Conquest, Oxford, 1948.

BELL, H. I., and SKEAT, T. C.   *Fragments of an Unknown Gospel and other Early Christian Papyri*, London, 1935.

BENTWICH, N.   *Josephus*, Philadelphia, 1914.

BERENDTS, A.   *Die Zeugnisse vom Christentum im slavischen "De Bello Judaico" des Josephus*, in *Texte und Untersuchungen*, herausgegeben O. v. Gebhardt und A. Harnack, Neue Folge xiv, Band 4, Heft, Leipzig, 1906.

BERENDTS, A., und GRASS, K.   *Flavius Josephus vom Jüdischen Kriege, Buch i–iv, nach der slavischen Übersetzung*; printed in *Eesti Varbariigi Tartu Ülikooli Toimetused*, Bd. 9, 10, Dorpat, 1926.

BERSANETTI, B. M.   *Vespasiano*, Rome, 1941.

BEVAN, E. R.   *Christianity*, London, 1938.
        "Hellenistic Judaism", article in *The Legacy of Israel*, Oxford, 1927.

BLACK, M.   *An Aramaic Approach to the Gospels and Acts*, Oxford, 1946.

BOUSSET, W.   *Kyrios Christos (Geschichte des Christusglaubens von den Anfängen des Christentums bis Irenaeus)*, Göttingen, 1913.

BRANDON, S. G. F.   "The Crisis of A.D. 70", article in *The Hibbert Journal*, vol. xlvi, London, 1948.
        "The Logic of New Testament Criticism", article in *The Hibbert Journal*, vol. xlvii, London, 1949.

BRIERRE-NARBONNE, J. J.   *Le Messie Souffrant dans la Littérature Rabbinique*, Paris, 1940.

BÜCHLER, A.   *The Economic Conditions of Judaea after the Destruction of the Second Temple*, London, 1912.

BULTMANN, R.   *Die Geschichte der synoptischen Tradition*, Göttingen, 1931.

BURCH, V.   *Jesus Christ and His Revelation*, London, 1927.

BURKITT, F. C.   *Christian Beginnings*, London, 1924.

Cambridge Ancient History, vols. x (1934), xi (1936), xii (1939).

CAMPBELL, J. Y.   "The Origin and Meaning of the Term Son of Man", article in *The Journal of Theological Studies*, vol. xlviii (1947), Oxford.

CARCOPINO, J.   *La Vie quotidienne à Rome à l'Apogée de l'Empire*, Paris, 1939.

CASE, S. J. (editor).   *Studies in Early Christianity*, New York, 1938.

CAVE, S.   *The Gospel of St. Paul*, London, 1928.

CHARLES, R. H.   *Studies in the Apocalypse*, Edinburgh, 1913.
        The Revelation of St. John, 2 vols., International Critical Commentary, Edinburgh, 1920 (abbr. Charles, *I.C.C.*).
        Between the Old and New Testaments, 9th ed., London, 1934.

CHARLESWORTH, M. P. (compiler).   *Documents illustrating the Reigns of Claudius and Nero*, Cambridge, 1939.

CLARKE, W. K. L.   *New Testament Problems*, London, 1929.

COHEN, A.   *Il Talmud* (Italian translation), Bari, 1935.

CREED, J. M.   *The Gospel according to St. Luke*, London, 1930.
        "The Slavonic Version of Josephus' History of the Jewish War", article in *The Harvard Theological Review*, vol. xxv (Oct. 1932).

CULLMANN, O.   *Le Problème littéraire et historique du Roman Pseudo-Clémentin*, Paris, 1930.
        Christus und die Zeit (Die urchristliche Zeit- und Geschichtsauffassung), Zürich, 1946.

CUMONT, F.   *Les Religions Orientales dans le Paganisme Romain*, 4th ed., Paris, 1929.

CURTIUS, L.—NAWRATH, A.   *Das Antike Rom*, Wien, 1944.

DALMAN, G.   *Jesus-Jeshua*, Eng. trans., London, 1929.

DAVIES, W. D.   *Paul and Rabbinic Judaism*, London, 1948.

DEISSMANN, A.   *St. Paul: A Study in Social and Religious History*, Eng. trans., London, 1926.

DEISSMANN, A. *(cont.)* *Licht vom Osten*, 4th ed., Tübingen, 1923.
  Light from the Ancient East, Eng. trans., London, 1927.
DE LABRIOLLE, P. *History and Literature of Christianity*, Eng. trans., London, 1924.
  La Réaction Païenne: Étude sur la Polémique Antichrétienne du Ier au VIe Siècle, Paris, 1942 (1934).
DELITZSCH, P. *Jewish Artisan Life in the Time of Christ*, Eng. trans., London, 1902.
DERENBOURG, J. *Essai sur l'Histoire et la Géographie de la Palestine (d'après les Thalmuds et les autres sources rabbiniques)*, Paris, 1857.
DE ZULUETA, F. "Violation of Sepulture in Palestine at the Beginning of the Christian Era", article in *Journal of Roman Studies*, vol. xxii (1932).
DIBELIUS, M. *Die Formgeschichte des Evangeliums*, Tübingen, 1933.
  From Tradition to Gospel (Eng. trans. from revised 2nd edition of *Die Formgesch. des Evangeliums*), London, 1934.
  Gospel Criticism and Christology, London, 1935.
DODD, C. H. *The Apostolic Preaching and its Developments*, London, 1944.
  History and the Gospel, London, 1938.
  The Epistle to the Romans, London, 1940 (1932).
  The Parables of the Kingdom, London, 1941.
DÖLLINGER, J. J. *The Gentile and the Jew*, vol. ii, Eng. trans., London, 1862.
DUCHESNE, L. *The Early History of the Christian Church*, vol. i, Eng. trans., London, 1914.
DUNCAN, G. S. *St. Paul's Ephesian Ministry*, London, 1929.
EASTON, B. S. *Christ and the Gospels*, New York, 1930.
EDERSHEIM, A. *History of the Jewish Nation*, London, 1896.
  The Life and Times of Jesus the Messiah, 2 vols., London, 1901.
EHRHARDT, A. A. T. "Jesus Christ and Alexander the Great", article in *The Journal of Theological Studies*, vol. xlvi (1945).
EISLER, R. *ΙΗΣΟΥΣ ΒΑΣΙΛΕΥΣ ΟΥ ΒΑΣΙΛΕΥΣΑΣ (Die messianische Unabhängigkeitsbewegung vom Auftreten Johannes des Täufers bis zum Untergang Jakobs des Gerechten. Nach der neuerschlossenen Eroberung von Jerusalem des Flavius Josephus und den christlichen Quellen)*, 2 Bände, Heidelberg, 1929–30.
  The Messiah Jesus and John the Baptist (according to Flavius Josephus' recently discovered "Capture of Jerusalem" and other Jewish and Christian sources), English edition by A. H. Krappe, London, 1931.
  The Enigma of the Fourth Gospel (Its Author and its Writer), London, 1938.
  Orpheus—The Fisher, London, 1921.
  Orphische-dionysische Mysteriengedanken in der christlichen Antike, Leipzig-Berlin, 1925.
  "The Sadoqite Book of the New Covenant: its Date and Origin", in the *Gaster Anniversary Volume*, ed. B. Schindler, London, 1936.
EPPEL, R. *Le Piétisme Juif dans les Testaments des Douze Patriarchs*, Paris, 1930.
ERMAN, A. *Die Religion der Aegypter*, Berlin-Leipzig, 1934.
FARRAR, F. W. *The Early Days of Christianity*, vol. 2, London, 1882.
FERRERO, G. e BARBAGALLO, C. *Roma Antica*, vols. ii and iii, Florence, 1932 (1922).
FESTUGIÈRE, A.-J. *La Révélation d'Hermès Trismégiste*, II, *Le Dieu Cosmique*, Paris, 1949.
GALL, A. VON. *ΒΑΣΙΛΕΙΑ ΤΟΥ ΘΕΟΥ*, Heidelberg, 1926.
GARSTANG, J. "Jerusalem under Herod the Great", article in *Wonders of the Past*, vol. iii, London, n. d.
GASTER, M. *The Samaritans* (Schweich Lectures, 1923), London, 1925.

GERNET, L., et BOULANGER, A. *Le Génie Grec dans la Religion* (Coll: *L'Évolution de l'Humanité*), Paris, 1932.

GINSBURG, M. S. *Rome et la Judée: Contribution à l'Histoire de leurs Relations politiques*, Paris, 1928.

GNECCHI, F. *Monete Romane*, Milan, 1935.

GOGUEL, M. *The Life of Jesus*, Eng. trans., London, 1933.
  Jésus et le Messianisme politique, Examen de la théorie de M. Robert Eisler (Extrait de la *Revue Historique*), Paris, 1931.
  La Naissance du Christianisme, Paris, 1946.
  L'Église Primitive, Paris, 1947.
  De Jésus à l'Apôtre Paul, article in *Revue d'Histoire et de Philosophie Religieuses*, t. xxviii (1948–9), Strasbourg et Paris.

GOODENOUGH, E. R. *The Politics of Philo Judaeus*, with a General Bibliography of Philo by H. L. Goodhart and E. R. Goodenough, Yale University Press, 1938.

GOODSPEED, E. J. *New Solutions of New Testament Problems*, Chicago, 1927.
  An Introduction to the New Testament, Chicago, 1937.

GRAETZ, H. *A History of the Jews*, Eng. trans., vol. ii, London, 1891.

GRANT, F. G. "The Economic Significance of Messianism", article in *The Anglican Theological Review*, vol. vii, Ohio, 1924.
  The Economic Background of the Gospels, Oxford, 1926.

GREEN, F. W. *The Gospel according to St. Matthew* (*Clarendon Bible*), Oxford, 1936.

GRESSMANN, H. *Die orientalischen Religionen im hellenistisch-römischen Zeitalter*, Berlin u. Leipzig, 1930.

GUIGNEBERT, Ch. *Le Monde Juif vers le Temps de Jésus* (Coll: *L'Évolution de l'Humanité*), Paris, 1935.
  Jesus, Eng. trans. (Coll: *The History of Civilization*), London, 1935.
  Le Christ (Coll: *L'Évolution de l'Humanité*), Paris, 1943.

GWATKIN, H. M. *Early Church History*, 2 vols., London, 1912.

HALLIDAY, W. R. *The Pagan Background of Early Christianity*, Liverpool, 1925.

HARNACK, A. VON. *Die Mission und Ausbreitung des Christentums in den ersten drei Jahrhunderten*, 2 Bände, Leipzig, 1906.
  Marcion: Das Evangelium vom Fremden Gott (*Texte und Untersuchungen zur Geschichte der altchristlichen Literatur*, herausgegeben von A. von Harnack und C. Schmidt, 3. Reihe 15 Band.), Leipzig, 1924.

HARRIS, J. RENDEL. *Some Interesting Syrian and Palestinian Inscriptions*, London, 1891.

HARRISON, P. N. *The Problem of the Pastoral Epistles*, Oxford, 1921.

HARTMANN, L. M. e KROMAYER, G. *Storia Romana* (Italian trans.), vol. i, Florence, 1942.

HENDERSON, B. W. *The Life and Principate of the Emperor Nero*, London, 1903.

HERFORD, R. T. *The Effect of the Fall of Jerusalem upon the Character of the Pharisees* (*Society of Hebraic Studies, No. 2*), London, 1917.

HOENNICKE, G. *Das Judenchristentum im ersten und zweiten Jahrhundert*, Berlin, 1908.

HOLTZMANN, O. *Das Ende des Jüdischen Staatswesens und die Entstehung des Christentums* (being part of *Geschichte des Volkes Israel von B. Stade*, Bänd ii), Berlin, 1888.

HORT, F. J. *Judaistic Christianity*, London, 1894.
  Notes Introductory to the Study of the Clementine Recognitions, London, 1901.

HOSKYNS, E., and DAVEY, N. *The Riddle of the New Testament*, London, 1931.

HOWARD, W. F. *The Fourth Gospel in Recent Criticism and Interpretation*, London, 1931.

HUNKIN, J. W. *Palestine in General History* (Schweich Lectures, 1926, with T. H. Robinson and F. C. Burkitt), London, 1929.

HUNTER, A. M. *Paul and his Predecessors*, London, 1940.

JACK, J. W. *The Historic Christ (An Examination of Dr. Robert Eisler's Theory according to the Slavonic Version of Josephus and Other Sources)*, London, 1933.

JACKSON, F. J. FOAKES. *Josephus and the Jews*, London, 1930.

Jewish Encyclopedia, New York, 1901.

JONES, A. H. M. *The Herods of Judaea*, Oxford, 1938.

JOUGUET, P. *L'Impérialisme Macédonien et l'Hellénisation de l'Orient* (Coll: *L'Évolution de l'Humanité*), Paris, 1926.

Judaism and Christianity, I, *The Age of Transition*, ed. W. O. E. Oesterley, London, 1937.

JUSTER, J. *Les Juifs dans l'Empire Romain*, Paris, 1914.

KAUTSKY, K. *Foundations of Christianity*, Eng. trans., London, 1929.

KENNARD, J. S. *Politique et Religion chez les Juifs au Temps de Jésus et dans l'Église Primitive*, Paris, 1927.

KIDD, B. J. *History of the Church*, vol. i, Oxford, 1922.

KILPATRICK, G. D. *The Origins of the Gospel according to St. Matthew*, Oxford, 1946.

KITTEL, G. *Die Stellung des Jakobus zu Judentum und Heidenchristentum*, article in *Zeitschrift für die Neutestamentliche Wissenschaft*, Giessen, 1931 (abbr. Kittel, *Z.N.T.W.*, 1931).

KLAUSNER, J. *Jesus of Nazareth*, Eng. trans., London, 1929.
   From Jesus to Paul, Eng. trans., London, 1942.

KLOSTERMANN, E. *Das Markusevangelium*, Tübingen, 1926.
   Das Lukasevangelium, Tübingen, 1929.
   Das Matthäusevangelium, Tübingen, 1927 (series: *Handbuch zum Neuen Testament*, ed. H. Lietzmann).

KNOX, W. L. *St. Paul and the Church of Jerusalem*, Cambridge, 1925.
   St. Paul and the Church of the Gentiles, Cambridge, 1939.
   Some Hellenistic Elements in Primitive Christianity (Schweich Lectures, 1942), London, 1944.
   "The Epistle of St. James", article in *Journal of Theological Studies*, vol. xlvi (1945).
   The Acts of the Apostles, Cambridge, 1948.

LAKE, KIRSOPP. *The Earlier Epistles of St. Paul*, London, 3rd ed., 1930.
   Landmarks in the History of Early Christianity, London, 1920.
   Paul, His Heritage and Legacy, London, 1934.

LAKE, K. and S. *An Introduction to the New Testament*, London, 1938.

LAWLOR, H. J. *Eusebiana*, Oxford, 1912.

LECLERCQ, H. "Josephus", article in *Dictionnaire d'Archéologie Chrétienne et de Liturgie*, Paris, 1927.

Legacy of Egypt, ed. S. R. K. Glanville, Oxford, 1942.

LEVY, R. "The Temples at Jerusalem", article in *Wonders of the Past*, vol. iii, London, n. d.

LEWIN, T. *Fasti Sacri*, London, 1863.
   The Siege of Jerusalem, London, 1863.

LIETZMANN, H. *Geschichte der alten Kirche*, Band I, *Die Anfänge*, Berlin u. Leipzig, 1937.
   An die Korinther, I, II, Tübingen, 1923 (*Handbuch zum Neuen Testament*, ed. H. Lietzmann).
   An die Galater, Tübingen, 1923 (*Handbuch zum Neuen Testament*, ed. H. Lietzmann).

LIGHTFOOT, J. *Horae Hebraicae et Talmudicae*, ed. R. Gandell, Oxford, 1859.

LIGHTFOOT, J. B.   *The Epistle to the Philippians*, London, 1868.
  The Epistle to the Colossians, London, 1875.
  The Epistle to the Galatians, London, 1881.
LIGHTFOOT, R. H.   *History and Interpretation in the Gospels*, London, 1935.
  Locality and Doctrine in the Gospels, London, 1938.
LIGHTLEY, J. W.   *Jewish Sects and Parties in the Time of Jesus*, London, 1925.
LODS, A.   *Les Prophètes d'Israël et les Débuts du Judaïsme* (Coll: *L'Évolution de l'Humanité*), Paris, 1935.
LOEWE, H.   " *Render unto Caesar* ".   *Religious and Political Loyalty in Palestine*, Cambridge, 1940.
LOHMEYER, E.   *Philipper, Kolosser, und Philemon*, Göttingen, 1930.
  Galiläa und Jerusalem, Göttingen, 1936.
LOISY, A.   *Les Mystères Païens et le Mystère Chrétien*, Paris, 1914.
  La Naissance du Christianisme, Paris, 1933.
  Le Origini del Cristianesimo (Italian trans.), Turin, 1942.
  Les Origines du Nouveau Testament, Paris, 1936.
LUCE, H. K.   *The Gospel according to St. Luke*, Cambridge, 1936.
MACCHIORO, V.   *Zagreus. Studi intorno all'Orfismo*, Florence, 1930.
McGIFFERT, A. G.   *A History of Christianity in the Apostolic Age*, Edinburgh, 1897.
McNEILE, A. H.   *The Gospel according to St. Matthew*, London, 1915.
  An Introduction to the Study of the New Testament, Oxford, 1927.
MADDEN, F. W.   *Coins of the Jews*, London, 1881.
  History of Jewish Coinage, London, 1864.
MANSON, T. W.   *The Teaching of Jesus*, Cambridge, 1935.
MANSON, W.   *Jesus the Messiah*, London, 1943.
MARTINETTI, P.   *Jésus Christ et le Christianisme*, Paris, 1942.
MERRILL, E.   *Essays in Early Christian History*, London, 1924.
MEYER, Ed.   *Ursprung und Anfänge des Christentums*, 3 vols., Stuttgart u. Berlin, 1921–3.
MICHAELIS, W.   *Judaistische Heidenchristen*, article in *Zeitschrift für Neutestamentliche Wissenschaft*, Giessen, 1931 (abbr. Michaelis, *Z.N.T.W.*, 1931).
MILMAN, H.   *History of the Jews*, 2 vols., *Everyman Edition*, London, 1909.
MOFFATT, J.   *Introduction to the Literature of the New Testament*, Edinburgh, 1933 (3rd ed. revised, 1918).
  The First Epistle of Paul to the Corinthians, London, 1943 (1938).
MOMIGLIANO, A.   *L'Opera dell'Imperatore Claudio*, Florence, 1932.
MOMMSEN, T.   *The Provinces of the Roman Empire*, 2 vols., Eng. trans., London, 1886.
MONTEFIORE, C. G.   *The Synoptic Gospels*, 2 vols., London, 1927.
MOORE, G. F.   *Judaism*, 3 vols., Cambridge (Mass.), 1927.
MORRISON, W. D.   *The Jews under Roman Rule*, London, 1890.
MURRAY, G.   *Five Stages of Greek Religion* (*Thinker's Library*), London, 1935.
NAIRNE, A.   *The Epistle of Priesthood*, Edinburgh, 1913.
A New Commentary of Holy Scripture, ed. C. Gore, H. L. Goudge, H. Guillaume, London, 1929.
NOCK, A. D.   *St. Paul*, London, 1938.
  "Early Gentile Christianity and its Hellenistic Background ", in *Essays on the Trinity and the Incarnation*, ed. A. E. J. Rawlinson, London, 1933.
  Conversion, Oxford, 1933.
OESTERLEY, W. O. E.   *A History of Israel*, vol. ii, Oxford, 1932.
OESTERLEY, W. O. E., and BOX, G. H.   *A Short Survey of the Literature of Rabbinical and Mediaeval Judaism*, London, 1920.

OESTERLEY, W. O. E., and ROBINSON, T. H.   *Hebrew Religion: its Origin and Development*, London, 1930.

OLMSTEAD, A. J.   *Jesus: In the Light of History*, New York, 1942.

Oxford Classical Dictionary, Oxford, 1949.

PARKES, J.   *The Conflict of the Church and the Synagogue*, London, 1934.

PEAKE, A. S.   *A Critical Introduction to the New Testament*, London, 1930.
      (Editor:) *Peake's Commentary on the Bible*, London, 1920.   *Supplement*, ed. A. J. Grieve, 1936.

PERETTI, A.   *La Sibilla babilonese nella Propaganda ellenistica*, Florence, 1943.

PIGANIOL, A.   *Histoire de Rome*, 3rd ed., Paris, 1949.

PIN, B.   *Jérusalem contre Rome (Un duel pour l'hégémonie en Mediterranée orientale)*, Paris, 1938.

POLAND, F., REISINGER, G., WAGNER, R.   *La Civilta antica*, Italian trans., Florence, 1924.

RACKHAM, R. B.   *The Acts of the Apostles*, London, 1901.

RAMSAY, W. M.   *The Church in the Roman Empire before A.D. 170*, 3rd ed., London, 1894.

RAWLINSON, A. E. J.   *St. Mark*, 5th ed., London, 1942.

REINACH, S.   *Orpheus*, Eng. trans., London, 1931.

RENAN, E.   *Antichrist*, Eng. trans., London, 1899.
      Marc-Aurèle, Paris, n. d.

RENDALL, G. H.   *The Epistle of St. James and Judaic Christianity*, Cambridge, 1927.

RICCIOTTI, G.   *Flavio Giuseppe. Lo Storico Giudeo-Romano*, Turin, 1937 (see Bibliography I under *Josephus*).

ROBERTSON, A.   *Jesus, Myth or History?*, London, 1941.

ROBINSON, J. A.   *Barnabas, Hermas, and the Didache*, London, 1920.

ROSTOVTZEFF, M.   *The Social and Economic Condition of the Roman Empire*, Oxford, 1921.

ROWLEY, H. H.   "The Herodians", article in *Journal of Theological Studies*, vol. xli (1940).

SANDAY, W., and HEADLAM, A. C.   *The Epistle to the Romans (International Critical Commentary)*, Edinburgh, 1900.

SCHAFF, P.   *History of the Christian Church*, vol. i, Edinburgh, 1893.

SCHLATTER, D. A.   *Geschichte Israels von Alexander dem Grossen bis Hadrian*, Stuttgart, 1925.

SCHMIDT, C.   *Studien zu den Pseudo-Clementinen, nebst einem Anhange: Die älteste römische Bischofsliste und die Pseudo-Clementinen*.   Herausgegeben von A. von Harnack und C. Schmidt in Texte und Untersuchungen, xlvi Band, Heft 1, Leipzig, 1930.

SCHMIDTKE, A.   *Neue Fragmente und Untersuchungen zu den judenchristlichen Evangelien. (Texte und Untersuchungen zur Geschichte der altchristlichen Literatur*, herausgegeben von A. von Harnack und G. Schmidt, 3. Reihe 17. Band.)   Leipzig, 1911.

SCHOEPS, H. J. I.   *Die Tempelzerstörung des Jahres 70 in der jüdischen Religionsgeschichte. III. Symmachusstudien (Coniectanea Neotestamentica, vi, Seminarium Neotestamenticum Upsalinse)*, Uppsala, 1942.

SCHONFIELD, H. J.   *History of Jewish Christianity*, London, 1936.

SCHÜRER, E.   *Geschichte des jüdischen Volkes im Zeitalter Jesu Christi*, 3 Bände, Leipzig, 1898–1901.

SCHWARTZ, E.   *Zu Eusebius Kirchengeschichte. I. Das Martyrium Jakobus des Gerechten*, article in *Zeitschrift für Neutestamentliche Wissenschaft*, Giessen, 1903 (abbr. Schwartz, *Z.N.T.W.*, 1903).

SCHWEITZER, A.   *Paul and his Interpreters*, Eng. trans., London, 1912.
      The Mysticism of Paul the Apostle, Eng. trans., London, 1931.

SCOTT, C. A. ANDERSON.   *Christianity according to St. Paul*, Cambridge, 1927.

SIEFFERT, F.   *Der Brief an die Galater*, Göttingen, 1899.

SIMON, M.   *Verus Israel: Étude sur les Relations entre Chrétiens et Juifs dans l'Empire Romain* (135–425), Paris, 1948.

SMITH, G. A.   *The Historical Geography of the Holy Land*, London, 1907.
   Jerusalem, 2 vols., London, 1907.

SMITH, P. GARDNER.   *The Narratives of the Resurrection*, London, 1926.

SPENGLER, O.   *The Decline of the West*, Eng. trans., 2 vols., London, 1928.

STAPFER, E.   *La Palestine au Temps de Jésus-Christ (d'après le Nouveau Testament, l'Historien Flavius Josèphe et les Talmuds)*, Paris, 1885.

STRACK, H. und BILLERBECK, P.   *Kommentar zum Neuen Testament aus Talmud und Midrasch*, Munich, 4 Bände, 1922–8.

STREETER, B. H.   *The Four Gospels*, London, 1924.
   The Primitive Church, London, 1929.
   "The Rise of Christianity", chapter vii, *Cambridge Ancient History*, vol. xi (1936).

Supernatural Religion (anonymous), London, 1902 (revised ed.).

SWAIN, J. W.   "Gamaliel's Speech and Caligula's Statue", article in *The Harvard Theological Review*, vol. xxxvii (1944).

TAYLOR, V.   *Behind the Third Gospel*, Oxford, 1926.
   The Formation of the Gospel Tradition, London, 1945 (1935).

THACKERAY, H. ST. JOHN.   *Josephus: the Man and the Historian*, New York, 1929.
   "Josephus", article in Hastings, *Dictionary of the Bible*, extra vol., Edinburgh, 1904.
   Selections from Josephus, London, 1919.

THOMSON, J. E. H.   *The Samaritans*, Edinburgh, 1919.

TOYNBEE, A. J.   *A Study of History*, vols. ii, v, Oxford, 1934, 1939.

WEBB, C. C. J.   *The Historical Element in Religion*, London, 1935.

WEINEL, H.   *Die Stellung des Urchristentums zum Staat*, Tübingen, 1908.

WEISS, B.   *Das Matthäus-Evangelium*, Göttingen, 1898.

WEISS, J.   *Das Urchristentum*, Göttingen, 1914.
   Der erste Korinthbrief, Göttingen, 1910.

WERNER, M.   *Der Einfluss paulinischer Theologie im Markusevangelium* (Beihefte I, z. *Zeitschrift für neutestamentliche Wissenschaft*, von H. Lietzmann), Giessen, 1923.

WESTCOTT, B. F.   *On the Canon of the New Testament*, London, 1870.

WILLIAMS, A. L.   *The Hebrew-Christian Messiah*, London, 1916.

WINDISCH, H.   *Der Untergang Jerusalems (Anno 70) im Urtheil der Christen und Juden*, article in *Theologisch Tijdschrift*, Leiden, 1914.
   Der zweite Korinthbrief, Göttingen, 1924.
   Die katholischen Briefe, Tübingen, 1930.
   Der Hebräerbrief, Tübingen, 1931.
   Der messianische Krieg und das Urchristentum, Tübingen, 1909.

ADDENDUM

Before he died Dr. R. Eisler was in the course of preparing a supplement to his *ΙΗΣΟΥΣ ΒΑΣΙΛΕΥΣ ΟΥ ΒΑΣΙΛΕΥΣΑΣ* which was designed to answer the criticisms made by scholars of various nationalities since its publication in 1929–30.   In justice to the memory of Dr. Eisler the attention of the reader who is interested in the issue may be drawn to his privately circulated brochure entitled *Flavius Josephus-Studien I. Das Testimonium Flavianum.   Eine Antwort an Dr. Walter Bienert* (Verlag Methuen and Co., Ltd., London, 1938). This monograph, although intended primarily to answer the objections advanced by Dr. W. Bienert in his book *Der älteste nichtchristliche Jesusbericht.   Josephus über Jesus.   Unter besonderer Berücksichtigung des altrussischen Josephus* (*Theol. Arbeiten z. Bibel-Kirchen-und Geistesgeschichte*, hg. v. D. Ernst Darmikol, Nr. IX, Akad Verlag Halle, 1936), contains a certain amount of new material and notices some points raised by other writers.   Dr. Eisler deposited a copy of this monograph in the library of the Warburg Institute, London; there is another copy in the library of Vienna University.

It may be noted also that Dr. Eisler had specially discussed the data relative to the Slavonic Josephus in an article entitled "*Die Slavische Uebersetzung der ΑΛΩΣΙΣ ΤΗΣ ΙΕΡΟΥΣΑΛΗΜ des Flavius Josephus*", which was published in *Byzantinoslavica* II/2, pp. 305–75, Prague, 1930.

APPENDIX

Jewish Christianity according to Professor H. J. Schoeps

The publication of Professor H. J. Schoeps' book entitled *Theologie und Geschichte des Judenchristentums* (Tübingen, 1949) will surely mark a decisive stage in the development of New Testament studies; for this great work, which is based upon an intensive study of the relevant material ranging over many years and which has been preceded by a series of monographs upon specific points, sets forth an interpretation of a vital aspect of primitive Christianity that must inevitably affect the study of Christian Origins as a whole. Its bearing upon the views advanced here is clearly of the highest importance, so that the valuable support which it affords to certain of these views merits notice, as its conflict with others demands attention.

At the outset Prof. Schoeps acknowledges that his interpretation may fairly be regarded as in some measure a rehabilitation of the nineteenth-century Tübingen school of New Testament criticism, but an important qualification must be made: "*In manchem werden unsere Bemühungen die späte Rehabilitierung eines geläuterten Tübinger Standpunktes darstellen, um so ein altes Unrecht wieder gutzumachen; aber von allen früheren Untersuchungen unterscheidet sich diese Arbeit fundamental dadurch, dass sie erstmalig das Problem auf eine viel breitere Basis stellt und Quellen heranzieht, an die man bislang noch gar nicht gedacht hatte*" (p. 5; cf. p. 70). Hence Prof. Schoeps enters upon his task with a careful consideration not only of the material studied by Baur and his followers, but also of the Bible translation of the Ebionite Symmachus, and of the relevant Rabbinical literature.

From such material he reconstructs the teaching of Jewish Christianity. His fundamental assumption is that the Ebionite documents concerned, especially the Pseudo-Clementine writings and those of Symmachus, truly represent the doctrine of the Jewish Christians prior to A.D. 70: "*Aber als gesichert darf uns—wie aller bisheriger Kirchengeschichtschreibung seit Eusebius— gelten, dass es die jerusalemer Urgemeinde, die Kinder und Enkel der ersten unmittelbaren Jünger Jesu waren, die um das Jahr 67 den Auszug ins Ostjordanland vornahmen und die bei den späteren Vätern als Sekten der 'Ebionäer' und 'Nazaräer' erscheinen*" (p. 7; cf. pp. 63–4). So far as the matter of historical fact is concerned this statement must be questioned in the light of the account which we have presented above of the fate of the Jerusalem *Urgemeinde*; however, a convincing case is made out for the view that Ebionite doctrine is in the true line of descent from that of the original Jerusalem Church, and this remarkably confirms the interpretation of the primitive Jerusalem Christology which has been advanced in the present work.

Prof. Schoeps finds that the Christology of the original Jewish Christians was thoroughly "Adoptionist": for them the Baptism and the Resurrection were the events of supreme importance in the career of Jesus (pp. 71–2). The doctrine was based upon two distinctive concepts, namely, that Jesus was the "*novus Moses*" and that he was the apocalyptic Son of Man (pp. 78–88). The death of Jesus accordingly had no essential significance: "*Jesu Kreuzestod war ihnen* (i.e. the Jewish Christians) *also nicht wie der Kirche das soteriologische Ereignis, sondern nur ein Frevel der Juden und im übrigen Erweis seines blossen Menschtums*" (p. 76). In this connection Prof. Schoeps notes that a distinct antipathy which shows itself in the Ebionite documents towards the animal sacrifices offered in the Temple undoubtedly reflected the Jewish Christian repudiation of Paul's doctrine of the sacrificial death of Jesus: "*Denn Pauli soteriologische Wertung des Todes Jesu als Sühnopfertod ist—ebionitisch gesprochen— das grösste Paradox, das gedacht werden kann, eine Lästerung solchen Stiles, dass sie allein schon ihn als Typus des Falschen Propheten erweist. Nicht durch alles umfassende Opfer des Gottessohnes, wie die Kirche in Pauli Nachfolge meint, ist die Christenheit von jüdischen Opferdienst frei geworden, sondern durch die Wasser der Taufe hat Jesus die Feuer des Opferkults—so ist ebionitischer Glaube zum Verlöschen gebracht*" (p. 157).

Throughout these Ebionite writings there breathes a profound hatred for Paul and his teaching, for behind the mask of the arch-enemy, Simon Magus, Prof. Schoeps perceives the figure of Marcion and behind that again the figure of Paul (pp. 128 *seq.*, 257, 420–1, 425–6); if his theory be accepted that the 7th book of the *Κηρύγματα Πέτρου* has preserved a fragment of the lost Ebionite *Acts of the Apostles*, this hatred extends to the impossible point of imputing to Paul the *Mordanschlags* on James, the Lord's brother and head of the Jerusalem Church (pp. 381–4, 417, 431, 435, 441, 446–7). However that may be, of special interest to our thesis is Prof. Schoeps' view that behind Peter's attack on the claims of Simon Magus to a true apostleship on the ground of his *ὀπτασίαι* and *ἀποκάλυψεις* (*Hom.* 17. 14) there lies an attack on the similar claims made by Paul in 2 Cor. 5. 16; 12. 1 ff. (pp. 425–7; cf. pp. 448–50).

Prof. Schoeps, believing that Stephen is an *Ersatzfigur* for James, sees in Stephen's speech before the Sanhedrin (Acts 7. 2–53) an original Jewish Christian polemic against the Temple cultus (pp. 236–7, 441, 446). Accordingly, the only significance which he finds for the Ebionites (does this mean also the original survivors of the *Urgemeinde*?) in the catastrophe of A.D. 70 is a demonstration of God's wrath on the Temple and its cultus: "*Und schliesslich ist den Ebioniten die Tempelzerstörung des Jahres 70 das grösste Argument dafür, dass Israel durch sein Festhalten an dem mit diesem Tempel verbundenen Opferkult Gott immer mehr erbittert* (exasperare) *habe. Die Tempelzerstörung ist geschehen, da die Israeliten nicht erkennen wollten, dass durch die Erscheinung des wahren Propheten* (i.e. Jesus) *die Zeit der Opfer endgültig vorüber wäre* (Rec. 1. 67)" (p. 241). This part of his interpretation seems to be very doubtful, because, as we have seen at length above, there is an abundance of evidence that the Jerusalem Christians continued faithful in their reverence for the Temple and in their observance of its cultus; indeed even Paul himself outwardly conformed to the ritual requirements of Judaism and, so far as his extant letters inform us, never criticized the Temple and the services performed there. Moreover, it is significant that Prof. Schoeps does not notice the problem which is constituted by the fact that in the Markan and Matthean Passion Narratives the charge that Jesus prophesied against the Temple is ascribed to "false witnesses", as indeed it also is in the Lukan account of Stephen's martyrdom (Acts 6. 13, 14).

As we have already noticed, it is a fundamental assumption of Prof. Schoeps' thesis that the Jerusalem Christians migrated *en masse*, or at least in effective part, to Pella. The evidence for this assumption is stated as follows: "*Ueber den Auszug der Urgemeinde ins Ostjordanland, der im Frühjar 66 oder 67—nach Ewald sogar erst Ende 67—erfolgt ist, besitzen wir zwei voneinander unabhängige Berichte von Eusebius und von Epiphanius sowie zwei noch nie herangezogene vaticinia post eventum in den K.Π.* (i.e. *Κηρύγματα Πέτρου*)" (p. 265); to these witnesses is added the possible testimony of Rev. 12. 6 ff., which we have noticed. The value of the evidence of Eusebius and Epiphanius we have examined critically, which Prof. Schoeps does not appear to have done, and we have concluded that it can only be accepted as witnessing to a late tradition that certain Christian communities in Trans-Jordania claimed to have descended from Jewish Christian refugees, not necessarily from Jerusalem, of the war of 66–70. Prof. Schoeps gives, as hitherto unnoticed evidence, two passages from the Pseudo-Clementine writings, *Rec.* 1. 37 (Syrus) and *Rec.* 1. 39 (Rufin); he seems to place the greatest reliance on the words in the latter: "καὶ οἱ αὐτῷ (the true Prophet, i.e. Jesus) πιστεύοντες θεοῦ σοφίᾳ εἰς ἰσχυρὸν τῆς χώρας τόπον εἰς σωτηρίαν συνηγμένοι, . . .", commenting thereon: "*Interessant ist die Betonung, dass Pella wegen der Sicherheit des Ortes gewählt wurde*" (p. 267; the passages are given *in extenso* on p. 47, notes 1 and 2). If the authenticity of the passage as evidence of a mass flight of the Jerusalem *Urgemeinde* to Pella is thus mainly to be based upon "*die Sicherheit des Ortes*", one can only wonder, after our study of the Jewish War above, in what sense Pella was notable for its security.

However that may be, the crucial problem which Prof. Schoeps fails to face in this connection is that constituted by the indisputable fact of the complete disappearance of the Mother Church of Jerusalem as an effective factor in the Christian movement after A.D. 70. The following obvious question which his views prompt calls forth its own equally obvious answer—if a substantial part of the *Urgemeinde* had fled from insurgent Jerusalem in obedience to a divine oracle and had established itself in Pella, would not its authority and prestige have continued undiminished, nay rather, have been enhanced by its signal faithfulness? Indeed, Prof. Schoeps himself provides a fitting answer to this question when, clearly puzzled by the fact that in so short a time "*diese Urzelle der Christenheit, die Nachkommenschaft der ersten Jünger Jesu*" (according to his interpretation), became the object of the orthodox scorn of the Catholic Christians, he exclaims: "*welches weltgeschichtliche Paradoxon!*" (p. 270)

This failure to account for the complete obliteration of the authority of the Mother Church of Jerusalem after A.D. 70 is undoubtedly connected with the complete ignoring of the political factor involved in the situation of the Jewish Christians up to A.D. 70 which is a notable feature of the work. The fact that Prof. Schoeps does not face this issue is especially curious since he is at pains to show that in the Ebionite literature there was a definite polemic against the Davidic descent of the Messiah and an emphasis upon the fact that the Kingdom of Jesus was to be "*himmlisch und engelisch*". Indeed he concludes: "*Die Wiedererrichtung des Thrones Davids war mit der ebionitischen Menschensohnvorstellung nicht mehr verknüpft, nachdem die etwaigen Hoffnungen auf ein politisches Messiaskönigtum durch die Ereignisse von 70 und 135 so gründlich enttäuscht worden waren*" (pp. 246–7). It might fairly be thought that a clue was provided here to the fate of those many Jewish Christians who must have made common cause with their compatriots in the great venture of the national faith in the years 66 to 70.

In his great study Prof. Schoeps has necessarily concentrated his attention upon the fortunes of Jewish Christianity after A.D. 70. This limitation has inevitably meant that he has explored the Christian situation prior to the Jewish revolt against Rome in 66 less thoroughly, especially in the matter of the reaction of the Pauline communities to their Apostle's arrest, in circumstances so compromising to himself and his doctrine, and the consequent policy of the Jerusalem Church towards those communities. In turn this has meant that Prof. Schoeps has not apparently considered the position of the Gentile Christians *vis-à-vis* the situation created by the Jewish War against Rome and the subsequent overthrow of the Jewish national state, or appreciated the clues afforded by the condition of the *Corpus Paulinum* and by the silence in the Lukan Acts about the beginnings and the nature of Alexandrian Christianity—problems of which the elucidation, as we have striven to show, is crucial for our understanding of Christian Origins.

INDEX OF MODERN AUTHORS

(References to the notes are shown in brackets.)

INDEX OF SUBJECTS

INDEX OF ANCIENT SOURCES